The Case for Animal Rights

The Case for Animal Rights

Tom Regan

UNIVERSITY OF CALIFORNIA PRESS

BERKELEY ● LOS ANGELES

University of California Press
Berkeley and Los Angeles, California

Copyright © 1983 by
The Regents of the University of California
Printed in the United States of America
2 3 4 5 6 7 8 9

Library of Congress Cataloging in Publication Data

Regan, Tom.
The case for animal rights.

Includes index.
1. Animals, Treatment of—Philosophy. I. Title.
HV4708.R43   1983   179'.3   83-1087
ISBN 0-520-04904-7

To Nancy
For Your Patience,
With My Love

Every great movement must experience three stages: ridicule, discussion, adoption.

—*John Stuart Mill*

Contents

Contents

Preface

No book can be all things to all people. This dilemma, common to all those who hope to write for different audiences simultaneously, has been especially acute in the present case. On the one hand, I wanted to write a book that would be accessible to all those who labor for the cause of the better treatment of animals, persons who, for the most part, have professions other than academic philosophy. My hope was to write, in clear, intelligible terms, a book that would lay the philosophical foundations of the animal rights movement as I conceive it. On the other hand, I hoped to write a book that would command the attention of my professional peers in philosophy, one that was more philosophical substance than shadow, inviting the critical application of philosophy's highest standards, including rigor, clarity, justification, analysis, and coherence. The dilemma faced, quite simply, was that a work that perks the attention of philosophers can put others to sleep, while one that keeps the non-philosopher interested runs the risk of philosophy's benign neglect. Add to this a third, larger audience I hoped I might reach, comprised of those whose daily work brings them into direct contact with animals—veterinarians and laboratory scientists, for example—and the difficulty of choosing an appropriate style, pace, and tone should be apparent. Understandably, I do not know how well I have struck a proper balance. But perhaps the following remarks, aimed at the several groups of prospective readers, might not be judged inappropriate.

To my professional peers in philosophy, I hope you will give this work your understanding indulgence when it spends time explaining ideas you already know well enough or, as in the "Summary" at the end of each chapter, it reiterates ideas you have already digested, but not when it comes to its arguments and analyses. In these latter places I assume you will subject what I say, as well as what I fail to say, to the closest critical scrutiny. Since, as I believe, the truth will withstand any fair criticism, what truth (if any) this book contains can only be decided by how well it stands up under the heat of informed efforts to refute its claims. That is the way the pronouncements of science are tested. I can see no reason why those of philosophy should differ in this respect.

To those nonphilosophers who work to improve the lot of animals, I ask your patience when the going gets rough—when, for example, there are pages of worry over whether animals have beliefs and even more over whether a given ethical theory is the best, all considered. To explore patiently these and related matters is the only way a reasoned case can be made for animal rights, in my view. Since all who work on behalf of the interests of animals are more than a little familiar with the tired charges of being "irrational," "sentimental," "emotional" or worse, we can give the lie to these accusations only by making a concerted effort not to indulge our emotions or parade our sentiments. And that requires making a sustained commitment to rational inquiry. If some of what follows sometimes takes more than a single reading to make sense, I hope you will spend the necessary time before moving on. I have tried my best to make difficult ideas clear; but even if I have succeeded, that does not make difficult ideas easy.

Finally, to all those who come to this book from outside the profession of philosophy and independent of involvement in animal welfare-related activities, your patience is especially to be solicited, all the more so if you are a participant in one of the uses made of animals that is subjected to criticism—for example, the use of animals in science or their treatment in agriculture. As Socrates said, "Not for the first time, but always, I am the sort of person who is persuaded by nothing in me except the proposition which seems to me the best when I reason about it." Two propositions—first, that animals have certain basic moral rights and, second, that recognition of their rights requires fundamental changes in our treatment of them—seem to me the best when I reason about them. It is not out of malice, then, that the use of animals in science, for example, or hunting and trapping are condemned in the sequel. It is out of respect for what "seems to me the best when I reason about it." I hope those of you who lack a philosopher's or animal activist's interest in these issues will persevere and help to test how well I have reasoned about these matters, even if—one might say, especially if—the conclusions reached are critical of what you do.

The positions defended in this book will be viewed as extremely radical by some and as too moderate by others. That is another respect in which no book can be all things to all people. Certainly some of the conclusions I reach have surprised even me, and, without having tried to do so, the book now appears to contain something to upset just about every special interest group. You will understand me when I say that I hope the conclusions reached will be assessed on their merits by subjecting my arguments to fair, informed criticism, rather than by seizing upon isolated claims and denouncing them as "too extreme" or "too radical," or as "too moderate" or "conservative."

The pages that follow contain comparatively few facts about how animals are treated. There already exist books not soon to be surpassed that cover these matters. These works are cited in the appropriate places. I have operated on the assumption that those who would take the time to read this book would either already be familiar with these factual works or would use the present work as a stepping-stone to them. I have not set out to rival them. What I have sought to do is articulate and defend, at greater length and in greater depth than others heretofore, what it means to ascribe rights to animals, why we should recognize their rights, and what are some of the principal implications of doing so. Though it should go without saying, it is necessary to add that others who claim to defend the rights of animals may have a quite different understanding of their rights. Indeed, not only might this be so, it clearly is so in some cases. In defending "the rights view," as I call it, therefore, I do not presume to speak for all those, whether individuals or organizations, who see themselves as champions of the rights of animals.

To make the case for animal rights is the dominant concern of the pages that follow, but not the only one. Short of allowing the miraculous a legitimate role in philosophical argument, no case can be made for the recognition of the rights of animals that fails to make the case for the rights of human beings, and a central objective of the present work is to do just that. At its most general level, therefore, the arguments set forth could, and should, be assessed both in terms of how well the case is made for recognizing the rights of human beings and in terms of how well the case is made for recognizing the rights of animals. Though I believe the case for the one is neither any weaker nor any stronger than the case for the other, that is a belief others might wish to contest. In any event, because the book attempts to make the case for certain human rights those who dismiss animal rightists as antihuman should be silenced. To be "for animals" is not to be "against humanity." To require others to treat animals justly, as their rights require, is not to ask for anything more nor less in their case than in the case of any human to whom just treatment is due. The animal rights movement is a part of, not opposed to, the human rights movement. Attempts to dismiss it as antihuman are mere rhetoric.

The rights view is not a complete theory in its present form. Not all its implications have been addressed, not all its challenges anticipated. Even in the area of justice, many difficult questions (for example, about justice in the distribution of harms and benefits between individuals) remain to be explored. The more modest claim made in its behalf is that it identifies, clarifies, and defends a set of ethical principles that must be accommodated by any theory that aspires to be the best theory, all considered. That is not the end-all of one's aspirations in ethical theory, but it is the begin-all of making the case for the rights of animals. And that is enough, given present purposes.

Hard thinking is humbling. Probably no one who has attempted to clear a path through thickets of difficult ideas has emerged brimming with confidence that every turn was the right one, made for the right reasons. We do our best with the time and talent we have, knowing we cannot avoid every error but hoping to shed some fresh light on the dark contours of human thought and institutions. Usually we have no cause to say this, or to say more than this, but the matter of animal rights is not usual in some respects. Not only are animals incapable of defending their rights, they are similarly incapable of defending themselves against those who profess to defend them. Unlike us, they cannot disown or repudiate the claims made on their behalf. That makes speaking for them a greater, not a lesser, moral undertaking; and this makes the burdens of one's errors and fallacies when championing their rights heavier, not lighter. With those who find mistakes in these pages that have eluded my grasp, therefore, may I take the unusual step to ask that you earnestly consider whether these mistakes can be avoided or corrected without weakening the kind of protection for animals sought by the rights view? The impotence of those about whose moral status we debate, when the merits of our arguments are at issue, imposes special constraints on those of us who debate them. By all means, then, let the bad arguments be identified and thrown out. But may those who find them look beyond them.

Many people have helped me write this book, including many of my past teachers and students. I thank them all. Ruth Boone and Ann Rives deserve special thanks for helping prepare the manuscript for publication, Carol Leyba for helping make the final draft more readable, and Sheila Berg, editor at the University of California Press, for her unfailing support and encouragement. Even greater is my debt to Dale Jamieson who over the years challenged my thought at every turn and helped save me from making some really foolish mistakes; his influence is present throughout. Most of the book was written during the academic year

1980–1981 during my tenure as a recipient of a Category B Fellowship from the National Endowment for the Humanities. My gratitude to the Endowment is very great indeed. I. T. Littleton, Director, and the staff of D. H. Hill Library at my university also have my thanks for making the facilities of the library available to me for purposes of my research. My children, Bryan and Karen, understood and accepted my preoccupation while writing the book with the wisdom of their youth, and my wife, Nancy, discussed every aspect of the project with me, well beyond the point I had the right to expect that anyone would or should. That the book will see the light of day is in no small measure due to her patience and support. She also deserves the lion's share of credit for selecting Stefan Lochner's *Saint Jerome in His Study* to serve on the book's jacket.

T. R.

Raleigh, N.C.
26 November 1981

Acknowledgments

*I*t is a pleasure to acknowledge permission to reprint material from the following sources. From work other than my own, there is Stephen Stich, "Do Animals Have Beliefs?" *Australasian Journal of Philosophy* 57 (1979), 15−17 and, from my own work, there is the following: "McCloskey on Why Animals Cannot Have Rights," *Philosophical Quarterly*, 26 (1976), 253−254; "Narveson on Egoism and the Rights of Animals," *Canadian Journal of Philosophy* 7 (1977), 179−186; "Cruelty, Kindness, and Unnecessary Suffering," *Philosophy* 55 (1980), 533−537, and "Broadie and Pybus on Kant" 51 (1976), 471−472; "Introduction," *Matters of Life and Death: New Introductory Essays in Moral Philosophy*, ed. Tom Regan (New York: Random House, 1980), pp. 10−14; "Utilitarianism, Vegetarianism, and Animal Rights," *Philosophy and Public Affairs*, 9 (1980), 306−314; "Vegetarianism and Utilitarianism Again," *Ethics and Animals* 2 (1981), 5−6, and "Duties to Animals: Rawls's Dilemma," 2 (1981), 76−82; "Introduction," *And Justice For All: New Introductory Essays in Ethics and Social Policy*, ed. Tom Regan and Donald VanDeVeer (Totowa, N.J.: Littlefield, Adams and Company, 1982), pp. 11−13, and "On the Ethics of the Use of Animals in Science," Tom Regan and Dale Jamieson, in *And Justice For All*, p. 170; and "Justice and Utility: Some Neglected Problems," *Journal of Value Inquiry* (in press). Lastly, Dr. Edgar Peters Bowron, Director, and the staff of the North Carolina Museum of Art, Raleigh, North Carolina, are to be thanked for granting permission to use Stefan Lochner's *St. Jerome in His Study*, a black and white reproduction of which appears on this book's jacket and as a frontispiece.

1

Animal Awareness

When the German painter Stefan Lochner (1400–1451) painted *Saint Jerome in His Study* (reproduced on the cover of this book), he conveyed through symbols some of the highlights of the life of the fourth-century saint. For example, Saint Jerome was a scholar, famous for his translation of the Bible from Greek into Latin (the Vulgate edition); the book at his desk symbolizes his scholarship. A more interesting use of symbols is the presence of a lion in the painting. According to legend, Saint Jerome had removed a thorn from a lion's paw, and the lion, grateful to his benefactor, remained with the saint. Those who saw Lochner's painting and knew the story of Saint Jerome and the lion understood the symbolism. We, who perhaps know little about Saint Jerome, initially know less about why the lion is present. Indeed, to our eyes the animal in the painting does not even look quite like a lion. The size is not the size of a lion, the tail is fixed in an unlionlike pose, the mane and feet belong to some other creature than the lions we know, the face and one visible ear are humanlike, and the demeanor of the animal is, one might say, more like that of a small dog, a puppy, than like that of the king of the beasts. One might attempt to explain the discrepancies between the lion in Lochner's painting and those lions with which we are familiar by speculating that lions in the fifteenth century were different than lions in the twentieth. But there is another, simpler explanation. Lochner, who was well versed in the story about Saint Jerome and the lion, had never seen a lion. The lion he painted was the work of his own imagination, constructed out of the scant information and anecdotal tales about lions available to him at the time.

Once we realize Lochner's handicaps, his failure to capture the likeness of a lion is both understandable and forgivable. It would be unreasonable to expect him to have an accurate conception of an animal he had never seen and about which he had little reliable information. Our situation differs. We have had time and opportunity enough to acquaint ourselves with what lions are like, not only their outward appearance but also their physiology and anatomy, their social structure and behavior. Anyone who today supposed that lions had the puppy-dog appearance Lochner gave them would rightly be accused of failing to become acquainted with information that is as well documented as it is easily accessible.

As Lochner used symbols in his work, so his work itself stands as a symbol of humanity's misconception of other animals. Pictured as "lawless beasts" by some[1] and "of the order of sticks and stones" by others,[2] humanity has done its best to keep its distance from recognizing, as the English philosopher Mary Midgley observes, that "we are not only a little like animals; we are animals."[3] How far our predecessors, and perhaps even some of our contemporaries, have gone in denying our kinship with other animals is no more evident than when we consider the debate over animal awareness.

For most of us, it is true, even to ask whether any nonhuman animals are conscious is to strain our robust sense of reality. What could be more obvious than that cats like stroking, dogs feel hungry, elks sense danger, and eagles spy their prey? The attribution of conscious awareness to animals is so much a part of the commonsense view of the world that to question animal awareness is to question the veracity of common sense itself. But though the belief in animal awareness accords with common sense, and though the attribution of consciousness to animals is in harmony with the ordinary language we use in everyday life (when we say that "Fido wants out," after all, it is not as if we were saying something like "The square root of 9 is angry" or "The Washington Monument is thirsty"), though both these facts are well established and relevant, the role they play in the debate over animal consciousness can be reasonably weighed only after, not before, we have examined both sides. Moreover, our investigation of this question will lay some necessary groundwork for our examination of the primary question explored in the next chapter—namely, whether any animals have beliefs and desires. That question is not settled just by defending an affirmative answer to the question about animal consciousness; but why we answer this latter question as we do has important implications for the question about animal beliefs and desires.

1.1 DESCARTES'S DENIAL

So accustomed are we to viewing animals as conscious that many are surprised to learn that anyone thinks otherwise. The seventeenth-century French philosopher René Descartes does, denying all thought, by which he means all consciousness, to animals. Animals, in his view, are "thoughtless brutes," *automata*, machines. Despite appearances to the contrary, they are not aware of anything, neither sights nor sounds, smells nor tastes, heat nor cold; they experience neither hunger nor thirst, fear nor rage, pleasure nor pain. Animals are, he observes at one point, like clocks: they are able to do some things better than we can, just as a clock can keep better time; but, like the clock, animals are not conscious. "It is nature which acts in them according to the disposition of their organs, just as a clock, which is only composed of wheels and weights, is able to measure the time more correctly than we can with all our wisdom."[4]

Recently a question has been raised about the textual evidence for interpreting Descartes as denying *all* consciousness to animals (the standard interpretation). In his essay devoted to this question,[5] the English philosopher John Cottingham suggests that some passages show that Descartes believes that animals are conscious of *some* things (for example, hunger or fear), denying only that they can have "thoughts about" what they are aware of (for example, that they can *believe that* there is food or something to fear nearby). And it is true that, in a letter to Henry More, for example, Descartes does write that "I am speaking of thought, not of life and sensation. I do not deny life to animals, since I regard it as consisting simply in the heat of the heart; and I do not deny sensation, in so far as it depends on a bodily organ."[6] The crucial question is, however, How does Descartes understand *sensation*? On this point the evidence seems overwhelmingly to support the standard interpretation.

Descartes, in his *Reply to Objections VI*, characterizes three "grades" of sensation:

> To the first (grade) belongs the immediate affection of the bodily organ by external objects; and this can be nothing more than the motion of the sensory organs and the change of figure and position due to that motion. The second (grade) comprises the immediate mental results, due to the

mind's union with the corporeal organ affected; such are the perceptions of pain, of pleasurable stimulation, of thirst, of hunger, of colours, of sound, savour, cold, heat, and the like. . . . Finally the third (grade) contains all those judgments which, on the occasion of motions occurring in the corporeal organ, we have from our earliest years been accustomed to pass about things external to us.[7]

The first grade of sensation is common to animals and humans; "it depends," in the words of Descartes's letter to More, "on a bodily organ," and so may be attributed to any being having the appropriate bodily organ, including animals. For example, a human being and a giraffe can both have sensations of sight, in this sense of "have sensations." But in *this* sense, to say that animals "have sensations" is only to say that they have sensory organs (e.g., eyes and ears) that can be stimulated by external stimuli; and this stimulation can occur, Descartes clearly implies, *without* "the mind's union with the corporeal organ affected" and thus without consciousness. To allow that animals "have sensations" of the first grade, therefore, in no way implies that they are conscious.

Unlike this first grade, the remaining two grades of sensation are possible only if a mind is present, either to form a "union with the corporeal organ affected" (the second grade) or to pass "judgments . . . about things external to us" (the third grade). Now, it is an essential part of Descartes's philosophy, as Cottingham himself freely acknowledges,[8] that animals have no mind. Thus, since, according to Descartes, having sensations other than those of the first grade requires the presence of a mind, Descartes's teaching must be that animals have no sensations of grades two and three. Cottingham, then, is correct to note that, as in his letter to More, Descartes does not deny that animals have sensations; but he is incorrect in thinking, as he evidently does, that Descartes's attribution of sensations to animals shows that Descartes thinks that animals are conscious, at least to some extent. It is perfectly possible, given Descartes's understanding of sensation, to say that animals "have sensations," on the one hand, and on the other, to deny that they are conscious. Cottingham's challenge to the standard interpretation thus misfires, and it is this interpretation of Descartes that will be considered in the argument that follows. When Descartes denies that animals "have thoughts," in brief, he denies that they are consciously aware of anything, those "sensations" they do have being nothing more than "the immediate affection of a bodily organ by external objects." While granting that, as Cottingham observes, "to believe that a dog with a broken paw is not really in pain when it whimpers is a quite extraordinary achievement even for a philosopher,"[9] there are adequate grounds for attributing this achievement to Descartes.

Descartes, in fact, is not alone in managing this achievement, neither among philosophers, as we shall see, nor among the scientists of his day, as the following passage, written by an unknown contemporary of Descartes's, amply attests.

> The (Cartesian) scientists administered beatings to dogs with perfect indifference and made fun of those who pitied the creatures as if they felt pain. They said the animals were clocks; that the cries they emitted when struck were only the noise of a little spring that had been touched, but that the whole body was without feeling. They nailed the poor animals up on boards by their four paws to vivisect them to see the circulation of the blood which was a great subject of controversy.[10]

Though Descartes himself is said to have had a pet dog that he treated well, *as if* the animal were conscious,[11] the practice of these physiologists was in keeping with the spirit of his teachings, which, he writes, "are not so much cruel to animals as they are indulgent to mankind . . . since it absolves them of the suspicion of crime when they eat or kill them."[12]

1.2 HOW NOT TO CHALLENGE DESCARTES

It is tempting to dismiss Descartes's position out of hand, as the product of a madman. But Descartes is far from mad, and his denial of animal consciousness cannot, and should not, be dismissed in an *ad hominem* fashion; we should not, that is, dismiss *what* he says by attacking *him* as a person. Descartes is well aware of the commonsense view that animals are conscious and that his denial is apt to excite stormy protests. But he denies it nonetheless, observing that the belief in animal consciousness is a "prejudice to which we are accustomed from our earliest years."[13]

It is significant that Descartes labels this belief a "prejudice." A prejudice is a belief we accept uncritically, without giving due attention to the need to justify it. For example, if people believe that the world is flat without inquiring into the reasons for accepting this, they are prejudiced. Descartes's point is that this same diagnosis applies to the belief that animals are conscious: we simply haven't taken the time to understand and justify it. If, in reply, we protest by saying that "everyone believes that animals are conscious," the impotence of our reply can be easily seen. We would not change our verdict about the belief in a flat earth just because all or most people happened to believe the earth is flat. Neither should Descartes change his verdict about the belief in animal consciousness for similar reasons. Even if it is true that "we all believe that animals are conscious" (and how can that be true, given Descartes's dissenting voice?), the appeal to what "we all believe" could, at this stage, simply wrap a naked prejudice in the cloak of respectability.

The need to engage Descartes head-on, rather than to seek to avoid the encounter by *ad hominem* devices, can be brought home in another way. Think of a dog's behavior at the sound of his master's footsteps. The dog behaves excitedly. There is no other word for it. He jumps, barks, scratches at the door, wags his tail—a veritable whirling dervish. Were Descartes to deny this, then his views about animals could be easily dismissed. It is a matter of ordinary perception that the dog behaves as described, and a correct use of ordinary language, under these circumstances, to say that the dog "is excited." But Descartes does not deny any of this. What he denies is that we must attribute consciousness to the dog to explain the dog's observed behavior. The difference between Descartes and those who accept animal consciousness is not a disagreement over any fact regarding overt animal behavior. The disagreement concerns *how we may best explain or understand* these facts.

Once this much is seen, we should also see that it is pointless to attempt to challenge Descartes's view of animals by reciting *any* fact about how animals behave—for example, that the dog behaves excitedly, that porpoises are loyal, or that a cat once traveled three thousand miles, on her own, to be reunited with her former owners. The recitation of these facts is no challenge to Descartes. *He* can accept them all. The question that separates Descartes and his critics is *how these facts are to be interpreted and explained.*

Anthropomorphism

There is a further consideration that militates against uncritical acceptance of common sense in the present context. This is the problem of anthropomorphism. Webster's defines the relevant sense of the verb, *to anthropomorphize*, as "to attribute human characteristics to things not human." Taken literally, the definition is unsatisfactory, since "being alive," for example, is a "human characteristic" and yet we are not guilty of anthropomorphism if we say that a tree or a squid "is alive." What the definition must mean is that we anthropomorphize if we attribute a characteristic that belongs *only* to humans to things not human, as in "the moon gazed in a mystical state" or "the grass made a contract with the rain." To anthropomorphize is not to talk nonsense; what is said is intelligible, and there is a point to saying it; it is just that what is said is not literally true. To anthropomorphize is to make more of the object spoken of than it really is. It is to speak of it as if it were humanlike, when it is not.

Now, if consciousness is a characteristic of humans only, then we are guilty of anthropomorphism if we regard animals as conscious; we make more of animals than what they are; we erroneously picture them as humanlike. Suppose the charge of anthropomorphism is made against those who view animals as conscious. How can it be met? Surely not by *repeating* the attribution, no matter how many times it is repeated, and no matter how many different people repeat it. All repeating the attribution could show is how many people view animals as conscious, and this fact, while of interest in some contexts, is impotent in the present one; however many people regard animals as conscious, it is quite possible that the view held by these people is anthropomorphic. Given the charge of anthropomorphism, and given the deficiency of trying to meet it by insisting oneself, or getting others to insist, that animals are conscious, it should be clear that another way must be found if this charge is to be met.

We have seen, then, that Descartes is not so mad as to deny that the dog behaves excitedly at the sound of his master's footsteps. What he denies is that this shows that the dog is consciously aware of anything, either the sounds made (sensations of grade two) or his belief that the sounds are those of his master (sensations of grade three). We have also seen that certain tempting ways to reply to him will not pass muster. Before developing a more reasoned response, we need to consider why Descartes—a man of substantial intelligence by any measure, truly a pioneering thinker in philosophy, mathematics and natural science—sets forth a view so much at odds with common sense. A survey of Descartes's thought reveals a variety of reasons, some of which we shall consider in the pages that follow.

1.3 THE PRINCIPLE OF PARSIMONY

To begin with, Descartes seems to accept the *principle of parsimony* or *simplicity* regarding the scientific explanation of phenomena. The fourteenth-century English philosopher William Occam expresses this principle with admirable simplicity when he states that we are "Never to multiply entities beyond necessity." This principle, frequently referred to as "Occam's razor," means that it is better (i.e., rationally preferable) to explain phenomena by making as few assumptions as possible. If we imagine that there are two theories before us, each one offering an intelligible explanation of an equal range of facts, and both equal in what they can predict, but one requiring that we make fewer assumptions than the other, then the principle of parsimony enjoins us to accept the simpler one, the one with fewer assumptions. Though the debates engendered by this principle are far from simple, it seems eminently reasonable. After all, how can it be reasonable to make more assumptions when fewer will do?

Now, Descartes can be understood as believing that we face a choice regarding the explanation of animal behavior. The first alternative (let us call this the *Mechanistic Alternative*) is to explain animal behavior in purely mechanical terms. Animals are viewed, in Descartes's words, as "nature's machines," differing from, say, pinball machines in that animals are alive while these machines are not, but still essentially like these machines in that neither animals nor pinball machines are conscious. In the case of pinball machines, we explain their behavior, to put it very crudely, in terms of the passage of electrical current through myriad circuits, the current having been activated by the impact of a metal ball, and there is no point in the pinball machine's behavior where it must be conscious in order to do what it does. A purely mechanical explanation suffices. Well, animals are like a pinball machine, according to the Mechanistic Alternative, though the mechanics of their behavior differ from those of nonliving machines. In place of electrical current passing through wires and circuits, animals have, so the science of Descartes's time taught, various "humors" or "animal spirits" which, coursing through their bloodstream, cause, when stimulated, various behavioral responses in the animal, one kind of stimulation of the animal spirits eliciting hunger-behavior, for example, while another causes behavior associated with fear. Today, it is true, belief in animal spirits or humors has been replaced by alternative physiological and neurological concepts to serve as terms in the stimulus-response explanatory model, but Descartes would likely view the advance in our understanding of the physiology of animals as adding credence to, rather than as casting doubt upon, the case for the Mechanistic Alternative. The more we understand what animals are like, Descartes would likely believe, the more reason we have to view them as essentially like man-made machines: not conscious, not aware of anything. Just as it is irrational to suppose that a pinball machine feels threatened, angry, humiliated or suffers pain when, because we play too vigorously, it lights up "Tilt!," so it is irrational to believe that animals feel threatened, angry, humiliated or suffer pain; *their* cries and whimpers are merely *their* machine's way of registering "Tilt!" The Mechanistic Alternative thus does not deny any observable fact about how animals behave. What it does is offer an explanation of this behavior, and of animal nature generally, that denies animal consciousness. Perhaps it is not so remarkable, not so "extraordinary (an) achievement," that a mind possessed of (or by) the Mechanistic View could, as the Cartesian scientists did, "administer beatings to dogs with perfect indifference."

That, very roughly, is the Mechanistic Alternative. The second (the *Nonmechanistic Alternative*) differs, not because it disputes any fact about animal anatomy or physiology, nor because it denies that animals behave as they do, but because it affirms that many animals, not just human beings, are conscious. This second alternative certainly appears to be less simple than the Mechanistic Alternative, since it involves two assumptions, not just one, about the basic makeup of animals: animals are not *just* more or less complicated "living machines"; they are also more or less conscious or aware.

Suppose we accept the principle of parsimony, and suppose we grant, for the sake of argument, that each of the two alternatives just explained provides an explanation of animal behavior equal to the other. Which alternative would it be most reasonable to choose? Given these assumptions, reason would be on the side of the Mechanistic Alternative, the one where animals are viewed as essentially like pinball machines. That is the alternative Descartes selects, and some but, as we shall shortly see, not all of his reasons for choosing it are based on considerations of parsimony or simplicity. We may find some flaw in Descartes's argument, but at least the foregoing should serve to show that Descartes does have reasons, does have an argument, for his denial of animal awareness. He does not make his denial in an argumentative vacuum.

Descartes's having reasons is no guarantee that he has good ones, however, and we must now inquire into the merits of the case for accepting the Mechanistic Alternative. Does it provide a simpler explanation of the facts? That is the central question before us. In answering it we must take special care not to beg the question by assuming that animals are conscious, and we must also avoid resting criticisms of Descartes's position just on appeals to common sense or "what we all believe," since these latter appeals would invite Descartes's predictable protest that they embody a "prejudice."

1.4 LA METTRIE'S OBJECTION

The eighteenth-century French philosopher and physician Julien Offay de La Mettrie suggests one way to challenge Descartes.[14] This consists of urging that the Mechanistic Alternative proves more than Descartes realizes. For if, as this alternative alleges, we ought not to view animals as conscious because we can explain *their* behavior mechanistically, why may we not do the same in the case of *human beings*? And if we can, must we not conclude that humans, not just animals, are "machines"? After all, what could be simpler, more in keeping with the principle of parsimony, than to explain all behavior, including that of humans, by reference to a single principle? In contrast to Descartes, La Mettrie takes the Mechanistic Alternative a step further, concluding that the "mental life" of humans is neither more nor less than the alterations of the "humors" in the human nervous system.

One reply Descartes might give is irrelevant. In a letter to the Marquis of Newcastle, Descartes writes that if animals were conscious as we are, "they would have an immortal soul like us. This is unlikely, because there is no reason to believe it of some animals without believing it of all, and many of them such as oysters and sponges are too imperfect for this to be credible."[15] What Descartes seems to be alleging here is that humans should, but animals should not, be viewed as conscious because we are immortal and they are not. Descartes is confused. The ascription of *consciousness* to any given individual does not entail that that individual has an immortal soul. People who deny that there is a "life beyond the grave" are not committed to denying their own consciousness in this life or to making a similar denial in the case of others. It may be true that it was largely owing to his religious convictions, or to the religious convictions of those ecclesiastics he was obliged to please,[16] rather than to his respect for the principle of parsimony, that Descartes attributes consciousness and thus, on his view, a mind or soul (he uses the terms interchangeably) to human beings while denying a mental life to animals. But whatever Descartes's reasons may be for equating the (conscious) mind and the (immortal) soul, there is no good reason why we must follow suit. Sponges and oysters may not be conscious; but whether they are or are not is an issue to be decided in their case, as in the case of human beings, independently of questions about immortal souls.

1.5 THE LANGUAGE TEST

Unlike the first, a second reply available to Descartes is germane to the objection raised by La Mettrie. Suppose we could point to a kind of behavior that can be explained only by postulating consciousness; and suppose, further, that it could be shown that humans, but not animals, exhibit this kind of behavior; then we could attribute consciousness to humans, but deny it to animals, independently of the irrelevant considerations about who or what is "perfect" enough to have an immortal soul.

One can find such an argument in Descartes: the kind of behavior is linguistic behavior, a kind, he thinks, that only humans can engage in. Among the relevant passages in Descartes's writings, the following is perhaps the clearest on this point:

> In fact, none of our external actions can show anyone who examines them that our body is not just a self-moving machine but contains a soul with thoughts, with the exception of words, or other signs that are relevant to particular topics without expressing any passion. I say words or other signs, because deaf-mutes use signs as we use spoken words; and I say that these signs must be relevant, to exclude the speech of parrots, without excluding the speech of madmen, which is relevant to particular topics even though it does not follow reason. I add also that these words or signs must not express any passion, to rule out not only cries of joy or sadness and the like, but also whatever may be taught by training to animals. If you teach a magpie to say good-day to its mistress, this can only be by making the utterance of this word the expression of one of its passions. For instance it will be the expression of the hope of eating, if it has always been given a tidbit when it says it. Similarly, all the things which dogs, horses, and monkeys are taught to perform are only expressions of their fear, their hope, or their joy; and consequently they can be performed without any thought. Now it seems to me very striking that the use of words, so defined, is peculiar to human beings. Montaigne and Charron may have said that there is more difference between one human being and another than between a human being and an animal; but there has never been known an animal so perfect as to use a sign to make other animals understand something which expressed no passion; and there is no human being so imperfect as to not do so, since even deaf-mutes invent special signs to express their thoughts. This seems to me a very strong argument to prove that the reason why animals do not speak as we do is not that they lack the organs but that they have no thoughts. It cannot be said that they speak to each other and that we cannot understand them; because since dogs and other animals express their passions to us, they would express their thoughts also if they had any.[17]

This and related passages[18] raise more questions than they answer. Some of these will be considered in what follows. For the present it is sufficient to emphasize that Descartes here recommends a particular test, henceforth referred to as *the language test*, to determine which individuals are conscious. Individuals who are able to express their thoughts by using a language, either words or their equivalent (e.g., the signs used by deaf-mutes), pass the test and thereby display their consciousness. Those who are unable to do this thereby flunk the language test and are thereby

proven to "have no thoughts" and thus, given the standard interpretation of Descartes's view of the relationship between thought and consciousness, to lack consciousness. It is Descartes's belief that no animal
can pass this test. It is worth asking, before testing the adequacy of the
language test itself, whether he is right.

Can Any Animals Use Language?

It would be unfair to Descartes to criticize him for failing to take note of
efforts to teach primates, including gorillas and chimpanzees, a language
such as the American sign language (ASL) for the deaf. Such efforts were
not undertaken—though they were imagined (e.g., by La Mettrie)—until
very recently. A number of books and essays have chronicled this enterprise, and many advocates of the Nonmechanistic Alternative have been
quick to give these early reports their enthusiastic support. Whether this
support might be a bit premature is a point to be discussed. The following
account of an interview, conducted in ASL, between *New York Times'*
reporter Boyce Rensberger and Lucy, an eight-year-old chimp who had
received instruction in American sign language, is typical of the early
results reaching the general public.

> Reporter (holding up a key): What is this?
> Lucy: (A) key.
> Reporter (holding a comb): What is this?
> Lucy: (A) comb (takes comb and combs reporter's hair, then hands comb
>   to reporter). Comb me.
> Reporter: O.K. (combs Lucy)
> . . . .
> Reporter: Lucy, do you want (to) go outside?
> Lucy: Outside, no. (I) want food, (an) apple.
> Reporter: I have no food. Sorry.

Regarding the interview, Rensberger writes:

> Brief. Not especially deep. But certainly communication. . . . After each
> exchange, Lucy and I would stare into each other's eyes for a few
> seconds. I do not know how she felt, but I was nervous. I was partici-
> pating in something extraordinary. I was conversing in my own language
> with a member of another species of intelligent being.[19]

There are many deep, troubling questions such accounts leave unanswered. Two in particular stand out. The first concerns the nature of
language. What is a language? Unless we know, the claim that Lucy is
"able to use a language" remains murky. Perhaps we are attributing to

her more than her behavior merits. If, for example, a language, properly conceived, involves not only a vocabulary (words, signs) but also rules of syntax governing how these words or signs can properly be strung together, then possibly Lucy's performance does not constitute a genuine use of language, or, alternatively, use of a genuine language. The issues are complicated, well beyond the reach of the present inquiry. Still, it is important to realize that this is a question that must be explored by anyone who views a chimp such as Lucy as a language-user.

Second, even assuming that Lucy qualifies as a language-user, one might ask how competent she is in comparison to, say, a human child who is in the early stage of language acquisition. Serious doubts have recently been raised about believing that chimps and these children display equal competence. The person raising the strongest doubts is hardly unqualified and cannot be pictured as one having a vested interest in discrediting animals' linguistic abilities. Herbert S. Terrace, professor of psychology at Columbia University, headed a four-year effort to teach American sign language to a chimpanzee named Nim Chimpski. Nim mastered the signs for well over a hundred words, including *finish, berry, hello, sleep, chair,* and *play.* All early interpretations of the chimp's success indicated considerable facility at language acquisition. Upon a more careful reconsideration of the evidence, however, including videotapes of sessions involving Nim and his teachers, Terrace came to question his earlier assumptions. A number of relevant facts emerged. For example, unlike children, including deaf children learning sign language, Nim never reached the point where he regularly extended the length of his sentences. "Having learned to make utterances relating a subject and a verb (such as 'Daddy eats')," Terrace writes, "and utterances relating a verb and an object (such as 'eats breakfast') the child apparently learns to link them into longer utterances relating the subject, verb, and object (such as 'Daddy eats breakfast'). Later, the child learns to elaborate that utterance into statements such as 'Daddy didn't eat breakfast' or 'When will Daddy eat breakfast?' and goes on to still further elaborations. Despite the steady increase in the size of Nim's vocabulary, the mean length of his utterances did not increase."[20]

Another pair of relevant findings were the degree to which Nim signed spontaneously (that is, without someone else initiating the conversation) and the frequency with which the signs Nim used had been used by the other party to the conversation. One statistical breakdown of what is called the *discourse analysis* of children learning a language, such as English, shows that children frequently are more apt to respond to, rather than to initiate, conversation (70 percent of the child's utterances were occasioned by what someone else said), but that "in most instances the child did not reply by simply repeating what the parent had said but added to the parent's utterances or created a new one from totally different words. Less than 20 percent of a child's utterances were imitations of its parent's utterance."[21] Terrace sees Nim's case as significantly different.

> During Nim's last year in New York only 10 percent of his videotaped utterances were spontaneous. Approximately 40 percent were imitations or reductions. If the conversations we videotaped and transcribed were representative of the thousands of conversations from which our corpus was derived—and I have no reason to believe that they were not—I must conclude that Nim's utterances were less spontaneous and less original than those of a child.[22]

Thus, Terrace writes that he

> must therefore conclude—though reluctantly—that until it is possible to defeat *all* plausible explanations short of the intellectual capacity to arrange words according to a grammatical rule, it would be premature to conclude that a chimpanzee's combinations show that same structure evident in the sentences of a child. The fact that Nim's utterances were less spontaneous and less original than those of a child and that his utterances did not become longer as he acquired more experience in using sign language, suggests that much of the structure and meaning of his combinations was determined, or at least suggested, by the utterances of his teachers.[23]

Of course, even if it were established that chimpanzees do not have the ability for language acquisition equal to that of young children, it would not follow that they have none at all. The issue of the extent to which chimps and other primates can "learn to talk" remains one worthy of further study, as does the question, What is a language? Neither issue can be pursued in detail here. It is sufficient for present purposes to remind ourselves that not all the evidence is in and that, until more is known, we would do well to remember Terrace's cautioning words, not to be "premature" in attributing significant linguistic abilities to non-humans such as Nim.

Quite apart from the problems relating to the use of language by chimps or gorillas, there is a further point that cries out to be made. Suppose that, contrary to Descartes's view, there are some animals who *are* able to use language to express their thoughts—chimps and gorillas, let us suppose, and perhaps a few others. That fact by itself—if it is a fact—carries no weight whatsoever for the many, many other species of animals whose members are not able to develop a facility for using a language such as American sign language. Thus, if, following Descartes, we were to agree that the use of a language to express one's thoughts is the decisive test for determining which animals are conscious, the very most we could do is correct Descartes for being too conservative. Besides humans, there would be a few other species whose members are conscious. As for cats and dogs, chickens and hogs, llamas and tigers, for example, since they give no evidence of being able to master the use of a relevant language, they would remain in the category assigned them by Descartes. They would remain in the category of "thoughtless brutes." This is not the outcome desired by many who accept the nonmechanistic view of animals, which should be enough to direct their critical attention to other, more fundamental issues. The question they should ask is not, How many animals can use language to express their thoughts? Rather, it is, Is the use of language a reasonable test for determining which individuals are conscious?

The Inadequacy of the Language Test

The language test holds that individuals who are unable to use a language lack consciousness. This cannot be true. If all consciousness depended on one's being a language-user, we would be obliged to say that children, before they reach an age when they can speak, cannot be aware of anything. This not only flies in the face of common sense—an appeal that, as noted earlier, Descartes is likely to dismiss as possibly an appeal to prejudice—but, more fundamentally, it makes utterly mysterious, at best, how children could learn to use a language. For if, prior to their mastery of a language, children are not conscious of anything—they are, that is, not aware of sound, or light, or tactile sensations—then how shall we teach them the rudiments of, say, English? Shall we write it out for them? But if they are not conscious of *anything*, there can be nothing for them to learn by means of their sight. Shall we speak it? But if they are *altogether* lacking in awareness, how shall our sounds reach them? The point is, instruction in language use requires *conscious reception* on the part of the learner. Unless we assume that, *before* learning a language a child can be aware of something, we shall be at a loss to explain how the child can learn it. When we dispute the adequacy of the language test as a test of consciousness, therefore, we should not be viewed as trying to combat Descartes's views merely by appealing to common sense. Since the language test implies that pre-language-using children are not conscious at all, and since this makes it mysterious (miraculous?) how they could learn to use a language, we have principled reasons for rejecting the test's adequacy. However, once we have come this far, we cannot treat the language test as a kind of double standard, allowing that humans do not have to pass it in order to be conscious while insisting that animals do. If a young child can be conscious independently of learning a language, we cannot reasonably deny the same of animals, despite the latter's inability to say what they are aware of.

One can anticipate the following objection. We cannot argue that dogs and cats must be conscious before they learn to use, say, English, since otherwise they could never learn to use it. And we cannot argue in this way for the simple reason that dogs and cats *never do learn* to use a language such as English. This disanalogy between the human and animal cases suggests an argument for denying consciousness to animals while ascribing it to humans.

1. Only those beings who have the potential to master a language are conscious without having to master it.
2. Animals (with the possible exception of chimps and gorillas, say) lack this potential.
3. Therefore, animals (with a few possible exceptions) are not conscious.

There are reasonable grounds for denying this argument's first premise. Certainly some mentally enfeebled humans, who lack the potential for language acquisition, seem nonetheless to be conscious of some things— for instance, sounds and pains. Thus, if some humans who lack the potential for language acquisition are conscious, then one cannot deny that animals who lack this potential can be. Moreover, even in the case of those humans who do have the potential to become language-users, it is unclear how this potential assures their actual prelinguistic consciousness. There are well-known problems involved in inferring what is actual from what is potential. When Henry Aaron was a wee toddler it was true that he was potentially the person who would set a record for the most career home runs hit in major league baseball, and, as things turned out, he actually set this record. But it does not follow that the-wee-toddler-who-is-Henry Aaron *at that time* actually holds this record; at most what follows is that he will in time set the record. Similarly, even if baby Jane has the *potential* to become a language-user, and even if it is true that to be an *actual* language-user one must be conscious, it does not follow that she is actually conscious because she has the potential to learn a language. At the very most what follows is that she will in time become conscious, which is a significantly different belief than the one expressed in this argument's initial premise.

But to concede even this much to this argument would be to concede to it more than it deserves, since the first premise assumes, without explaining, that there is an essential connection between, on the one hand, being able to use a language, including having the potential to do so, and, on the other, being conscious. Whether there *is* such a connection, however, is precisely the question at issue. As things stand, therefore, premise (1) of this argument is question-begging: it assumes the truth of the very thing it is called upon to prove. For this reason, if for no other, this argument fails to justify the belief that the only beings who are conscious are those who pass the language test or who have the potential to do so.

1.6 SKEPTICISM

At this juncture, Cartesians in particular face a serious problem. Since (a) they claim that the behavior of animals is to be explained by the Mechanistic Alternative but favor the Nonmechanistic Alternative for explaining the behavior of human beings; since (b) appeal to immortal souls is irrelevant to questions about who or what is conscious (1.4), and since (c) the language test has been shown to be less decisive than Descartes assumes (1.5), how are Cartesians to avoid the conclusion that human beings too, not just animals, are "thoughtless brutes"? As noted earlier (1.4), this is the conclusion La Mettrie thinks Descartes should reach. And perhaps he is right. That issue is beyond the range of the present work. The same is true of another, related question. This latter question asks how any one person can know that there are "other minds," other human beings in particular, who are consciously aware of anything. There is a vast and ever expanding literature devoted to this problem. But though skeptical challenges to our claims to knowledge deserve a respectful hearing when voiced in appropriate contexts, the present work is not one of them. Here we must side with Descartes, at least in one respect, and part company with La Mettrie. Human beings, we shall assume, are not "thoughtless brutes" who only "respond" to "stimuli," not "mindless machines," but are creatures who have a mental life. This is a necessary assumption for any work in moral philosophy. If human beings do not experience pleasure and pain, for example, or do not prefer some things over others, or cannot make decisions and act intentionally, or are incapable of understanding what is involved in treating others with respect, then there could not be anything for ethical theory to be a theory of. Our attempt to understand the morality of our acts or institutions, in other words, must be premised on certain assumptions about the sort of creature we are, and a minimal assumption in this respect is that we are creatures with a mental life. In concert with Descartes, therefore, and in this respect in opposition to La Mettrie, we will assume that humans have a mental life (have, that is, sensations of grades two and three or, alternatively, that we perceive, believe, remember, expect, desire, prefer, etc.). Skeptical challenges to this assumption will have to be aired and addressed on some other occasion.

1.7 EVOLUTIONARY THEORY AND CONSCIOUSNESS

Given the assumption that we humans are conscious, the question must still arise concerning what other creatures, if any, are. If the answer depended on which creatures have immortal souls or have the ability to pass the language test, the Cartesian answer (all and only human beings are conscious, at least among terrestrial creatures) might yet be defensible. But these ways of approaching the question of creature consciousness have been shown to be inadequate. How else might this question be approached?

Evolutionary theory provides a significantly different approach to the question of animal awareness than the one offered by Descartes. If we assume, as Descartes does, that human beings are conscious, then it would be quite remarkable indeed, given the basic thrust of that theory, if *Homo sapiens* were the *only* species whose members had this attribute. Darwin, for one, is quite emphatic in denying a privileged status to human beings in this regard. "There is," he writes, "no fundamental difference between man and the higher mammals in their mental faculties."[24] And, again: "The difference in mind between man and the higher animals, great as it is, certainly is one of degree and not of kind."[25] Within evolutionary theory, this similarity between human and animal mental life rests on a number of related considerations. One concerns the visible complexity of, and similarities between, human and animal anatomy and physiology. Another concerns the basic belief that more complex forms of life have evolved from more simple forms, a belief that implies that both humans and some animals evolved from simpler life forms, though not necessarily the same life forms in every case (it is possible that there are several different branches of evolutionary development or lines of descent which, though they began at the same point, diverged at different times in response to local environmental conditions). For present purposes, however, the crucial point is *the survival value of consciousness*. If consciousness had no survival value—if, in other words, it was of no or little assistance in the struggle of species to adapt to and survive in an ever changing environment—then conscious beings would not have evolved and survived in the first place. But we know from the human case that conscious beings exist. Thus, given evolutionary theory and given the demonstration of the survival value of consciousness the human case provides, we have every reason to suppose that the members of other species also are conscious. Given the survival value of consciousness, in other words, one must expect that it would be present in many species, not in the human species only. The contemporary animal physiologist Donald R. Griffin states this point forcefully when he writes as follows:

> It thus becomes almost a truism, once one reflects upon the question, that conscious awareness could have great adaptive value, in the sense that this term is used by evolutionary biologists. The better an animal understands its physical, biological, and social environment, the better it can adjust its behavior to accomplish whatever goals may be important in its life, including those that contribute to its evolutionary fitness. The basic assumption of contemporary behavioral ecology and sociobiology . . . is that behavior is acted upon by natural selection. . . . From this plausible assumption it follows that—insofar as any mental experiences animals have are significantly interrelated with their behavior—they, too, must feel the impact of natural selection. To the extent that they convey an adaptive advantage on animals, they will be reenforced by natural selection.[26]

Of course, to argue that animals "have a mental life" does not by itself establish the relative complexity of their mental life. That is an issue that will occupy our attention in the following chapter. What attributing conscious awareness to animals on the basis of evolutionary theory does do, is provide us with a theoretical basis for making this attribution to animals *independently of their ability to use a language*. The ability to use a language no doubt also has significant survival value. But evolutionary theory does not imply that the emergence of consciousness either does or must coincide with the emergence of this capacity; indeed, if it did imply this, evolutionary theory would be at a loss to explain how language could be taught or learned. If, as seems reasonable to suppose, linguistic ability is a higher-order cognitive capacity, one that presupposes consciousness, then evolution will support our viewing other animals as having both consciousness as well as other, lower-order cognitive capacities from which the higher-order capacities required for language mastery have evolved. The application of the principle of parsimony to the evolutionary process supports this view, as Griffin makes clear in the following passage:

> Accepting the reality of our evolutionary relationship to other species of animals, it is unparsimonious to assume a rigid dichotomy of interpretation which insists that mental experiences have some effect on the behavior of one species of animals but none at all on any other. It would be absurd to deny that mental experiences are important components in human behavior and human affairs in general.[27]

If, then, "mental experiences *are* important components in human behavior and human affairs in general"—and recall that, in the present work, as in any other work in moral philosophy, we assume that human beings have a mental life, that we can know that there are other (human) minds, and that, in Griffin's words, our mental experiences play an important role "in human behavior and human affairs generally"—*if* this much is conceded, then it would be unparsimonious, given the major thrust of evolutionary theory, to deny that the mental life of animals plays a similar role in their behavior and our understanding of it. Granted, accepting this much does not by itself settle the thorny question of *which* animals are most reasonably viewed as having a mental life, a question addressed below (1.9). What it does provide is a theoretical basis, independent of the ability to use language, for viewing some nonhuman animals as conscious.

There is another advantage garnered from approaching the question of animal awareness from the vantage point of evolutionary theory. Frequently people approach this question as if it could be settled just by observing how animals behave. The issue is often thought to be resolved, once and for all, *merely* by citing the dog's excited behavior at the sound of his master's footsteps on the stairs, for example, or by *just* noting the loyal behavior of dolphins. It is well to remember what was said earlier about the impotence of such examples (1.2). How animals are observed to behave may be compatible with disparate, incompatible explanations of their observed behavior—for example, with Descartes's and Darwin's. Because this is so, it is a plain mistake to suppose that one can prove that dogs and dolphins are conscious *just* by citing any one or any number of examples of how they behave. The attribution of consciousness to animals must rest on grounds *in addition to* how they behave, though how they behave must surely be consistent with any viable theoretical explanation of why they behave as they do. Though how animals are observed to behave may initially give rise to the belief that they have a mental life, the validity of the attribution of consciousness to them must ultimately rest on a theory about the nature of those animals to whom consciousness is attributed. And this theory, like any other, must be assessed *as a theory*, something we fail to do if we content ourselves with citing facts that are themselves consistent with inconsistent theories.

1.8 DESCARTES'S DOWNFALL

Evolutionary theory provides a theoretical basis for attributing a mental life to animals; Descartes's theory does not. Which theory is preferable? Obviously, this is a complicated question, since how theories are to be assessed is itself a highly controversial issue. However, there are two kinds of considerations that are relevant in the present case. The first is that of simplicity: other things being equal, it is reasonable to select a theory that makes fewer assumptions over one that makes more. A second is explanatory power: other things being equal, it is reasonable to select the theory that explains a broader range of facts. Both considerations will become clearer as we apply them to an assessment of Descartes's theoretical position.

As was implied by the earlier discussion, Descartes is a dualist. He views reality as consisting of two basic, independent, and irreducible kinds of things: minds and bodies. Minds he regards as having no physical properties; they have no size, weight, shape and the like; minds are immaterial or spiritual and thus have no location in space. My mind is not to the left or right of anything; literally speaking, my mind is not any*where*. Moreover, according to Descartes, minds are "things which think," and a thing which thinks, he states, is something "which understands, which conceives, which affirms, which denies, which wills, which rejects, which imagines also, and which perceives."[28]

Bodies, by contrast, according to Descartes, have physical properties. They have size, shape; they are extended. What bodies do not have are thoughts. Bodies are "dumb," in the sense that they completely lack thought; they are *non*mind; they are *non*consciousness. This is true of all bodies and true equally of each. A rock lacks consciousness (thought) just as much as a tree, a dog's body, or, for that matter, a human body. All are equally "dumb."

Human bodies thus do not differ essentially, in and of themselves, from any other kind of body. Where they differ is that they are associated with minds—human minds. All other bodies, according to Descartes, lack a mind with which they are associated; and the reason why we feel pain, whereas a dog feels none, according to Descartes, is not because our bodies are in any essential way different from a dog's; it is because our bodies are, whereas a dog's is not, associated with a non-bodily, immaterial mind.

Descartes's dualism encounters well-known problems. Only one shall concern us here. This is the problem of interaction. To set the stage, it is a commonplace of ordinary experience that (1) what happens in or to our bodies frequently makes a difference to what we are aware of, and (2) what transpires in our mental life frequently makes a difference to our bodily behavior. As illustrative of (1), consider stepping on a tack. A sharp metal object pierces my skin and lodges itself in my foot. This happens to my body. In ordinary circumstances (e.g., assuming my foot has not been anesthetized) I also experience a sensation of pain. This experience of pain is not, according to Descartes, another thing that happens in or to my body. On the contrary, since I am consciously aware of the pain, I must be aware of it in my mind. Thus, it at least appears to be the case that something that happened in my body (a pin enters my foot) *causes* a sensation in my mind; the sensation arises, to use the words of Descartes quoted in an earlier connection (1.1), as an "immediate mental result, due to the mind's union with the corporeal organ affected."

One aspect of the problem of interaction is that Descartes's theory of the mind and the body provides no earthly clue concerning how this alleged union of the two, this presumed causal interaction between them, could possibly take place. Physical processes, such as those that take place within our nervous system, can bring about physical changes. That much is clear, and Descartes certainly can allow this. What is not clear at all is how a physical process can bring about changes in something that is not physical, which, according to Descartes's theory, is what happens when the tack's intrusion into my foot causes a sensation of pain. The question is not, How *does* this occur? It is, How *can* this occur? By insisting, as he does, that the mind is immaterial and the body material, Descartes is unable to explain how what evidently does occur can occur. There is, within his theory, no plausible, intelligible way of explaining the possibility of "the mind's union with the corporeal organ affected."

The situation for Descartes is no less serious when viewed the other way around. Suppose that I know I must get out of bed if I am to make it to a dentist appointment, something I do not look forward to with particular relish. Still abed, I review the options and, despite my disinclination, decide to get up. Now, this decision is, on Descartes's theory, a mental event: it is something that occurs in my mind. What follows, after I have made my decision, is that my body behaves in a particular way—for instance, I throw back the covers and climb out of bed. But how *could* my decision, which is a mental event in my mind—and thus, according to Descartes, one that takes place in an immaterial medium—cause my body, which is material, to move as it does? An event that occurs in my mind presumably could cause another mental event; but it is mysterious at best, and contrary to the laws of nature at worst, to hold that an immaterial something (my decision) caused a material something (my bodily movement). Whichever direction the mind and the body interact, whether a bodily process causes a mental event, or a mental event causes bodily behavior, Descartes's view of the mind and the body is quite unable to explain how this can occur. If the mind (consciousness) and the body interact, and if any adequate theory of the mind and body must explain how this interaction is possible, then Descartes's theory of the mind and the body is inadequate. On the present criticism, in short, Descartes's dualism fails the test of explanatory power.

There is a way to avoid this outcome, one taken by some of Descartes's followers. This is to deny that the human mind and body interact. It is clear how recourse to this expedient, if successful, could rescue Cartesian dualism from the criticism just given. If the mind and body don't really interact, then it is no objection to Descartes to point out that he fails to explain how they do. Only now, however, there is another problem, no less serious than that of interaction itself. If it is not the tack in my foot that causes my pain, from whence does this sensation come? And if it is not my decision to get up that leads me to throw back the covers, from whence does this physical movement originate?

One reply favored by some Cartesians is known as *occasionalism* and may be taken as illustrative of the difficulties attempts to defend dualism encounter. On this view, the tack's entering my foot does not cause my sensation of pain; rather, its entering my foot is *the occasion for God's causing my sensation of pain*, just as my decision to get up does not itself cause my body to move but is, rather, *the occasion for God's causing* it to do so. Since God is omnipotent (all-powerful), he can do anything, including cause my body to get up and my foot to hurt; and since God is omniscient (all-knowing), he certainly knows when I have stepped on a tack just as surely as he knows when I have decided to get up. Theoretically, therefore, there is no reason why an omniscient, omnipotent God could not do what the occasionalists say he does.

But this merely pushes the problem back a step. The question remains, How does interaction take place, if not between the human mind and body, then between God and the human mind and God and the human body? To be told that the "mechanics" of the interactions are obscure and elude our intellectual grasp ("God works in mysterious ways, His wonders to perform") is not to be given any explanation; we are not, that is, any closer to understanding how my stepping on a tack is related to my experiencing pain. Indeed, we are further away from understanding this. One mystery is not explained by another. The Greeks had an expression for the artificial rescue of a character in a play who is in perilous danger and cannot secure his safety by relying on his own resources: *deux ex machina*, "god in a machine," so named because a person playing a god was actually lowered onto the stage by a machine, so that the hero of the drama might make an expeditious escape (like the heroine who, tied to the train tracks and facing certain death, is rescued at the last possible second by "the good guy"). Well, philosophers are not above attempting to rescue theories by similar means. The attempt to save Cartesian dualism by calling upon the machinery of god's intervention, after the fashion of occasionalism, is a classic instance of this phenomenon in philosophy.

A further point is worth making. The principle of parsimony, we know, requires that we not make any more assumptions than we need to make to explain what we want to explain. Before the introduction of God as a mediating causal agent between the human mind and body, dualism does not appear to make a great many assumptions. There are minds, and then there are bodies. Things look pretty simple. Once God is introduced, however, a third, extremely controversial assumption is added. And when, in addition to merely postulating his existence, God is called upon to fill the role of a sort of cosmic switchboard operator, completing all the calls to all the bodies from all the minds, and vice versa, a theory that once seemed a model of simplicity can now be seen to be swamping itself in the weight of its own assumptions. If every time anyone experiences physical pain, for example, we have to assume that "God completes the call," the superficial simplicity of dualism has gone by the boards.

There is a lesson to be learned from Descartes's downfall. It is that viewing the mind as an "immaterial something," as a soul, is certain to land us in trouble. For unless we are prepared to argue that, despite all appearances to the contrary, *everything* is immaterial, the problem of interaction will arise, and we will be left with a theory that is in principle unable to provide an intellectually satisfactory answer to the question of whether and, if so, how interaction takes place. One of the virtues of accepting an evolutionary view of the origin and development of con- sciousness is that it does not commit one to dualism regarding the mind and the body, and though this does not prove evolutionary theory true, it at least removes a possible source of objection. Viewed against the backdrop of evolutionary theory, to say that animals "have minds" is not to say that they "have immaterial, immortal souls."

1.9 THE CUMULATIVE ARGUMENT FOR ANIMAL CONSCIOUSNESS

As noted at the beginning of this chapter, the belief in animal awareness is part of the commonsense view of the world. To say this is not to settle the question of animal awareness, however, since it may be true in any given case that the commonsense view of things is mistaken. Still, compelling reasons must be given against a commonsense belief before it is reasonable to abandon it. The role of appeals to common sense, in other words, both in the particular case of the question of animal awareness and in general, is not to guarantee the truth or reasonableness of a given belief, but to put the burden of proof on those who would deny it to show why it should be denied. Descartes, for the reasons given in the above, fails to meet this requirement when it comes to the issue of animal consciousness. He provides us with no good reason to give up our commonsense belief. The arguments he presents against this belief are seriously deficient and have been shown to be so without begging the question—that is, without assuming the truth or reasonableness of the commonsense belief in animal awareness. In this regard, at least, Descartes's attempt to unseat the verdict of common sense fails.

A second point, also noted earlier, is that ordinary language is not strained by talking of animals in a way that implies that they have a mental life. Everyone who is conversant in, say, English understands perfectly well what it means to say that Fido is hungry, or that a mother lion is annoyed by her overly playful cub. Once again, however, it does not follow that we ought to speak a certain way just because we ordinarily do. Possibly ordinary language stands in need of correction or improvement. However, as in the case of appeals to common sense, so also in the case of appeals to ordinary language: the burden of proof falls to those who would change our ordinary speech habits to provide compelling reasons why they should be changed. For example, if it could be shown that speaking as we ordinarily do in a given connection is a barrier to clear and effective communication, then perhaps we ought to modify or replace the way we ordinarily speak. But does our speaking in ways that attribute a mental life to animals stand in the way to clear and effective communication? Is there a clearer, more circumspect, less "anthropomorphic" way to speak about animals? Here we can do no better than to relate the findings of the contemporary psychologist D. O. Hebb, who, together with others involved in a two-year project involving adult chimpanzees at the Yerkes Laboratory of Primate Biology, attempted to avoid "anthropomorphic descriptions in the study of temperament."[29] "A formal experiment was set up," Hebb writes, "to provide records of the actual behavior of adult chimpanzees, and from these records to get an objective statement of the differences from animal to animal." When the "anthropomorphic descriptions" were dispensed with, the results were less than useless. "All that resulted," Hebb continues, "was an almost endless series of specific acts in which no order or meaning could be found." When the "anthropomorphic descriptions" of emotion and attitude were allowed, however, "one could quickly and easily describe the peculiarities of the individual animals, and with this information a newcomer to the staff could handle the animals as he could not safely otherwise." Commenting on Hebb's findings, the contemporary American philosopher Gareth B. Matthews remarks that, once "relieved of methodological scruples, the staff found that they could rather easily agree among themselves that one animal was fearful, another nervous, a third shy. They naturally characterized one as friendly to human beings, though quick-tempered, whereas they found another to *hate* human beings, as they quite naturally put it."[30]

What the experience of Hebb and his colleagues points to is that there is nothing to be gained, and a good deal to be lost, if, in place of the mentalistic language we ordinarily use in talking about many animals, we institute a different, supposedly objective, nonmentalistic vocabulary. In themselves, the adequacy of ordinary language to this task and the failure of a language stripped of "anthropomorphic descriptions" do not show that animals have a mental life. What they do show is that we have no good reason to change how we ordinarily talk about certain animals on the grounds that doing so stands in the way of clear, effective communication. Indeed, just the opposite is true, if the experiment of Hebb and the others can be taken as illustrative. While it is possible that ordinary language requires correction in some cases, this is not one of them.

A third point that bears on the case for attributing a mental life to certain animals is the failure of a position like Descartes's, one that attempts to limit consciousness just to human beings (at least among the inhabitants of *terra firma*). To view humans as unique in this regard will oblige one who holds this view to provide an argument for accepting it. But what shape must such an argument take? It must insist upon a strict dichotomy between humans and animals, a dichotomy that involves attributing a nature to humans that differs in kind from that of all other animals. Clearly, this "unique nature" could not be explained in evolutionary terms, since an evolutionary view denies that humans have a unique nature. More particularly, those who would view humans as the only conscious beings could not adequately ground this belief in considerations about human biology, physiology, and anatomy, since there is nothing in these aspects of human nature that is both relevant to our being conscious and uniquely human. How else, then, if not in this way, could one attempt to defend the thesis that humans, and humans alone, are conscious? Only by having recourse to some allegedly nonbiological, nonphysiological, nonanatomical or, in a word, nonphysical peculiarity of humans. This is the option Descartes selects, and we can perhaps understand why, given his views about the immortality of the (immaterial) human soul. But to select this option is, to use John Cottingham's apt phrase, to land one in "a philosophical mess."[31] This view of human consciousness (that consciousness is a defining characteristic of mind or soul, which is immaterial) will make the most common occurrences of ordinary life, such as feeling pain when one steps on a tack, *in principle* mysterious.

Of course, if how animals were observed to behave was at odds with viewing them as having a mental life, the plot would thicken. For example, if mice behaved in random, unpredictable ways when presented with some cheese after having gone without food for a day or so, non-Cartesians would have to wonder whether these animals weren't rather unruly "machines" after all. In fact, however, animal behavior is not random, is not in principle unpredictable. For example, the mice will eat the cheese, as one would naturally expect of conscious creatures, or if they do not, their unexpected behavior would be due to some untoward condition (e.g., a lack of sensory powers). So, while it is true that how animals behave does not by itself prove that they have a mental life, their behavior does provide a reason for viewing them in this way.

This finding, as well as the verdict of common sense and the demonstrable utility of talking about certain animals in mentalistic terms, accords with the implications of evolutionary theory. Roughly speaking, this theory implies that many animals, not just human beings, are conscious, not because (or only if) they possess an immaterial soul; certain animals are rightly deemed to be conscious because we (humans) are conscious *and* because, given the main thrust of evolutionary theory, the mental life of humans (our psychology) does not differ in kind from these animals.

There is, then, no *single* reason for attributing consciousness or a mental life to certain animals. What we have is *set* of reasons, which, when taken together, provides what might be called the *Cumulative Argument for animal consciousness*, the main tenets of which can be summarized in the following way:

1. The attribution of consciousness to certain animals is part of the commensense view of the world; attempts to discredit this belief, if Descartes's attempt is taken as illustrative, have proven to lack adequate justification.
2. The attribution of consciousness to certain animals is in harmony with the ordinary use of language; attempts to reform or replace this way of speaking, as the experiment of Hebb and his associates illustrates, also have proven to lack adequate justification.
3. The attribution of consciousness to animals does not imply or assume that animals have immortal (immaterial) souls and thus can be made and defended independently of religious convictions about life after death.
4. How animals behave is consistent with viewing them as conscious.
5. An evolutionary understanding of consciousness provides a theoretical basis for attributing awareness to animals other than human beings.

The preceding does not constitute a strict proof of animal awareness, and it is unclear what shape such a proof could take. What it provides is a set of relevant reasons for attributing consciousness to certain animals. If it could be shown that the claimed relevance of these reasons is illusory, or that, though relevant, the claims made about consciousness in 1 through 5 are false, or that, though relevant and true, there are better reasons for denying consciousness in animals while affirming it in the case of human beings, *then* the Cumulative Argument would be exposed as deficient. Unless or until such challenges are made and sustained, we have principled reasons for parting company with Descartes and attributing consciousness—a mind, a mental life—to certain animals.

1.10 WHICH ANIMALS ARE CONSCIOUS?

The Cumulative Argument provides a basis for attributing consciousness to beings other than humans while leaving it an open question which animals are conscious and how highly developed the consciousness of various animals is. This latter problem will occupy our attention in the following chapter. It is the former problem, the one concerning which animals are conscious, that shall now concern us.

The Cumulative Argument justifies attributing consciousness to an animal when the attribution is underwritten by points 1 through 5 above. That is, we are justified in viewing certain animals as conscious if (1) doing so accords with the commonsense view of the world; (2) speaking of them in mentalistic terms is in harmony with ordinary language; (3) viewing them thus does not commit us to attributing an immaterial mind (soul) to them; (4) their behavior is consistent with the attribution of consciousness to them; and (5) both the commonsense beliefs about these animals and our ordinary way of talking about them and their behavior can be given a principled defense in terms of evolutionary theory. The members of *many* species of animals are reasonably viewed as conscious given these conditions, including all species of mammalian animals in particular. Certainly these are the animals concerning whom common sense and ordinary language are most at home in regarding as conscious; and it is also in the case of these animals that evolutionary theory provides the strongest case for the attribution of consciousness.

The explanation of this latter point is as follows: The point from which we must decide which animals are conscious is the case we know best, and it is human beings that provide the paradigm of conscious beings, setting skeptical challenges to our knowledge of "other minds" to one side. Now, from what we know about the relationship between human consciousness and the structure and function of the human nervous system, there is good reason to believe that our consciousness is intimately related to our physiology and anatomy. Damage to the spinal cord, for example, can make it impossible for us to receive sensations from affected parts of our bodies, and persons whose brains have been severely damaged may cease to give any evidence of consciousness at all. Given that our consciousness is intimately related to our physiology and anatomy, that mammalian animals are most like us physiologically and anatomically, and that consciousness has an adaptive value and has evolved from less complex forms of life —given all this, and, as a work in moral philosophy may do, setting to one side skeptical doubts about human consciousness, it is reasonable to conclude that mammalian animals are likewise conscious. This does not mean that only those animals most like us anatomically and physiologically can *possibly* be conscious. It means, rather, that these are the animals for whom the attribution of consciousness is most well founded.

Ought we to go further than this and attribute consciousness to nonmammalian animals? A systematic answer to this question is well beyond the scope of the present inquiry. All that can be noted here is a point that has gone undiscussed previously, namely, that there is the possibility of conflict between what is hospitable to common sense and ordinary language, on the one hand, and the possible implications of evolutionary theory, on the other. Normally we neither think nor say, for example, that a snail clinging to the side of a tree "wants" to be there, or is "angry" when removed, or (though this is less clear) "feels pain" if squashed. Certainly we are even less tempted to say or think these things about animals less developed than a snail. Earlier, however, it was conceded that just because a given belief is part of the commonsense view of the world, and just because we speak a certain way, it does not follow that our belief is true. It may be that the snail and animals even less like us are conscious, despite our disinclination to say or think so. If they are, the theoretical grounds for thinking that they are must come from the same source that underpins the attribution of consciousness to mammalian animals. It must come from the systematic application of evolutionary theory, or some other theory, if a better theory can be found.[32] *Where one draws the line* regarding the presence of consciousness is no easy matter, but our honest uncertainty about this should not paralyze our judgment in all cases. We cannot say exactly how old or tall someone must be, to be old or tall, respectively, but it does not follow that we cannot recognize that some people are old or tall. Our ignorance about the shadowy borders of attributions of consciousness is no reason to withhold its attribution to humans *and* those animals most like us in the relevant respects. (The problem about where one draws the line surfaces in several places below, e.g., in 2.6, 8.5, 10.4).

Anthropomorphism and Human Chauvinism

Anthropomorphism, as previously explained (1.2), is the attribution to things not human of characteristics that apply only to humans. There can be no doubt that some talk about animals is anthropomorphic. If the widow Ames says that her cat has not been eating because he is concerned about Middle East tensions and the problem of storing nuclear waste, then the widow seems a bit excessive in her view of feline intellectual sophistication, to put the point as politely as possible. To acknowledge that *some* of the things that *some* people say or believe about animals is correctly gauged as anthropomorphic, however, is not to imply that this is true of the attribution of consciousness to some animals. The Cumulative Argument offers a set of relevant reasons for believing that consciousness is not restricted to human beings. It is not the attribution of consciousness to these animals that should raise our intellectual eyebrows, but the refusal to make it. Donald R. Griffin, the animal physiologist whose views were cited earlier, again squarely addresses the point presently before us:

> The possibility that animals have mental experiences is often dismissed as anthropomorphic. . . . *This belief that mental experiences are a unique attribute of a single species is not only unparsimonious; it is conceited.* It seems more likely than not that mental experiences, like many other characteristics, are widespread.[33]

Of special interest is Griffin's use of the word *conceit*. It is not, he is saying, any defect in animals that bars us from recognizing that they have a mental life; the bar to this recognition is our own conceit, our presumed uniqueness, a supposed privileged status that, while it possibly could be accepted on religious grounds, can hardly be defended on scientific ones. What Griffin does is prick the balloon of our puffed-up species pride by reminding us that it is an expression of conceit that is unwarranted by the facts.

There is a neglected other side to the anthropomorphic coin. This is human chauvinism.[34] The anthropomorphic side reads: "It is anthropomorphic to attribute characteristics to nonhumans that belong *only* to humans." The human chauvinism side reads: "It is chauvinistic *not* to attribute characteristics to those nonhumans who have them and to persist in the conceit that only humans do." Human chauvinism, that is, like all other forms of chauvinism, involves a failure or refusal to recognize that those characteristics one finds most important or admirable in one's self, or in members of one's group, are also possessed by individuals other than one's self or the members of one's group, as when male chauvinists fail, or refuse, to see that they are not alone in possessing admirable qualities. With the argument of the present chapter serving as the backdrop, the conclusion we reach is that to deny consciousness or a mental life to mammalian animals is an expression of human chauvinism.

1.11 SUMMARY AND CONCLUSION

This chapter explored the question of animal awareness and sought to defend the reasonableness of viewing some animals as like us in being conscious. Descartes's famous denial of animal awareness was characterized (1.1) and various ways not to challenge his position were sketched (1.2). The central disagreement between Descartes and his critics was shown to concern the explanation of why animals behave as they do. Descartes believes that animal behavior, like that of any machine, can be explained in purely mechanical terms (1.3). La Mettrie pushes Descartes's reasoning a step farther (1.4): human, not just animal, behavior can be described and explained without making any reference, explicit or implied, to a mind or consciousness. Descartes denies this, believing that the linguistic behavior of human beings shows that humans are unique among terrestrial creatures in being conscious (1.5). Against Descartes, it was argued that to make language-use the decisive test of consciousness not only opens the possibility that some animals (e.g., chimpanzees and gorillas) have a mental life, it also, and more fundamentally, relies on a demonstrably inadequate test of consciousness, since individuals could not learn to use a language if they were not conscious before, and thus independently of, their acquisition of this understanding.

One might, at this juncture, side with La Mettrie and argue that human beings, not just animals, are "thoughtless brutes." Though a theoretical possibility that warrants extended examination in some contexts, the present work is not one of them. Any recognizable moral theory assumes that human beings have a mental life (for example, that we have desires or goals, are satisfied or frustrated, feel emotions, and experience pleasure and pain). Without this assumption, there is nothing for a moral theory to be a theory of, so that to make this assumption here, without addressing the skeptical challenges others might raise (1.6), is not peculiar to a work that aspires to make the case for animal rights.

Evolutionary theory provides a reasonable theoretical option to Descartes's position (1.7), maintaining that consciousness is an evolved characteristic, with demonstrable adaptive value, something that is therefore reasonably viewed as being shared by the members of many species in addition to the members of the species *Homo sapiens*. When assessed as a theory (1.8), Descartes's position comes up short. If it is kept simple (i.e., if we suppose that there are just two basic kinds of terrestrial realities, bodies [both human and nonhuman] and human minds), Descartes's position fails to give a rational explanation of how the mind, which he regards as immaterial, can interact with the body, which he regards as material. If, in response to its failure to satisfy the requirement of explanatory power, the Cartesian occasionalist has recourse to the intervention of an omnipotent, omniscient deity to explain how the human mind and body appear to interact, then the theory loses all semblance of simplicity. In the contest of theories between Cartesianism and Darwinism, when it comes to the question of the nature of mind and which creatures have a mental life, Cartesianism loses.

Those who reject the Cartesian view in favor of a more catholic position regarding consciousness have several reasons, not just a single one, to marshal in support of their position (1.9). Common sense and ordinary language favor the attribution of consciousness and a mental life to many animals; possession of consciousness is logically independent of questions about who or what has an immaterial (immortal) soul, so that the question involving consciousness can be approached independently of religious predispositions; animal behavior is consistent with viewing them as conscious; and evolutionary theory supports viewing those animals most like paradigmatic conscious beings (namely, human beings) as being like us in being conscious. To attribute conscious awareness to mammalian animals, leaving open the possibility that other kinds of animals might also be conscious (1.10), is not anthropomorphic nor, in Descartes's words, does this show that one is in the grip of a "prejudice to which we are accustomed from our earliest years." Just the reverse is true, in fact. Those who refuse to recognize the reasonableness of viewing many other animals, in addition to *Homo sapiens*, as having a mental life are the ones who are prejudiced, victims of human chauvinism—the conceit that we (humans) are *so* very special that we are the only conscious inhabitants on the face of the earth. The arguments and analysis of the present chapter sought to unmask this conceit.[35]

2

The Complexity of Animal Awareness

T he Cumulative Argument advanced near the end of the previous chapter (1.8) supports more than the attribution of consciousness to certain animals. That argument can also be used to defend the view that mammalian animals[1] have beliefs and desires and that the explanation of why they behave as they do can frequently be given in terms of those beliefs and desires they have. Both common sense and ordinary language underwrite this view; the attribution of beliefs and desires to these animals is logically independent of questions about their having or lacking immortal (immaterial) souls; the behavior of these animals is consistent with attributing beliefs and desires to them; and evolutionary theory supports the view that animals frequently behave as they do because they desire what they desire and believe what they believe. As Griffin observes, "accepting the reality of our evolutionary relationship to other animals, it is unparsimonious to assume a rigid dichotomy of interpretation which insists that mental experiences have some effect on the behavior of one species of animals but none at all on others."[2] So strong is the cumulative support provided by the Cumulative Argument that we are justified in using it to pose a burden-of-proof challenge to those who deny that animals have beliefs and desires. Unless or until these critics show that the reasons for denying that animals have beliefs and desires are better reasons than those supplied by the Cumulative

Argument for affirming that they do, we are rationally justified in believing that they do.

Not a few philosophers aspire to meet this challenge. True, none attempt to meet it by denying that either common sense or ordinary language is on the side of attributing beliefs and desires to animals, both domestic and wild varieties.[3] And few, if any, are today likely to make the Cartesian assumption that consciousness is possible only for those who have immaterial, immortal souls and on this basis attempt to meet the burden of proof. Yet there is no scarcity of objections that contest, either in whole or in part, the propriety of attributing beliefs and desires to animals or of explaining their behavior in these terms. Not all these objections can be considered, and not all the controversies unearthed along the way can be examined fully. Nevertheless, the objections considered are a fair representation of the strongest, not the weakest, and the examination of controversial ideas, though far from complete, has, it is hoped, a degree of thoroughness appropriate to the occasion.

2.1 THE BELIEF-DESIRE THEORY

Let us begin with a fuller description of the position to be defended. Stephen Stich, a philosopher at the University of Maryland and, as we shall see more fully below (2.3), one who raises some doubts about attributing beliefs to animals, offers an especially perspicuous characterization of this position, which he designates "our intuitive 'belief-desire' theory." It will be useful to quote his remarks at length:[4]

> The theory postulates two different sorts of functional states, beliefs and desires, with normal subjects having a large store of each. Desires can arise in a variety of ways. One way in which they typically arise is as a result of deprivation. An organism deprived of food, water or sexual release, will acquire a desire for food, water or sexual release, the strength of the desire generally increasing with the length of time the organism has been deprived. Also, organisms generally have a strong desire to escape from painful stimuli. Desires can, in addition, be generated by the interaction of beliefs with other desires. Thus, for example, if a dog wants something to eat and if it believes there is a meaty bone in the next room, it may well acquire a desire to go to the next room. It need not acquire this desire, however. It may, for example, also believe that it would be severely shocked if it were to go into the next room, and thus not desire to go into the next room despite the presence of the bone. Alternatively, it might fail to form the desire without the influence of some overriding desire, like the desire to avoid pain. For it might simply be a rather stupid

dog, or perhaps (like all of us from time to time) it may simply fail to make use of its beliefs about the bone. The belief might "slip its mind".

Desires, or at least a certain subset of them, are capable of causing behaviour. Generally, if an organism now wants to move its body in a particular way and if it has no incompatible wants, it will move its body in this way. Higher level desires, like the desire to get its master to open the door, can result in behaviour by generating (in collaboration with appropriate beliefs) one or more of these low level desires that are capable of causing bodily movement. . . .

Like desires, beliefs have a variety of causes. The two most perspicuous ones are perception and inference. If our canine's master puts a meaty bone in the dog's dish, if the dog has a clear view of the proceedings, if it is paying attention and is psychologically normal, then the dog will form the belief that there is a meaty bone in its dish. It will also, no doubt, form a variety of further beliefs, some enduring and some ephemeral, as a result of observing its master's activity. In a similar way, perception also leads to the removal of beliefs from an organism's store of beliefs. . . .

Beliefs can also be generated by other beliefs. When tolerably coherent, the process by which beliefs generate further beliefs counts as inference. Thus, for example, Fido may believe that if he scratches at the door his master will open it, and also that if the door is opened he will be able to reach a bone. From that pair of beliefs he may infer that if he scratches at the door he will be able to reach the bone.[5]

Stich makes it plain that the preceding is not a detailed psychological theory; it is the barest, and broadest, outlines of such a theory. Even so, his remarks are enough to give meaning to the claim that "the best psychological explanation of animal behaviour will be provided by a theory which follows the general pattern of our intuitive belief-desire theory."[6] Echoing La Mettrie's challenge to Descartes (1.4), Stich observes that "it would be remarkable indeed if a theory could be produced which explains the behaviour of higher animals without appeal to beliefs and desires, and if this theory could *not* be adapted to explain *human* behaviour as well"[7] and, echoing Griffin's observations about the implications of evolutionary theory, Stich remarks that "in light of the evolutionary links and behavioural similarities between humans and higher animals, it is hard to believe that belief-desire psychology could explain human behaviour, but not animal behaviour. If humans have beliefs, so do animals."[8]

It is significant that Stich ends the argument just quoted on a conditional note: *If* human beings have beliefs, so do animals. Stich himself offers no argument to support ascribing beliefs to human beings, and neither shall we. As previously noted (1.6), there are some assumptions about the mental life of human beings that must be made in any work in moral philosophy, including the assumptions that human beings sometimes want certain things, that they sometimes act as they do because they believe doing so is necessary if they are to satisfy their desires, that they sometimes consider the beliefs and desires of others, and so forth. The challenge to defend these assumptions, like the challenge to defend our belief in the existence of other (human) minds, cannot be undertaken, let alone met, here. Here it must suffice to note that these assumptions are common to any work in moral philosophy, not ones that are peculiar, and this in a perverse or damaging sense, to a work on animal rights. A view of human nature that reduces all human behavior to "innate" or "conditioned" "responses" to external or internal "stimuli" is, let us agree, a theoretical possibility whose merits (or lack of them) deserve our sustained critical attention on some occasion. But let us also agree that the present occasion is not that occasion.

Assuming, then, what the advocates of alternative ethical theories will assume, that our intuitive belief-desire theory applies to human beings and our behavior, and in view of the collective force of the Cumulative Argument as outlined above, we are right to insist that the burden of proof falls to those who deny the application of this theory to animals and their behavior. To meet this challenge it is not enough, for example, to assert that animal behavior *might* be uniformly explicable in terms of a stimulus-response theory, or to have recourse to any other theory that denies the presence of beliefs and desires in the case of animals while affirming them in the case of humans. The challenge is met *only if* one can show that it is reasonable to deny that the belief-desire theory applies to animal behavior without implying that the same is true in the case of human behavior.

There are at least two ways in which those who aspire to meet this burden of proof might endeavor to do so. First, they might argue that animal behavior cannot be explained by the belief-desire theory for the simple reason that animals, unlike humans, not only do not but cannot have beliefs or desires; second, they might argue that even though animals do have beliefs, we cannot say *what* they believe and so are unable to explain their behavior by making reference to what they believe and, if desires presuppose beliefs, what they desire. Stich argues in the latter way; R. G. Frey, senior lecturer in philosophy at the University of Liverpool, argues in the former. Though the arguments these philosophers offer do not exhaust all the possible attempts to meet the burden of proof posed by the Cumulative Argument, they are, as remarked earlier, a fair representation of these arguments, so that it would be unfair to object to the argument that lies ahead that "the real issues are avoided" or that it deals with ideas raised by straw (as distinct from real) men. The hope is that the strongest, not the weakest, contrary positions are examined. We shall consider Frey's arguments first (2.2). After Stich's position has been characterized and critically evaluated (2.3), a number of further objections that challenge our ability to say what animals believe will be considered (2.4), and the positive approach to questions about the content of animal beliefs, set forth in 2.3, will be defended. The results of this account, and its defense, will then (2.5) be brought to bear on questions dealing with related cognitive capacities of animals (e.g., memory) and with whether animals are reasonably viewed as intentional agents.

2.2 LANGUAGE AND BELIEF

Animals, Frey concedes, do have needs, including, for example, the need for food, water, and sexual release. However, needs are distinct from desires, and the possession of the former does not presuppose or imply possession of the latter. Plants need water, as do car radiators, yet we do not suppose that either plants or radiators desire water. The same is true, in Frey's view, of animals: they have needs but lack desires. The belief-desire theory thus has no valid application in their case. Lacking as they are when it comes to possession of desires, their behavior is not to be explained in ways that assume that they have them.

Frey offers a number of arguments against attributing desires to animals. One (let us call it *Frey's Main Argument*) takes the following form:

1. Only those individuals who can have beliefs can have desires.
2. Animals cannot have beliefs.
3. Therefore, animals cannot have desires.

I have elsewhere contested Frey's arguments in support of premise 1.[9] I shall not reproduce them here. Instead, critical attention will be mainly of premise 2. Premise 1 implies that anytime anyone desires anything, there is and must be a belief lurking in the background, so to speak. For example, I may be said to desire to eat a raspberry tart or to be warmed by the heat of the fire; but I could not be said to desire these things, it may be claimed, if I did not believe that the tart was edible or that the fire would give me warmth, or if I did not have some other belief (e.g., that either the tart or the fire or both were conducive to my health). More generally, my desire for X may be supposed to require beliefs of the form 'If I want X, then I must do Y' or 'Since I want X, and Y appears to be X, then I must get

Y.'[10] On this view, what neither I nor anyone else can do is desire something without believing something about what is desired. Where the appropriate belief of the appropriate kind is missing, there the desire must be missing also. And since, on Frey's view (see premise 2 of his Main Argument), animals cannot believe anything, they cannot, on his view, desire anything either.

But why can't animals believe anything? According to Frey, animals lack beliefs because *what* is believed (the object of belief) is that a given sentence is true; and since animals lack linguistic proficiency, they cannot believe that any sentence is true. That being so, they cannot believe anything and so, given that beliefs are necessary for desires, they cannot desire anything.

Frey's reasons for excluding animals from the class of believers are more than a little reminiscent of Descartes's language test (see sec. 1.5). But there is a relevant difference. Descartes, it will be recalled, holds that being able to use a language is the decisive test for consciousness. Frey concedes that animals are conscious.[11] What he contends is that the ability to use a language is necessary if one is to have beliefs; and since, on his view, having beliefs is necessary for having desires, the ability to use a language is also necessary if one is to have desires. Thus, since animals lack the ability to use a language, they lack both beliefs and desires. The burden of proof, in Frey's view, has been met: the belief-desire theory does not apply to animals and their behavior.

Some critics might challenge Frey by citing the linguistic competence of chimpanzees and other primates as showing that these animals do not "lack language" and so can have beliefs and desires. But there are two points to notice about casting one's criticism of Frey in these terms. First, as mentioned in the previous chapter (1.5), there is a good deal of controversy surrounding the attribution of linguistic competence to these animals; there is some question, then, whether we would be on stable ground if we credited them with linguistic capacities. Second, and more fundamentally, even if primates show that they are able to use a language, they would prove to be the exception rather than the rule. Certainly most animals, including even most mammals, give no indication that they now possess or can acquire the use of language, in the sense of "language" central to Frey's argument. If we are looking for grounds on which to challenge Frey, grounds that would underwrite the attribution of beliefs to mammals generally, then Frey's position needs to be challenged at another place and in another way. That place is his view that *what* is believed (the object of belief) is that a sentence is true. This claim is absolutely crucial to Frey's position, since unless he can persuade us that what is believed is that a given *sentence* is true, we have no reason to agree with him concerning which individuals do or do not, or can or cannot, have beliefs.

We turn now to the reasons Frey offers in support of his view that what one believes, whenever one believes something, is that a certain sentence is true. Frey introduces his first reason by way of an example. We are to imagine that Frey desires to own a Gutenberg Bible, a desire he would not have, we are further to assume, if he did not believe that he lacked a Gutenberg Bible. The question is then put, "What is it that I believe?" to which Frey replies:

> I believe that my collection lacks a Gutenberg Bible; that is, I believe that the sentence "My collection lacks a Gutenberg Bible" is true. In expressions of the form "I believe that . . . ," what follows the "that" is a sentence, and what I believe is that that sentence is true. The same is true with expressions of the form "He believes that . . ." What follows the "that" is a sentence, and what the "he" in question believes is that that sentence is true. [12]

This is the whole of Frey's first argument in defense of his view that what is believed is that certain sentences are true. The structure of this argument is not transparent; indeed, it is not clear that an argument is given. What Frey says seems to be more in the nature of a declaration. But, in fairness to Frey, perhaps what he believes is that (1) because particular sentences follow the "that" in sentences of the form "I believe that . . ." and "He believes that . . . ," *it follows that* (2) what is believed is that the sentence following the "that" is true. And it is because Frey perhaps believes that (2) follows from (1) that he also perhaps thinks that he has provided an argument for his account of what is believed.

Before assessing this argument, it is worth noting that Frey is not saying that we *sometimes* have beliefs about sentences, something that is uncontroversial. For example, suppose I believe that the sentence "Jack and Jill went up the hill" is a sentence in English. Then my belief in this case is a belief about a sentence. This is not Frey's view. *Whenever* I believe *anything*, on his view, *what* I believe is that a certain sentence is true, and this is a position that is distinct from, and is not entailed by, the uncontroversial view that sometimes people have beliefs about sentences.

Frey's view is not only controversial, it is false. Imagine that my son has a rubber snake and that, while waiting for a train, he takes the snake out of his pocket and sets it on the floor. Another traveler walks by, sees the snake, jumps away, and lets out a scream. I pick up the snake, apologize to the traveler, and counsel my son, explaining that the man believes the snake will harm him. All this is perfectly intelligible, and we should require of any philosophical account of the object of belief, Frey's included, that it explain how what is plainly true (we know that the traveler believes that the snake will harm him) can be true. Frey's stated position cannot explain this, if we add the following possibility: The man who is frightened by the snake, the one who believes that the snake will harm him, speaks only, say, Portuguese, while I speak only English. For if, as Frey would have us suppose, *what* this man believes is that the sentence "The snake will harm him" is true, and given that the man in question is totally ignorant of the English language, it follows that he cannot believe that *any* English sentence is true, including, in particular, the English sentence "The snake will harm him." Frey's view, as stated by him, fails to explain how it is possible to do what sometimes we plainly are able to do—namely, correctly attribute beliefs to people who do not understand a particular language and who thus cannot believe that sentences in that language are true.

A possible reply to the criticism just made points out that the traveler is assumed to be conversant in some language (Portuguese). So perhaps it will be objected that Frey's view is not that the traveler must be able to believe that the *English* sentence "The snake will harm him" is true, if he is to believe that the snake will harm him; perhaps what he must believe is that *the equivalent sentence in Portuguese* is true. More generally, perhaps what Frey believes is this: Whenever we say that some individual (A) believes something, what we affirm is that A believes that *some* sentence is true, that sentence being a particular sentence in English, or its equivalent in Portuguese, in German, or in some other language. In this way, it might be claimed, Frey could revise his somewhat unguarded characterization of what is believed and thereby respond to the criticism raised in the previous paragraph.

Thus revised, Frey's position, which initially seemed noteworthy for its simplicity, now runs the risk of being buried by its unadvertised complexity. If different people who speak different languages can believe the same thing, despite expressing their beliefs in different words from different languages, then *what* is believed by any one of them cannot be reduced to the belief that a particular sentence in a particular language is true (e.g., the *English* sentence "The snake will harm him"). And if what is believed is not reducible to the belief that a particular sentence in a particular language is true, it is very unclear what sense it can make to persist in claiming that what is believed is that *a* sentence is true. The idea that sentences are what are believed, but that these sentences are not sentences in any particular language, strains one's powers of comprehension, to say the least.

A further objection to Frey takes the following form. Suppose the man who, upon seeing the snake, jumps away in terror, happens not to be able to speak or comprehend any language. Both physically and intellectually, let us suppose, he lacks the necessary wherewithal to acquire the use of language. On Frey's view, even when revised, what we cannot do is attribute any belief to this man. Since he is totally bereft of any linguistic competence, he cannot believe that any sentence, in any language, is true (or false). On Frey's view, he cannot believe anything. So, here we have this man: his eyes bulge, he jumps away, his face wears an expression of extreme terror; but does he believe anything? Is there something about what our fellow traveler perceives that leads him to believe that there is something to be afraid of? On Frey's view, there is not. Lacking in language, the traveler is lacking in beliefs also. Not only does he not believe anything, he *cannot* believe anything.

What shall we say of a view that leads to a conclusion such as this? Reason would not look with disfavor on its rejection. Unless we can be shown why it is a mistake to attribute beliefs to individuals who lack the ability to formulate or comprehend sentences (and Frey fails to show why this is a mistake), the traveler's behavior, understood in concert with the other tenets of the Cumulative Argument, is sufficient reason to attribute beliefs to him, and those who demur, denying the propriety of speaking in this way, would not show that the traveler lacks beliefs; what they would show is that they do not understand the ordinary use of sentences of the form "He believes that *p*."

Frey is likely to view this last objection with a jaundiced eye.[13] He is likely to say that his "linguistic intuitions" differ, alleging that, in his view, we ought not to say that the traveler "believes that the snake will harm him." But this, he will say, settles nothing, since it fails to settle *whose* "linguistic intuitions" are correct. Besides, the case of the linguistically deficient traveler is likely to be judged a "deviant case" by Frey, one that departs significantly from "normal cases" of belief attribution. And it is precisely because it is, in Frey's view, a deviant case that he is likely to dismiss it or downplay its relevance to the analysis of belief. If Frey's analysis fits the normal cases well, then how can it be reasonable to challenge his analysis by dredging up deviant cases? That, very likely, is the sort of response Frey would make to the argument involving the linguistically deficient traveler.

This likely response of Frey's assumes that there are "normal cases" of the attribution of belief—that is, cases where, in attributing beliefs to certain individuals, the attribution of belief is clearly justified.[14] "Deviant cases" are cases where beliefs are attributed to individuals who, in one way or another, are relevantly unlike those individuals to whom beliefs are attributed in these normal cases. Which individuals are those to whom beliefs are attributed in these normal cases? Frey's position is that these individuals are normal, adult human beings, individuals who, so it turns out, happen to be able to use a language and who, by this means, are able to express their beliefs linguistically. The linguistically deficient traveler of our earlier example represents a deviant case: he is not a normal, adult human being and lacks language. And, Frey is likely to argue, one ought not to contest the adequacy of a proposed analysis of belief, one that fits the normal cases well, by, in his words, "seizing upon . . . (the case of) . . . those deviant humans among us. . . ."[15]

Three replies must suffice here. First, what counts as a "normal" or a "deviant" case is not the neutral matter Frey evidently assumes that it is. On Frey's understanding of these notions, the linguistically deficient traveler is a deviant case. But this is to assume the greater part of what Frey is obliged to show, since, on some accounts of the grounds for the attribution of belief (for example, if a given organism's behaving in a certain way is sufficient for attributing beliefs to it), the traveler provides us with a normal, not a deviant, case. In other words, *before* Frey could be justified in marking off as the *only normal* cases, those cases where beliefs are attributed to individuals who express their beliefs linguistically, he should be required to show that alternative accounts of the grounds of belief attribution are deficient. The mere advocacy of Frey's favored view regarding the object of belief does not show that this view is correct. That is the first point to be made regarding Frey's understanding of normal cases.

Second, quite apart from the specific question of animals' beliefs, Frey's general understanding of how to assess proposed analyses of difficult ideas is radically conservative. Essentially, what Frey believes is this: If a proposed analysis fits the "normal" cases, *then that is enough*, and it is quite improper to contest its adequacy by dredging up this or that "deviant" case. This is a quite remarkable view for a philosopher to take, since it rules out the familiar, proper method of testing proposed analyses of ideas by considering possible counterexamples, cases that, in one way or another, depart from "normal" cases and thus are in that sense "deviant." Frey's view would presumably countenance, for example, an analysis of a human being that included "has two arms" since this is the "normal" condition of those who are human. If we were to contest this analysis by citing one-armed humans, one who accepts Frey's position presumably could dismiss our challenge on the grounds that one-armed humans are "deviant" cases and so have no role to play in the dispassionate assessment of proposed analyses. Such a view of how rival analyses are to be tested should find no favor among philosophers. Part of what conceptual analyses seek to lay bare are the conditions that must be met if a given concept can possibly be properly applied; one wants to know the *limits* of its intelligible application, not just what applications are "normal." To suppose that its limits can be found *just* by getting clear on its "normal" applications is fundamentally confused (in some ways like supposing that we can discover the age of the oldest living person by determining the "normal" life expectancy of people alive today). Even though it is true that "normal" adult human beings (a) have beliefs and (b) can, and sometimes do, express their beliefs linguistically, it does not follow that it is a *logical* truth that only those individuals who can express beliefs in language can have them. Begged questions to one side, Frey's reasons for dismissing the relevance of "deviant" cases bespeaks a too narrow view about the point of, and the proper way to assess, proposed analyses of concepts or ideas.

Third, Frey's understanding of "normal" cases, when coupled with his view about the object of belief, leads to the conclusion that no one can learn a language. And this in turn leads to the unwelcome result that no one can believe anything, *if* the object of belief is, as Frey says it is, that a particular sentence is true. The first part of the argument showing this can be formulated as follows:

1. If, in order to believe anything, one must believe that certain sentences are true, then those individuals who do not understand sentences cannot believe anything.
2. Young children, before they learn a language, do not understand sentences.
3. Therefore, young children cannot believe anything.

The first step merely restates Frey's view regarding the object of belief; the second sets forth an evident truism; and the third states the conclusion that follows from 1 and 2. Where does this argument lead? This is brought out by the following steps, which build upon the previous ones:

4. If young children cannot have beliefs, then they cannot be taught to use a language.

5. Therefore, young children cannot be taught to use a language.

The crucial step is step 4, and its defense involves the following observations, observations that are in some ways reminiscent of the discussion in the previous chapter of Descartes's language test (1.5). Consider what is involved in teaching young children the use of words in a language such as English. Characteristically we begin by holding up or pointing to objects and giving their names—*ball, mother, dog, bottle*. If Baby Jane picks up on what we are attempting to teach, the time comes when she is able to give the correct name: she says "ball" when the object we hold or point to is a ball. To explain how Baby Jane learns to do this would be no mean accomplishment certainly, and it is well beyond the range of the present work to undertake this task. The sole point that needs to be made here is this: unless Baby Jane comes to believe that there is a particular thing we are referring to, when we say the word *ball*, all manner of instruction in the use of the word *ball* will be for naught. She simply will not come to learn the meaning of the word. Without a *preverbal* belief on her part, one that picks out the ball as the thing to which we are referring when we say *ball*, her linguistic education cannot get underway. As step 5 declares, she will be in a situation where she simply "cannot be taught to use a language."

Frey's view of the object of belief consigns Baby Jane to just this fate. Given his view, Baby Jane not only will not, she cannot, acquire linguistic proficiency. This is because, according to Frey, to believe something is to believe that a certain sentence is true, something Baby Jane most certainly is incapable of doing before acquiring the use of language. Accordingly, since to learn a language Baby Jane must have beliefs about what we are referring to, and since, on Frey's view, to have a belief is to believe that a certain sentence is true, it follows that Baby Jane cannot have any beliefs about what we are referring to before she learns to speak or think in sentences. And from this it follows, given that Baby Jane *must* have such beliefs if she is to acquire the use of language, that she cannot be taught to use a language and, indeed, that she never can come to have any beliefs, given Frey's view of the object of belief. Unless we were to assume that humans come into the world already knowing the meanings of words and already knowing which words refer to which things—assumptions that no one, Frey included, will accept—Frey's position leads to the conclusion that no one can ever believe anything.

The preceding criticisms of Frey, if sound, show that something is radically wrong with his analysis of belief. Quite apart from what he thinks about "deviant" cases, Frey surely must think that normal, adult human beings do have beliefs and that the acquisition of linguistic proficiency by children is an everyday occurrence. Not even Frey, that is, can be assumed to accept views that so flagrantly fly in the face of common sense. This being so, Frey must give up his view about the object of belief. In particular, as reflection on the possibility of language acquisition shows, Frey must recognize that human children must have the ability to form beliefs *before* they learn to use a language, since otherwise they could not learn to use one. More generally, Frey must recognize that there are nonlinguistic beliefs—beliefs, that is, that individuals have independently of their mastery of a language. Before she learns to speak any language, Baby Jane must believe enough about what we refer to by our words and gestures to understand what it is that we refer to. This much granted, animals cannot consistently be viewed otherwise. If humans can have nonlinguistic beliefs, so can animals. To allow this possibility in the former case while denying it in the latter would be doctrinaire.

At this point, if not before, Frey might complain that what he calls "a further argument" in support of his view that animals cannot believe anything has been systematically ignored. For in order to believe that something is the case, Frey maintains, one must be able to distinguish between true and false beliefs, something that animals are unable to do. Lacking in this respect, they are similarly lacking in beliefs.[16]

This "further argument" is disputable on at least two counts. The first concerns Frey's grounds for denying that animals can distinguish between true and false beliefs. According to Frey, animals are unable to do this because they "lack language."[17] But if this is why animals are alleged to lack the ability to distinguish between true and false beliefs, Frey's "further argument" is not a further argument at all. It *assumes* that to believe that something is the case, one must believe that this or that sentence is true. Since this is a position of Frey's we have sound reasons to reject, we are similarly entitled to dismiss arguments that would require its acceptance. (For further comments on the ability of animals to distinguish between true and false beliefs, see sec. 2.4.)

A second reason for disputing Frey's "further argument" is this. The view that belief requires one's distinguishing between true and false beliefs leads to an infinite regress. This can be shown by considering what Frey says about our grasp of the connection between language and "the world." On Frey's view, we must "grasp (the) relationship" between true and false sentences, on the one hand, and "the world," on the other, if we are to believe anything about the world. This grasp is "essential."[18] It is, Frey writes, "difficult to capture" this "link."[19] What is certain is that, unless we have "grasped" it, we can have no beliefs about the world.

For Frey to say that it is difficult to capture this link is to understate the difficulty for one who holds a view like his. Any credible account of what my "grasp of this link" involves will involve my *having beliefs about* how language and the world are linked; to credit me with "grasping this link," on the one hand, and, on the other, to deny that I have *beliefs about* how language and the world are "linked," will be irredeemably unintelligible. If I "grasp the link," I must have beliefs about the "link" between the two. That much is certain. Now, these beliefs I have (that is, my beliefs about how language and the world are linked), given Frey's view, inasmuch as they *are* beliefs, must be beliefs that certain sentences are true. This must be true, given Frey's view, because what one believes, whenever one believes something, is that a given sentence is true. However, if I am to have beliefs about the link between language and the world, I must do in their case what Frey implies I must do in the case of any other belief: I must distinguish between (a) my believing that this link is thus-and-so and (b) my possibly being mistaken in believing what I do. In other words, I must distinguish between my believing that (a') a sentence of the form " 'Language and the world are linked in such and such a way' is true" and (b') " 'Language and the world are linked in this way' is false." If I fail to grasp the idea that I might be mistaken in believing what I do, then I will have failed to grasp the distinction between true and false beliefs about what I believe is the link between language and the world. And if I fail to grasp *this* distinction in the case of my beliefs about this link, there is every reason to deny that I have any beliefs about this link, given Frey's views about the concept of belief.

But now there is a problem. For if I distinguish between (a') and (b'), then I must believe something about the former that I do not believe about the latter. To credit me with *"grasping the distinction"* between believing (a') and believing (b'), on the one hand, and, on the other, to deny that I *have different beliefs about the two*, is unintelligible. So, in order for me to "grasp the link between language and the world," given Frey's views, not only must I have beliefs about the "link" between the two, I must also have beliefs about my beliefs about the "link" between the two. And there is no stopping here, given a position like Frey's. Since I must distinguish between what I take to be my true beliefs about my beliefs about the link in question and what I take to be false beliefs about this link, if I am to believe anything about this link, I must also have beliefs about my beliefs about my beliefs about this link. And beliefs about these beliefs. And beliefs about these, and so on, ad infinitum. The result is that if I am to "grasp the link between language and the world," I *must* distinguish between an infinite number of beliefs that I take to be true and an infinite number that I take to be false. And since no one can satisfy this requirement, the view—that one must grasp the distinction between true and false beliefs in order to "grasp the link" between language and the world—precludes the possibility of anyone's grasping this link and thus, given Frey's views about the relationship between belief and language, precludes anyone's believing anything about the world. It can be no valid objection to attributing beliefs about the world to animals to urge that they cannot meet a requirement that no one can possibly satisfy. Since Frey's requirement has this unsalutary feature, it provides no good reason against attributing beliefs to animals.

There is a way to halt the regress outlined in the preceding paragraph. This is to show that there are some beliefs that we can have that do not require that we distinguish between our belief that they are true and the belief that their negation is false or, alternatively, between our belief that they are true and our recognizing the possibility that we may be mistaken in believing what we do. For example, suppose it could be shown that in order for any individual, A, to have a belief about the world, A had to distinguish between his believing that something is the case, on the one hand, and that thing's not being the case, on the other. And suppose it was then claimed that although this is necessary in the case of beliefs about the world, it is not necessary in the case of beliefs we have about the relationship between language and the world, or in the case of beliefs about such beliefs, and so forth. If that were shown, then the regress could be stopped and, given a view like Frey's, we could then maintain that animals, because they are languageless, cannot have beliefs about the world.

Perhaps this is what Frey believes. In any case, what one would be right to insist upon is a supporting argument. What is there about "beliefs about the world" that makes it reasonable to require that one distinguish between true and false beliefs *in their case*, if one is to be said to have such beliefs, but *not in the case of any other belief* (e.g., beliefs about the link between language and the world)? Without some argument to support limiting this requirement to *just* beliefs about the world, limiting it just to these beliefs will be arbitrary in the extreme. Frey, it seems fair to say, fails to advance a supporting argument, and it is extraordinarily unclear what shape any argument could take if, as is required, the charge of arbitrariness is to be met. Setting to one side the criticism that Frey begs the question when he denies that animals are unable to distinguish between true and false beliefs because they "lack language," his own views on what is involved in having beliefs about the world either lead to an infinite regress or, if this regress is stopped at a point that excludes animals from those who have beliefs, does so arbitrarily. In either case Frey's "further argument" for denying that animals have beliefs fails.

Neither of Frey's arguments examined in the present section provides a reasonable defense of his denial that animals can have beliefs. Neither, therefore, provides an adequate defense of his denial that animals can have desires, if desires presuppose beliefs. The burden of proof the Cumulative Argument places on those who deny the application of the belief-desire theory to animals has not been met by Frey.

2.3 THE CONTENT OF BELIEF

As was remarked earlier (2.1), Frey is not the only one to challenge the application of the belief-desire theory to animals and their behavior. Stich also believes there is reason to resist applying this theory in their case. But the principal difficulty, according to Stich, is not, as it is according to Frey, that animals cannot believe anything; it is that we cannot say *what* they believe and so cannot describe or explain their behavior by making reference to what they believe and, if beliefs are necessary for desires, by making reference to what they desire. Because Stich's reasons for denying the validity of applying the belief-desire theory to animals differ from Frey's, their adequacy or inadequacy must be assessed on their merits, independently of the criticisms raised against Frey's arguments. The present section undertakes this necessary assessment.

To make his position clearer, Stich distinguishes between what he calls "two quite different sorts of properties" that we attribute to beliefs. Here is what he says:

> On the one hand, we take beliefs to be functional or psychological states of quite a special sort. Beliefs are states which interact with desires, with perception and with each other. . . . Thus a psychological model of a subject who has beliefs (and desires) would have to fit the (belief-desire theory). On the other hand, beliefs are states with content; they are propositional attitudes. If a state is a belief we expect it to be a belief *that* something or other; we expect there to be some way of expressing its content.[20]

Now, the problem about animal belief—what Stich at one point calls "the dilemma of animal belief"[21]—is, according to Stich, that we simply cannot specify the content of what, on the belief-desire theory, we say that animals believe. On reflection, that is, Stich thinks that "we find ourselves quite unable to say what (animals) believe,"[22] and, since we are unable to say this, we simply do not know *what* we are attributing to animals, if and when we say that they believe something. Stich does not conclude from this that animals do not or cannot have beliefs. He concludes his essay by asking the same question with which he begins, "Do animals have beliefs?" and answers it by writing, "To paraphrase my son: 'A little bit they do. And a little bit they don't.' "[23] Our interest lies in Stich's reasons for the "little bit they don't" part of his answer—with, that is, his arguments that are supposed to show that we cannot specify the content of animal beliefs. (Frey, as we shall see, raises similar objections, which also will be considered.)

In his initial statement of his case Stich deploys two different arguments.[24] The first is that, since Fido the dog sometimes gets confused when it comes to bones—failing occasionally to recognize that some bones (e.g., bones of the middle ear) *are* bones, while at others he is fooled by imitations—it follows that Fido must not have the concept of a bone. The second argument urges that, even were Fido better at recognizing a bone when he saw one, we still ought not to credit him with understanding the concept of a bone because he is ignorant of elementary facts about bones, including, for example, that bones have an anatomical function and originate in the way they do. Against both arguments it is tempting to respond that Fido is not alone in these matters.[25] Many human beings, not just dogs, are fallible when it comes to recognizing bones, and many people once did, and a good many still do, believe that, say, dinosaur bones were part of God's original creation. But though these responses have a point, they fail to address the fundamental assumption Stich brings to his discussion of animal belief—namely, his steady reliance on there being *the* concept of such and such, such as *the* concept of a bone. Unless or until we have examined this assumption, the tempting objections we might want to raise against Stich's two initial arguments against attributing beliefs to animals might just slide by his position.

What, then, is *the* concept of a bone, according to Stich? The answer Stich provides undermines itself in an interesting way. What Stich evidently believes (see, for example, his two arguments) is that for any x, the concept of x consists of a set of beliefs about x's. For example, the concept of a bone consists of a set of beliefs about bones, including, say, the beliefs that they have a certain anatomical function and that they originate in a certain way. There is, however, an obvious difficulty for this interpretation of *the* concept of a bone: what has been and is believed about bones varies considerably, both at the same time but in different places, and in the same places but at different times. To understand *the* concept of x as consisting of *a* set of beliefs about x's undermines thinking that there is *the* concept of anything. To think of concepts in this way is to suggest or assume a permanence in what is believed that history will not tolerate. Rather, we ought at most to speak of "the concept of a bone" (or "of the earth," "of the stars," etc.) as these are understood by various individuals, at the same or different times or places. When, therefore, Stich writes of "*the* concept of a bone," he must be interpreted to mean not "the set of beliefs about bones accepted by everyone who has ever lived," an interpretation that, since there is no unanimity as regards beliefs about bones (or anything else), would cause *the* concept of a bone to evaporate before our very eyes; he must mean, instead, "the set of beliefs about bones shared by those who happen to hold the same beliefs about bones as I do (i.e., as Stich does)." Now, since Stich assumes that his readers are likely to have the same beliefs about bones as he does and thus to have the same concept of a bone, he might also refer, and in fact sometimes does so refer, to this concept as "our concept."

Let us assume that we do share Stich's beliefs; when Stich refers to "*the* concept of a bone" he means "*our* concept of a bone." And let us briefly note, before proceeding, how interpreting his talk of "the concept of a bone" in this way makes it clear how Stich should reply to the tempting objections, mentioned earlier, concerning his two initial arguments against attributing beliefs to animals. Were we, for example, to object that some humans do not know anything about the anatomical function of bones and claim that Stich would be playing favorites if he denied that Fido lacked our concept of a bone because he lacked this belief but allowed that the humans in question have our concept, Stich's reply should be clear. It is that *neither* Fido *nor* the humans have our concept of a bone. Moreover, since, as Stich observes, "this argument may be reiterated, *mutatis mutandis*, for meat, yards . . . burying," and so forth, Stich will urge that we ought not to attribute these concepts to Fido *or* "to a human who is as irredeemably ignorant as Fido."[26] Stich, in short, plays no favorites when it comes to who does, and who does not, have our concepts. Some humans, not just all animals, are losers. The tempting objections to Stich's initial arguments overlook this and, he implies, therefore pose no real objection.

There are two divergent critical approaches one might take at this point. The first is to challenge Stich by arguing that, though animals and some humans do not have *our* concept of a bone or the other family of concepts we share with Stich, these animals and humans have concepts nonetheless—*their* concepts—so that it is, therefore, no serious deficiency in their case that they come up short of the standards one must meet to have our concepts. The second approach is to argue that at least some animals *do* have our concept of a bone and, if this much could be shown, that they have our concepts of much else besides. This second challenge may seem unpromising, and it is a measure of its initial implausibility that Frey thinks it can be dismissed out of hand. He writes as follows:

> If we are to attribute beliefs to animals, then how are we accurately to capture the content of their beliefs? When we say 'The cat believes that the ball is stuck', do we really wish to maintain that the cat possesses our concepts of 'ball' and 'stuck'? Plainly not.[27]

But why is this "plainly not" the case? Well, Frey goes on to say, the cat does not have *our* concept of "ball" since "it is highly unlikely that the cat possesses . . . *our* notions of 'physical object' or 'material object' or 'independent thing' or 'substantial entity in my visual field'. . . ."[28] On Frey's view, as on Stich's, the reason why the cat "plainly" lacks our concept of a bone, a ball, or what have you, is that the cat, like any other nonhuman animal, lacks our beliefs about bones, balls, and so on; or at least it is "highly unlikely" that these animals have these beliefs. For these reasons, the second challenge one might raise against Stich and, by implication, against Frey, in this regard may seem to be anything but promising. Yet one can imagine how Stich, like Frey, might argue that it is only this second, not the first, challenge that can pose a serious threat. For since, in order to credit animals with beliefs in a full-blooded way, we must be able to specify the content of what they believe, and since, in the attempt to specify this, we must use a language that encapsulates *our* concepts (e.g., of "ball" or "bone"), and assuming that our concept of a bone includes, say, the beliefs that bones have certain anatomical functions and originate in certain ways (beliefs we have no reason to assume that animals share), then it looks fairly certain that no animal can have our concept of a bone or of anything. This being so, to persist in attributing beliefs to animals, beliefs that involve *their* (supposed) concepts—as those who would criticize Stich's position in the first way are wont to do—seems illogical at best. To use Frey's observation about the cat who, though presumably lacking our concepts of "ball" and "stuck," is nevertheless alleged to believe that "the ball is stuck," what this first approach would leave us with are supposed "feline concepts, though without any idea as to what these are or how they are formed."[29] This first critical approach to Stich's views, therefore, seems destined to fail to do what it set out to do— namely, to specify *the content* of animal beliefs. This can be done, Stich could argue, only if we had reason to believe that animals share our concepts. And *this* can be argued not by attempting to challenge Stich's position along the lines of the first critical approach but only by pressing the second.

It is not certain that Stich would reply in just these terms, but it is certain that he could. In any event, it is the second way of critically approaching Stich's views on animal beliefs (and, as we shall see more clearly, Frey's as well) that will be pursued in what follows. Before commencing my critical assessment, a cautionary word is in order. As in other controversial areas in philosophy, there is no scarcity of alternative views in the particular case of the analysis of the concept of concepts. It will not be possible to examine all the competing alternatives, but neither would it be fair to require that we do so. The motivation of the present discussion is *to examine the merits of major arguments that explicitly address the question of animal beliefs and desires*, and though there are other positions regarding the concept of concepts that have interesting implications for this question, it is not unreasonable to limit the scope of our inquiry here to an assessment of the major arguments at hand—namely, to Stich's and, as we shall see, Frey's. To try to do more would be to accomplish less.

One final preliminary point. In contesting the views of those who deny that we can say what animals believe even if we assume that they believe something, one can either accept the type of analysis of the concept of concepts on which these views depend or reject this analysis. To do the latter is certain to meet with objections from Stich (and Frey), and the debate over whose analysis of the concept of concepts is "the right one" is, it seems, certain to carry us further away from the question that inspires the controversy presently before us—namely, whether we can say what animals believe, assuming that they have beliefs. Better, then, for present purposes, to grant to these critics the type of analysis they themselves rely upon and then to show that *even if* we concede this much, it does *not* follow that we cannot say what animals believe. This may be to concede more to these critics than we should, but to concede less, it seems, would be certain to be counterproductive.

The Concept of Concepts

Among the questions we need to consider is the following: Suppose there are two groups of individuals, G_1 and G_2, who do not share all of the same beliefs about a given x (e.g., about bones). Is this difference by itself sufficient for concluding that they do not have the same concept of a bone? It would be sufficient if we accept what we might call *the all-or-nothing view* of concepts and their acquisition. On this view, *any* difference in the beliefs held about x's as between G_1 and G_2 is enough to rule out their having the same concept. For example, if the Stichians (those of us who believe all that Stich believes about bones) believe all that we do, while the Prechemists believe all that we do except that, because of their ignorance of chemistry, they do not believe that bones contain calcium, then, on the all-or-nothing view, we Stichians have one concept of a bone while the Prechemists have an entirely different one. An alternative to the all-or-nothing view is the *more-or-less* view. This view holds that having a given concept is not the you-either-have-it-or-you-lack-it situation the all-or-nothing view entails. On the more-or-less view, different groups and different individuals can have the same concept to a greater or lesser degree. On this view, the Prechemists have the Stichian (our) concept of a bone, though not *in toto*, and another group, similarly lacking in chemical knowledge but also in the dark about how, say, dinosaur bones originated, also has our concept of a bone, but to an even less degree than the Prechemists. *Who* has *what* concept, in short, is a matter of degree, according to the more-or-less view. It bears noting, however, that even the more-or-less view will allow us sometimes to say that a given group or individual completely lacks a given concept of ours. For example, if the Boneheads believed that bones came into existence by a sort of magical spontaneous generation when and only when a living body was injured or died, and explicitly denied that bones have the anatomical function we Stichians affirm, denied that bones originated in the way we believe, and similarly denied everything else that we take to be definitive of a bone, then, even if we accept the more-or-less view, we ought to say that the Boneheads lack our concept of a bone—totally.

We shall return to the case of the Boneheads later (2.4). For the present there is a more fundamental issue to decide. The all-or-nothing and the more-or-less views give us two different ways of regarding, two alternative ways of describing, what is involved in possessing the same concept. Assuming that one's concept of x is one's set of beliefs about x's which view ought rationally to be preferred? The more-or-less view seems clearly rationally preferable. Not only does it enable us to mark the difference we want to mark between the Prechemists and the Boneheads vis-à-vis their having our concept of a bone (for we *do* want to say that the Prechemists and the Boneheads *are not equally deficient* when it comes to their respective possession of our concept), it also enables us to explain how it is possible for individuals to increase their understanding of a given concept in stages, incrementally, a little at a time. This is a possibility the more-or-less view allows and the all-or-nothing view excludes.

Suppose, for illustrative purposes, that Mitch has a quite limited understanding of what it is to be a bone, making all the errors a beginner is prone to make—taking a long time to hear the difference between, say, "bone" and "phone," with predictable attendant mistakes. From these meager beginnings, imagine Mitch has progressed and now knows a good deal about bones, though still not an expert by any means, and still woefully ignorant when it comes to matters chemical. It would be very natural to say that Mitch's understanding of our (the Stichian) concept of a bone had progressed, from very little to a good deal more, that his grasp of this concept had improved. The more-or-less view can account for this, but the all-or-nothing view cannot. On this latter view, Mitch did not start with a limited understanding of our concept of a bone and then come steadily to increase his understanding of this concept as he learned more about what we believe about bones. According to the all-or-nothing view, when Mitch had only a few of our beliefs about bones, he did not have our concept at all because he did not as yet have *all* the beliefs about bones that, on the all-or-nothing view, he must have in order to have our concept in the first place. Nor did Mitch add to his understanding of our concept as he acquired additional beliefs we have about bones; rather, just he was totally lacking in our concept when he had only a few of our beliefs about bones, so he failed to increase his grasp of our concept as he acquired additional beliefs. With every increase, Mitch acquired a new, a different concept. It was only on that fateful day when, let us assume, Mitch came to have all the beliefs about bones that, on the all-or-nothing view, one must have in order to have our concept of a bone, that Mitch acquired his first grasp of our concept. On that fateful day, in short, the all-or-nothing view entails that Mitch went from having nothing (that is, from having no grasp of our concept of a bone) to having everything (that is, to having our concept completely).

It is difficult to understand how—unless, to use a wonderful expression of Frey's, one is "in the grip of a theory"—anyone could claim that the all-or-nothing view is a credible view about concepts and their acquisition. Mitch *clearly* has made some sort of progress before he arrives at that banner day when he completes the list of our beliefs about bones. Toward the end of his adventure in learning Mitch clearly is closer to *completing his grasp* of our concept of a bone, *not* closer to acquiring our concept, to any extent, for the first time. If it is the beliefs we have about bones that define our concept of a bone, the reasonable thing to say is that Mitch has increased his understanding of our concept along the way. The more-or-less view will countenance our saying this, but the all-or-nothing view will not. Since, then, one wants an account of concepts and concept acquisition that enables us to say this, there are principled reasons for selecting the more-or-less view in preference to its rival.

Asking the Right Question

Now, acceptance of the more-or-less view enables us to give a clear formulation of the question we need to answer if we are to attribute our concept of a bone to Fido. For if individuals can have this concept to a greater or lesser degree, the possibility presents itself that it would be *enough* to show that Fido has this concept if we had reason to maintain that he had just *one* of the beliefs among the set of beliefs that defines our concept. Granted, were Fido to have just one such belief, his understanding of this concept would be meager, impoverished, elementary, and so on, in comparison to those who have this concept *in toto*. But this would only show that his understanding was less than others', not that he has no understanding at all. The question we need to ask, then, granting the reasonableness of the more-or-less view, is this: Is there any reason to maintain that Fido has at least one of the beliefs about bones that is definitive of our concept of a bone? It would seem not. The two most obvious attempts to provide an affirmative answer prove woefully ineffective. The first attempt begins by noting that, though not infallible, Fido nonetheless is reasonably good at discriminating when it comes to bones. Normally, that is, Fido knows a bone when he sees one. Might we not conclude from his success in this regard that he therefore has our concept of a bone, at least minimally? The answer must be, no. For though Fido is good when it comes to recognizing a bone when he sees one, his success in this regard does not by itself tell us anything about *his* concept of a bone—does not, that is, *by itself* inform us about what it is for something to be a bone, from Fido's point of view. Let his powers of discrimination be as good as you please, we are still as far from saying what Fido believes, when he believes that something is a bone, as we were before. Even assuming that the more-or-less view of concepts and concept acquisition is to be preferred, and even granting that Fido is a skillful bone discriminator, we have as yet no reason to maintain that Fido has *our* concept of a bone, even to a minimum degree.

A natural response to the failure of this first argument is to attempt to determine the properties of those bones Fido recognizes as bones. This could be approached in a scientific manner: bones could be weighed and chemically analyzed, and shapes could be recorded; we would then, let us assume, eventually arrive at a sort of "Fido Bone Profile," a report that sets forth the chemical, geometric, and other properties of "Bones Fido Recognizes" as against "Bones Fido Doesn't Recognize." However, even were we to achieve our objective, this would not provide a basis for attributing any part of our concept of a bone to Fido, since, as Stich argues against a comparable enterprise,[30] we could not view Fido's concept of a bone in terms of the dog's beliefs about the chemical, geometric, and other theory-laden properties we find in the bones Fido recognizes. This we could not do because there is no good reason to believe, and profoundly good reason to deny, that Fido himself understands anything whatever about chemistry, geometry, and the other factors that figure in his "Bone Profile."

What Stich calls "the dilemma of animal belief," then, comes to this: *Fido's* ability to recognize a bone when he sees one *by itself* does not reveal what it is that Fido believes are the properties of bones by virtue of which he recognizes those bones he does; and *our* efforts to say what these properties are, it seems, can only supply us with a list of properties there is no reason to suppose that Fido can understand, let alone believe, that bones possess. Neither of these approaches, in short, can move us any closer to the goal of specifying the *content* of what Fido believes when he believes that something is a bone. Now, later on (2.4), the point will be made that our ignorance regarding Fido's beliefs about the properties bones have is a two-edged sword; and we shall want to explain how sharp its second edge is. For the present, it may look as if there is no possible way to specify the content of Fido's beliefs about bones and thus no possible ground on which to attribute our concept of a bone to the dog.

Enfranchising Fido

Though the most obvious efforts to enfranchise Fido in this respect fail for the reasons given, to conclude that Fido cannot share any belief about bones with us would be premature. For there is a belief about bones that (1) is a member of the set of beliefs that defines our concept of bones and that (2) we have ample reason to maintain that Fido has. The belief in question does not concern some theory-laden property of bones, such as their chemical composition. Nor is the belief reducible to Fido's discriminatory capacity when it comes to bones. Rather, the belief concerns how bones relate to desires and their satisfaction, more particularly, how, in certain circumstances, the choice of a bone is the preferred choice—that is, is the choice to be made if a desire is to be satisfied. To make this clearer, we need first to remind ourselves that occasions arise in the sphere of human activity where the choice of a bone is the choice to be made if we are to satisfy certain desires or fulfill certain purposes. What these desires or purposes are can vary, from, say, wanting to illustrate how a bone decays over time to desiring to concoct a hearty beef stew. Nevertheless, bones being what they are, circumstances do arise where, given that we have those desires and purposes we have, the selection of a bone is called for if we are to satisfy these desires or fulfill these purposes. Now, to recognize this connection between bones and satisfying desires *is* to have a belief about bones—not, to be sure, a belief about their chemical composition or their anatomical function but a belief about bones nonetheless. Moreover, this belief—the belief that a bone is to be chosen if a given desire is to be satisfied—*is* one member of the set of beliefs that collectively define our concept. This can be seen by imagining that Mitch has progressed in his understanding of this concept to the point where he understands that bones have an anatomical function but, when asked what to add to the pot, a meaty beef bone or a maple limb, given his keen desire for a tasty beef stew, he replies that he does not know which should be added and disclaims any understanding of there being any connection between the taste of stews and the flavor of bones. If Mitch were to display so grievous a lack of understanding of this connection, we would be right to say not that he has no grasp of our concept of a bone but that he has not quite got the whole of that concept: he simply fails to grasp the connection between the flavor bones have, on the one hand, and, on the other, how this fact bears on why, in circumstances of a sort in which he finds himself, bones are to be chosen in preference to other things if he is to satisfy the desire we assume he has. Put another way, the belief that is grounded in one's understanding of this connection (let us call this *the preference-belief*) is, to this point in time at least, missing from Mitch's repertoire of beliefs concerning bones.

But what of Fido? Does he have the preference-belief Mitch lacks? Does he believe that there is a connection between (a) satisfying his desire for a certain flavor and (b) choosing a bone? Lacking as he is in language, Fido of course cannot tell us, or reasonably be expected to tell us, whether he has this belief.[31] In the nature of the case, *his* having the preference-belief Mitch lacks can be fairly judged by attending to the only thing we have to go on—namely, his nonverbal behavior. What we want to ask, then, is whether by observing Fido's behavior we may ever reasonably conclude that he believes that bones are to be chosen if he is to satisfy his desire for a certain flavor. (Recall, before an answer to this question is offered, that representative arguments that deny that animals can believe or desire anything were examined and found wanting in the previous section [2.2]. Thus, those who, for example, are enamored of a stimulus-response explanation of animal behavior cannot rely on those arguments to support their view that Fido in particular and animals in general neither believe nor desire anything.)

Once the question is put in the appropriate terms, and once we command a clear view of the conceptual and empirical terrain from the vantage point of the argument that has progressed to this point, the answer is clear. All indications are that Fido does from time to time desire a flavor he finds that bones have. This is, on the view recommended here, a fact about Fido, something we know of him, not wild speculation or unbridled anthropomorphism. (These claims are defended more fully in section 2.4.) Moreover, we can also observe, by attending to how he behaves, what Fido selects by way of fulfilling his desire. This is not the refrigerator, say, or the neighbor's lawnmower. What he selects by way of fulfilling his desire is—a bone! On the basis of his behavior, therefore, we have reason to maintain that Fido believes that bones are related to his desires or preferences in the following way: Bones satisfy certain desires he has and are to be chosen to satisfy those desires. Granted, our accepting that Fido has this one belief about bones does not settle the question about the full range of properties bones have, from Fido's point of view, by virtue of which he recognizes a bone when he sees one. There may be and indeed most certainly probably are many such properties, including, most obviously, certain olfactory properties, that Fido associates with being a bone. But what these properties are, however interesting that question may be, is not a question that must be answered *before* we can credit Fido with believing that there is a connection between choosing bones and satisfying his desire for the flavor they have. Whatever the full range of these properties might be, we have ample reason to maintain, on the basis of how the dog behaves, when viewed against the backdrop of the Cumulative Argument, that Fido sometimes chooses a bone in the belief that it will satisfy his desire for a given flavor. And to know this of Fido is to know enough for present purposes, since, knowing this much, we can say something specific about *what* Fido believes about bones—we can, that is, *specify the content* of his concept of a bone, at least to some degree. When Fido believes that something is a bone, at least part of what he believes is that it will satisfy his desire for a particular flavor and so is to be chosen if that desire is to be satisfied.

Now, it is not irrelevant that Fido should have this belief about bones. On the contrary, as was already noted, the preference-belief is part of *our* concept of a bone. For if Mitch uniformly fails to recognize that, bones being what they are, and his desires being what we have imagined them to be, a bone is to be chosen if he is to satisfy his desire for a particular flavor, then Mitch simply hasn't quite grasped our concept of a bone. Given, however, that *Fido* has the preference-belief about bones that Mitch lacks; given, further, that this belief is one of the beliefs that define the content of *our* concept of a bone; and given, finally, the reasonableness of the more-or-less view of concepts and their acquisition; then it follows that Fido *does* have *our* concept of a bone, at least to some degree. What Frey maintains is "plainly not" the case regarding our attributions of beliefs to animals—namely, that it is "plainly not" the case that animals have *our* concepts of anything—turns out to be otherwise (even if not "plainly"). Though his grasp may be limited, Fido has *our* concept of a bone, assuming, as we have, that our concept of *x* is understood as our beliefs about *x*'s.

2.4 THREE OBJECTIONS

A number of objections can be anticipated, one each concerning, respectively, what concepts, what experiences, and what beliefs we are entitled to say Fido has. Each will be considered separately, in the order just given. When we reach the third we will be able to supplement the previous remarks about Fido's grasp of the preference-belief.

Lacking Beliefs and Lacking Concepts

First, it might be objected that Fido's possessing (at least so far as has been argued in the above) only one of the beliefs that define our concept of a bone is an insufficient basis on which to attribute our concept to him, even assuming the more-or-less view is rationally preferable. Certainly Stich is likely to make this objection, since he states at one point that "if a subject *lacks* enough of our beliefs . . . content attribution is undermined."[32] This position, however, rests on a failure to distinguish between two senses in which a subject may be said to "lack enough of our beliefs." The first is what we might term *the denial sense*, the sense in which the Boneheads, as discussed earlier (2.3), "lack enough of the beliefs" about bones we Stichians accept. For the Boneheads, it will be recalled, *deny* all the beliefs we Stichians affirm when it comes to bones; *they* certainly "lack enough of our beliefs" about bones and do not, therefore, have our concept. A second sense of "lack enough beliefs" is the *nondenial sense*. In this sense a subject who "lacks our beliefs" does not *deny* any of them; rather, the subject simply *does not have* the beliefs in question. Mitch, for example, in the early stages of his education in our concept of a bone, certainly lacks a great many of our beliefs about bones but does not deny any of these remaining beliefs. Unlike the Boneheads, Mitch does not deny that bones have the anatomical function we believe they have; the matter of bones *having or not having* an anatomical function is an idea yet to be broached in Mitch's early education. While it is true that we ought not to attribute our concept of a bone to the Boneheads because they "lack enough of our beliefs" about bones in the denial sense, it by no means follows that we should do the same in Mitch's case. Indeed, given the reasonableness of the more-or-less view, we have principled reasons for maintaining that Mitch does have our concept, to a limited degree, even though he lacks many of the beliefs definitive of that concept, in the nondenial sense of "lacks our beliefs." So long as Mitch has at least one of the beliefs definitive of our concept, and so long as we have no reason to suppose that he holds other beliefs about bones that either explicitly deny our other beliefs or entail their denial, there is sufficient reason to attribute our concept to him.

To object that we cannot attribute our concept of a bone to Fido because Fido "lacks enough of our beliefs" about bones *can* be a valid objection, given what has just been argued, only if we have reason to believe that Fido "lacks enough of our beliefs" in the *denial* sense; that is, we cannot deny that Fido has our concept *unless we have reason to suppose that Fido has other beliefs about bones, in addition to the preference-belief, that explicitly deny our remaining beliefs or entail their denial.* So let us ask whether we have ample reason to believe this of Fido. It is here that the second, the neglected edge of our claimed ignorance about the remaining beliefs Fido has about bones shows itself. For our ignorance is genuine, if Stich is correct. As remarked earlier, *Fido's* success at recognizing bones does not by itself reveal what those properties are by virtue of which he recognizes a bone when he sees one, and *our* attempts to discover what these properties are by our own devices can only give us a list of properties (e.g., chemical and geometric) which there is no reason to suppose that Fido can understand, let alone believe, bones have. But *our presumed ignorance* in this regard, if genuine, shows that we cannot be justified in maintaining that Fido, though he has the preference-belief, *lacks* our remaining beliefs about bones, in the *denial* sense of "lacks." Since we do not know *what* (other) beliefs Fido has about bones, given Stich's view, we do not know that any or all of these beliefs explicitly or implicitly deny our remaining beliefs. And since we do not know this, we have no reason to deny that Fido has this concept, assuming, as always, that Fido does have the preference-belief, that this belief is partially definitive of our concept of a bone, and that the more-or-less view of concepts and concept acquisition is accepted. Were we to accept all this *and still* maintain that

Mitch does, while Fido does not, have our concept of a bone, then we *would* be playing favorites, and this in a rather nakedly prejudicial way.

It might be thought that this charge of prejudice could be met if an argument was at hand that showed that the beliefs defining our concept of a bone themselves have varying logical properties. In particular, suppose it is claimed that having the anatomical belief about bones is a logically necessary condition of having our concept of a bone. If this were shown to be so, then one could see how Fido would lack our concept of a bone, even though he shared at least one belief about bones with us. Moreover, since logic plays no favorites, it might seem that Fido has been excluded nonarbitrarily. But has he? One would want to know precisely how we are supposed to arrive at the conclusion that having the anatomical belief is a necessary condition of having our concept of a bone. If we were told that this is so *because* Fido cannot have this belief, then the prejudicial basis on which the issue is being decided would be obvious. Once we deny the reintroduction of the very prejudice under suspicion, however, there can be no argument that could convert anyone not already committed to the conclusion that the anatomical belief is necessary. *If* it were, then we would be obliged to say that Mitch did not have our concept of a bone, no matter how many other beliefs about bones he shared with us, if he lacked this particular belief. For reasons already adduced, this is an unsatisfactory view in the particular case of the anatomical belief.

What is true of the anatomical belief may be true of any other belief about bones. Given any particular belief we have about bones, that is, it may be true that having that particular belief is not a necessary condition of having our concept of a bone, at least to a certain degree. What is true of the anatomical belief, however, may not be true of every other belief we have about bones. There remains, that is, the possibility that at least one belief we have about bones is necessary, is essential, if someone is to have our concept. But what belief, if any, might this be? *If* there is such a belief, none can have a greater claim to the title "essential belief" than the preference-belief. After all, the question about who has our concept of a bone arises within the larger context of discussions about the belief-desire theory. So, again, *if* there is one belief about bones that is essential for possessing our concept, that belief should concern the relationship between believing that something is a bone, on the one hand, and, on the other, the bearing that having this belief has on choosing that thing (that is, the thing believed to be a bone) to satisfy a given desire. And *that* is precisely what characterizes the preference-belief, since to have that belief *is* to believe that those things one believes are bones are to be chosen in preference to other things if one is to satisfy one's desire for a particular taste or flavor. Accordingly, if there is no belief about bones that is essential for having our concept of a bone, then Fido cannot be disenfranchised from having our concept on the grounds that he shares only one belief (the preference-belief) with us, whereas if there is some one belief that is essential for possessing our concept of a bone, the preference-belief has at least as strong a claim to that title as any other belief. Whichever alternative is chosen, we have rational grounds to attribute a grasp of our concept of a bone to Fido. Fido is no Bonehead when it comes to bones.

Animal Experience

A second objection holds that, if we knew what it would be like to have a desire or taste a bone in the way Fido does, then we could attribute the preference-belief to the dog and thereby give content to what he believes when he believes that something is a bone. In fact, however, we do not know what it is like for Fido to experience anything, which rules out attributing the preference-belief to him.

Aside from discredited Cartesian grounds for denying consciousness to animals, what could be the basis for the skepticism that infuses this objection? One possibility is that since Fido is not a language-user, and since our own attempts to describe his experience *necessarily* will be expressed in language, it follows that we cannot know what it would be like for Fido to experience desires, tastes, and the like. Let us call this *the language argument*. It is a specious argument. Were we to accept it, we would be committed to the view that language-users cannot know that any description of anything that lacks a language is true. When, for example, we say a penny is brown, we, who are language-users, offer a partial description of the coin, which is not a language-user. If it were claimed that we cannot know what it would be like for Fido to experience desires and the like because our descriptions are linguistic and the dog is not a language-user, then we should also have to say that we cannot know that the penny is brown, because it, too, lacks language. But this is absurd. Equally absurd, therefore, is the view that leads to it. It cannot be reasonable to be skeptical of what we can know about Fido's experience because we do, while he does not, use a language. To give a slight twist to an argument of Jonathan Bennett's, a philosopher at Syracuse University, if we could not know anything about canine experience because we use language and dogs don't, then we could not even give a knowledgeable description of the canine digestive system.[33]

Perhaps it will be replied that it is the limits of our imagination, not language, that blocks the way to our being able to understand what it would be like for Fido to experience desires and the like. We cannot, we might be told, put ourselves imaginatively into Fido's world, cannot experience the world as Fido does. All efforts to do so are doomed since, even were we to imagine ourselves looking out at the world through the dog's eyes, so to speak, all we will have succeeded in doing is imagining *ourselves* looking out through his eyes, not *Fido's* doing so. Because we lack the necessary imaginative wherewithal, we just can't understand what it would be like for Fido to experience things as he does.

This argument (*the imagination argument*) also has skeptical implications few could live with. If I cannot imagine what it would be like to taste something as Fido does because all I can possibly bring off is imagining *myself* tasting things while (imaginatively) inhabiting Fido's body, how could it be any different were I to try to imagine myself being, say, Fidel Castro? Let my imaginative efforts and success be as robust as you please, I am still not going to have Fidel's experiences; at most I will have experiences of mine that I take to be like those of the Cuban leader. Am I to say that I therefore do not know what it is like for Fidel to want a cigar or to taste some brandy? I *must* say this, if my knowledge of how he experiences things stands or falls on my ability to imagine my being him to such a degree that what I experience are *his* experiences. But of course we do not suppose that skepticism should be given so free a rein. We do not believe that we are obliged to say that we do not know something because we are unable to fulfill a requirement for knowledge that it is impossible to fulfill. It cannot be reasonable, therefore, to be skeptical about how Fidel experiences desires, tastes, and so on, because we cannot imagine his experiences as ours. Neither, then, can it be reasonable to be skeptical about Fido's experiences on similar grounds.

"Still," someone will protest (and here we come to *the species argument*), "Fidel's and Fido's cases are different. Granted, I cannot experience Fidel's desires, only my own. Nevertheless, I know enough about what it is to be a human being—I have a first-hand acquaintance, after all—that I know that, when Fidel wants a cigar, his experience is like mine when, say, I want a pinch of snuff. The case of Fido is markedly different. I share no common fund of experience with the dog and thus do not know how he experiences anything. Fido is a dog, not, like Fidel, a member of my own species."

But is it true that different individuals, because they belong to different species, do not share any common experience? We would be in a fine fix, both practically and theoretically, if it were so. No one, presumably, believes that because dogs and cats belong to different species that *they* therefore share no common experience—for example, that canine and feline pain, or canine and feline sexual desires, are *entirely* different phenomena. Granted, it is *logically* possible that, though these animals exhibit similar pain and sexual behavior, they nonetheless have entirely different accompanying mental states. Both our common practice and respect for parsimony, however, are against regarding this possibility as true. Not only do we behave in ways that attest to our belief that animals from different species have similar experiences (for example, we act *as if* cat and dog pain are the same or relevantly similar); and not only does our behaving in this way "work" (treating cats and dogs as if they had the same or similar experiences enables us to interact with them in a practically efficacious way, as when, for example, we offer efficacious medical treatment to a cat with a broken leg that is analogous to the efficacious treatment we give a dog); more than this, regarding canine and feline experience as relevantly similar also has sound theory on its side. For we ought not to multiply kinds of experience (canine, feline, etc.) beyond necessity. If the belief that animals from different species share common or relevantly similar experiences is consistent with their observed behavior, then it is reasonable, for reasons of parsimony, to accept this belief. The belief that animals from different species do have the same or relevantly similar experiences frequently is consistent with their observed behavior, which is why, in addition to our having practical reasons for accepting this belief, we have theoretical reasons besides. We would throw respect for simplicity to the wind if we thought otherwise.

But is the attribution of common experiences to *humans* and animals consistent with human and animal behavior? This is a question to be settled on the basis of observing how humans and animals behave. What we want to know is whether animals ever behave in ways that resemble how humans behave, when we know that humans, say, desire water, warmth, food, or rest. Given the other tenets of the Cumulative Argument, and setting skeptical doubts about our knowledge of "other minds" to one side, it can only be, in Hume's words, "from the resemblance of the external actions of animals to those we ourselves perform, that we (can) judge their internal likewise to resemble ours."[34] If their behavior does resemble ours, and given the other tenets of the Cumulative Argument, then simplicity again will be on the side of attributing shared experiences. Now, none will deny that animal behavior does resemble human behavior, when, for example, it comes to the behavior associated with the known human desires just mentioned. If I know that you are thirsty and desire some water, I naturally expect you to drink a glass of water rather than down a cup of sand, when given the choice. Human-thirst behavior has its animal counterpart, and so I expect that animals would make a similar selection. In claiming that human-thirst (or taste, etc.) experience and animal-thirst (or taste, etc.) experience are similar, what we claim is not inconsistent with the observable facts about human and animal behavior. Once again, therefore, since, on grounds of simplicity, I ought not to multiply kinds of experience beyond necessity, I ought not to postulate a human-taste experience, say, that is totally different from canine-taste experience. On the contrary, I ought to postulate a shared, a common taste experience, even though dogs belong to one species of animals and humans to another.

This is not to say—and one need not say this—that every human experience has its animal counterpart, or even that every animal experience always is relevantly similar to some human experience. It is not to say the former because, for example, there is no reason to suppose that Fido has anything like the political worries I have or delights in Steeler victories as I do. And it is not to say the latter because there may be some forms of animal experience so alien to our own that we not only do not share relevantly similar experiences with them, we may not even be able to understand what it would be like to do so. This latter point is forcefully made by the American philosopher Thomas Nagel in his provocative essay, "What is it like to be a Bat?" "We know," observes Nagel,

> that most bats (the microchiroptera, to be precise) perceive the external world primarily by sonar, or echolocation, detecting the reflections, from objects within range, of their own rapid, subtly modulated, high frequency shrieks. Their brains are designed to correlate the outgoing impulses with the subsequent echoes, and the information thus acquired enables bats to make precise discriminations of distance, size, shape, motion, and texture comparable to those we make by vision. But bat sonar, though clearly a form of perception, is not similar in its operation to any sense that we possess, and there is no reason to suppose that it is subjectively like anything we can experience or imagine.[35]

The question at hand, however, is not whether *some* animals have *some* experiences radically dissimilar from human experience. That may be conceded by all the parties to the dispute. The question is whether we have any reason to believe that *any* animals have *any* experiences relevantly similar to some human experiences, most especially whether any, including Fido, experience desires and tastes in a way similar to how we do. Because the relevant animal behavior resembles human behavior, because we have independent reasons for viewing animals like Fido as having a mental life, and because simplicity requires that we not multiply kinds of experience beyond necessity, there is a strong presumptive reason for viewing these animal experiences as being like their human counterparts. It is a strong *presumptive* reason because we allow that arguments *may* be forthcoming that show that the inference to similar mental states is unwarranted—for example, because, in some cases, human and animal behavior is not sufficiently similar. Three arguments that, if sound, would block this inference have been considered—the language argument, the imagination argument, and the species argument. Each has been found wanting. There may, of course, be other arguments. Unless or until some argument is given that shows that this inference is rationally defective, however, the similarity of behavior between conscious beings from different species, coupled with the other tenets of the Cumulative Argument, warrant making it.

Behavior and the Content of Belief

A final objection concerns our ability to specify the content of animal belief on the basis of animal behavior. The point at issue is not whether animal behavior *by itself* suffices as a basis on which to rest the claim that animals have beliefs, understood as functional or psychological states. Earlier discussions have argued that the attribution of a mental life to animals rests on considerations *in addition to* how they behave (e.g., on considerations about the ordinary use of such words as *wants, believes, hates,* etc., as well as on the implications of evolutionary theory). The point presently at issue concerns our alleged inability to say *what* animals believe, to specify the *content* of their beliefs, on the basis of their observed behavior. Stich, because he denies that we can specify the content of animal beliefs, implies that we cannot say what they believe on the basis of how they behave. Stich's grounds for his denial have been considered and disputed (2.3). Frey also addresses the question at issue and offers a negative answer. Even if we were to suppose that animals have beliefs (i.e., beliefs in the sense of functional or psychological states), Frey claims that we could not say *what* animals believe on the basis of how they behave. His reasons for this denial are set forth in the following passage.

> I do not understand how behaviour can *show* that my dog possesses the belief *that p* unless that behaviour is connected with the belief *that p* in such a way that that same behaviour is not compatible with the belief *that q* or *that r* or *that s*. For if the dog's behaviour is compatible both with the belief *that p* and with these other beliefs, then I do not understand how it

can be concluded on the basis of that behaviour that it is the belief *that p*
that the dog has. For example, several months ago, my dog wagged its
tail furiously when its master was at the door but also when its lunch was
about to be served and when the sun was being eclipsed by the moon. So
far as I could see, its behaviour was the same on the last two occasions as
it was on the first, and I am not at all clear how, on the basis of that
behavior, it can be concluded that it was the belief that his master was at
the door which the dog had. . . .[36]

A number of questions arise here, the most important being whether
Frey has a sufficiently rich understanding of behavior, especially as this
bears on the behavioral grounds for the attribution of particular beliefs, in
his dog's case or in any other. Suppose Mary (a human) hears a noise and
we observe her walk to the door. Can we rationally attribute any particular belief to her, concerning who or what she believes is at the door, just
on the basis of her going toward it? Our answer must be that we clearly
cannot. But this is not because we know all we would want to know about
her behavior and still find ourselves rationally unable to say what Mary
believes. It is, rather, that we cannot understand individual bits of behavior in isolation from the broader context in which they take place, either
now, in the past, or in the future. Abstracted from its contextual home,
Mary's going-to-the-door behavior hardly constitutes *behavior* at all; it is
little more than a series of movements in a certain direction. But to what
end? Was the noise a familiar noise? Was she expecting someone? Does
she hesitate before opening the door? These are the sorts of questions one
would have to have answered before one could rationally begin to say
who or what Mary believes is at the door. We need what might be termed
a holistic view of behavior, not an atomistic view, if we are to make
reasonable attributions of particular beliefs on the basis of how individuals behave, not only in the case of animals, as shall shortly be explained,
but also in the case of humans.

Frey's dog, we are told, wags his tail furiously under quite different
circumstances, not only when his master is at the door. That being so,
Frey wants to know how the tail-wagging "can *show*" that Fido believes
that his master is at the door. But this is to ask an improper question, not
only in Fido's case, but in any case. Behavior must be understood in
context, holistically, if it is to be understood at all. When we say that the
dog believes his master is at the door, we imply that the dog has certain
expectations, expectations which, if the dog has them, will be manifested
by the dog's future behavior. If the dog has this belief, then he expects a
certain person to enter, one with whom, let us suppose, he has an amiable
relationship and thus one the dog looks forward to seeing with pleasur-

able anticipation. The attribution of this belief to Fido *can* only be understood in terms of our having reason to believe that the dog has these expectations, and *our* having reason to believe this *can* only come from our past observation of how the dog behaves (or how other dogs like Fido behave) in relevantly similar circumstances—when, for example, there is a familiar sound on the stairs or at the door. For we can no more say with reason who or what Fido believes is at the door without this sort of background information than we can with reason say who or what Mary believes is at the door if we are similarly ignorant. Let us assume we know the dog well and so interpret his tail-wagging, when there is a familiar sound at the door, as a sign that he has those expectations that, from our past observations, we have come to recognize the dog has when the sound of his master is in the air. It is *not* the tail-wagging alone, considered in isolation from everything else under the sun, that serves as the basis for attributing the belief to Fido that his master is at the door. It is the known association between his wagging his tail, given relevantly similar circumstances, *and* his having shown by his past behavior in such circumstances that he has certain expectations associated with his master's being at the door, that provides the grounds for our attributing this belief to him now. We are right to attribute this belief to him if we have reason to believe that he now has those expectations he would have if he believes that it is his master, just as we would be right to attribute to Mary the belief that her friend Nora is at the door if we have reason to believe that she has those expectations she would have if she believed it was her friend at the door. But just as we cannot say that Mary believes this solely on the basis of her walking to the door when a noise has been heard, so we cannot say *what* Fido believes just by viewing his tail-wagging as a piece of isolated behavior.

    This account of the behavioral basis on which to attribute particular beliefs to animals gains additional support when we recognize three further points. First, the account recommended here provides us with a way to test the accuracy of belief attributions. Since we imply that Fido has certain identifiable expectations when we attribute to him the belief that his master is at the door, the attribution of this belief will be shown to be accurate (verified, confirmed) if, by his future behavior, Fido shows that he had those expectations he would have if he believed that it was his master who was at the door. If he displays his recognition of his master, shows his excitement at his return and, say, engages in other customary "ritual" greeting behavior, then we have all the reason we could have, and all that we should be required to have, to say that he did believe that it was his master at the door. For this is *just* the way Fido would behave if he expected his master, and he would expect his master if he believed that it was his master at the door. If, however, he greets the entering person with snaps, growls, barks and a bite or two, we have all the reason we could have, and all the reason we should be expected to have, to conclude that he did not believe it was his master who was at the door. Unless there is more than a little antagonism between Frey and his dog, this is not the way the dog would behave if he thought his master was about to enter. In either case, it is how the dog behaves, not only *before* but *after* someone enters through the door, that will determine whether our attribution is accurate. His preentrance behavior gives us a sign as to what his beliefs and, thus, what his expectations are; but his postentrance behavior provides the crucial test for determining whether we have read the signs accurately.

Second, this same account of attributions of particular beliefs to animals illuminates what it means to say, and how to test the accuracy of, the attribution of beliefs to animals in intentional contexts. Let us say that animals behave intentionally whenever they do one thing in order that they may do another. For example, if Fido scratches at the door, is let out, immediately runs to the spot where he saw us burying something, and begins to dig furiously, his behavior looks for all the world like intentional behavior: he wants out *in order to* get to the burial spot, and he digs there *in order to* find what was buried. It would be natural to say that Fido behaved as he did because he had certain beliefs—for example, the belief that a bone was to be found *and* that he had to get out and dig to find it. Is it reasonable to attribute such (intentional) beliefs to the dog? It is, if we have reason to believe that the dog has those expectations he would have, if he has the beliefs we attribute to him; and our attribution will be reasonable if, on the basis of our past observations of the dog's behavior, we have come to recognize that he behaves in certain ways in relevantly similar circumstances and thus displays that he has relevantly similar expectations. The accuracy of our attribution also is testable by observing how the dog actually behaves. If it is a Coke bottle we have buried in the yard, and if Fido is a normal dog, he will behave quite differently when he unearths it than he would have behaved had he found a bone, and it will not take a trained ethologist's eye to note the difference. Were he to find the bottle while expecting a bone, he would behave as anyone would whose expectations had been dashed. If Fido is a normal dog, his disappointment will be evident. His behavior will be what we would expect (predict) it to be, if he discovered that his belief ("There is a bone") were false, so that we may, in the absence of a sound argument against this, and Frey's denial to the contrary notwithstanding (2.2), credit Fido (and similar animals) with the ability to distinguish between true and false beliefs.

Third, because of the general features of the account of the grounds for attributing, and testing the attributions of, particular beliefs to animals, more can now be said vis-à-vis Fido's grasp of the preference-belief than was initially possible (2.3). When we say that Fido has this belief we claim that he grasps the connection between choosing bones and satisfying his desire for the flavor bones provide. But can we be right to attribute this belief to him? This will depend on whether we ever have any reason to say that Fido has those expectations regarding bones that he would have if he believed that bones satisfy his desire for a certain taste. These expectations will include getting his mouth on it, chewing it, licking it, tasting a certain flavor, and finding the congeries of these experiences generally pleasant. The *accuracy* of our attribution of this belief to him will depend on whether we ever find that Fido relates to bones in the way he would if he had these expectations. Here is a simple test to decide. Produce a meaty bone and, in full view of Fido but while another person is holding him, put the bone down. Observe how the dog behaves. Does he show any interest in the bone? Does it seem that he would like to get his mouth on it pronto? Or does he bark angrily at it, fall asleep, or cower in the corner at the mere sight of this dreaded object? If Fido is a normal dog, we know full well what to expect, because we know full well what Fido expects: he expects to have a pleasant time chewing on that bone. Whether, then, we are accurate when we attribute the preference-belief to Fido can only be decided by whether we have adequate grounds for thinking that he has those expectations he would have if he has that belief. A crucial part of the test for accuracy will depend on what he does after he is released. Chances are he will show by his behavior that he had those expectations we thought he did when we attributed the preference-belief to him.

It is important to emphasize that the connection claimed here, between believing *that p* and having certain expectations, is not one of identity. It is not being claimed that "A believes *that p*" *means* "A expects thus and so." To maintain identity in this case would undermine the intelligibility of citing our beliefs as a way of explaining or justifying what we expect. Suppose that, when Mary heard the noise at the door, she opened it without checking first to see who was there, and a total stranger rushed in and stole her most valuable possessions. Suppose we ask her why she opened the door without first checking, and she replies that she was expecting her friend Nora. It then is perfectly reasonable to ask her *why* she was expecting her, and what we will want from Mary is a recounting of those *beliefs* that were relevant to her having that expectation. Now, if the beliefs on which her expectation depended were the *same* as this expectation itself, all she could be doing when recounting her beliefs would be saying that she had the expectation she had because she had that expectation. This she is manifestly not doing. Her beliefs are the basis for her having the expectation she has; her believing *that p, that q,* and the like is thus not identical with her expecting what she does. When, therefore, it is claimed that it is our knowledge of Fido's expectations on which our attributions of particular beliefs to him must be based, and when, further, it is claimed that the accuracy of these attributions must be tested on the basis of whether Fido behaves as he would behave if he had those expectations he would have if he believed what we attribute to him, it is not being claimed that Fido's believing *that p* is identical with his expecting thus and so. Like the rest of us, he expects what he does *because* he believes what he does, so that to say what expectations he has is distinct from, though related to, saying what he believes.

When the attribution of particular beliefs to animals is understood in the way argued for in the preceding, and when we bring a holistic perspective to bear on the interpretation of animal behavior, Frey's worries can be assuaged. Fido wags his tail under various circumstances. That is agreed. It is also agreed that the dog's doing *just* this is compatible with attributing any number of different beliefs to him. And it is also agreed that we therefore cannot say, just on the basis of observing his wagging tail, what it is that Fido believes. Our inability to say what Fido believes just on the basis of his wagging tail, however, does not signify some deficiency in Fido's behavioral repertoire or a lack of behavioral grounds on which we can say what it is that the dog believes; rather, the supposition that we should *even try* to say what the dog believes by focusing our attention just on one feature of the dog's behavior, viewed in isolation from the context in which it occurs, points to a failure on Frey's part to understand what behavior is and how a more sensitive appreciation of it can provide the needed grounds for attributing, and for testing the attributions of, particular beliefs to animals.[37] A holistic view of animal behavior allows us to decide when to attribute beliefs to animals, what beliefs to attribute, and whether the beliefs we have reason to attribute at one time, in one set of circumstances, are the same or different from those we have reason to attribute at another time, in another set of circumstances. If Fido is a normal dog, for example, he will have beliefs about his lunch, and these will differ from those beliefs he has about his master; he will, therefore, have different expectations when he believes that lunch is at hand than those he has when he believes that his master is at the door. And he will behave differently, because he has these different beliefs. If Frey's dog is a normal dog, he will eat his lunch, not his master.

2.5 THE COMPLEXITY OF ANIMAL CONSCIOUSNESS

In the previous section three types of objections against attributing the preference-belief to Fido were considered and found wanting. In the present section I indicate, though sketchily, some of the more important implications that follow if, as has been argued, we have good reason to attribute, and have a reliable way of deciding the accuracy of the attribution of, the preference-belief to the dog. As we shall see, a great deal, much of it of great importance to our understanding of the mental life of animals, not just Fido in particular, flows from making the minimal case that Fido has the preference-belief.

The first point worth making is that the argument regarding Fido's grasp of the preference-belief obviously can be generalized to provide the content of many other beliefs the dog has, not only about how certain things are to be chosen if he is to satisfy his desire for certain tastes but also how various other things are to be chosen to satisfy other desires he has—for example, for rest, or warmth, or companionship. Second, this same form of argument obviously can be generalized and applied to other mammals. If Fido is enfranchised into the class of believing animals because he has the preference-belief regarding bones, then cats, cows, pigs, horses, llamas, tigers, giraffes, hippos, and cetaceans, for example, cannot be far behind.

In the case of those animals who, like Fido, have beliefs, a good deal more follows concerning the cognitive powers they must have. The way to proceed is via a transcendental argument: Given that Fido has the preference-belief, how is this possible? It is preposterous to hypothesize that he came into the world with this belief. No one will seriously maintain that dogs are born *knowing* how bones taste. To find this out, Fido, like the rest of us, had to get his mouth on one. Suppose he does, and suppose the dog lacks memory. Then Fido could not form the preference-belief or behave as he does because of what he believes about the connection between the taste of bones and the satisfaction of his desires. This he could not do because the preference-belief is a general belief about this connection. If dogs lacked memory, then they could not form any general belief and thus could not grasp the preference-belief. Because Fido can be reasonably viewed as having this belief, he is reasonably viewed as having the ability to remember the relevant experiences—bone-tasting ones—even if, unlike us, he cannot say that he does.

Fido must be able to do more than remember, however, if he is to grasp the preference-belief: he must be able to recognize a bone. But to recognize a bone Fido must not only be able to perceive (not merely "detect by its senses")[38] individual bones, he must also have the ability to abstract from individual cases, form general concepts (e.g., the concept of a bone), and apply this concept to particular cases. Without these abilities there could be no rational account of how Fido grasps the preference-belief. Since, then, we have good reason to attribute this belief to him and to refer to this belief of his when we seek to explain why he behaves as he does, we also have good reason to attribute the ability to form general concepts to him as well.

But can Fido have beliefs about the future? If, as has been argued, Fido has expectations about what will occur and beliefs correlated with these expectations, then he certainly has beliefs about the future, a finding that is reinforced by considering a related question—namely, whether Fido can reasonably be viewed as acting intentionally. If we are reasonably to view any individual, A, as having this ability, we must show that it is reasonable to view A as acting with the intention of achieving a given purpose (e.g., satisfying a certain desire). Is Fido able to do this? If we had good reason to deny that Fido can have beliefs, we would have equally good reason to deny that he can act intentionally, and if we had good reason to deny that we can specify what it is that the dog believes, then we would have equally good reason to deny that we are able to say with what intentions he acts, even assuming that he does so. But we have no good reason to deny any of this. The Cumulative Argument provides defensible grounds for viewing Fido and other mammalian animals as being like us in having beliefs, understood as functional or psychological states, and their behavior provides us with the needed basis for saying *what* they believe. That being so, there is nothing that logically stands in the way of viewing Fido, for example, as wanting out *in order that* he may dig where he believes a bone is, *and* as wanting out, digging, and getting hold of that bone *in order that* he may satisfy his desire for the flavor bones provide. There is, in short, no logical barrier to viewing Fido as acting with the intention of fulfilling *his* purposes. Not only *may* we view him thus, however, we *ought* to, *if* we view humans as being capable of intentional agency, something which, it bears repeating, is an essential presupposition of any work in moral philosophy. Once we have accepted this in the human case, once the major challenges to crediting animals with awareness and beliefs have been met, and once we have explained how their behavior may be intelligibly described and parsimoniously explained by making reference to what they believe and desire, *then* we have done all that we can reasonably be required to do to make the case for viewing them, too, as individuals who act intentionally. And once we have made this case we have additional reasons for crediting Fido and similar animals with beliefs about the future, if we do so in the human case, since to act in the present with the intention of satisfying one's desire in the future (as Fido does when he acts in a way that leads us to let him out in order that he may satisfy his desire by getting his mouth on the bone he believes we have buried) requires that Fido and these other animals have such beliefs.

To recognize the status of mammalian animals as intentional agents paves the way for recognizing that they should also be viewed as self-conscious. For an individual, A, to act now in order to bring about the satisfaction of his desires at some future time is possible only if we assume that A is self-aware at least to the extent that A believes that it will be *his* desires that will be satisfied in the future as a result of what he does now. In other words, intentional action is possible only for those who are self-conscious. Since Fido and relevantly similar animals are reasonably viewed as capable of acting intentionally, it must likewise be reasonable to view them as self-aware and thus, in this case, as in others, to view them as "models" of human mental capacities. As in the case of beliefs, desires, intentions and the like, self-consciousness is not the exclusive property of *Homo sapiens*. In sympathy with Gareth Matthews's position, the preceding supports acceptance of what he calls *the Principle of Psychological Continuity*: "The psychology of human beings is part of the psychology of animals generally."[39]

A final implication of the preceding is worth noting. The validity of attributions of belief to animals and our ability to specify the content of their beliefs underpin the propriety of viewing animals as having an emotional life, a point upon which Darwin, for instance, repeatedly insists and one that can only be reinforced if we recall the lessons learned by Hebb and his associates (see 1.8). Except for pathological cases, which in the nature of the case are the exception not the rule, to be afraid, for example, is to fear *that something in particular will occur*, while to feel anger is to feel anger *toward someone or something* because of what has been done.[40] Normally, that is, one does not, for example, fear that something will happen without believing that it will, or is likely to occur. Not surprisingly, Frey "doubts" that animals can or do have emotions because he denies that they can or do have beliefs. But while Frey seems to be on the side of the truth when he claims that emotions, or "at least . . . a good many (of them),"[41] are not possible without belief, he is not similarly positioned when he denies an emotional life to animals or "doubts" that they have one because they lack beliefs. No good argument has been given to support this denial, and there are strong presumptive reasons for attributing beliefs to them. When, therefore, Darwin refers to the terror, suspicion, affection, and jealousy of mammalian animals,[42] what he writes cannot rationally be dismissed as the breezy anthropomorphism of a mind with its scientific guard down. "The recognition of emotion in man and animals," in Hebb's words, "is not fundamentally different"[43]

Finally, a problem analogous to one considered in the previous chapter must be discussed. The earlier problem (see 1.8) concerned where to draw the line between those animals that are, and those that are not, conscious or aware. The answer offered was that this is to be decided by appeal to the Cumulative Argument, including the implications of evolutionary theory. The greater the anatomical and physiological similarity between given animals and paradigmatic conscious beings (i.e., normal, developed human beings), the stronger our reasons are for viewing these animals as being like us in having the material basis for consciousness; the less like us a given animal is in these respects, the less reason we have for viewing them as having a mental life. Because some animals frequently differ from us in quite fundamental ways in these respects, it is not unreasonable to view them as utterly lacking in consciousness. Like automatic garage doors that open when they register an electronic signal, or like the pinball machine that registers the overly aggressive play of a competitor and lights up "Tilt!" some animals may be reasonably viewed as making their "behavioral moves" in the world without any awareness of it. Certainly to claim that some animals are conscious is not to commit oneself to the view that all animals are.

The present problem concerns where one draws the line regarding the relative complexity of the conscious lives of various animals. To claim that *some* animals are aware of their environment, have beliefs and desires, possess memory and expectations about (and thus a sense of) the future, and are able to act intentionally in seeking to fulfill their desires or purposes, does not commit one to the view that *all* conscious animals are similarly endowed. Not only is it possible, it is highly probable, given the major thrust of evolutionary theory, that some conscious animals have a rudimentary mental life, living, we might conjecture, in a perpetual specious present, having no memory of the past nor conscious anticipation of the future, yet experiencing, for example, something akin to pleasure when certain things happen in or to their bodies, and something akin to pain when other events take place. If we assume what evolutionary theory implies, that the more complex forms of conscious life evolved from the less complex, then the existence of animals having a rudimentary mental life is inescapable. Where we draw the line in these and related cases is, of course, certain to be controversial. And yet we can be as certain as we reasonably can be that, say, single-celled animals are utterly lacking in consciousness and that animals with a primitive central nervous system have the bare minimum for rudimentary consciousness. However, for our purposes, the crucial question is not where we draw the line in every case; it is whether we have good reasons to draw the line in a way that implies that mammalian animals not only are conscious and sentient but also have beliefs, desires, memory, a sense of the future, self-awareness, and an emotional life, and can act intentionally. The reply the present chapter has sought to clarify and defend may be summed up in two words: we do.

The problem over line-drawing actually is more complicated than has been indicated up to now. For though it is reasonable to view mammalian animals as individuals having a complex mental life of the sort described, it is neither necessary nor reasonable to view them in this way at every stage of their physical development or deterioration. At the moment of conception, for example, or after having suffered massive brain damage, neither cats nor dogs are reasonably viewed as having beliefs or desires, goals or preferences, sensations or emotions. Whether they have a mental life approaching this complexity when they are first born also is controversial. Precisely when this family of mental abilities emerges or recedes during the biological life of a given mammalian animal—exactly where, that is, we draw the line in *this* regard—is as vexing a question as is its companion query concerning human beings. Few, if any, even including the most avid champions of the fetus's right to life, will claim that the human fetus has beliefs and emotions, for example, at the moment of conception, or that a physically mature human being continues to have a sophisticated mental life when in an irreversible coma. Like mammalian animals, in short, humans can both acquire and lose the family of mental abilities discussed in the present chapter. As is true in the case of these animals, we cannot erase the difficult problem of where to draw the line concerning an individual human's acquisition or loss of these abilities.

But though this problem cannot be erased, its difficulty can be lessened without begging any essential questions at this point. Whether a human fetus at the later stage of its development has memory, beliefs, or desires is, let us agree, a controversial question. But whether a child of a year or more has these abilities, assuming the child is not very seriously mentally enfeebled, is not open to serious doubt, unless one is the victim of a mistaken analysis of the concepts of belief, desire, and the like. Similarly, whether a fetal or newborn dog has these abilities is perhaps open to informed debate; not so in the case of a normal dog of a year or more, assuming the soundness of the analyses and arguments advanced in the preceding. That much granted, we can adopt a conservative policy at this point, one that leaves the line-drawing question unanswered when it arises at the level of individuals, but a policy that enables us to move forward in spite of leaving this question unresolved. The policy is simply this: Henceforth, when either humans or animals are referred to, it is to be assumed that those to whom we refer are individuals *well beyond* the point where anyone could reasonably "draw the line" separating those who have the mental abilities in question from those who lack them. Unless otherwise indicated, that is, the word *humans* will be used to refer to all those *Homo sapiens* aged one year or more, who are not very profoundly mentally retarded or otherwise quite markedly mentally impoverished (e.g., permanently comatose). And, unless indicated otherwise, the word *animal* will be used to refer to mentally normal mammals of a year or more. To stipulate at this point how the words *human* and *animal* will be used allows for economy of expression in the sequel and should not occasion misunderstanding. Just to be on the safe side, some reminders will be posted along the way. Here it will serve the interests of communication well to note that, though the argument for animal rights offered in the sequel applies most clearly to those animals covered by the stipulated use of the word *animal*, related considerations will be offered to explain why important moral constraints also apply to our dealings with other animals (see, especially, 9.3–9.4).

2.6 SUMMARY AND CONCLUSION

A variety of reasons make it reasonable to view mammalian animals as individuals who, like us, have beliefs and desires. Common sense and ordinary language support this, as does evolutionary theory; their behavior is consistent with this view; and the question of the relative mental sophistication and powers of these animals is only confusedly tied to asking whether they have immaterial, immortal souls. These reasons taken together (the Cumulative Argument) provide the basis for a burden-of-proof argument: unless or until we are shown that there are better reasons for denying that these animals have beliefs and desires, we are rationally entitled to believe that they do. What Stephen Stich calls "our intuitive belief-desire theory" wins, one might say, unless those who dispute it show that it loses.

R. G. Frey is one philosopher who endeavors to meet the burden of proof. On Frey's view, animals do not have desires because they cannot have them. They cannot have desires, properly conceived, he thinks, because to have desires involves having beliefs, and only those individuals who "have language" can have beliefs. Frey's position, that beliefs are impossible for those who "lack language," was shown to be untenable (2.2) because, among other reasons, it leads to the absurd consequence that no one can believe anything. On Frey's view, since there can be no beliefs without one's having mastered a language (at least to the point where one can frame or understand sentences) and since learning a language requires that one have preverbal beliefs about what is being taught, we must conclude that no one can learn a language and so, on his view, no one can believe anything. To exclude animals from the class of individuals who have beliefs by means of an account of belief that entails that this class is empty is a pyrrhic victory at best.

Stich is representative of a second type of challenge to applying the belief-desire theory to animals. Beliefs and desires are, Stich allows, psychological states, and Stich evidently concedes that the Cumulative Argument supports viewing normal mammalian animals, aged one or more, as having, in his words, "a large store" of both desires and beliefs. But beliefs and desires also have content: to believe something is to *believe that* something is the case. And it is in this connection, he thinks, that animal belief eludes our grasp. We simply cannot say *what* they believe despite having more than ample reason to suppose that they have beliefs, understood as psychological states. The belief-desire theory, one might say on Stich's behalf, is half a theory at best when applied to animals.

Stich's grounds for claiming that we cannot say what animals believe were shown (2.3) to rest on an unsatisfactory understanding of when individuals have the same concept. Two individuals can have the same concept more or less; they need not share all and only the same beliefs about a given x in order to share the same concept of x. A child, for example, who knows nothing about chemistry does not therefore have an entirely different concept of milk or bottle than we do. When viewed in this way, normal mammalian animals aged one or more are reasonably viewed as sharing many of our concepts. Fido's concept of a bone was used to illustrate the general point at issue. Since at least one of the beliefs that informs our concept of a bone (namely, the preference-belief: bones are to be chosen to satisfy the desire for a certain flavor) *is* a belief we have good reason to believe that Fido shares, and since, assuming Stich is right, we have no good reason to maintain that *Fido* denies any of the other beliefs about bones that comprise our concept, the dog is reasonably viewed as having our concept, at least to a limited degree. The content of Fido's concept of, and beliefs about, bones and, generalizing on the dog's case, the content of, and beliefs about, many other things on the part of mammalian animals generally, is thus in principle determinable—at least "a little bit." In a broad range of cases, they believe what we believe.

This finding might be challenged in a variety of ways. Among the challenges considered (2.4), one disputed our ability to say what animals believe on the basis of how they behave; a second disputed our ability to say what their experience is like since all we have to go on is their nonverbal behavior. With regard to the latter objection it was argued that it is unparsimonious to multiply kinds of experience (canine, feline, human, etc.) beyond necessity, something we would be guilty of if we assumed that, say, canine taste-experience must differ from our own. In reply to the former objection, the point was made that behavior must be understood holistically, not atomistically. If we are to use animal behavior to fix the content of animal belief, we must be certain not to fix our attention, as Frey implies we should, on isolated bodily movements (e.g., the wag of a dog's tail). We must ask whether animals behave as they predictably would *if* they had those beliefs we attribute to them, a question that can be answered only if we take the time to view the animal's behavior holistically (e.g., if we investigate what else the dog does in addition to wagging his tail, how he wags it, when he does it, etc.). The accuracy of our attributions of belief to animals depends upon, and is testable by making reference to, whether their behavior shows that they have those expectations they would have, if they have the beliefs attributed to them, something that is in principle determinable by determining whether the animals in question behave as they reasonably could be predicted to behave if they had the appropriate expectations. At least in a great many cases, in short, the content of animals' beliefs is empirically determinable.

Having made the case for viewing animals such as Fido as individuals who have beliefs and desires, assuming (as always) that human beings do, some of the more important implications were then sketched (2.5). These animals are reasonably viewed as having the ability to act intentionally if humans are similarly conceived. *They* initiate action because they want this or seek that, and they act as they do *in order to* satisfy these desires; they do not merely react to external stimuli, as plants bend toward the light. Moreover, because beliefs such as the preference-belief are general beliefs about the connection between choice and the satisfaction of desire, these animals must not only be able to perceive individual objects (e.g., this bone); they must also be able to remember and, on the basis of past experience, form general concepts. And since many of the beliefs they have involve their having expectations about the future, these animals must also have a sense of the future—indeed, a sense of their own future. As individuals who initiate a chain of events now (in the present) with the intention of bringing about the satisfaction of their desires in the future, these animals are reasonably viewed as having a grasp of (i.e., beliefs and correlative expectations about) *their own* future. Thus are they reasonably viewed as being not only conscious but self-conscious.

Perception, memory, desire, belief, self-consciousness, intention, a sense of the future—these are among the leading attributes of the mental life of normal mammalian animals aged one or more. Add to this list the not unimportant categories of emotion (e.g., fear and hatred) and sentience, understood as the capacity to experience pleasure and pain, and we begin to approach a fair rendering of the mental life of these animals. To deny a mental life of this complexity to these creatures in favor of, for example, a stimulus-response theory of their behavior, while affirming a complex mental life to human beings is, let us agree, a *theoretical* possibility. But one wants arguments to support viewing humans and animals so differently, arguments that meet the burden of proof issued by the Cumulative Argument. This chapter examined major arguments that explicitly address the question of animal beliefs and desires. Though not all the options could be examined, and while it was freely conceded that not all the controversies discussed along the way were settled with philosophical finality, enough was considered and argued, it is to be hoped, to show that these major arguments fail to meet the burden of proof. To continue, in the face of the failure of these arguments, to apply a stimulus-response theory to animals but to favor the application of the belief-desire theory to humans, or, worse still, to disparage those who subscribe to this latter understanding of animals and their behavior as "anthropomorphizers," is to bespeak a prejudice rather than to unmask one. To cling to and perpetuate a vision of the world that concedes a "primitive" mental life to animals or—for there are closet Cartesians in our midst—to deny *any* mental life to them is as far removed from having an accurate conception of what these animals are like as the lion in Stefan Lochner's painting is from representing a real lion.

3

Animal Welfare

M ammalian animals have a welfare. They fare well or ill during the course of their life, and the life of some animals is, on balance, experientially better than the life of others. All this is platitudinous. As is so often the case, however, these platitudes paper over difficult questions. One example in the present case concerns questions about identity. The idea that Fido fares well or ill throughout his life presupposes that the dog is the same dog from one day to the next and at different stages of his life. This is not remarkable. If the dog's present discomfort is diagnosed as being due to worms, if we administer the proper medication, and if the animal's discomfort is alleviated, then the dog in whose interests we act, the one who in the future does not experience the discomfort Fido presently copes with, is not some animal *other than* Fido, is not a *different* dog. It is Fido for whom we act; we do what we do to improve the quality of *his* life. Judged on the basis of common sense and ordinary practice, it is not remarkable that Fido should be the same dog in the future as he is in the present. What would be remarkable is if he were a different dog.

This unremarkable view is not without its remarkable philosophical problems. The central one is the age-old problem of explaining how some thing can change and yet remain the same. By the time the dog reaches the age of ten, there is a not a solitary hair on his body that is the same as one of the hairs with which he was born; the cells in his body are not numerically the same; behaviorally, he is different; his sight is likely to be less keen and the acuity of other senses diminishing. Amid all these changes, where may we point, as it were, and say, "There is the Fido who does not change; this is what makes him the same dog today as he was yesterday and, in all likelihood, will be tomorrow"?

This troubling question is no different in kind from other questions about identity, whether these questions concern the identity of a chair, for example, or a tree, or a human being. But like other questions mentioned along the way, this one, too, cannot be explored in the present work. Here we must assume that individuals, including both individual animals like Fido and individual human beings, retain their identity over time. The assumption that this is true in the case of human beings is common to all moral theories and begs no substantive moral question (that is, no question about what is morally right or wrong, good or bad). Similarly, therefore, in assuming that the same is true in the case of animals like Fido, no substantive moral question is begged. We do not, that is, assume that certain ways of treating animals are wrong or that certain animals have moral rights just by assuming that these animals retain their identity over time. However, since, for reasons advanced at length in the previous chapter, animals like Fido are creatures with a sophisticated mental life—a mental life that differs from ours, in Darwin's words, in degree, not in kind—we can say something about any potentially viable account of the identity of these animals. Accounts of their identity must address, as they seek to illuminate, the psychological, not merely the physical, identity of these creatures. Accounts that deal *exclusively* with the latter could give us at most half a story of the identity of these animals, since they would at most deal with only half the animal.

A second question, one that will be explored in some detail, concerns the nature of animal welfare. The notions of interests, benefits, and harms will be explored (3.2–3.4) and, before that (3.1), the grounds for ascribing autonomy to animals will be identified. As will become clearer as we proceed, animals, as individuals who retain their psychophysical identity over time, have a welfare that is not unrelated to their ability to act autonomously (i.e., as they prefer). The role of death in the analysis of animal welfare will be examined (3.5), as will two further questions— first, whether it is possible to act paternalistically toward animals (3.6) and, second, how the notion of euthanasia, as applied to animals, should be understood (3.7). Though no moral conclusions are reached in the present chapter, the issues examined will play a prominent role in the moral conclusions argued for in subsequent discussions. To ask about the proper analysis of euthanasia, for example, should not be dismissed as a case of making much ado about nothing. Unless we are clear about this and the other ideas canvassed in the present chapter, our grasp of the moral questions that await us will be impoverished. Moreover—and this signals the central objective of the present chapter—the analysis of the idea of animal welfare will reveal that it is in essential respects like that of human welfare. The examination of the idea of animal welfare, therefore, will reveal another important similarity between humans and animals, a similarity that can hardly be irrelevant to understanding both.

3.1 THE AUTONOMY OF ANIMALS

Autonomy can be understood in different ways. On one interpretation, which finds its classic statement in Kant's writings, individuals are autonomous only if they are capable of acting on reasons they can will that any other similarly placed individual can act on. For example, if I am trying to decide whether I morally ought to keep a promise, I must, Kant believes, ask whether I could will that everyone else who is similarly placed (i.e., who has made a promise) can act as I do for the same reasons as I have. In asking what I ought to do, in other words, I must determine what others can do, and it is only if I have the ability to think through and reflectively evaluate the merits of acting in one way or another (e.g., to decide to keep the promise or to break it), and, having done this, to make a decision on the basis of my deliberations, that I can be viewed as an autonomous individual.

It is highly unlikely that any animal is autonomous in the Kantian sense. To be so animals would have to be able to reason at a quite sophisticated level indeed, bringing to bear considerations about what other animals (presumably those who belong to their own species) can or ought to do in comparable situations, a process that requires assessing the merits of alternative acts from an impartial point of view. Not only is it doubtful that animals have the requisite abilities to do this; it is doubtful that we could confirm their possession of these abilities if they had them. There is, after all, a limit to how much we can reasonably attribute to animals on the basis of the Cumulative Argument, even when this is supplemented by a holistic interpretation of animal behavior; and it at least seems to be the case that we would be attributing more even to mature mammals than reason would allow if we ascribe autonomy, in the Kantian sense, to any of them.

But the Kantian sense of autonomy is not the only one. An alternative view is that individuals are autonomous if they have preferences and have the ability to initiate action with a view to satisfying them. It is not necessary, given this interpretation of autonomy (let us call this *preference autonomy*), that one be able to abstract from one's own desires, goals, and so on, as a preliminary to asking what any other similarly placed individual ought to do; it is enough that one have the ability to initiate action because one has those desires or goals one has and believes, rightly or wrongly, that one's desires or purposes will be satisfied or achieved by acting in a certain way. Where the Kantian sense requires that one be able to think impartially if one is to possess autonomy, the preference sense does not.

Both the Kantian and the preference sense of autonomy obviously exclude some of the same individuals from the class of autonomous beings. Rocks, clouds, rivers, and plants, for example, lack autonomy given either sense. But the preference sense includes some individuals excluded by the Kantian sense, most notably many animals. For reasons advanced toward the end of the last chapter (2.5), mammalian animals, at least, are reasonably viewed as creatures meeting the requirements for possession of preference autonomy. These animals are reasonably viewed as possessing the cognitive prerequisites for having desires and goals; they perceive and remember, and have the ability to form and apply general beliefs. From this it is a short step to acknowledging that these animals are reasonably viewed as being capable of making preferential choices.

Two types of cases illustrate the propriety of viewing these animals in this way. The first involves cases where they regularly behave in a given way when given the opportunity to do one thing or another. For example, if, when Fido is both hungry and has not recently had an opportunity to run outdoors, he regularly opts for eating when given the choice between food or the outdoors, we have adequate behavioral grounds for saying that the dog prefers eating to running in such cases and so acts (i.e., chooses) accordingly. A second type of case involves situations where there is no regular behavioral pattern because of the novelty of a given set of circumstances. If Fido is hungry, if we place before him both a bowl of his regular food and a bowl of boiled eggplant, and if, as is predictable, Fido opts for his regular food, then we again have adequate behavioral grounds for saying that the dog prefers his normal food to the eggplant and so acts (i.e., chooses) accordingly. And this we may reasonably contend even if this is the only time Fido is presented with the choice in question.

When autonomy is understood in the preference sense, the case can be made for viewing many animals as autonomous. Which animals it is reasonable to view as autonomous will turn, first, on whether we have reasonable grounds for viewing them as having preferences, understood as desires or goals, and, second, on whether we find that how they behave in various situations is intelligibly described and parsimoniously explained by making reference to their preferences and the choices they make because of the preferences they have. Like other comparable issues, where one draws the line is certain to be controversial. But at least in the case of normal mammalian animals, aged one or more—even if not in the case of any others—the conclusions reached in the previous two chapters, including the need to view their behavior holistically, underwrite the reasonableness of ascribing preference autonomy to them.

We have, then, two senses of autonomy—the Kantian and the preference sense—each differing significantly from the other. If it could be shown that the Kantian sense is the only true sense of autonomy or that the preference sense is silly, or muddled, or worse, then one could rightfully claim that animals lack autonomy. But none of these options hold any promise. The Kantian interpretation of autonomy does not give us a condition that must be met if one is to be autonomous in any sense. It provides a condition that must be met if one is to be an autonomous *moral agent*—that is, an individual who can be held morally accountable for the acts he performs or fails to perform, one who can rightly be blamed or praised, criticized or condemned. Central to the Kantian sense of autonomy is the idea that autonomous individuals can rise above thinking about their individual preferences and think about where their moral duty lies by bringing impartial reasons to bear on their deliberations. These two ideas (that of individual preferences, on the one hand, and, on the other, one's moral duty) are distinct. Just because I prefer your death or public shame, for example, it does not follow that either I or anyone else has a moral duty to terminate your life or bring about your public disgrace, and there are many things I might be morally obligated to do that I personally do not prefer doing (e.g., keeping a promise). Suppose it is agreed that one must be autonomous in the Kantian sense to have the status of a moral agent. (For additional remarks on the notion of moral agency, see 5.2.) It does not follow that one must be autonomous in *this* sense to be autonomous in *any* sense. So long as one has the ability to act on one's preferences, the ascription of autonomy is intelligible and attributions of it are confirmable. Though normal mammalian animals aged one or more are not reasonably viewed as moral agents because they are not reasonably viewed as autonomous in the Kantian sense, they are reasonably viewed as autonomous in the preference sense.

3.2 INTERESTS

Recognition of the intellectual propriety of regarding animals as autonomous has important implications for the proper understanding of their welfare. These implications are seen most clearly by examining the generic notion of welfare as this applies both to humans and to these animals. A helpful place to begin is by noting the ambiguity of talk about someone's (A's) "having interest in" something (X). At least two different things we can mean by this are (1) that A is interested in X and (2) that X is in A's interests. These ideas are logically distinct. Our friend Jones, for example, can be interested in something that is not in his interests—for example, he might be interested in taking drugs that are injurious to his health. And our friend Smith might not be interested in something that is in his interests—for example, he might not be interested in exercising despite the benefits he would derive. Suppose we mark this distinction by speaking of *preference-interests* and *welfare-interests*. By the former we shall mean those things that an individual is *interested in*, those things he likes, desires, wants or, in a word, prefers having, or, contrariwise, those things he dislikes, wants to avoid or, in a word, prefers not having. It is this sense of interests—preference-interests—that the American philosopher Ralph Barton Perry evidently has in mind when he characterizes interests as "a certain class of acts or states which have the common characteristic of *being for or against.*"[1] Perry's characterization does not seem entirely satisfactory, however. What he evidently has in mind is what we might term *episodic interests*—such as, my *presently* being in a mental state which, if asked to describe it, I might be characterize as wanting a banana. However, individuals might have a preference-interest in something without it being true that they *now* are in a mental state of being for or against it and without it being true that they *now* are performing a comparable mental act. Some of my friends are interested in plants; but when I say, "Don is interested in plants," the truth of what I say does not depend on what Don's present mental states are or what mental acts he is presently performing. Preference-interests can be *dispositions* to want, like, and so forth, not just episodes in one's mental life, and it is this sense of preference-interests, the dispositional sense, that is involved when I say that my friend Don is interested in plants. The dispositional character of preference-interests seems to be left out by Perry's characterization.

Welfare-interests differ from preference-interests. In the case of welfare-interests, to say that A has an interest in X is not to say (nor necessarily to imply) that A has a preference-interest in X either in the episodic or dispositional sense. What, then, are we saying? The following: that having or doing X would (or we think it would) benefit A, that having or doing X would make a contribution to A's well-being. In this sense of "interests," a necessary condition of literally speaking of an individual as having an interest is that the individual have a well-being, a welfare. Since animals and humans like them in the relevant respects meet this requirement, we may speak literally of their having welfare-interests, and since, for reasons offered at length in preceding chapters, both are reasonably viewed as having desires, we may also speak literally of their having preference-interests. Some things are *in their interest*, and there are some things they are *interested in*. Now, since what is in an individual's (A's) interests is a benefit to A, while what is not in A's interests harms A, to understand the generic notion of individual welfare requires examining the notions of benefits and harm.

3.3 BENEFITS

Benefits make possible, or increase opportunities for, individuals attaining the kind of good life within their capacities. To say that what makes an individual's (A's) welfare *possible* is a benefit to A means that, unless certain conditions are met, A's chances of living well, relative to the kind of good life A can have, will be impaired, diminished, limited, or nullified. In other words, certain conditions are necessary, certain basic requirements must be met, if an individual who *can* live well is to have a realistic chance of doing so. What these conditions are will vary to some degree, depending on the varying abilities of different individuals and the broader circumstances of their life. If A is a typical human being, for example, a certain level of educational achievement is essential for having a realistic chance to live well. What level is necessary can vary because of where one lives (e.g., a village in Tibet or in the Bronx), just as what one will need to know can differ as a result of the cultural ambience in which one finds oneself. (One doesn't need to know how to plant corn in order to take the subway, or vice versa.) Despite many possible differences, however, certain conditions are universal for all humans and animals, if each is to have a reasonable chance to live well. Adequate nourishment, shelter, water, and rest, for example, are such conditions. They constitute basic biological needs of both humans and animals. Frey, we may recall, contends that we can attribute needs to things without implying that they have desires. This is true. As was noted earlier (2.2), we can make sense of saying that cars and flowers need water without implying that they desire it. Once we have moved beyond Frey's denial of desires to animals, however, there is no reason to deny that they are like us in having both episodic and dispositional interests relative to their basic needs. Like flowers, animals have a basic biological need for water and nourishment; but like us, and in this respect unlike flowers, they *prefer* to have these needs satisfied rather than unsatisfied. Correlated with their basic needs, in short, animals, like us, have desires. They are *interested in* food and water, just as food and water are *in their interests*.

It may be that the only desires or preferences some "lower" animals have are desires to satisfy their basic biological needs. If this is so, then their individual welfare will be a function of the degree to which these desires are harmoniously satisfied. The notion of harmonious satisfaction is crucial. It is not enough for an animal to have all the water she wants but no food, or all the food but no water. Neither is it enough that she satisfy all her desires on rare occasions. To live well, relative to one's capacities, is to have one's several desires satisfied in a harmonious, integrated fashion, not occasionally but regularly, and thus not just today but generally, throughout the time one retains one's psychophysical identity. An animal's welfare, like a human being's, refers to the general tenor, the dominant quality of ongoing life as lived and experienced, not to isolated occasions. In either case, human or animal, one's chances to live well, relative to the kind of good life within one's reach, will depend on the degree to which one has the opportunity harmoniously to satisfy one's desires. If animals lack this opportunity, either because of natural circumstances (e.g., flood, draught, fire) or because of human intervention (e.g., destruction of natural habitat), their chance to live well is correspondingly diminished.

Regardless of what might be true of some nonhuman animals, typical human beings clearly have preferences that go beyond those associated with basic biological needs. The network of desires and goals bound up with interests in art, music, and literature are conspicuous examples. The more complicated a conscious organism is (that is, the greater the number and sophistication of its desires and goals), the more complex must be the notion of its living well *and* the greater the number of conditions that must be met if it is to have a realistic chance to do so. Since living well involves the harmonious satisfaction of one's desires and goals over time, the greater the number of desires and goals one has, the more difficult it will be to satisfy them in a harmonious fashion. Indeed, the greater the number and sophistication of the desires and goals, the more difficult it will be to establish anything helpful about the specific nature of the good life available to such individuals. The supreme difficulty we have in saying what it is for a human being to live well, a difficulty more than vouchsafed by the voluminous literature on this question coming down through the ages, is a fair index of the complexity of the idea of "the good life" for humans. Where the nexus of desires and goals are the most complex, as in the case of typical human beings, we should not be surprised that the nature of that creature's "good life" should be open to heated debate.

This debate cannot be resolved, or even adequately aired, in the present work. What is within our reach is a general discussion of some of the more important ideas that are bound up with the notion of human welfare, in addition to those ideas involving such basic biological needs as the need for water or shelter. As we shall see, a survey of these ideas also goes some way toward illuminating the notion of animal welfare. For reasons that will be advanced as we proceed, some of the elements of a good human life, over and above considerations of basic biological needs, have a counterpart in the case of these animals.

Psychological and Social Needs

However much people might disagree over the specific nature of "the good life" for humans, most agree that typical humans have a family of psychological and social needs, including the need for companionship, security and liberty. These needs obviously can interact. An individual deprived of companionship (a neglected child, for example) is likely to be insecure in his dealings with others and to fear his freedom, whereas those raised in circumstances that foster a strong sense of security, backed by supportive companions, are more likely to have the confidence necessary to act on their own. These human needs find their counterparts among animals. Psychological and social needs, not just basic biological propensities, are as much a part of their nature as is true in the human case. For example, as was argued previously (2.5), animals have an emotional life, a life that includes affection and hate, fear and anger, security and loneliness. To the extent that animals live in an environment that provides opportunities for the satisfaction of those preferences correlated with their needs, to that extent they are benefited. To be situated in such an environment, in other words, is a welfare-interest of these animals.

An individual's welfare does not consist merely in having those benefits that make living well possible. Whether humans or animals, individuals must take satisfaction in living as they do if they are to have a good life, all considered. And this will require that they get what they want, prefer, desire and the like, more often than not, since without this their life will be characterized by frustration and all that this is heir to. But while the welfare of individuals involves the harmonious satisfaction of their desires or preferences, there is no guarantee that the satisfaction of each and every desire, on each and every occasion it makes itself known, will contribute to their welfare or be in their interests. As was noted earlier (3.2), getting what an individual is interested in (that is, wants or desires) may not be in that individual's interest, and it sometimes happens that the individual is not the best judge of the latter even if she is the best judge of the former. I know of no one, for example, who is more interested in my health than I am, not even my doctor, and yet, as Nicholas Rescher, a philosopher at the University of Pittsburgh, notes, my doctor is often better equipped than I am to determine what I need to do in order to regain or retain my physical well-being.[2] When it comes to welfare-interests, the American legal philosopher John Kleinig observes, "judgment" and "expertise" are required, "and though a person's own feelings . . . are not be left out of account, they are not decisive."[3] In the case of what is in my interests (my welfare-interests), as distinct from what I happen to be interested in (my preference-interests), other people sometimes are better judges than I am. As this is true in the case of human beings, there is no reason why it cannot be true in the case of animals. Fido, for example, is not the best judge of what will promote the quality of his life, a point we shall return to below (3.6).

To acknowledge that human beings are not always the best judge of what is in their interests is not to commit oneself to the view that we are ever, least of all that we are frequently, entitled to interfere in the life of a competent human being because we believe the outcome of her acts will be contrary to her interests. A meddling paternalism, in other words, is not justified merely on the grounds that competent humans sometimes act in ways that we know are detrimental to their individual welfare. One reason why we should resist overactive paternalistic intervention in the lives of others is because allowing maximum personal liberty is itself a benefit, making possible for those who possess it a sense of self-directedness in the unfolding of their lives. To allow extensive individual liberty is thus to make possible the satisfaction that comes from choosing well (that is, getting what one wants by one's own lights), a source of satisfaction that would be denied or diminished to the degree that individual liberty itself was denied or diminished. If the notion of individual autonomy could not be meaningfully applied to animals, it would be similarly meaningless to view them as individuals for whom extensive individual liberty is a benefit. In the opening section of the present chapter (3.1), however, the case was made for the rational propriety of viewing them as creatures with a kind of autonomy—namely, preference autonomy: they are able to initiate action to satisfy their desires and preferences. As such, there is no reason not to assume that they, too, are capable of taking satisfaction, not only in reaching their goals or fulfilling their desires but also in doing so "by their own lights." A captive wolf who is regularly fed by his keeper doubtless has his desire for food satisfied. But a wolf who must exert some effort and ingenuity to satisfy his desire for food satisfies not only his desire for food; in principle, there is no reason to deny that he also finds satisfaction, in collaboration with other members of his pack, in doing what needs to be done to have his desire for food satisfied.

In the human case, as in the case of animals, benefits and satisfactions should be kept distinct.[4] Benefits are profitably viewed as being what make satisfactions possible, or as what increase the opportunity for satisfactions, rather than as being satisfactions themselves. For example, if wealth, leisure, and natural talents are benefits to those humans who have them, they are benefits because they expand the range of possible sources of satisfaction in their lives. They may be squandered or neglected, in which case the range of satisfactions they make possible is never realized or realized to a less than optimal extent. Such individuals, we say, waste their talents, money, leisure, and the like. They make less of their benefits, and thus less of their life, than they could.

Though benefits and satisfactions are distinct, one can take (or find) satisfaction in having or securing a benefit. If I desire wealth, or if I work very hard in the hope of receiving a promotion, then I am likely to take satisfaction in achieving my objective (though I need not; sometimes we discover that it was the struggle for something, not its attainment, that was a source of satisfaction, and sometimes we discover that a goal for which we have worked, once achieved, was not what we really wanted and so is not a source of satisfaction). There is also the possibility that the mere possession of a given benefit, apart from the role its possession has in multiplying the possible sources of satisfaction for its possessor, is a source of satisfaction in its own right, as when, for example, a person in top-notch physical health takes satisfaction just in being in that condition. While we can and sometimes do take satisfaction just in having or securing certain benefits, however, it remains true that these benefits have a value that is not reducible merely to the satisfaction one might take in possessing them. Health, wealth, talent, and kindred human benefits *are* benefits because they enlarge the scope of satisfaction those who possess them can find in life, which is why we judge that a wealthy miser, for example, misunderstands and misuses his wealth. He fails to enrich his life by making optimal use of the benefit he has (money), impoverishing his life by limiting the range of his satisfaction to its mere possession.

The same kind of distinction applies in the case of our thought about animal welfare. Benefits for animals are distinct from satisfactions. A benefit enlarges the range of possible sources of satisfaction. Physical health, for example, is a benefit for those animals who have it; it contributes to their welfare. But the major contribution it makes is to be understood in terms of what it makes possible, not in terms of the state or condition it is. Healthy animals, can do more than sick animals, and because they can do more they have a greater range of possible sources of satisfaction. That is what makes health the benefit it is, both for these animals and for us.

Though it is beyond the limits of the present work to specify the essence of the good life for human beings, it is possible to generalize on the basis of the preceding and sketch a partial formal characterization of what it is for a human being to live well. Humans live well if (1) they get or pursue what they prefer, (2) they take satisfaction in pursuing and getting what they prefer, and if (3) what they pursue or obtain is in their interests. These conditions apply both to normal and deviant humans who have an experiential welfare. Humans who are handicapped, either physically or mentally, have diminished opportunities for pursuing what they prefer and, in some cases, are unable even to understand that some things they prefer are, while others are not, in their long-term (welfare) interests. But though the good life of which these humans are capable is, to a greater or lesser degree, diminished in comparison with that available to those of us who have been luckier with respect to the genetic lottery and the whims of accident, this only shows that we have been luckier, not that these humans lack a welfare or that the formal characterization offered above fails to apply in their case.

The same is true in the case of the animals. Like us, they live well relative to the degree to which (1) they pursue and obtain what they prefer, (2) they take satisfaction in pursuing and getting what they prefer, and (3) what they pursue and obtain is in their interests. That the range of possible satisfactions in their case is less than in ours shows not that their welfare is in all essential respects unlike ours but that *some* of the things we have an interest in (e.g., arts and sciences) are, so far as we know, peculiar to us, with the result that the contributions satisfying these interests makes to our welfare are lacking in their case. Differ though animals and humans do in some respects, however, the resemblances are just as noteworthy. We share with animals a set of biological, social, and psychological interests. As we are benefited to the extent that we have increased opportunities to satisfy these interests harmoniously, so, too, are they.

3.4 HARMS

Individuals are harmed when their welfare is seriously diminished. Not all harms harm equally, and not all harms harm in the same way. Two types of harm can be distinguished—inflictions and deprivations.

Inflictions

Acute or chronic physical or psychological suffering is the paradigm of a harm understood as an infliction. Suffering is not just pain. If I experience an acute but momentary pain from a cramp in my foot, then I will be in pain but I need not suffer. This is true even if I *suffer from* foot cramps (that is, if I am predisposed to have cramps in my feet). If I have this predisposition, then I will have cramps more often than is normal. But to suffer from a particular condition is not the same as, and does not entail, that one suffers as a result. Suffering involves prolonged pain of considerable intensity. It is not possible, and neither is it necessary, to give precise quantitative parameters regarding how long or how intense pain must be before it constitutes suffering. Regarding humans, paradigm cases include severe burns, amputations, starvation, paralysis, such diseases as intestinal cancers and emphysema, brutal torture, the death or serious illness of a friend or loved one, loss of self-esteem, public shame or ridicule, severe depression. In saying that these are paradigm cases of human suffering we convey *both* that we find it psychologically impossible to doubt that those who endure these hardships suffer as a result *and* that we readily empathize with their suffering. In such cases the sufferer does not "make more" of his/her pain than is reasonable, as hypochondriacs are wont to do. Moreover, those whose lot it is to endure such suffering are prima facie harmed; the quality of their life or welfare, that is, is diminished *unless* their suffering is directly causally related to a subsequent improvement in the quality of their life, an improvement that exceeds, to a quite considerable degree, the quality their life would have had, had they been spared their suffering. It is, of course, extremely difficult to know that this is true in any given case, or even to say how we could establish that it is. Yet some people who suffer *say* this. Suffering sometimes awakens people to the shallowness of their previous way of life and is the occasion for their striking out in a new, fuller, and more satisfying direction. It is in this sense that even suffering can be "a good thing," a "blessing in disguise," and, considered in the overall estimation of an individual's welfare, can be more than offset by the future satisfaction it makes possible. Not all suffering has a happy ending, however. Suffering can, and not infrequently does, take the bottom out of people's lives, marking in some cases the point from which their welfare steadily declines. In these cases suffering is not only prima facie harmful; it is genuinely harmful.

Since animals, like us, have a welfare, it would be highly unusual to deny that suffering for them can be a harm as it is for us, and it is significant that Jeremy Bentham, a nineteenth-century English philosopher, in an oft-quoted passage in which he sets forth some of his views regarding the moral status of animals, relies on the notion of animal suffering, not that of animal pain. He writes as follows:

> The day *may* come when the rest of the animal creation may acquire those rights which never could have been withholden from them but by the hand of tyranny. The French have already discovered that the blackness of the skin is no reason why a human being should be abandoned without redress to the caprice of a tormentor. It may one day come to be recognized that the number of legs, the villosity of the skin, or the termination of the *os sacrum*, are reasons equally insufficient for abandoning a sensitive being to the same fate. What else is it that should trace the insuperable line? Is it the faculty of reason, or perhaps the faculty of discourse? But a full grown horse or dog is beyond comparison a more rational, as well as a more conversable animal, than an infant of a day or a week, or even a month, old. But suppose they were otherwise, what would it avail? The question is not, Can they reason? nor Can they *talk*? but, Can they *suffer*?[5]

Bentham is astute in posing the question in terms of suffering rather than pain. Though no individual can suffer who is incapable of experiencing pain, not all painful experiences constitute suffering. Mild headaches, sore muscles, and skinned knuckles are (more or less) painful, but one would have to have a hypochondriac's predilections to find them occasions for suffering. Pains are not reasonably viewed as occasions for suffering unless they are severe enough, and prolonged enough, to constitute prima facie harms.[6]

Remarks of the same kind apply to the pain and suffering of animals. Like us, they do not prefer pain. But to cause them pain is not the same as, and does not entail, making them suffer. Whether the pain they endure occasions suffering depends on its severity and duration, and though we cannot say *exactly* how long and how severe pain must be to constitute suffering for an animal, there are paradigms in their case as in ours (e.g., extensive burns or deep cuts). Viewed in this light, Bentham's posing his question about "the insuperable line" in terms of suffering, as distinct from pain, takes on a new significance. In our dealings with animals, he may be interpreted as saying,[7] the question is not merely, Can we cause them pain?, to which the answer, except for closet Cartesians, is that we can. Rather, the question is, Can we cause them pain so intense and long lasting as to make them suffer? That is a more central moral question since, if we can cause animals to suffer, then what we do to them not only can hurt them, it can harm them; and if it can harm them, than it can detract from the experiential quality of their life, considered over time; and if it can do that, then we must view these animals as retaining their identity over time and as having a good or ill of their own. For Bentham to put the question in terms of suffering rather than pain suggests that he recognizes a deeper and, in view of the arguments that have gone before, a truer resemblance between us and them than that we both may be hurt. It is that we both may be harmed.

It is important to realize that harm is not exclusively a moral notion, as it would be if "only people (can) do harm."[8] To restrict the concept of harm to something only people can do is arbitrary. Nature, not just persons, can harm. The vast amount of suffering brought about by natural causes, including floods, hurricanes, typhoons, earthquakes, fires, disease, and congenital abnormalities can be, and frequently is, harmful. Prima facie, I am just as much harmed (that is, my welfare is just as much adversely affected) if a falling tree breaks my leg as if my neighbor does. True, to suffer "at the hands of nature" is not to be wronged. Nature is not a moral agent, and so cannot do what is wrong any more than it can do what is right. But to suffer as a result of natural occurrences is prima facie to be harmed. Even if it were true that all who wrong me harm me, it is not true that everything that harms me wrongs me, a point we shall have occasion to recall in the following discussion of harms viewed as deprivations.

Harms as Deprivations

Individuals can be harmed in ways that do not involve causing them to suffer. If, for example, a father recklessly gambles away his wealth, so that his son is subsequently denied an opportunity to secure the education that would be in his (the son's) interests, then the son's welfare is prima facie diminished (the son, that is, is prima facie harmed) even if he does not suffer as a result. Or, again, if a bright young woman is reduced to the condition of a contented imbecile by painless injections of debilitating drugs, then she is significantly harmed though she does not suffer. There are, in short, more ways to harm than simply to hurt. Not all harms hurt, just as not all hurts harm.

How should we understand harms that do not hurt? The most promising approach is to think of them as *deprivations* or *losses* of those benefits that make possible or enlarge the sources of satisfaction in life.[9] Thus, the gambler's son is harmed because he is deprived of the opportunity to secure an education, something that, because it would have enlarged the sources of satisfaction available to him, would have been a benefit to him; and the young woman who is the victim of the administration of drugs is harmed because, as a result of her mental deterioration, she loses those benefits she formerly possessed (e.g., her ability to act autonomously, in the Kantian sense). In general, then, individuals are prima facie harmed when benefits they have are taken from them or when circumstances, including the acts of others, preclude their having some benefit that is necessary if they are to have a realistic opportunity to live well relative to their abilities. To deny children equal access to an education because of race, religious affiliation, or sex, or to deny competent adult humans access to employment for similar reasons, is to harm them by denying them access to essential benefits. The victim does not have to be aware of these harms or to suffer physically or psychologically as a result. A "contented" housewife and a "happy" domestic slave may have been harmed without their knowing it. Indeed, sometimes the harm is all the greater precisely because those who have been harmed are *unaware* of the harm that has been done.

That individuals can be harmed without knowing it has important implications for the proper assessment of the treatment of animals. Modern farms (so-called factory farms), for example, raise animals in unnatural conditions.[10] The animals frequently are crowded together, as in the case of hogs, or kept in isolation, as in the case of veal calves. Since the only environments these animals ever see are the artificial ones in which they live, it sometimes is claimed that they don't know what they are missing and so cannot be worse off for having to forego an alternative environment they know nothing about. The unspoken assumption is not that what you don't know can't hurt you; it is that what you don't know can't harm you. This assumption is false. If I were to raise my son in a comfortable cage, in isolation from other human contact, though seeing to it that his basic biological needs were satisfied, and if, in all of my dealings with him, I went to considerable trouble to insure that he experienced no unnecessary pain, then I could not be faulted on the grounds that I was hurting him. However, I would have quite obviously harmed him and this in a most grievous way. How lame would be my retort that my son "didn't know what he was missing" and so wasn't harmed by me. That he doesn't know what he's missing is part of the harm I have done to him. Those animals who are raised intensively, then, let us assume, do not know what they're missing. But that does not show that they are not being harmed by the conditions under which they live. Quite the contrary, just as would be true in the case of my son, what we should say is that part of the harm done to these animals by factory farming *is* that they do not know this.

That harms can take the form of deprivations, independent of considerations about suffering, and that animals can be the subjects of such harm, is readily seen if we recall that many animals have needs and attendant desires over and above the basic biological ones for food, water, rest, and the like. Humans are, we say, social animals, but we are not the only ones. The more we learn about animals, both domesticated and wild, the more we must be impressed with the social needs and arrangements that characterize their lives. To the untutored eye, a pack of wolves might seem to be a mere collection of specimens from the species *canus lupus*, with neither bonds of affection between any of its members nor any structure to their common pursuits, as in the hunt. The day is now past when persons presuming to even a modest understanding of these animals can continue to believe this.[11] Even so "lowly" a creature as the chicken has a discernible social structure and behaves in ways that suggest social needs and attendant desires. To place animals with such desires in situations in which these desires cannot be fulfilled—as is done by caging wolves in, say, roadside zoos—is to cause them prima facie harm, whether they suffer or not, because it is to deny them the opportunity to satisfy their desires for companionship or physical freedom of movement. It is not just the suffering caused intensively raised or caged animals, if or as they are made to suffer, that harms them; also *prima facie* harmful is the loss of opportunities for satisfaction caused by being severely confined. Even if these animals were not made to suffer, that would show only that they were not hurt, not that they were not harmed. Moreover, in the absence of a considerable gain in their individual welfare traceable to their confinement (a gain that would not be possible for them except as a result of their captivity), these animals *are* harmed, just as my son in the earlier example would be. It is difficult to imagine how anyone could deny that massive harm is done to wolves, or hogs, or the other animals whose lot it is to be kept in solitary or close confinement.

Harms viewed as deprivations need not cause or involve pain or suffering. That point is clear. But harms as deprivations frequently do cause or involve this. In many cases, in other words, deprivations are double-barreled harms: there is, first, the harm done to the individual because that individual is denied opportunities to obtain satisfaction from various sources; but there is also the harm done because of the suffering caused by the methods used to deprive the individual of these opportunities. Solitary and close confinement of animals again provide clear cases of both types of harm, for though a caged wolf, say, could be harmed just by being denied the opportunity to exercise his autonomy even if he suffered not (say he was drugged into a near stuporous state), it is clear that wolves normally suffer as a result of being caged, as do many zoo animals. It is also clear that suffering, though distinct from harms viewed as deprivations, can have effects that include deprivations. Farm animals raised intensively, for example, not only suffer from, and as a result of, various digestive ailments—including ulcers and chronic watery bowel movements caused by diets ill-suited to their nature and needs[12]—their suffering itself and the debilitating consequences of their condition diminish their ability to do what they want to do and what they would find satisfaction in doing. Dairy cows who suffer acutely when they stand on a wire-mesh or concrete floor not only must bear the harm as infliction (the acute pain that comes from standing) but also the harms as deprivations that flow from their diminished activity.

3.5 DEATH

The recognition that harms need not hurt has important implications regarding the death and killing of animals. It is sometimes said that so long as animals are put to death painlessly, so long as they do not suffer as they die, we should have no moral objection. This view frequently is advanced in debates about the "humaneness" of alternative methods of slaughtering animals for food and the ethics of using animals for scientific purposes. For example, in this latter case we frequently are told that if animals are anesthetized, so that they feel nothing and so do not suffer, and if, after the test, experiment or demonstration is completed, the animal is "sacrificed" before regaining consciousness, then everything is morally above board. The accounts of benefit and harm developed in this chapter enable us to explain why this view is seriously deficient. It assumes that the only harm we can do to animals is to cause them to suffer; it completely overlooks the other type of harm we may visit upon them—namely, the harm done by deprivation. And an untimely death *is* a deprivation of a quite fundamental and irreversible kind. It is irreversible because, once dead, always dead. It is fundamental because death forecloses *all* possibilities of finding satisfaction. Once dead, the individual who had preferences, who could find satisfaction in this or that, who could exercise preference autonomy, can do this no more. Death is the ultimate harm because it is the ultimate loss—the loss of life itself. It may not be the worst harm. Some things are worse than death. A life of protracted, intense, untreatable suffering, one that promises no relief, is an obvious example. This does not mean that we must (ought to) choose death in preference to continuing to endure such a life, if given the choice, or that we must (ought to) terminate someone else's life in that condition even if she wishes to remain alive. It is only to say that we *understand* that, though death is the ultimate harm because the ultimate loss, it may not be the worst harm there is.

Professor Ruth Cigman disputes this way of viewing the death of an animal:[13] It will be instructive to examine her reasons. In order for death to be, in her terms, a "misfortune" for a given individual, that individual must have the capacity to have what Cigman, following Bernard Williams, calls "categorical desires."[14] Such a desire, she writes,

> is a desire which does not merely presuppose being alive (like the desire to eat when one is hungry), but rather answers the question whether one wants to remain alive. It may answer this question affirmatively or not. Williams discusses what he calls a rational forward looking desire for suicide; the desire is categorical because it resolves (negatively), rather than assumes, the question of one's continued existence. Alternatively one may resolve this question affirmatively with a desire, for example, to raise children or write a book. Such desires give one reason to go on living, they give life so-called point or meaning. Most persons have some such desires throughout substantial periods of their lives.[15]

Animals, Cigman contends, although they "manifest acute fear when their lives are threatened," "blindly clinging on to life," lack the capacity to have categorical desires.[16] This is because animals lack the necessary understanding of life and death that having categorical desires presupposes. One cannot see death as a misfortune or harm unless "one possesses the related concepts of long-term future possibilities, of life itself as an object of value, of consciousness, agency and their annihilation, and of tragedy and similar misfortunes." Since "such understanding is necessary for a subject of categorical desires," and since animals lack this understanding and the capacity to have such desires, it follows that death for them is no misfortune—is no harm.[17]

There is a good deal that is unclear here, perhaps ineradicably so in some cases. For death to be a misfortune for a given individual, that individual, Cigman contends, must have a sense of "long-term future possibilities." But how long is "long-term"? The question is not idle. Grounds have been advanced in the preceding for viewing animals as having a sense of their own future; they act in the present with a view to bringing about the satisfaction of their desires in the future. Is their grasp of their future ever long enough to qualify as a grasp of "long-term future possibilities"? When, for example, wolves run for many hours, possibly even days, in a given direction and then, upon reaching a given place, stop and wait; and when in time the wandering herd of caribou comes into view, may we not parsimoniously describe and explain the wolves' behavior in terms of their sense of "future possibilities"?[18] If so, is their grasp of these possibilities sufficiently future-oriented to satisfy Cigman's requirement that they involve a sense of *long-term* possibilities? Clearly we cannot say one way or the other unless or until Cigman herself sheds some light on this shadowy idea.

Suppose, however, that animals fall short in this regard: their sense of future possibilities never involves their grasp of long-term future possibilities. What follows from this? What follows is that animals would be unable to make long-term plans or set themselves distant goals and then proceed to act in the present with the intention of actualizing these plans or fulfilling these goals. The writing of a book, to use Cigman's example, is a long-term project; one begins with a goal one sets before oneself, and one must work on the project as the future unfolds. If one had no sense, no understanding, of long-term future possibilities, one could not set such a goal for oneself. That much is reasonably clear. But it does not follow that individuals who lack any grasp of long-term future possibilities *have* no long-term future possibilities. On the contrary, even if we assume that animals fail to have a sufficiently rich grasp of long-term future possibilities, in Cigman's sense, animals do have a psychophysical identity over time. Barring unforeseen developments, Fido will be the same dog tomorrow, and tomorrow, and so on into the indefinite future, as he is today. The untimely death of such an animal, therefore, does cut that individual's life short, not only in the sense that a living organism ceases to be biologically alive, but, more pertinently, in the sense that a particular psychological being ceases to be. And it is this latter fact, not whether animals themselves have a sense of their long-term future possibilities, that is decisive in giving an account of the harm or misfortune death can be for them. Death for them is a misfortune, a harm, when death for them is a deprivation, a loss, and it is the latter when their death is contrary to their welfare-interests, even assuming that they themselves have no preference-interest in remaining alive or in avoiding death.

Aside from the inadequacy of Cigman's grounds for denying that death is a misfortune for *animals*, one ought also note how newly born and soon-to-be-born *human beings* fare, given her position. Everything turns on how she understands the notion of having (in her words) the *capacity* to have categorical desires. By this she could mean *potential*, so that, for example, human fetuses and young children have the capacity to have categorical desires although they have yet to have any. But she might mean, instead, *ability* to have such desires, so that one has the capacity to have categorical desires if, and only if, one actually has them. How she understands this crucial notion of capacity does make a difference. If the latter interpretation is the one she accepts, then not only human fetuses but also young children and many mentally enfeebled and senile humans would be in the same category regarding death as the one in which Cigman places animals: since, like animals, these humans lack the ability to have categorical desires, *their* death, like the death of animals, would be no misfortune. This is strongly counterintuitive. Few people would endorse the view that the untimely death of a young child is no harm, no misfortune. Most will find the untimely death of a young child the very paradigm of the tragic face of death—death's ugly sting at its worst. Cigman could accommodate this view by accepting the potentiality interpretation: since young children have the potential to have categorical desires, death is a misfortune for them. Unfortunately, this option would cause more problems than it would solve, given Cigman's position, since human fetuses, not just young children, have the potential to have categorical desires. And it is *quite* clear that Professor Cigman does not believe that death is a misfortune for the fetus.[19]

There is a still more fundamental question to be raised, however, and this concerns how Professor Cigman understands the central notion of death as a misfortune. Characteristically she writes of the misfortune of death in terms of its being a "tragedy," as something "tragic." To view death in this way is fairly certain to exclude the death of at least most animals from being a misfortune, since to view the death of each and every animal as "a tragedy," as "tragic," is to strain anyone's credulity. The inference we should draw from this, however, is not that the death of an animal can be no misfortune or harm to that animal; it is that there is something fundamentally unsatisfactory in requiring that death be "tragic" if it is to be a harm or misfortune.

To regard all *human* death as tragic is to cheapen the notion of tragedy. This is clearest in the case of those humans for whom death is a merciful release from a life of constant, untreatable pain and torment. It is the condition of their life, not their death, that is more aptly viewed as tragic. The fullness of one's life, especially when compared with one's promise, also makes a difference. Van Gogh's death was tragic: he had so much to give and so little time to give it. But no one looking for tragedy will find it in, say, Picasso's death. Mozart's death was tragic, but not Handel's. The deaths of the Kennedy brothers, tragic, but the death of the Wright brothers? What for many is the very paradigm of the tragedy of death, the death of young children, *is* tragic, when it is, because death irrevocably and irretrievably denies them any opportunity to have a full life. The tragedy of the death of these children, despite their inability to have "categorical desires" except potentially, shows that having such desires is not a necessary condition of one's death being a tragedy, just as the absence of tragedy in Picasso's death shows that having such desires, or dying before one fulfills them, is not a sufficient condition of death's being a tragedy.

It does not follow from this that deaths that are not tragic are not harms or misfortunes. These notions—tragedy, on the one hand, and harm and misfortune, on the other—are not equivalent. To say that Picasso's death was not a tragedy is not to say that it was not a harm or misfortune. It is quite possible that living longer would have been in Picasso's interests, in which case his death, whether painful or not, was a harm because of the loss it represented. But to apply the notion of tragedy to his death is to force it where it does not fit. All deaths that are tragic are harms or misfortunes, but not all deaths that are the latter are the former. Even assuming, then, that we were to grant to Professor Cigman her view that the death of an animal is never a tragedy (and it is unclear that we should make this major concession to her),[20] it would not follow that we are committed to denying that death can be, and frequently is, a harm or misfortune for individual animals. To bring about the untimely death of animals will not hurt them if this is done painlessly; but they will be harmed. And it is the harm that an untimely death is, not just the painful methods frequently used, that should occasion our ethical curiosity.

3.6 PATERNALISM AND ANIMALS

Earlier (3.2) it was noted that what we are interested in is not always in our interests and that we are not always the best judge of what is in our interests. Neither of these points justifies a meddling paternalism in the case of competent adults, however, since our having extensive personal autonomy is itself a great benefit, making possible the satisfaction we can derive from directing the course our life will take. But what of paternalism as regards animals? Clearly to allow them to do what they want is not always in their best interests. The raccoon may *want* the food he finds, but the fatal clamp of the leghold trap that would ensnare him if he went for the food would scarcely be in his interests. If we frighten the raccoon away, we have intervened in his life in a way that is in his interests. But have we acted paternalistically?

The contemporary philosophers Bernard Gert and Charles M. Culver deny that we can literally act paternalistically toward animals. While allowing that "there is . . . an *analogue* to paternalism in our treatment of some animals and infants," these writers insist that "it simply muddies the conceptual waters to allow for paternalistic action toward animals and infants."[21] Animals and infants, Culver and Gert argue, fail to satisfy a necessary condition for paternalistic action. On their view, we can act paternalistically toward a given individual (S) *only if* we have reason to believe that S believes, perhaps falsely, "that he (S) generally knows what is for his own good."[22] Like human infants, animals fail to satisfy this condition (henceforth referred to as *the belief requirement*), according to Culver and Gert, which is why we cannot act paternalistically toward them.

Gert and Culver are not alone in excluding animals and infants in this way. The contemporary American political scientist Ann Palmeri confides that she "has no quarrel" with the belief requirement. "Clearly," she writes, "we cannot be acting paternalistically towards those who cannot even think about what is in their own behalf," which is why, in Palmeri's view, as in the view of Culver and Gert, "to say that I act paternalistically towards my plants when I prune them because I often will claim that it is 'for their own good' certainly extends paternalism too far."[23]

Now, there *is* a good deal of "conceptual muddying" going on here, only it is not to be found where Culver, Gert, and Palmeri locate it, nor is it to be cleared up in the way they propose. Part of the muddying process flows from lumping together highly disparate classes of individuals and things—infants, animals, plants. Neither infants nor animals *are plants*, and it is extraordinarily misleading to suppose or suggest that normal, mature, mammalian animals should be regarded as, so to speak, the mental equivalent of permanent human infants. For reasons that will become clearer as we proceed, while it is not true that we can literally act paternalistically toward plants, it is true that we can act paternalistically, literally, toward animals.

Central to the notion of paternalistic action, as Culver and Gert realize, is the presence of a certain kind of motivation. To act paternalistically toward S, I must be motivated to act for S's good or welfare, not so that I (or others) might benefit. Paternalistic acts, properly so-called, must be other-regarding, not self-regarding, and the other for whose benefit one acts must be the same individual in whose life one intervenes. Let us say that acts that satisfy this requirement are *paternalistically motivated*. Thus, for example, legislation requiring motorcyclists to wear protective headgear is paternalistically motivated if the intended beneficiaries are the motorcyclists (rather than, say, helmet manufacturers) and if the legislation is motivated by a regard for what is believed to be in their interests. It would not follow, of course, that this (or any other) act would be justified, just because it was paternalistically motivated. All that would follow is that this (and other similarly motivated acts) could qualify as paternalistic, whether justified or not.

Having the proper motive is a necessary, not a sufficient, condition of an act's being paternalistic, according to Culver and Gert. Also necessary, in their view, is the belief requirement. That is, not only must we intend to benefit the individuals in whose life we intervene and be motivated to do so because we want to benefit them, we must also believe that they generally know what is for their own good. This is the requirement that infants and animals fail to satisfy. Though we can and sometimes do intervene in their lives for their good, so that our intervention sometimes shares the motivational feature required of paternalistic acts, such intervention fails to count as genuine paternalism and is at most an "analogue."

Culver and Gert offer no argument in defense of their view that animals fail to satisfy the belief requirement. Yet an argument is called for. Because animals not only have beliefs but also are reasonably viewed as sometimes having beliefs about their beliefs (e.g., the belief that a given belief was false; see 2.5), we should not *assume* that animals cannot satisfy the belief requirement either because they are incapable of believing anything or because they are incapable of having any second-order beliefs (that is, beliefs about beliefs). Moreover, though it may be true that animals fail to show by their behavior that they have a conception of their long-term self-interest, and so fail to show by their behavior that they believe that they usually know what is for their long-term good, it is less clear that they are incapable of having similar beliefs about the short-term. Certainly there is no good reason to deny that predatory animals, for example, are capable of remembering successful hunt strategies or of using these strategies to get what they want in the present. Why, then, *must* they be incapable of believing that they "generally know" that reliance on beliefs rooted in past success will be "for their good" in the present? An argument is needed to foreclose this possibility if, like Culver and Gert, we accept the belief requirement and deny that animals satisfy it.

That requirement, as it turns out, should not be accepted because of its highly paradoxical implications. Not just plants, human infants, and (if Culver and Gert are right) animals fail to satisfy the belief requirement; young children also fail, so that if satisfaction of the belief requirement was a necessary condition for paternalistic action, it would follow that we cannot act paternalistically toward *them*. And that is to distort the concept of paternalism rather than to illuminate it. To make this clearer, imagine that your three-year-old son wants to "fly" off the roof of your house. You try all manner of dissuasion, pointing out that such flights defy gravity, that he is not a bird or Superman, and that he will be seriously hurt if he tries to fly. Because of his limited experience of the world and his limited imaginative capacities, the lad is unable to accept or imagine what, for us, are the foreseeable consequences of many of his acts, especially novel ones, including his maiden flight. Your attempts to dissuade him are unsuccessful; off he steps, in the belief that he will fly—only to be grabbed by you at the last instant, thereby preventing the unhappy landing that was almost certain to befall him.

Was your intervention in your son's life paternalistic? The position of Culver and Gert arguably implies that it was not. For though *you* may have been motivated to prevent your son's acting as he desired in the way required by paternalistic acts, it is very unclear that *he* meets the belief requirement. For if your son is as lacking in experience of the world and in imaginative capacity as we assume is normal for a three-year-old, we have no reason to believe that he has yet formed the concept of what is for his good (i.e., what is conducive to his overall welfare), from which it follows that he cannot believe that he generally knows what is in his own interests. Like everyone else, your son cannot have beliefs about something he has no conception of. Assuming, then, what seems reasonable, that your son lacks the concept of his own good, and in view of Culver and Gert's claim that "we cannot act paternalistically toward someone whom we do not regard as believing that he knows what is for his own good,"[24] it follows that you not only did not act, but you could not have been acting, paternalistically when you stopped your son.

This finding must strike us as strongly counterintuitive. It is not enough to say, what Culver and Gert contend, that "one can act paternalistically toward children, especially *older* children."[25] One *must* say this or else be faced with the devastating paradox that a father cannot act paternalistically toward his children, a gross corruption of the root meaning of the word *paternalism* (from the Latin *paternus*, meaning "of or relating to a father; evincing a father's care or solicitude," according to *Webster's Third New International Dictionary*). One must say more than this, if we may safely generalize on your son's example. One must also say that it is possible to act paternalistically in regard to *young* children, children who, for the reasons given in the above, arguably fail to meet the belief requirement. That requirement, in short, cannot incorporate an acceptable necessary condition of an act's being genuinely paternalistic.

To reject the belief requirement does not by itself illuminate why your intervention in your son's affairs counts as a genuine instance of paternalism, rather than as an analogue of the genuine article. The following set of conditions, taken jointly, are sufficient for paternalism, and provide an alternative to the analysis of paternalism offered by Culver and Gert, one that sheds light where theirs fails to do so.

An act by an individual (A) is paternalistic if A intervenes in the life of another individual (S) and the following conditions are satisfied.

a) A knows that S has a particular preference;

b) A knows that S has the capacity to act in a way that S believes will bring about the satisfaction of his (S's) preference;

c) A knows that, unless prevented, S will act in the way S believes will bring about the satisfaction of his preference;

d) A knows that S's acting in this way will bring about results that are detrimental to S's welfare; and

e) A intervenes to prevent S from acting as S would choose to act, if not prevented by A, in the belief that such intervention is for S's own good and out of concern for S's good.

The previous example of your intervening to prevent your son's stepping off the roof satisfies these conditions and thus is, on the view recommended here, genuinely paternalistic. Not so in the case of "acting for the good of plants." Since we have no adequate reason to believe that plants have preferences (desires), let alone that they can act to satisfy them, we have no basis for thinking that, to use Palmeri's words, "I act paternalistically toward my plants when I prune them because I often will claim that it is 'for their own good.' " The view recommended here, in short, which has the desirable implication that we do act paternalistically toward young children when we act for their good with the proper motivation, does not imply that we act paternalistically in the case of plants when we act "for their good."

The situation with regard to animals (e.g., the raccoon of the earlier example) is like the situation of your son and unlike that of plants. The case has been made (3.1) for the view that these animals are reasonably viewed as having a kind of autonomy, namely, preference autonomy: they not only desire some things, they can and do act, when not thwarted, to secure what they want or prefer. That being so, we clearly can and, as a matter of fact, frequently do intervene in their lives in ways that frustrate their dominant present desires. Sometimes this intervention is done without our being motivated by a concern for the well-being of the animals themselves. The people who slaughter animals in packing houses, for example, usually do not slaughter them because they are motivated to act in the animals' interests. In such cases human intervention can only erroneously be characterized as paternalistic. Sometimes, however, our intervention is appropriately other-regarding, as when, for example, sick or injured animals, despite their behavioral protestations, are subjected to painful examinations or treatment in the course of receiving proper medical care. In these cases we are on solid conceptual ground—we "muddy no conceptual waters"—if we characterize our acts as paternalistic. For they are in all relevant respects like the case of your paternalistic intervention in your son's flight plans, satisfying conditions (a) through (e) above of genuine paternalism.

It might be objected that there is a relevant difference between your son's case and that of any animal, the claim being that, though your son lacks the ability to entertain beliefs about his long-term future possibilities and, with this, also lacks the concept of his own overall good, he nevertheless does have beliefs, even if they happen to be false, about what he expects his immediate future will be like and about what he believes is in his short-term interests. In this sense and to this degree, it might be claimed, your son does have a concept of "his own good" and does, or at least can, believe that he usually knows what is for his own good. That much granted, so this objection concludes, your son can, but animals cannot, satisfy the belief requirement.

This move to save the belief requirement can succeed only at the price of enfranchising animals along with your son and other similar human children. We have no more, and probably less, reason to suppose that your son has the conceptual and intellectual wherewithal to satisfy the belief requirement, when modified to include beliefs about short-term good, as we do in the case of those animals that have been, and will continue to be, of particular interest to us—namely, normal mammalian animals aged one or more. The upshot, then, is that if the belief requirement were modified so that young children can meet it, these animals could meet it also, whereas if that requirement were not modified, thereby excluding paternalistic acts toward animals, it would also exclude paternalistic acts toward young children. In neither case, it seems fair to say, is it likely that the truth about paternalism and its implications, especially as this relates to animals, lies where Culver and Gert think they find it.

3.7 EUTHANASIA AND ANIMALS

The results of the preceding analyses of preference autonomy, death, and paternalism illuminate the idea of euthanasia as it applies to animals. It is well to remind ourselves of the number of animals said to be "euthanized." Conservative estimates place the total of cats and dogs annually "euthanized" in the United States at 15 million. Moreover, it is fair to assume that a large percentage of the estimated 60–80 million animals used for scientific purposes in America, and the 200 million used worldwide, are "euthanized" upon completion of nonfatal uses. The practice of "euthanizing animals" clearly affects a large number. Our present interest lies not in resolving the morality of this practice but in understanding whether and, if so, when the intentional termination of an animal's life is *properly classifiable as* euthanasia. To anticipate the main conclusion of the argument that lies ahead, what we shall see is that most, but not all, cases where animals are *said* to be "euthanized" are not cases of euthanasia, properly conceived.

The word *euthanasia* comes from two Greek words that are perhaps best translated as meaning "good death." To euthanize an individual is to bring about that individual's "good death" either by direct killing (so-called active euthanasia) or by letting die (so-called passive euthanasia).[26] Cases of passive euthanasia characteristically arise in situations where individuals are kept alive by extraordinary means (e.g., artificial respirators or kidneys). To remove the patient from these essential life-support systems, to "pull the plug," is to allow the patient to die by allowing nature to run its course. Except for rare exceptions (e.g., a valuable race horse might be kept alive by artificial means), the practice of euthanizing animals involves actively terminating their life, not passively allowing them to die. For this reason, only active euthanasia will concern us in what follows.

Euthanasia requires more than killing another painlessly or with a minimum of suffering. If Cedric kills his Aunt Bertha without causing her any pain or suffering (say he injects a lethal dose of sodium pentothal into her bloodstream while she sleeps) but does so in order to collect the inheritance in store for him upon her death, then Aunt Bertha's passing from this life is not a case of euthanasia. It is a case of murder. For the concept of euthanasia to apply to the active termination of an individual's life, that individual's life must be terminated *for the right reason*, not merely by the right (that is, the least painful) means. Actively to euthanize another requires that one kill the other in the belief that this is for his/her own good *and* out of concern for that individual's good. Euthanasia thus requires that one's motives be other-regarding, not self-regarding, and that the other for whose sake one acts must be the one who is killed. Were Cedric to bring about Aunt Bertha's death painlessly but do so in order that his children might get their inheritance, without any thought of what he personally stood to gain, his act would be other-regarding but it would still be murder.

For a case of actively terminating the life of a given individual to qualify as a case of euthanasia, therefore, at least the following conditions must be met:

1. The individual must be killed by the least painful means available.
2. The one who kills must believe that the death of the one who is killed is in the interests of the latter.
3. The one who kills must be motivated to end the life of the one who is killed out of concern for the latter's interests, good, or welfare.

Though even these conditions do not go far enough (the second will be strengthened momentarily), they suffice to show why many cases of "euthanizing animals" fall short of genuine euthanasia. In some (for example, when dogs are "put to sleep" in the decompression chamber), the *means used* to kill the animals are not the least painful available, while in others (for example, when laboratory rats have their life terminated by striking their heads against a sharp edge, such as the edge of a table), the *motivation* is not appropriately other-regarding. To persist in calling such practices "euthanizing animals" is to wrap plain killing in a false verbal cover.

Reflection shows that condition (2) is too weak as it stands. It is not enough that *we believe* that it is in another's interests to die if terminating his life is to constitute euthanasia. The belief *must be true*. The verb *to euthanize*, in other words, is an achievement verb, and one does not achieve (perform) euthanasia unless the belief that death is for the good of the victim is true. "He thought that he euthanized her, but he didn't; she would have been better off if she had lived" makes perfectly good sense and is just what we should say if someone painlessly killed another out of well-intentioned concern for the victim but in the mistaken belief that death was in the victim's interests. Though the killing is motivated by a concern for the victim's welfare, though the means used are the least painful available, and though the deed is done in the belief that the victim will be better off dead than alive, the killing is not a case of euthanasia if this latter belief is false. Condition 2, then, should be modified to read as follows:

2. The one who kills must believe, and it must be true, that the death of the one who is killed is in that individual's interests.

As will shortly be noted, the requirement this condition imposes frequently is not met by those who profess to euthanize animals.

In the literature on euthanasia, a distinction is sometimes drawn between (a) voluntary and (b) nonvoluntary euthanasia. (If there were such a thing as "involuntary euthanasia," it would be killing others *against their will, in open disregard for their expressed wishes.* This would be murder, not euthanasia, which is why "involuntary euthanasia" will not figure in the analysis given in what follows.) The clearest cases of voluntary euthanasia are those where, in addition to conditions 1 through 3 being satisfied, the individual who is killed is competent, is going to die soon anyway, and requests to die. The request might take different forms, from formally written instructions, explicit verbal pleadings, or recognizable nods to appropriate questions. Whatever we might think about the morality of acceding to such explicit requests in any given case, it is clear that it *would* muddy conceptual waters if we were to characterize voluntary euthanasia as paternalistic. To comply with a competent individual's request when death is requested, cannot be anymore paternalistic than to pass him the salt when salt is requested. In both cases we comply with the individual's own explicit request and so cannot be said to be acting paternalistically if we comply.

Whatever form requests for one's own death take, it is clear that such requests can only be made by those who (a) understand their own mortality and (b) have the means to articulate the desire that their life be terminated. It is doubtful that any animals can satisfy these two conditions, and it is uncertain at best how, lacking in linguistic competence as they all are or may be, we could have any basis for deciding whether they can or do meet them. Though, to use Cigman's words, animals "cling . . . to life," when they find themselves in a life-threatening situation, it is unclear whether they do so in order to avoid death or in the belief that the pain, terror, or anguish they are presently experiencing will end. Because their behavior is intractably ambiguous in this crucial respect, it cannot be shown on behavioral grounds that animals can satisfy conditions (a) and (b). It is not implausible to maintain, therefore, that the concept of voluntary euthanasia, as typically understood, is inapplicable to cases where animals are euthanized, and it would thus appear that, when animals are euthanized, the kind of euthanasia in question must be nonvoluntary euthanasia.

But there are serious conceptual problems here. Paradigm cases of nonvoluntary euthanasia are those where the lives of irreversibly comatose human beings are terminated, whether actively or passively. Because of their condition, these individuals can neither request their own death, which is partially definitive of voluntary euthanasia, nor request that they be allowed to live. Because of their condition, they cannot request anything. Of course, human beings who are reduced to the state of a "vegetable" may have issued instructions in the past about what was to be done to them in the event that they became irreversibly comatose. If they did, and if they requested death under such circumstances, to kill them now, because it would be to comply with their known wishes, could qualify as a form of voluntary euthanasia, whereas if they previously asked not to have their life actively terminated, then to kill them now would seem to qualify as a form of involuntary euthanasia. These considerations, plus questions about our ability to know what persons *would* want, *if* they could say what they preferred in their irreversibly comatose condition, complicate matters certainly, and any examination of euthanasia that aspires to completeness would have to explore these matters in detail. For our purposes, however, the striking fact, and the one to be emphasized, is that in their condition as irreversibly comatose human beings, the individuals in question experience no preferences. They are not the experiencing subjects of occurrent desires or aspirations, nor do they retain any dispositions in this regard. Psychologically, they have ceased to be. Psychologically, they are dead. And it is in just these respects that paradigm cases of nonvoluntary euthanasia, when these involve human beings, differ from the standard cases where animals are said to be euthanized. For the animals who are routinely "put to sleep" at pounds or shelters, and many of those who are "humanely sacrificed" in the laboratory, are *not* irreversibly comatose—are not comatose at all. To kill them is thus relevantly dissimilar from killing irreversibly comatose human beings. Though neither these human beings nor these animals can request their own death or request that they be allowed to live—and thus resemble each other in not qualifying as possible recipients of voluntary or involuntary euthanasia, as these notions are usually understood—they nonetheless differ from each other in that the animals continue to retain, while the humans in question have lost, their psychological identity. To classify cases of euthanizing *both* these humans *and* these animals as nonvoluntary euthanasia is to conceal, rather than to illuminate, this crucial difference. Previously unmarked categories of euthanasia need to be noted if we are to understand the idea of euthanizing animals. Two such categories are sketched in what follows.

Preference-Respecting Euthanasia

It sometimes happens that animals are in conditions of acute, untreatable suffering (for example, cats in advanced stages of feline leukemia). Animals in such conditions not only will be aware of their pain at present, they will also desire to be rid of their pain as soon as possible, a desire that relates to their preferences about their immediate future. In the type of case in question it is a brute fact that, unless the animals are killed or rendered permanently unconscious by the use of various drugs, their future condition will be just as painful and just as untreatable as their present one. What we know, then, is that their future conscious life will be the same and that their overriding future desire will continue to be the same as the desire they have at present. However long they may live, their dominant desire will be to have their acute suffering end. To kill animals in these circumstances would seem clearly to be in their interests, for there are fates worse than death, and the condition of these animals is one. Better for them to be dead than to live a life of relentless physical agony. Suppose that the three conditions cited earlier as a partial analysis of euthanasia are satisfied: we kill the animals as painlessly as we can; we do so in the true belief that their death is in their interests; and we are motivated to terminate their life for other-regarding reasons, out of concern for what is in their interests. For reasons already adduced, the merciful killing of these animals is not a case of voluntary euthanasia, since the animals themselves cannot request their own death, nor is it a case of nonvoluntary euthanasia, since, unlike the permanently comatose, the animals retain their psychological identity. What is needed, then, is a new category of euthanasia, one that may be literally applied to the case of these animals. Let us call the needed category *preference-respecting euthanasia*. The propriety of calling it preference-respecting can be defended in the following way.

What the animals in the condition we have imagined want, what they prefer, is that their pain cease. And this is something these animals will continue to want as long as their pain continues. Thus, since, *ex hypothesi,* their pain will continue unabated as long as they remain conscious, they will continue to want their pain abated into the foreseeable future. The only way we can respect what will be *their* overriding preference, therefore, is to terminate their lives as conscious individuals. In killing these animals, therefore, we respect *their* preference—not their desire to die, to be sure, since we have agreed that animals cannot desire what they do not understand, so that, assuming that animals do not understand their own mortality, they cannot desire their own death; rather, we honor or respect the preference of these animals, both their present preference and the preference we foresee they will continue to have, by doing the only thing we can do to satisfy it—namely, by killing them. It is in this sense and for these reasons that euthanizing an animal or, by extension, a young child whose life has been reduced to acute, untreatable physical agony is properly viewed as preference-respecting euthanasia.

Preference-respecting euthanasia is not paternalistic. When we terminate the lives of individuals because this is the only way to bring about what it is that they now want and will continue to want, we respect *their* preferences. Though we do for them what they cannot do for themselves, *we do not impose our will on them* "for their own good." Rather, because we do what must be done if they are to have their preferences satisfied, *we comply with their will*, as this is known to us. What we do *is* for their good, but what do is *not* paternalistic.

Paternalistic Euthanasia

While it is possible to kill animals for their own good without acting paternalistically, the range of cases in which this is possible is limited and does not include the more common kind of case in which domesticated animals are said to be euthanized. For the most common case involves killing *healthy* animals—strays and unwanted pets, for example. Since the condition of these animals differs importantly from the condition of those whose euthanasia is preference-respecting, we need to ask how we should understand the practice of "euthanizing" healthy but unwanted animals.

Though animals have preferences, they may lack the necessary cognitive prerequisites for having a conception of their own long-term good. Assuming they do, it follows that animals themselves can have no preference regarding their long-term future: they cannot have preferences about what they have no conception of. Except in cases where we know that an animal's dominant present and future desire can be satisfied only by terminating his psychological being—except, that is, for cases where euthanizing an animal is preference-respecting—to kill an animal "for his own good" is paternalistic: we impose *our* will and *our* judgment on the animal, for the animal's own good, as we conceive it. *Paternalistic euthanasia* is an appropriate label for this type of euthanasia.

As is true of euthanasia generally, paternalistic euthanasia requires more than that death be caused by the least painful available means, more than that one's motive be appropriately other-regarding, and more than that one believe that death is in the interests of those who are killed. That belief must be true. Otherwise we have (at most) well-intentioned killing, not euthanasia. Virtually all cases where healthy, unwanted pet animals are said to be euthanized fail to qualify as euthanasia. Because these animals are healthy, killing them can only erroneously be classified as preference-respecting. And because those who kill these animals could refuse to do so, instituting instead the policy, as a few shelters do, of keeping animals until they are adopted into a responsible person's home, it is false that *these* animals (that is, the ones already in the shelter, the ones who would be killed) are better off dead than they would be alive. On the contrary, there is every reason to believe that *these* animals would be better off alive, if those who ran the shelter took proper care of them until they were adopted.

A critic will object that the preceding overlooks the dismal life prospects of the many unwanted animals to whom shelters would have to deny admittance if shelters instituted the policy of keeping animals until they were adopted or euthanizing them only when it was a case of preference-respecting euthanasia. Realistically, this critic will note, there is a limit to the space, budget, and personnel shelters can provide, so that while the policy advocated in the preceding would provide a safe haven for those animals lucky enough to find a place within a shelter, it would consign many, many more to the wretched fate of trying to fend for themselves in the streets. Better to serve the many who are helpless than to cater to the fortunate few.

This objection misses the mark. The question at issue is not which policy is *morally* preferable—the one where healthy animals are, or the one where they are not, routinely killed, if they have not been adopted in a given length of time. The question at issue is *conceptual*. It is *whether* animals are *euthanized* when shelters rely on the practice of killing animals if they have not been adopted after a given length of time. The answer must be, no. Even assuming they are killed by the least painful means available, assuming those who do the killing have appropriate other-regarding motives, and granting that they believe they are acting in the interests of the animals they kill, *what they do* is not euthanasia, properly conceived. It is no more true to say that healthy dogs and cats are euthanized when they are "put to sleep" to make room for other cats and dogs at animal shelters than it would be true to say that healthy derelicts would be euthanized if they were "put to sleep" to make room for other derelicts at human shelters. This does not entail that "putting (healthy) animals to sleep" *must* be wrong. It is simply to remove a piece of the rhetoric standing in the way of commanding a clear view of the ethics of this practice. To acknowledge that these animals are *not* euthanized but *are* killed will not resolve the moral dilemma faced by those who work in animal shelters. It might, however, help occasion a fresh reexamination.

3.8 SUMMARY AND CONCLUSION

Mammalian animals have and, in the normal course of events, retain a psychophysical identity over time. That being so, we use language literally, not metaphorically, when we speak of the good, or welfare, of these animals. Like us, they fare well or ill during the course of their experiential life. The present chapter's central objective was to offer an analysis of the idea of welfare that helped explain why, differ though we do from these animals, human and animal welfare do not differ in kind.

Included in the analysis and estimation of animal welfare is autonomy (3.1). As individuals with desires, beliefs, and the ability to act in pursuit of their goals, animals have a kind of autonomy—preference autonomy. One aspect of animals' faring well or ill is the degree to which they are able to exercise their autonomy, since to thwart their will by denying them the opportunity to do what they prefer is to cause them frustration, while to allow them to do what they prefer is to make it possible for them not only to obtain what they want but to take satisfaction in obtaining it by their own devices.

Preference autonomy provides a starting point for thinking about the interests of animals (3.2). As was noted, not only are animals interested in (that is, want, desire, prefer) various things, but a variety of things also are in their interests (that is, contribute to their good or welfare). The two kinds of interests (respectively, preference-interests and welfare-interests) are distinct. Though they differ, however, both sorts of interest have a role to play in the analysis of animal (and human) welfare. This was shown by noting that the notion of an individual's welfare is partly analyzable in terms of benefits and harms. Benefits make possible, or increase opportunities for, individuals attaining the kind of good life within their capacities (3.3), while harms negate these possibilities, or otherwise decrease, these opportunities (3.4). Mammalian animals, as is true of humans, have biological, social, and psychological interests. To the extent that these animals (or we humans) are in circumstances that answer to this family of interests, to that extent they (and we) are benefited, while to the extent that either is denied these benefits, to that extent is each harmed.

To live well, relative to one's capacities, involves more than having benefits. One must also take satisfaction in having, or in using, one's benefits, not only sporadically, but on balance, over time. To live well is to have a life that is characterized by the harmonious satisfaction of one's desires, purposes, and the like, taking account of one's biological, social, and psychological interests. More generally, animals (and humans) live well relative to the degree to which (1) they pursue and obtain what they prefer, (2) they take satisfaction in pursuing and obtaining what they prefer, and (3) what they prefer and obtain is in their interests.

Harms are classifiable as either inflictions or deprivations (3.4). Paradigmatic inflictions are acute physical or mental suffering. Though both involve pain, it is false that pain always constitutes suffering or harm. Pain must be intense enough, and last long enough, to reasonably be viewed as suffering or harm.

Despite the importance of reducing animal suffering, it is essential that we recognize that not all harms hurt. Harms understood as deprivations detract from an individual's welfare independently of their occasioning pain or suffering. As deprivations, these harms are to be understood as losses of benefits (e.g., losses of opportunities to develop or exercise one's autonomy). In the case of both humans and animals, it was argued, what we don't know can harm us, even if what we don't know can't hurt us. It is, therefore, no defense of consigning either humans or animals to environments that ignore their biological, social, or psychological interests, or that cater to some (e.g., the desire for food) at the expense of others (e.g., the interest in autonomy or social relations) to claim that these individuals do not know what they are missing and so cannot be any worse off for not having it. Environments that deny humans or animals the sort of benefits necessary for their welfare are to that extent harmful to their interests, whether they cause suffering or not.

When we recognize that harms can take the form of deprivations, we are able to understand why death is a harm, when it is (3.5). Death is the ultimate, the irreversible harm because death is the ultimate, the irreversible loss, foreclosing every opportunity to find any satisfaction. This is true whether death is slow and agonizing or quick and painless. Though there are some fates worse than death, an untimely death is not in the interests of its victims, whether human or animal, independently of whether they understand their own mortality, and thus independently of whether they themselves have a desire to continue to live. Though young children, like animals of comparable mental development, arguably lack any conception of their long-term welfare, lack the ability to formulate categorical desires, and lack any sense of their own mortality, the untimely death of either is a harm. To attempt to avoid this finding by requiring that death must be "tragic" in order to be a harm or misfortune, is to distort rather than to illuminate when and why death is the harm or misfortune that it is. Moreover, because the harm that an untimely death, viewed as a loss, is for any given individual is independent of the pain involved in dying, the ethical questions concerning, for example, the slaughter of animals for food and their use in science are not limited to how "humane" are the methods used to kill them. When these questions are examined (they are explored in detail below, 9.1 and 9.4, respectively), the ethics of causing animals an untimely death must also be considered.

Because animals have a welfare, and because we sometimes intervene in their life in the name of their welfare-interests and contrary to their known present preference, there is a strong presumption to believe that we can act paternalistically toward them. This presumption is denied by Professors Culver, Gert, and Palmeri, but the grounds for their denial, it was argued (3.6), are defective. Just as it is not necessary to have a conception of one's long-term future possibilities for it to be true that some things are in one's long-term future interests, so it is unnecessary that one believe that one usually knows what is in one's interests for it to be true that others can act paternalistically toward one. When we prevent animals or young children from doing what they want because doing so would be harmful to them, and when we intervene on their behalf out of concern for their welfare, then we practice genuine paternalism toward them, not a mere analogue.

One of the paternalistic acts we may do to animals is cause their death when death is in their interests. To explore these matters required analyzing the notion of euthanasia (3.7). Standard varieties of euthanasia in the case of human beings (namely, voluntary and nonvoluntary euthanasia) are ill suited to casting light on euthanasia in the case of animals. Since voluntary euthanasia requires that someone requests to die, animals are excluded for the simple reason that they cannot make the relevant request; and since nonvoluntary euthanasia paradigmatically applies in cases where individuals fail to request death because they are psychologically dead, most animals are excluded for the simple reason that most animals who are said to be euthanized are psychologically alive. In an effort to make the notion of euthanasia intelligible when applied to animals, two further forms of euthanasia were characterized: preference-respecting euthanasia and paternalistic euthanasia. Both assume that (1) the animals euthanized are killed by the least painful means available; (2) they are killed in the true belief that death is in their interests; and (3) they are killed out of concern for them and for what is in their interests. Preference-respecting euthanasia occurs when, in addition to meeting these three conditions, we know that an animal's future will be characterized by constant, acute pain. To euthanize this animal is to do what must be done if this animal's present and foreseeable preferences are to be satisfied. Since this type of euthanasia does what must be done if the victim is to get what the victim wants (namely, relief from suffering), it is not paternalistic. Paternalistic euthanasia involves killing animals for their own good but in circumstances where their foreseeable future will not be characterized by constant suffering.

Though millions upon millions of animals annually are said to be euthanized, the results of the analysis offered in this chapter contest the accuracy of saying this. Sometimes animals who are killed are not euthanized because the least painful available means are not used; sometimes they are not euthanized because the required other-regarding motivation is not present; sometimes they are not euthanized because it is false that they are better off dead than they would be alive (for example, when they are "put to sleep" to make room for additional animals in city pounds or animal shelters). If any (or all) these conditions obtain, any animal "put to sleep" is killed, not euthanized. To persist in referring to acts that culminate in the untimely death of these animals as "euthanasia" is as inaccurate as the acts are regrettable.

If the analyses and arguments of the present chapter are sound, we have more than ample reason to deny that human and animal welfare differ in kind. Both animals and humans have preference- and welfare-interests, some biological, some psychological, some social; both are capable of acting intentionally in pursuit of what they want; both may be benefited or harmed and, if the latter, harmed either because of what they are made to experience (harms as inflictions) or because of what they are denied (harms as deprivations); both have lives that are characterized by pleasure or pain, satisfaction or frustration; and the overall tone or quality of the life of each, to a greater or lesser degree, is a function of the harmonious satisfaction of those preferences that it is in the interests of each to have satisfied. Granted, the sources of satisfaction available to most humans are at once more numerous and varied than those available to animals; even granted, in Mill's memorable words, that it is "better to be a human being dissatisfied than a pig satisfied";[27] nevertheless, the same categories of thought (interests, benefits, harms, etc.) that illuminate the most general features of human welfare are equally applicable to animal welfare. Though some may find this similarity surprising, they shouldn't. In view of our own animality, surprise would be appropriate only if things were otherwise—only if, that is, human welfare *differed in kind* from animal welfare. Seen in this light, it is at least a small measure of the possible truth of the major conclusions reached in the present chapter that, at its end, we find no surprises.[28]

4

Ethical Thinking and Theory

The first three chapters have examined questions about the nature of animals. Some animals arguably lack consciousness, while others are conscious and sentient but evidently lack beliefs and all that this makes possible. Still others not only are conscious and sentient; their behavior is intelligibly described and parsimoniously explained by attributing to them beliefs and desires, memory and a sense of the future, an emotional life, a kind of autonomy (namely, preference-autonomy), intentionality, and self-awareness. Where one draws the line between those animals belonging to the various categories is a difficult question, but at least in the case of normal mammalian animals, aged one or more, the preceding argument provides the grounds for viewing them as belonging in this final category. Moreover, given the morally uncontroversial assumption that animals retain their identity over time, it is reasonable to view them as psychophysical individuals who have an individual welfare. For the notion of having a welfare, of faring well or ill, is a notion that has perspicuous application to those individuals whose life *over time* is better or worse for them, considered as individuals, logically independently of their being the object of the interests of any other individual. Animal welfare, it was argued, is no different in kind than human welfare.

Beginning with this chapter, attention must be focused on a new set of questions—namely, moral ones. The approach will be as follows: I will begin by first characterizing some ways not to answer moral questions (4.1). Then I will characterize the notion of an ideal moral judgment (4.2). This latter inquiry will in turn lead to the idea of a moral or ethical (the terms will be used interchangeably) principle, and this will oblige me to say something about how such principles may be rationally evaluated (4.3). After I have done this I will characterize some leading ethical theories (4.4, 4.5) and indicate how previous remarks about evaluating moral principles apply to the evaluation of competing ethical theories (4.6). No conclusion will be reached in the present chapter about the adequacy of these competing theories. That question will occupy us in subsequent chapters. The object of the present chapter is to lay the foundation for this later inquiry.

4.1 SOME WAYS NOT TO ANSWER MORAL QUESTIONS

Moral Judgments and Personal Preferences

Some people like classical music; others do not. Some people think bourbon is just great; others detest its taste. Some people will go to a lot of trouble to spend an afternoon in the hot sun at the beach; others can think of nothing worse. In all these cases disagreement in preference exists. Someone likes something; someone else does not. Are moral disagreements, disagreements over whether something is morally right or wrong, the same as disagreements in preference?

It does not appear so. For one thing, when a person (say, Lee) says he likes something, he is not denying what another person (Jane) says if she says she does not like it. Suppose Lee says "I [Lee] like bourbon," and Jane says "I [Jane] do not like bourbon." Then clearly Jane does not deny what Lee says. To deny what Lee says, Jane would have to say "You [Lee] do not like bourbon," which is not what she says. So, in general, when two persons express conflicting personal preferences, the one does not deny what the other affirms. It is perfectly possible for two conflicting expressions of personal preference to be true at the same time.

When two people express conflicting judgments about the morality of something, however, the disagreement is importantly different. Suppose Lee says, "Abortion is always wrong," while Jane says, "Abortion is never wrong." Then Jane is denying what Lee affirms; she is *denying* that abortion is always wrong, so that, if what she said were true, what Lee said would have to be false. Some philosophers have denied this. They have maintained that moral judgments should be understood as expressions of personal preferences. Though this view deserves to be mentioned with respect, it is doubtful that it is correct. When people say that something is morally right or wrong, it is always appropriate to ask them to give reasons to support their judgment, reasons for accepting their judgment as correct. In the case of personal preferences, however, such requests are inappropriate. If Lee says he likes to go to the beach, it hardly seems apt to press him to give reasons to support his judgment; indeed, it hardly seems that he has made a *judgment* at all. If he says abortion is always wrong, however, a judgment has been expressed, and it is highly relevant to press Lee for his reasons for thinking what he does. If he were to reply that he had no reasons, that he just does not like abortions, it would not be out of place to complain that he speaks in a misleading way. By saying that abortion is wrong, Lee leads his listeners to believe that he is making a judgment about abortion, not merely expressing some fact about himself. If all that he means is that he personally does not like abortions, that is what he should say, not that abortion is wrong.

This difference between conflicting expressions of personal preference and conflicting moral judgments points to one way not to answer moral questions. Given that moral judgments are not just expressions of personal preference, it follows that moral right and wrong cannot be determined just by finding out about the personal preferences of some particular person—say, Lee. This is true even in the case of our own preferences. Our personal preferences are important certainly, but we do not answer moral questions by saying what we like or dislike.

Moral Judgments and Feelings

Closely connected with personal preferences are a person's feelings, and some philosophers have maintained that words like *right* and *wrong* are devices we use to express how we feel about something. On this view, when Jane says that abortion is never wrong, what she conveys is that she has certain positive feelings (or at least that she does not have any feelings of disapproval) toward abortion, whereas when Lee says abortion is always wrong, what he conveys is that he does have feelings of disapproval. This position encounters problems of the same kind as those raised in the previous section. It is always appropriate to ask that support be given for a moral judgment. It is not appropriate to ask for support in the case of mere expressions of feeling. True, if Lee is sincere, one can infer that he has strong negative feelings about abortion. But his saying that abortion is always wrong does not appear to be simply a way of venting his feelings. As in the case of a person's preferences, so also in the case of a person's feelings: neither by itself provides answers to moral questions.

Why Thinking It Is So Does Not Make It So

The same is true about what someone thinks. Quite aside from his feelings, Lee, if he is sincere, does think that abortion is always wrong. Nevertheless, if his judgment ("Abortion is always wrong") is a moral judgment about the wrongness of abortion, what he means cannot be "I [Lee] think that abortion is wrong." If it were, then he would not be affirming something that Jane denies when she says, "Abortion is never wrong." Each would merely be stating that each thinks something, and it is certainly possible for it *both* to be true that Lee thinks that abortion is always wrong *and*, at the same time, that Jane thinks that abortion is never wrong. So if Lee is denying what Jane affirms, then he cannot merely be stating that he thinks that abortion is always wrong. Thus, Lee's thinking that abortion is wrong is just as irrelevant to establishing its wrongness as his feeling a certain way about it. And the same is true concerning what we happen to think. Our thinking something right or wrong does not make it so.

The Irrelevance of Statistics

Someone might think that though what one person happens to think or feel about moral issues does not settle matters, what all or most people happen to think or feel does. A single individual is only one voice; what most or all people think or feel is a great deal more. There is strength in numbers. Thus, the correct method for answering questions about right and wrong is to find out what most or all people think or feel; opinion polls should be conducted, statistics compiled. That will reveal the truth.

This approach to moral questions is deficient. All that opinion polls can reveal is what all or most people happen to think or feel about some moral question—for example, Is capital punishment morally right or wrong? What such polls cannot determine is whether what all or most people think about such an issue is reasonable or whether what all or most people feel is appropriate. There may be strength in numbers, but not truth, at least not necessarily. This does not mean that what we think (or feel) is irrelevant to answering moral questions. Later on, in fact (4.3), it will be shown that, given that certain conditions have been met, what we think provides us with a place from which to begin our search for what is right and wrong, as well as one test of the adequacy of competing ethical theories (4.6). Nevertheless, *merely* to establish that all (or most) people think that, say, capital punishment is morally justified is not to establish that it *is* morally justified. In times past, most (possibly even all) people thought the world was flat. And possibly most (or all) people felt pleased or relieved to think of the world as having this shape. But what they thought and felt did not make it true that the world was flat. The question of its shape wasn't answered merely by finding out what most people happened to think or feel. There is no reason to believe moral questions differ in this respect. Questions of right and wrong cannot be answered just by counting heads.

The Appeal to a Moral Authority

Suppose it is conceded that we cannot answer moral questions just by finding out what someone (say, Lee) thinks or feels; or by finding out what all or most people think or feel. After all, a single individual such as Lee, or most or all people like him, might think or feel one way when he or they should think or feel differently. But suppose there is a being who never is mistaken when it comes to moral questions: if this being judges that something is morally right, it *is* morally right; if it is judged wrong, it *is* wrong. No mistakes are made. Let us call such a being a *moral authority*. Might appealing to a moral authority be a satisfactory way to answer moral questions?

Most people who think there is a moral authority think that this being is not an ordinary person but a god. This causes problems immediately. Whether there is a god (or gods) is a very controversial question, and to rest questions of right and wrong on what an alleged god says (or the gods say) is already to base morality on an intellectually unsettled foundation. The difficulties go deeper than this, however, since even if there is a god who is a moral authority, very serious questions must arise concerning whether people have understood (or can understand) what this authority says about right and wrong. The difficulties that exist when Jews and Christians consult the Bible ("God's revelation to man") can be taken as illustrative. Problems of interpretation abound. Some who think that drinking is wrong think they find evidence in the Bible that God thinks so too; others think they find evidence that He does not. Some who think that homosexuality is declared wrong by God cite what they think are supporting chapters and verses; others cite other chapters and verses they think show God does not think homosexuality is wrong, or they cite the same passages and argue that they should be interpreted differently.

The gravity of these and kindred problems of interpretation should not be underestimated. Even if there is a moral authority, and even if the God Jews and Christians worship should happen to be this authority, that would not make it a simple matter to find out what is right and wrong. The problem of finding out what God thinks on these matters would still remain. In view of the fundamental and long-standing disagreements concerning the correct interpretation of the Bible, this would be no easy matter.

Problems of interpretation aside, it is clear that the correct method for answering moral questions does not consist in discovering what a moral authority says. Even if there is a moral authority, those who are not moral authorities can have no reason for thinking that there is one unless the judgments of this supposed authority can be checked for their truth or reasonableness, and it is not possible to check for this unless what is true or reasonable can be known independently of reliance on what the supposed authority says. If, however, there must be some independent way of knowing what moral judgments are true or reasonable, the introduction of a moral authority will not succeed in providing a method for answering moral questions. That method will have to illuminate how what is morally right and wrong can be known independently of the supposed moral authority, not how this can be known by relying on such an authority. This is why we will dispense with appeals to a moral authority throughout this work.

4.2 THE IDEAL MORAL JUDGMENT

The results of the argument to this point are largely negative. They concern how *not* to answer moral questions. If we are to make progress in our moral thinking, we must have more than negative results. A positive account of how to approach moral questions must be provided. That is the challenge we must now face. I shall begin by attempting to answer the question, What requirements would someone have to meet to make an ideal moral judgment? Considered ideally, that is, what are the conditions that anyone would have to satisfy to reach a moral judgment as free from fault and error as possible? Now, by its very nature, an *ideal* moral judgment is just that—an ideal. Perhaps no one ever has met or ever will completely meet all the requirements set forth in the ideal. But that does not make it irrational to strive to come as close as possible to fulfilling it. If we can never quite get to the finish, we can still move some distance from the starting line.

There are at least six different ideas that must find a place in a description of the ideal moral judgment. A brief discussion of each follows.

Conceptual Clarity

The importance of conceptual clarity is obvious. If someone tells us that euthanasia is always wrong, we cannot determine whether that statement is true before we understand what euthanasia is. Similar remarks apply to other controversies. In the case of abortion, for example, many think the question turns on whether the fetus is a person; and that will depend on what a person is—that is, on how the concept "person" should be analyzed. Clarity by itself may not be enough, but thought cannot get far without it.

Information

We cannot answer moral questions in our closets. Moral questons arise in the real world, and a knowledge of the real-world setting in which they arise is essential if we are seriously to seek rational answers to them. For example, in the debate over the morality of capital punishment, some people argue that convicted murderers ought to be executed because, if they are not, they may be (and often are) paroled; and if they are paroled, they are more likely to kill again than are other released felons. Is this true? Is this a fact? We have to come out of our closets to answer this (or to find the answer others have reached on the basis of their research); and answer it we must if we are to reach an informed judgment about the morality of capital punishment. The importance of getting the facts, of being informed, is not restricted just to the case of capital punishment by any means. It applies all across the broad sweep of moral inquiry.

Rationality

Rationality is a difficult concept to analyze. Fundamentally, however, it involves the ability to recognize the connection between different ideas, to understand that if some statements are true, then some other statements must be true while others must be false. Now, it is in logic that rules are set forth that tell us when statements do follow from others, and it is because of this that a person who is rational often is said to be logical. When we speak of the need to be rational, then, we are saying that we need to observe the rules of logic. To reach an ideal moral judgment, therefore, we must not only strive to make our judgment against a background of information and conceptual clarity; we must also take care to explore how our beliefs are logically related to other things that we do or do not believe. For example, imagine that Lee thinks all abortions are morally wrong; and suppose that his wife, Mary, recently has had an abortion. Then Lee is not being rational or logical if he also believes that there was nothing immoral about Mary's abortion. Rationally he cannot believe this while believing the other things we assume he believes. Logically, it is impossible for both of the following statements to be true: (1) All abortions are morally wrong, and (2) Mary's abortion was not morally wrong. Whenever someone is committed to a group of beliefs that cannot possibly all be true at the same time, that person is said to be committed to a *contradiction*. Lee, then, is committed to a contradiction. To fall short of the ideal moral judgment by committing oneself to a contradiction is to fall as short as one possibly can.

Impartiality

Partiality involves favoring someone or something above others. For example, if a father is partial to one of his children, then he will be inclined to give the favored child more than he gives his other children. In some cases, perhaps, partiality is a fine thing; but a partiality that excludes even thinking about or taking notice of others is far from what is needed in an ideal moral judgment. That someone has been harmed, for example, always seems to be a relevant consideration, whether this someone is favored by us or not. In striving to reach the correct answer to moral questions, therefore, we must strive to guard against extreme, unquestioned partiality; otherwise we shall run the risk of having our judgment clouded by bigotry and prejudice.

The idea of impartiality is at the heart of what sometimes is referred to as the *formal principle of justice*, the principle that justice is the similar, and injustice the dissimilar, treatment of similar individuals. This principle is said to express the formal principle of justice because by itself it does not specify what factors are relevant for determining what makes individuals similar or dissimilar. To decide this, one would have to supplement the formal principle of justice with a substantive or normative interpretation of justice. Alternative interpretations will be assessed in chapter 7. Even at this juncture, however, we can recognize the rich potential the formal principle of justice can have in arguments about moral right and wrong.

For example, if someone were to say that causing suffering is wrong when humans are made to suffer but not wrong in the case of animals, it would be apposite to ask why the two cases are dissimilar. For they must be dissimilar if, as we are assuming, dissimilar treatment is allowed. If, in reply to our question, we were told that the difference is that human beings suffer in the one case but animals suffer in the other, then it would again be apposite to ask why a biological difference, a difference that relates to the species to which humans and animals happen to belong, can make any moral difference to the morality of the treatment in the two cases. If to cause suffering is wrong, then it is wrong no matter who is made to suffer, and the attempt to limit its wrongness only to human beings is a symptom of one's showing unquestioned partiality for the members of one's own species. While the formal principle of justice does not by itself tell us what are the relevant factors for determining when treatment is similar or dissimilar, that principle must be observed if we are to make the ideal moral judgment. Not to observe it is a symptom of prejudice or bias, rational defects that must be identified and overcome if we are to make the best moral judgment we can. I will have occasion to refer to the formal principle of justice in a number of places in what follows.

Coolness

All of us know what it is like to do something in the heat of anger that we later regret. No doubt we have also had the experience of getting so excited that we do something that later on we wish we had not done. Emotions are powerful forces, and though life would be a dull wasteland without them, we need to appreciate that the more volatile among them can mislead us; strong emotion is not a reliable guide to doing (or judging) what is best. This brings us to the need to be "cool." *Being cool* here means "not being in an emotionally excited state, being in an emotionally calm state of mind." The idea is that the hotter (the more emotionally charged) we are, the more likely we are to reach a mistaken moral conclusion, while the cooler (the calmer) we are, the greater the chances that we will avoid making mistakes.

The position is borne out by common experience. People who are in a terribly excited state may not be able to retain their rationality. Because of their deep emotional involvement, they may not be able to attain impartiality; and because they are in an excited emotional state, they may not even care about learning what happened or why. Like the proverb about shooting first and asking questions later, a lack of coolness can easily lead people to judge first and ask about the facts afterwards. The need to be cool, then, seems to merit a place on our list.

Valid Moral Principles

The concept of a moral principle has been analyzed in different ways. At least this much seems clear, however: for a principle to qualify as a *moral* principle (as distinct from, say, a scientific or a legal principle), it must prescribe that all moral agents are required to act in certain ways, thereby providing, so we are to assume, rational guidance in the conduct of life. More will be said about moral principles and moral agents in the sequel (see, for example, 5.2). For the present it will suffice to say that moral agents are those who can bring impartial reasons (i.e., reasons that respect the requirement of impartiality) to bear on deciding how they ought to act. Individuals who lack the ability to understand or act on the basis of impartial reasons (e.g., young children) fail to qualify as moral agents: they cannot meaningfully be said to have obligations or to do, or fail to do, what is morally right or wrong. Only moral agents have this status, and moral principles apply only to the determination of how moral agents may behave.

How does the idea of a valid moral principle relate to the concept of an ideal moral judgment? In an ideal moral judgment, it is not enough that the judgment be based on complete information, complete impartiality, complete conceptual clarity, and so forth. It is also essential that the judgment be based on a *valid* or *correct* moral principle(s). Ideally, one wants not only to make the correct judgment but to make it for the correct reasons. But which among the many possible moral principles we might accept are the correct or most reasonable ones? This is a question we cannot answer merely by saying which principles we *happen* to prefer, or which ones all or most people *happen* to accept, or which principles some alleged moral authority issues. These ways of answering moral questions have previously been eliminated from serious consideration. What is needed are criteria for rationally evaluating and choosing between competing ethical principles. In the section that follows various criteria are characterized and their appropriateness defended. No claim to completeness is made, nor are the several criteria ranked systematically in terms of their respective weight or importance, though some suggestions will be made in this regard. It will be enough for our present and future purposes to make the case for the reasonableness of the criteria about to be discussed.

4.3 CRITERIA FOR EVALUATING MORAL PRINCIPLES ·

Consistency

A minimum requirement for any ethical principle is that it be consistent. Consistency concerns the *possible conjoint* truth of two or more statements. Any combination of two or more statements (let us refer to this as *any set of statements*) is consistent if and only if it is possible that all the statements constituting the set can be true at the same time. Here is an example of a consistent set. (It is assumed that "Jack" refers to one, and "Jill" refers to another, individual, at the same time, in the same circumstances).

Set A (1): Jack is taller than Jill.
        (2): Jill is shorter than Jack.

Here is an example of an inconsistent set.

Set B (3): Jack is taller than Jill.
        (4): Jill is taller than Jack.

Set A is consistent because it is possible for both (1) and (2) to be true at the same time: there is nothing involved in (1)'s being true that automatically or necessarily makes (2) false, and vice versa—the conjunction of (1) and (2) is *not* a contradiction—though neither (1) nor (2) must be true (for it might be that Jack and Jill are the same height). Set B is inconsistent, however, because if (3) were true, then (4) would have to be false, and if (4) were true, then (3) would have to be false; necessarily, that is, (3) and (4) cannot both be true; the conjunction of (3) and (4) *is* a contradiction.

Now, a valid moral principle must be consistent. This is true because such a principle aims at providing us with a basis by reference to which we may rationally decide which actions are right and which are wrong. If, however, a proposed principle turns out to be inconsistent, then its failure in this regard would undermine the very point of having an ethical principle in the first place—namely, to provide rational guidance in the determination of what is right and wrong.

One way of arguing that a proposed principle is inconsistent is to show that it implies that the very same act can be both right and wrong. One (but by no means not the only) interpretation of the view called *ethical relativism* has this implication. On this interpretation, an act is right or wrong whenever the majority in any given society approves or disapproves of it, respectively. It is important to be clear about what, on this interpretation, ethical relativism comes to. The claim is not that a given act is *thought* to be right in a given society if the majority approves of it; nor is it that the act of which a given society's majority approves is right *in that society*; rather, an act *is unqualifiedly right*, according to the interpretation presently under review, whenever the majority of the members of any given society happen to approve of it.

This way of viewing right and wrong does imply that the very same act can be both right and wrong. To make this clearer, suppose that the majority in one society happens to approve of killing and eating foreigners, while the majority in another society happens to disapprove of it. Then it follows, given the interpretation of ethical relativism we are discussing, both that (a) killing and eating foreigners is right, and that (b) it is not the case that killing and eating foreigners is right. The principle implies, that is, that *both* (a) *and* (b) are true. However, since (a) and (b) are *inconsistent*, they *cannot* both be true. Neither, then, can ethical relativism, as understood here, be a valid ethical principle.

Adequacy of Scope

A further legitimate requirement is that an ethical principle have adequate scope. The reason for this should be clear when we recall that ethical principles are supposed to provide us with practical guidance in the determination of what is right and wrong. Since we find ourselves in a great variety of circumstances in which we have to make such determinations, a given principle will succeed in providing guidance to the extent that it can be applied in these circumstances, and this will depend on the principle's scope. The wider a principle's scope, the greater its potential use; the narrower its scope, the narrower its range of applications. Though it is not possible to legislate exactly how wide a principle's scope must be if it is to qualify as adequate, the case for viewing adequacy of scope as a relevant criterion is reasonable, something we will see more clearly as we proceed.

Precision

What we want from an ethical principle is not vague direction concerning a broad range of cases: we expect specific or determinate direction. Without this precision, a principle's usefulness will be seriously diminished. It is of little help, for example, to be told to "Love your neighbor" or "Do no harm" if we are not told, in a clear and helpful way, what "love" and "harm"—and "neighbor," for that matter!—are supposed to mean. If a principle is vague in what it requires, in a significant range of cases, we will be uncertain of what it requires; and to the extent we are uncertain, we will also be unsure about what we must do to follow the principle's direction in the present or whether we have complied with the principle by acting as we have in the past. A reasonable degree of precision, then, is a legitimate requirement for any ethical principle. At the same time, too much precision, or precision of the wrong sort, are illegitimate requirements. Ethics is not geometry. We should not expect or require definitions of moral concepts (e.g., of "love" or "harm") to be as exact as definitions of geometrical concepts (e.g., of "square" or "circle"); nor should we require that moral principles be as precise, or that they be demonstrable in the same way, as the Pythagorean Theorem. Always we must keep Aristotle's sage advice in mind: "It is the mark of an educated man to look for precision in each class of things just so far as the nature of the subject admits."[1] We shall have occasion to remind ourselves of this elemental wisdom on more than one occasion in the sequel.

Conformity with Our Intuitions

One final basis for evaluating competing ethical principles concerns whether they conform with our moral intuitions. This is by far the most controversial criterion we will discuss and use. Some philosophers flatly reject it as a reasonable test. Others insist on its validity. Whichever position one does or should take, it is essential to clarify what it means in the present context. This is more than idle semantic curiosity. The notion of intuition has been understood in different ways in moral philosophy, some of which are logically distinct from, and thus ought not be confused with, the sense in which this notion is used when "appeals to intuition" are recognized as a legitimate way to test ethical principles. The highly influential twentieth-century English philosopher G. E. Moore, for example, uses the word *intuition* to refer to those ethical propositions that, on his view, are "incapable of proof,"[2] while a contemporary of Moore's, W. D. Ross, characterizes moral intuitions as "self evident" moral truths.[3] Whatever else one might wish to say about either Moore's view of intuition, or Ross's, or both, it is abundantly clear, as will be seen more fully in what follows, that neither Moore's sense nor Ross's is what is meant when one asks whether a given ethical principle conforms with our moral intuitions or holds that conformity with them is a legitimate test of an ethical principle's rational credentials.

A third sense in which 'intuition' is sometimes used in moral philosophy is to mean "our unexamined moral convictions," including our initial response or immediate reactions to hard moral cases. It is in this sense that the word is used when people are asked, What are your intuitions?, after an unusual case or situation has been described (e.g., a case where a man has to kill and eat his own grandson in order to survive, and the question is whether he ought to). This sense of 'intuition' certainly is distinct from either Moore's or Ross's, since in responding to the question by giving our initial response we are far from committing ourselves to the view that what we say is self-evidently true or that it is unprovable. Even more important, our intuitions in this sense are our *pre*reflective judgments about what is right or wrong. When we are asked about our intuitions in this sense, in other words, we are not being asked to say what we think *after* we have given the question a good deal of thought—*after* we have tried, to the best of our ability, to make an ideal moral judgment about the case. On the contrary, what we are being asked is what we think *before* we have thought about the case in any considerable detail and thus before we have made a concerted effort to make an ideal moral judgment about it. For convenience, let us refer to intuitions in this sense as *prereflective intuitions*. Like Moore's and Ross's understanding of intuition, this prereflective sense also is not the sense involved, when we require that ethical principles conform to our moral intuitions.

The sense that is involved is what we shall term *the reflective sense*. In this sense, our intuitions are those moral beliefs we hold *after* we have made a conscientious effort to satisfy five of the previously listed criteria of making an ideal moral judgment. It is to be assumed, that is, that we have conscientiously endeavored to think about our beliefs coolly, rationally, impartially, with conceptual clarity, and with as much relevant information as we can reasonably acquire. The judgments we make *after* we have made this effort are not our "gut responses," nor are they merely expressions of what we *happen* to believe; they are our *considered* beliefs, beliefs we hold when, and only when, we have done our best to be impartial, rational, cool, and so forth. To test alternative moral principles by how well they conform with our reflective intuitions is thus to test them against our considered beliefs, and, other things being equal between two competing moral principles (i.e., assuming that the two are equal in scope, precision, and consistency), the principle that matches our reflective intuitions best is rationally to be preferred.

Theoretically, however, it is possible that a given principle might pass all the tests for evaluating an ethical principle and yet fail to match one or a few of those beliefs we initially regard as considered beliefs. Moreover, it may also be true that we know of no other moral principle demonstrably better than this principle when it comes to meeting the appropriate criteria for evaluating moral principles, that can account for these intuitions. In that case we should be highly skeptical of those beliefs initially construed as considered beliefs. If no otherwise satisfactory moral principle can be shown to match them, then wisdom would dictate that we agree that, try as we have, we have erred in our initial assessment of these beliefs. Those beliefs we initially identify as considered beliefs, in other words, can themselves be shown to stand in need of revision or abandonment. What we must strive to achieve, to use a helpful expression of the Harvard philosopher John Rawls,[4] is "reflective equilibrium" between our considered beliefs, on the one hand, and our moral principles, on the other. Some of these beliefs may have to be discounted because they cannot be made to fit any principle that is satisfactory in other respects, and some of these principles will have to be dismissed because they fail to match intuitions that can be accommodated by principles that are otherwise satisfactory. No principle is shown to be invalid, therefore, *merely* on the grounds that it fails to match each and every reflective intuition. But a principle *is* shown to be invalid if it fails to match our intuitions *in a broad range of cases*, assuming that these intuitions *are* matched by an alternative principle that is validated by appeals to other relevant criteria. When "the appeal to our intuitions" is understood as an appeal to our considered beliefs, beliefs that stand up under the heat of our best reflective consideration, in the sense and in the manner explained, we should not surrender requiring conformity with these beliefs as a legitimate test of the validity of moral principles unless we are given a good argument against doing so.

I shall consider some criticisms momentarily. First, though, a second use we can make of our reflective intuitions is worth noting. Suppose we have identified a variety of our considered beliefs. Having done this, we may then seek to unify them by formulating ethical principles that identify their plausible common ground. For example, if we count among our considered beliefs the belief that it is wrong to force some persons to pursue particular careers when such pursuit is contrary to their own welfare, wrong to deny citizens the opportunity to discuss the troubling political and social problems of the day, wrong to deny some citizens of a democratic society the opportunity to vote because of the color of their skin or their place of national origin, and wrong to deny the members of similar groups access to educational, recreational, and cultural opportunities, then it is reasonable to view the following principle (the liberty principle) as a principle that unifies, by identifying the relevant common ground of, these several intuitions: it is wrong, other things being equal, to limit an individual's liberty. The adequacy of this principle, of course, is not vouchsafed by its mere articulation. We would be obliged to test it very carefully indeed—for example, by inquiring into its consistency and by asking how well it matches other considered beliefs. The reasonableness of the liberty principle is not the issue here (it will concern us later, 8.1); it is mentioned at this juncture only by way of illustrating a second role appeals to our reflective intuitions can play in moral theory.

Some Criticisms

Critics of using appeals to intuition as a test of a principle's validity think they have good arguments against allowing such appeals to count. Some of these arguments are seriously muddled. They involve a failure clearly to distinguish between the several senses in which the notion of 'intuition' has been used in moral philosophy. This seems a fair interpretation of some of the arguments offered by the Oxford philosopher R. M. Hare and a past student of Hare's, the Australian philosopher Peter Singer. Hare, for his part, repeatedly castigates appeals to intuition as appeals to prejudice.[5] It is understandable why he should do this, since, as has been explained, appeals to intuitions sometimes are invitations to say what we think, without our having thought about what we believe coolly, impartially, and so forth. When such appeals are understood in *this* way, they *are* indistinguishable from appeals to prejudice. If, however, we have thoughtfully considered our beliefs by making a conscientious effort to be rational, informed, and the like, then appeals to our intuitions are *not* appeals to what we just happen to think; they are appeals to those beliefs that withstand the test of such reflection. It is exceedingly unclear how a belief that we hold *after* we have made a conscientious effort in this regard could properly be called a prejudice. In its clearest meaning, *prejudice* means a belief we accept without having critically thought about the reasons for accepting it. If, *after* we have made a conscientious effort to think about our beliefs ideally, we are still said to be prejudiced, the notion of prejudice has lost any clear or helpful meaning. Interpreted in this way, everything that anyone believes would qualify as a prejudice. When we appeal to our intuitions, in the reflective sense, there is ample reason not to view them as prejudices.

Singer also is impatient with appeals to intuition. In his latest book, *The Expanding Circle: Ethics and Sociobiology*, he criticizes those philosophers who believe "that philosophy can do no more than systematize our moral intuitions,"[6] a position that *might* be held not only by those who understand intuitions in the way that, say, Ross does (as "self-evident truths") but also by those who understand intuitions in the way favored here, as considered beliefs. Arguments aimed at the reasonableness of Ross's understanding of intuitions and his general approach to moral philosophy, however, will not strike the heart of this latter understanding and approach. To argue, therefore, as Singer does (here we come to the second argument urged against appeals to intuition) that "discovering biological origins for our intuitions should make us skeptical about thinking of them as self-evident moral axioms" or as "self-evident moral absolutes"[7] may cast doubt on *Ross's* understanding of our moral intuitions. Such discoveries do not cast doubt on the propriety of appealing to intuitions in the *reflective* sense, however, since intuitions *in this sense* are not understood as "self-evident moral truths," or "self-evident moral absolutes."

A third criticism lodged against appeals to intuition is that it fosters moral conservatism. Witness Singer, who objects to those who think that moral philosophy should "match the data of our settled convictions" by decrying "the in-built conservatism of this approach to ethics, an approach which is liable to take relics of our cultural history as the touchstones of morality."[8] This criticism rests on the view that our reflective intuitions are the product of our particular culture's system of values at a given time, together with the environmental influences of our immediate family and social group. These influences, it is supposed, will tend to be morally conservative because the values imparted will tend to be those that favor the moral status quo. For example, if we had been born into the white propertied class of slave owners in the South prior to the American Civil War, the values we would have been taught would have reflected the values of that class and would have been conservative in nature. Instead of being taught values that threatened the moral status quo (e.g., that all humans are equal) we would have been taught values that fostered it (e.g., that whites are superior in value to blacks). Once this instruction had taken root, we would have regarded it as "obviously true" that whites are superior to blacks, and this belief would have been incorporated into our body of "moral intuitions."

This argument of Singer's merits two replies. The first is *ad hominem*. Some critics of *his* position have disputed its adequacy for the very same reason he disputes the legitimacy of appeals to intuitions—namely, because of *its* in-built moral conservatism. In his essay "Utilitarianism," the American philosopher Dan W. Brock disputes preference utilitarianism, which is the position Singer holds, on this ground, arguing as follows:

> A person's desires or preferences are the product of biological needs and the socialization process by which he or she is inducted into society, state, and various social groups. They are importantly determined by and will tend to reinforce the existing social arrangements, power and authority relations, and expectations in one's environment. Consequently, utilitarianism formulated so as to require maximal satisfaction of prefer-

ences as they exist, in turn serves to reinforce the existing social structure; it will have a significant conservative bias. For example, a racist, sexist society may foster racist or sexist preferences in its members, and preference utilitarianism seems committed to seeking the satisfaction of these preferences.[9]

The seriousness of the problem caused by the "significant conservative bias" built into preference utilitarianism will be touched upon in my subsequent critique of Singer's attempt to ground the obligation to be vegetarian (see 6.4).

Second, and more fundamentally, to test moral principles by asking whether they "match the data of our settled moral convictions" need not be conservative in the disparaging sense in which Singer levels this charge. Beliefs are "conservative" to the extent that they are not subject to alteration. There is, however, no reason to suppose that, when the appeal is made to our intuitions, the beliefs appealed to are conservative in this sense. Some prereflective beliefs can be seen to stand in need of revision, once we have taken the time and expended the effort to make the best judgment about them we can—for example, the belief that Native Americans are not human beings and so are not covered by principles that specify what can be done to humans. And those beliefs we do retain, or come to hold, as a result of our making this effort are not held *simply* because we have been taught to believe what we believe; they are retained, or we come to hold them, because they pass the appropriate tests for distinguishing between prereflective and reflective intuitions.

A further objection raised against using conformity with reflective intuitions as a test of a moral principle's validity is that this makes ethical thinking ineradicably subjective.[10] Not everyone has the same prereflective, or reflective, intuitions, it is claimed, so that the very most we can arrive at, if we use this test, are principles that fit our individual intuitions, not principles that fit everyone's. The upshot is that there will be as many "valid" moral principles as there are different individuals with different intuitions. This result, these critics allege, destroys the very possibility of there being a *valid* moral principle, since a valid moral principle must apply to all moral agents.

This objection fails to recognize the differences between (a) an ethical principle's *being* valid for all rational beings and (b) our *knowing* that a given principle is valid for all moral agents. The importance of this difference can be explained as follows. When we have subjected an ethical principle to the tests of consistency, scope, precision, and conformity with our reflective intuitions, and when we have done this while making a conscientious effort to make an ideal moral judgment, we have done all we can reasonably be required to do to be in a position to justify our belief that the principle is binding on all moral agents. Because of our common human fallibilities, however, we must recognize that we are liable to be mistaken at every turn in the process of validation—an elementary logical mistake may pass unnoticed, for example, or an intuition we regard as a reflective intuition may stand in need of revision. Thus, though principles that, given our best judgment, pass the tests of consistency, precision, and so forth are those that we can *with good reason* claim are binding on all, we cannot with good reason *claim to know* that their universal application has been validated. What we can claim, with good reason, is that the principles we validate in the manner outlined in the preceding are those that *would* be accepted by all who make ideal moral judgments about which principles to accept. What we claim, in other words, is *a consensus among all ideal judges* concerning what principles are binding on all.

To claim, with good reason, that such a consensus would be forthcoming is one thing; to claim to know that it would be realized is quite another. Because the consensus is claimed to obtain among all ideal judges, and because we can never ourselves fully satisfy all the conditions of making an ideal judgment, we are never ourselves in a position to claim to *know* what principles any or all ideal judges would select. In my case, I must recognize that, despite my best efforts to judge ideally, I might be mistaken in selecting those principles I do; and you, who, let us assume, select different principles, must recognize a similar possibility of error on your part. But it does not follow from our admission of fallibility in this regard that the principles we accept must bespeak "subjectivism" in the sense charged by the criticism under review. Having admitted my fallibility, it does not follow that I am advocating principles *valid for me alone*, nor does it follow from your similar admission that you are advocating principles *valid only for you*. That *would* be subjectivism in ethics of the most pernicious sort. But the criteria for validating ethical principles outlined above, including the appeal to our reflective intuitions, entails nothing of the sort. When we have done all that we reasonably can do to validate an ethical principle, including testing it against our reflective intuitions, each of us is claiming, with good reason, that the principle *is valid for everyone*. What we are not claiming is that we know that it is. We who, try as we might, can never completely fulfill the requirements of an ideal moral judgment, are in no position to claim to know this, and we must, therefore, if we are honest, recognize and live with an ineradicable element of uncertainty regarding which ethical principles are valid. All we can do is the best we can do, which is less than what ideally could be done; but to recognize our shared limitations in this regard is not to authorize, any more than it is to imply, ethical subjectivism. Whatever difficulties testing ethical principles against our reflective intuitions may fairly have to face, the charge that it entails ethical subjectivism is not one of them.

A final criticism against using appeals to intuition as a means of validating ethical principles—and this perhaps is the most basic criticism—is that this way of viewing our intuitions has things backwards. Rather than appealing to intuitions to test ethical theories, we ought rather to appeal to a sound ethical theory to test our intuitions. This is the view Singer advocates. "We should," he writes, "work from sound theories to practical judgments, not from our judgments to our theories."[11] The assumption Singer makes is that we *can* arrive at a sound ethical theory without making appeals to our reflective intuitions. But can we? The proof that we can must surely consist in someone's having done so, since without its having been done the claims that we can (and should) work in the direction Singer advocates lack adequate backing. For reasons that will be explained in detail when we examine Singer's ethical theory (6.3ff.), Singer himself fails to provide us with a "sound theory," even if it were true, as in fact it is not, that he himself is uniformly successful in not testing ethical theories against "our intuitions."[12]

The reply to Singer offered in the preceding paragraph might be formulated in terms of a burden-of-proof argument, where the burden of proof falls squarely on the shoulders of those who, like Singer, would have us construct a sound ethical theory independently of appeals to our intuitions. What Singer must show is that (a) he can develop an ethical theory that does not involve appeals to our reflective intuitions and (b) the theory he advocates is a sound one. Since, as will be argued in the sequel, Singer fails to satisfy condition (b), and in view of the weaknesses of the previously mentioned objections against regarding appeals to our reflective intuitions as a legitimate means of validating ethical principles, we have solid, even if not conclusive, grounds to resist his protests.

4.4 CONSEQUENTIALIST ETHICAL THEORIES

This last criticism obliges me to broach the topic of ethical theory. An ethical theory seeks to bring maximum order to ethical thinking, and, as is the nature of any such enterprise, there is no scarcity of options vying for our rational assent. It is now customary to distinguish between two major classes of ethical theories—*consequentialist* (also sometimes called *teleological*) ethical theories and *nonconsequentialist* (also sometimes called *deontological*) ethical theories. I shall begin by characterizing and illustrating theories of the former type, postponing a discussion of the latter until later (see 4.5).

Consequentialist ethical theories hold that the rightness or wrongness of what we do ultimately depends on the consequences (the effects, results) of what we do and *only* on the consequences. Theories of this type enable us to distinguish between (a) what is morally obligatory, (b) what is morally right, and (c) what is morally wrong. To make this clearer, suppose we must choose between performing one of three acts, one of which will produce better consequences than the other two. Leaving the idea of "better consequences" vague for the moment, consequentialist theories hold that we have a positive moral obligation to perform that act and a negative obligation not to perform either of the other two. In contrast, suppose that two of the alternatives will produce consequences that are equally good *and* both will produce better consequences than those that would result from performing the third alternative. Then we are morally obliged not to perform this third act, but we are not obliged to perform *one rather than the other* of the former options. *Either* option would be morally right—that is, either would produce consequences that are as good as those produced by the other. Thus, our duty lies in doing one or the other of those acts that are right, but we have no duty to perform the one rather than the other.

A number of alternatives are available to anyone who would advance a consequentialist ethical theory. First, there are options regarding *whose* consequences one takes into account in the determination of which alternative has the best consequences. *Ethical egoism* (also sometimes called *rational egoism*) is the view that it is only the consequences for the individual agent that are of direct moral significance. On this view, whenever I ask myself what I morally ought to do, the answer lies in my determining which one among the options available to me will bring about the best consequences for me, whereas when you ask yourself this question the answer lies in your determining which will bring about the best consequences for you. How what I do will affect you is morally irrelevant except in those cases where how you are affected by what I do will end up affecting me. And the same is true concerning how what you do will affect me; this can have no bearing on what you ought to do unless my being affected by what you do will affect you. I shall have occasion to consider ethical egoism in more detail in the next chapter (5.3).

Utilitarianism is a second option available to consequentialists. Rather than restricting consequences that have direct moral significance only to the individual agent, utilitarianism holds that the consequences for everyone affected by the outcomes of alternative choices are of direct moral significance. For the utilitarian, it is the *principle of utility* that determines moral right, wrong, and obligation: what we morally ought to do is act so as to bring about the best total consequences for everyone affected by the outcome, not just the best consequences for the agent who acts.

Now, one question that arises for utilitarians concerns the scope of "everyone affected by the outcome." Which individuals are included? Some commentators on utilitarianism picture it as a human-centered ethical theory, so that human beings, and only human beings, are included within the scope of "everyone." How far this is from being a correct characterization of the leading forms of utilitarianism will be seen more clearly after we have explored the need all consequentialists have for a theory of intrinsic value.

Those who favor any version of consequentialist theory must provide a companion theory of intrinsic value. This is because they hold that moral right, wrong, and obligation depend on the best consequences, and what makes some consequences better than others ultimately depends on what consequences are intrinsically valuable (good) or disvaluable (evil). The idea of intrinsic value has been defined in a variety of ways, including "what is desired for its own sake," "what would be good even if it existed in isolation from everything else," "what ought to exist for its own sake," and "what is valued or preferred in itself." Differ though these characterizations do, each attempts to articulate the difference between (a) something's being of positive value *only* as a means to something else and (b) something's being good *independently* of its being a means to something else. Those things of instrumental value fall into the former category; what is of positive intrinsic value falls into the latter. Whatever is both useful as a means and good in itself has both instrumental and intrinsic value.

What is intrinsically valuable or disvaluable, according to consequentialists? Not all consequentialists offer the same answer. Two answers offered by utilitarians are of particular importance for our purposes, since both will figure in the subsequent discussion of utilitarianism in chapter 6. The first is *value hedonism*. On this view pleasure and pleasure alone is intrinsically valuable, while pain and pain alone is intrinsically disvaluable. This is the theory of value advocated by the classical utilitarians, Jeremy Bentham and John Stuart Mill. The second theory is what we shall term *the preference theory*. It holds that what has positive intrinsic value is the satisfaction of preferences, understood as desires or goals, while what has negative intrinsic value is their frustration. This is the theory of value implied by recent utilitarian thinkers, including in particular Singer and Hare. Acceptance of either theory of value by utilitarians provides the grounds for criticizing the view that utilitarianism is "human-centered." This cannot be an accurate portrayal of the major thrust of utilitarian thought since (a) most utilitarians subscribe to either value hedonism or the preference theory and because (b) these utilitarians acknowledge that nonhuman animals can experience pain or pleasure *or* have preferences that can be satisfied or frustrated.[13] The scope of the "everyone" in the utilitarian's injunction to bring about "the best total consequences for everyone affected by the outcome," in short, should not be understood as being limited only to human beings but should be read to include all those who can experience pleasure and pain (the view of the hedonistic utilitarians) or all those who can have preferences that may be satisfied or frustrated (the view of the preference utilitarians).

Utilitarians differ in more ways than one. Not only do they offer conflicting views about what makes some consequences better than others, they also have different, incompatible views about how to use the principle of utility. So-called rule utilitarians hold, roughly speaking, that this principle should be used to determine what rules of conduct we should all follow; so-called act utilitarians maintain that, roughly speaking, the principle of utility should be used to determine what, in each and every individual case, the obligatory, right, and wrong acts are, independently of appeals to those rules favored by rule utilitarianism. Both of these characterizations are somewhat crude; neither does full justice to the subtlety of the positions available to those who favor act or rule utilitarianism. This will become clearer when, in the subsequent discussion of these theories, they are subjected to sustained critical review (for act utilitarianism, see 6.2–6.3; for rule utilitarianism, see 7.7). For our immediate purposes it is only necessary to realize that utilitarians differ not only over what makes some consequences "the best" but also over what appeals to the principle of utility are supposed to evaluate—the moral status of individual acts (act utilitarianism) *or* the moral status of certain rules (rule utilitarianism).

4.5 NONCONSEQUENTIALIST ETHICAL THEORIES

Nonconsequentialist ethical theories can be defined negatively. These theories deny that moral right, wrong, and duty depend *only* on the value of consequences of what we do, either for ourselves individually (ethical egoism) or for everyone affected by the outcome (utilitarianism). Not all nonconsequentialist theories agree, however, on whether the value of consequences has any role to play in the determination of what we ought to do. Some theories (what we might call extreme deontological theories) hold that the value of consequences is entirely irrelevant to this determination, while others (moderate deontological theories) hold that, though the value of consequences is relevant, other things are relevant too. The German philosopher Immanuel Kant (1724–1804) provides us with an example of an extreme deontological ethical theory. Kant holds that there is one supreme principle of morality, which he calls "the categorical imperative." This principle can be formulated in alternative but equivalent ways, he thinks. What has come to be called *the Formula of Universal Law* states that we are to act so that the maxim of our action can be willed to be a universal law. By "the maxim" of our action Kant means our reasons or intentions for acting as we do. What this formula requires that we do, then, is ask ourselves whether everyone can do what we do, for the reasons or with the intentions that we have. If we cannot will that everyone follow our example, so to speak—if our maxim cannot be willed as a universal law that everyone could follow—then what we are doing is wrong. The question about the value of the consequences of acting as we do, either for ourselves individually or for everyone, is strictly irrelevant. The decisive test, at least according to this formulation of the categorical imperative, is whether we can will that our maxim become a universal law.

An example Kant himself gives may make his position clearer. Suppose I ask to borrow some money from you and, despite promising to repay, I haven't the slightest intention of doing so. Now, to determine whether my deceitful promise is right or wrong what I must not do is ask about the beneficial consequences for me if I am successful in getting you to lend the money (the ethical egoist's counsel), nor should I ask about how good the consequences will be for everyone as a result of the transaction, including how your pleasures or preferences will be affected (the utilitarian's approach). Instead I must ask whether everyone could follow my maxim if it were made into a universal law. Could there be a universal law, that is, according to which, whenever someone wanted something (e.g., money) they would ask another to borrow it while not having the slightest intention of returning it? Kant believes that all we need do is ask the question in order to see that such a law is impossible. If anytime anybody wanted something they asked for it, promised to return or repay it, but never had the slightest intention of carrying out their promise, then no one would ever believe anyone's promise in the first place; indeed, if it is true, as it may well be, that no one can even make a promise unless it is believed by someone, then making my maxim into a universal law would destroy the very possibility of making a promise in the first place. It is therefore wrong, according to Kant, to make a deceitful promise, and the wrongness of doing so can be established entirely independently of our determining how good or bad the consequences of making one happen to be in any given case. Considerations about the value of consequences are totally irrelevant to the determination of where our duty lies, according to Kant.

A second example of a nonconsequentialist ethical theory is what we shall term *the rights view*. According to this theory, certain individuals have moral rights (e.g., the right to life) and they have these rights independently of considerations about the value of the consequences that would flow from recognizing that they have them. For the rights view, in other words, rights are more basic than utility and independent of it, so that the principal reason why, say, murder is wrong, if and when it is, lies in the violation of the victim's moral right to life, and not in considerations about who will or who will not receive pleasure or pain or have their preferences satisfied or frustrated, as a result of the deed. Those who subscribe to the rights view need not hold that all moral rights are absolute in the sense that they can never be overridden by other moral considerations. For example, one could hold that when the only realistic way to respect the rights of the many is to override the moral rights of the few, then overriding these rights is justified. Even were one to hold that moral rights are overridable in such circumstances, however, that would not be tantamount to compromising the nonconsequentialist basis for recognition of these rights in the first place. Individuals have the moral rights they do, according to the rights view, for reasons that are independent of the value of consequences, either for them individually or for everyone else.

4.6 EVALUATING ETHICAL THEORIES

Like the other theories mentioned in the preceding, both Kant's view and the rights view will be examined at greater length in subsequent chapters (chaps. 5 and 8, respectively). The brief characterization of these theories is enough for present purposes, since it provides examples of nonconsequentialist ethical theories. Moreover, the four theories I have sketched should make it plain that we suffer from a luxury of riches when it comes to alternative ethical theories. A *number* of such theories vie for our rational assent, not just one, and the problem we face is that of having reasons—reasonable standards or criteria—for evaluating these alternatives. With such standards, the task of selecting from among the alternatives the one that, all considered, is the most adequate is at least approachable. Without such standards, the task of rational assessment cannot even get underway. But what standards *are* appropriate or reasonable? Part of the answer is provided by the earlier discussion (4.3) of the criteria appropriate for evaluating *any* moral principle—the criteria of consistency, adequate scope and precision, and conformity with our reflective intuitions. These criteria are appropriate tests since (1) these are criteria any proposed moral principle must satisfy, and (2) all ethical theories advance their favored moral principle(s) as rationally preferable to their competitors. It must be just as reasonable, therefore, to evaluate and test those principles claimed to be fundamental moral principles against the criteria of scope, consistency, precision, and conformity with our reflective intuitions as it is to evaluate and test any other moral principle in this way. At the level of evaluating competing ethical theories, however, there is at least one other criterion that is reasonable to invoke. This is the criterion of simplicity. Its role in theory assessment can be explained as follows.

Competing scientific theories sometimes explain the same range of facts with comparable precision. If one theory is also able to predict future occurrences better than the other, thus having what is termed greater predictive power, then its having greater predictive power is a reason for choosing it in preference to its competitor. It sometimes happens, however, that two competing theories are relevantly similar in terms of consistency, scope, precision, and predictive power. When this occurs it is customary to invoke another standard for evaluating the competing theories—namely, *the principle of simplicity* (also referred to as *the principle of parsimony*). As explained in a previous chapter (1.3), that principle affirms that, other things being equal, the simpler theory should be chosen. Now, the simpler theory is the one that makes the fewest assumptions or that requires that we accept the fewest unproven, and perhaps unprovable, premises. The standard of simplicity seems eminently wise. After all, how can it be reasonable to make more assumptions (in the case of science, assumptions about what exists) when fewer will do? Why overpopulate the world with entities whose existence is demonstrably unnecessary to explain what one wants to explain?

Simplicity also is a relevant criterion for evaluating ethical theories. Theoretically, the fewer ethical assumptions and principles we require, the better. The more principles we have, the more we need to remember and the greater the chances for significant conflict between them. This can make a mess of our ethical decision-making, something that is nicely illustrated by Jesus' reply to the request that he summarize the laws of the prophets. Jesus, it will be recalled, answers by citing just two laws—to love God, and to love thy neighbor as thyself. Observance of these two laws will suffice, Jesus implies, if one is to do what is right and avoid doing what is wrong, a truly radical move on his part in the direction of simplicity, when one recalls that there were over two hundred separate and distinct ethical principles that were then recognized as codifying the laws of the prophets. It does not follow from the simplicity of Jesus' summary that the two principles he set forth provide an adequate theory, all considered (for one thing, they will lack precision unless the notion of love is carefully explained). Simplicity, though *a* criterion for evaluating ethical theories, is not the only criterion. Nevertheless, other things being equal between two competing ethical theories (i.e., assuming that they both meet the other criteria for evaluating such principles equally), the simpler theory—the one that makes the fewest unproved (and perhaps unprovable) assumptions—should be chosen in preference to the more complex. That is as eminently wise and rationally well founded in the case of evaluating competing ethical theories as it is in the case of evaluating competing scientific ones.

4.7 SUMMARY AND CONCLUSION

This chapter marked my initial approach to thinking about moral questions. I examined some ways not to answer moral questions (4.1) and then traced the conditions someone would have to meet to make an ideal moral judgment (4.2). An ideal judgment would not only be the correct judgment; it would be correct for the right reasons. Ethical theories attempt to specify what "the right reasons" are for judging acts right, wrong, and obligatory. Such theories fall into two major classes. Consequentialist theories (4.4) hold that right, wrong, and obligation depend on the value of the consequences of what we do, and *only* on the value of the consequences. Nonconsequentialist theories (4.5) hold that right, wrong, and obligation do not depend only on the value of the consequences, either not at all (extreme nonconsequentialist theories) or not entirely (moderate nonconsequentialist theories). Two examples of consequentialist theories were provided, ethical egoism (the theory that right, wrong, and obligation are to be determined by what brings about the best consequences for the individual agent) and utilitarianism (the view that right, wrong, and obligation are to be determined by what brings about the best total consequences for everyone affected by the outcome, where by "everyone" the leading utilitarian theories include not only humans but many nonhuman animals). Two theories of intrinsic value were sketched (4.4), value hedonism—which holds that pleasure and pleasure alone is intrinsically good, while pain and pain alone is intrinsically evil—and the preference theory—which holds that it is the satisfaction of preferences, understood as desires or purposes, that is intrinsically good, while their frustration has negative intrinsic value. Of the two nonconsequentialist ethical theories, one (Kant's) maintains that we can determine moral right, wrong, and obligation totally independently of asking about the value of the consequences of what we do and asking instead whether the maxims of our actions (our reasons or intentions for doing what we do) could be willed to be universal laws. The second nonconsequentialist theory (the rights view) asserts that certain beings have certain moral rights (e.g., the right to life) and that the grounds for recognizing their possession of these rights are independent of utilitarian or other consequentialist considerations; an act is wrong, then, on this view, if it violates an individual's moral rights.

In view of the plurality of ethical theories each claiming to have identified the right reasons for judging acts right, wrong, or obligatory, we stand in need of criteria for rationally choosing between them. Five criteria were listed and explained (4.3, 4.6): (1) consistency, (2) adequacy of scope, (3) precision, (4) conformity with our intuitions, and (5) simplicity. The fourth criterion was shown to be especially divisive, some philosophers rejecting it as a legitimate test of ethical theories in particular and of any moral principle in general, and others defending it. Emphasis was placed on being clear about what the "appeal to intuitions" means, and, in particular, a distinction was drawn between our prereflective intuitions (our "gut responses") and our reflective intuitions (our considered beliefs). When understood in this latter way, appeals to intuition, it was argued, have a legitimate role to play in rationally assessing moral principles, the principal arguments against this view proving deficient. The general approach to the construction and testing of an ethical theory argued for, then, may be summarized as follows. We are to begin by considering our prereflective intuitions—those beliefs about right and wrong that we happen to have. We then make a conscientious effort to make the best review of these judgments we can, and we do this by striving to purge our thought of inconsistency and unquestioned partiality, and by thinking as rationally and coolly as we can, with maximum conceptual clarity and on the basis of the best relevant information we can muster. Those moral beliefs we hold *after* we have made an honest effort to meet these requirements are our considered beliefs, our reflective intuitions, and any ethical theory that fails to match our considered beliefs, in a broad range of cases, cannot be reasonably judged the best theory, all considered. Properly understood, ethical theories *are* to be assessed in terms of how well they "systematize our considered beliefs." That theory is best, all considered, that does this best, and the theory that does this best is the one that (1) systematizes the maximum number of our considered beliefs, thereby having maximum scope; (2) systematizes them in a coherent fashion, thereby achieving consistency; (3) does this without compromising the degree of precision it is reasonable to expect and require of any moral principle(s); and (4) satisfies these other criteria of evaluation while making the fewest possible assumptions necessary to do so, thereby meeting the criterion of simplicity.

5

Indirect Duty Views

No serious moral thinker accepts the view that animals may be treated in just any way we please.[1] All agree that legitimate moral constraints apply to our treatment of them. When we inquire into the grounds of these constraints, however, agreement quickly gives way to conflict, and we are faced with the task of reflectively assessing the adequacy of the competing views. Though the positions examined in this and the following chapter differ in important respects, all share one important feature. Each position affirms or implies that we may adequately account for the wrongs done to animals without having recourse to animal rights. The present chapter begins the task of critically examining the major, but certainly not the only, attempts to dispense with animal rights.

5.1 INDIRECT AND DIRECT DUTY VIEWS

The major options to the rights view, if we might put matters in these terms, fall into two divisions. First, there are what will be termed *indirect duty views*. Common to these views is the proposition that we have no duties directly to animals; rather, animals are a sort of medium through which we may either succeed or fail to discharge those direct duties we owe to nonanimals, either ourselves, other human beings, or, as on some views, God. We have, then, according to these views, duties *involving* animals, but no duties *to* them. An example from another quarter might help to make this clearer. It might be held (and some do hold)[2] that we have no duties directly to works of art—say, to Picasso's *Guernica*. Rather, we have, in this case, direct duties to human beings, including future generations of human beings, to preserve and protect the best examples of art presently in our trust. Thus, we do have a duty *involving Guernica*, but we have no duty *to* that work itself. The duty to preserve the painting is an indirect duty to humanity. Similarly indirect, then, according to indirect duty views, are our duties involving animals. In the case of rare or endangered species, for example, if we have a duty to preserve them, this is not a duty we owe to the animals themselves but rather an indirect duty owed, for example, to humanity. We owe it to human beings, both present and future generations, to take the necessary steps to insure that presently endangered species of animals continue to exist so that these humans might, say, take pleasure in viewing them or increase their knowledge of the world by studying them.

The second major classification of theories at odds with the rights view is what will be termed *direct duty views*. Like the indirect duty views to be considered, the direct duty views attempt to dispense with appeals to the rights of animals as a ground on which to rest our moral dealings with them. Unlike indirect duty views, however, direct duty views hold that we have duties directly to animals. These views may differ over what direct duties we have, and do differ over why we have those we do. It is thus possible, for example, that two direct duty views might give conflicting accounts of the grounds of our duty to preserve rare or endangered species, while agreeing that the preservation of, say, Siberian tigers is a duty we have directly to these animals and not a duty owed directly only to humanity or, say, God. Utilitarianism and attempts to ground duties to animals on considerations about cruelty and kindness are the most noteworthy and influential examples of direct duty views. They will be examined in the following chapter. The present chapter is limited to the reflective assessment of representative indirect duty views.

5.2 MORAL AGENTS AND MORAL PATIENTS

A helpful place to begin is to distinguish between moral agents and moral patients (the former idea was briefly explained earlier, 4.2). Moral agents are individuals who have a variety of sophisticated abilities, including in particular the ability to bring impartial moral principles to bear on the determination of what, all considered, morally ought to be done and, having made this determination, to freely choose or fail to choose to act as morality, as they conceive it, requires. Because moral agents have these abilities, it is fair to hold them morally accountable for what they do, assuming that the circumstances of their acting as they do in a particular case do not dictate otherwise. If an action is the result of duress, coercion, unavoidable ignorance, or a psychological impairment (e.g., temporary insanity), then the individual may fairly be excused from being held responsible for acting as he or she does in those circumstances. In the absence of such excusing conditions, however, moral agents are justly and fairly held accountable for their deeds. Since it is they who ultimately decide what they do, it is also they who must bear the moral responsibility of doing (or not doing) it. Normal adult human beings are the paradigm individuals believed to be moral agents. To defend this belief would take us far afield from the present inquiry, involving us in debates dealing both with the existence of free will, for example, and with the extent to which we are able to influence how we act by bringing reason to bear on our decision-making. Though it is a large assumption to make, the assumption will be made that normal adult humans are moral agents. To make this assumption in the present case plays no theoretical favorites, since all theories examined in this and the following chapter share this assumption.

Now, moral agents not only can do what is right or wrong, they may also be on the receiving end, so to speak, of the right or wrong acts of other moral agents. There is, then, a sort of reciprocity that holds between moral agents. I can do what is right or wrong, and my doing either can affect or involve you; and you can do what is right or wrong, and what you do can affect or involve me. Let us define the notion of *the moral community* as comprising all those individuals who are of direct moral concern or, alternatively, as consisting of all those individuals toward whom moral agents have direct duties. Then one possible specification of who belongs to the moral community is that *all and only moral agents belong*. This is the conception of the moral community common to all indirect duty views. Any individual who is not a moral agent stands outside the scope of direct moral concern on these views, and no moral agent can have any direct duty to such individuals. Any duties involving individuals who are not moral agents are indirect duties to those who are.

In contrast to moral agents, *moral patients* lack the prerequisites that would enable them to control their own behavior in ways that would make them morally accountable for what they do. A moral patient lacks the ability to formulate, let alone bring to bear, moral principles in deliberating about which one among a number of possible acts it would be right or proper to perform. Moral patients, in a word, cannot do what is right, nor can they do what is wrong. Granted, what they do may be detrimental to the welfare of others—they may, for example, bring about acute suffering or even death; and granted, it may be necessary, in any given case, for moral agents to use force or violence to prevent such harm being done, either in self-defense or in defense of others (see 8.7). But even when a moral patient causes significant harm to another, the moral patient has not done what is wrong. Only moral agents can do what is wrong. Human infants, young children, and the mentally deranged or enfeebled of all ages are paradigm cases of human moral patients. More controversial is whether human fetuses and future generations of human beings qualify as moral patients. It is enough for our purposes, however, that some humans are reasonably viewed in this way.

Individuals who are moral patients differ from one another in morally relevant ways. Of particular importance is the distinction between (a) those individuals who are conscious and sentient (i.e., can experience pleasure and pain) but who lack other mental abilities, and (b) those individuals who are conscious, sentient, and possess the other cognitive and volitional abilities discussed in previous chapters (e.g., belief and memory). Some animals, for reasons already advanced, belong in category (b); other animals quite probably belong in category (a). The moral status of these latter animals will be addressed in subsequent chapters (7.4, 9.2, 9.4). Our primary interest, in this and in succeeding chapters, concerns the moral status of animals in category (b). When, therefore, the notion of a *moral patient* is appealed to in the discussions that follow, it should be understood as applying to *animals in category (b) and to those other moral patients like these animals in the relevant respects*—that is, those who have desires and beliefs, who perceive, remember, and can act intentionally, who have a sense of the future, including their own future (i.e., are self-aware or self-conscious), who have an emotional life, who have a psychophysical identity over time, who have a kind of autonomy (namely, preference-autonomy), and who have an experiential welfare of the kind clarified in chapter 3. Some *human* moral patients satisfy these criteria—for example, young children and those humans who, though they suffer from a variety of mental handicaps and thus fail to qualify as moral agents, possess the abilities just enumerated. Where one draws the line between those humans who have these abilities and those who do not is a difficult question certainly, and it may be that no exact line can be drawn. (On this problem, see 9.4.) But how we should approach the question in the case of human beings is the same as how we should approach it in the case of animals. Given any human being, what we shall want to know is whether his/her behavior can be accurately described and parsimoniously explained by making reference to the range of abilities that characterizes animals (desires, beliefs, preferences, etc.). To the extent that the case can be made for describing and explaining the behavior of a human being in these terms, to that extent, assuming that we have further reasons for denying that the human in question has the abilities necessary for moral agency, we have reason to regard that human as a moral patient on all fours, so to speak, with animals. As previously claimed, some human beings *are* moral patients in the relevant sense, and *it is only those individuals who are moral patients in this sense (who have, that is, the abilities previously enumerated), whether these individuals be human or nonhuman, who are being referred to, in this chapter and in the sequel, when reference is made to "moral patients."*

Moral patients cannot do what is right or wrong, we have said, and in this respect they differ fundamentally from moral agents. But moral patients can be on the receiving end of the right or wrong acts of moral agents, and so in this respect resemble moral agents. A brutal beating administered to a child, for example, is wrong, even if the child herself can do no wrong, just as attending to the basic biological needs of the senile is arguably right, even if a senile person can no longer do what is right. Unlike the case of the relationship that holds between moral agents, then, the relationship that holds between moral agents, on the one hand, and moral patients, on the other, is not reciprocal. Moral patients can do nothing right or wrong that affects or involves moral agents, but moral agents can do what is right or wrong in ways that affect or involve moral patients.

Now, indirect duty views, we have said, limit the membership of the moral community to all and only moral agents. Thus, moral patients, even paradigm moral patients (children and the mentally enfeebled) are of no direct moral significance; we have no *direct* duties to them. Rather, if or as we have duties involving moral patients, even human moral patients, these are indirect duties we have to moral agents.

It is against this backdrop that we can understand why indirect duty views place animals outside the class of individuals of direct moral concern. They stand outside the boundaries of the moral community because, according to these views, they are moral patients *and* because only moral agents, only those who stand in the reciprocal kind of relation in which moral agents stand to one another, are members of this community. This does not mean that there are no moral constraints on what we may do to animals, any more than it means that there are no moral constraints on what we may do to those humans who are moral patients. It is simply to say that the grounds for why we may treat animals in some ways but not in others, like the grounds for why we may do this in the case of, say, young children, are *not* to be located in how our actions directly affect them. It is only if or as what we do to them affects *moral agents* that we can have a moral basis for deciding that some ways of treating animals are permissible while others are not.

Indirect duty views, as understood here, are not *speciesist*,[3] if by that term we understand the attempt to draw moral boundaries *solely* on the basis of biological considerations. A speciesist position, at least the paradigm of such a position, would take the form of declaring that no animal is a member of the moral community because no animal belongs to the "right" species—namely, *Homo sapiens*. To deny animals membership in the moral community because they are not moral agents, however, is not to deny them membership solely on the basis of their failing to belong to the right species; it is to deny them membership because they lack the necessary cognitive and other prerequisites that underpin the reciprocal relationship that holds between the only individuals who, according to indirect duty views, are members of the moral community—namely, moral agents. That this way of arbitrating who is, and who is not, of direct moral concern is not speciesist should be abundantly clear once we remind ourselves that *some human beings* fail to qualify for membership, despite the fact that they are *Homo sapiens*. There may be other prejudices at work in the attempt to limit membership in the moral community to all and only moral agents, but speciesism, at least in its paradigmatic form, is not one of them.

Indirect duty views invite different kinds of criticism, some applying to individual theories, others to all such theories equally. Objections of the latter kind are the most fundamental but also the most controversial, since they rely on appeals to intuitions, in the reflective sense, a procedure that, as we saw in the previous chapter (4.3), some philosophers regard as defective. I shall postpone lodging these fundamental objections until after we have examined representative indirect duty views on their individual merits. My initial goal will be to expose the inadequacies of representative indirect duty views without relying on appeals to intuition, or relying on them only when the philosopher whose views are under examination recognizes the legitimacy of doing so; that way I cannot be charged with stacking the deck against proponents of indirect duty views.

Two preliminary points are in order. The first concerns completeness. Certainly there are other indirect duty views besides those examined in the following pages. In terms of the number of theories considered, therefore, my examination must be judged to be incomplete. In terms of the comparative importance of the positions discussed, however, the discussion can lay claim to reasonable completeness, since the positions we are about to examine are the strongest, not the weakest, examples of indirect duty views.

Second, though much of the discussion that lies ahead is devoted to the moral status of animals, it is not only animals whose moral status is at stake. *Human* moral patients, like animals in the relevant respects, occupy a position of the same kind as these animals, given indirect duty views. In endeavoring to dismantle these views so that we might come to recognize the direct moral significance of animals, we are also endeavoring to do the same for these human beings. Though some who criticize the concern about the moral status of animals evidently do not realize this, to be "for" animals is not to be "against" humans. On the contrary, the refutation of indirect duty views not only goes some way toward insuring that we think about the moral status of animals properly, it also assists our understanding of the moral status of human moral patients. What one is "against" is not humanity but the assumption that *some* humans—those who are moral agents—have a privileged moral status. To secure a better understanding of why this assumption is arbitrary by itself will not guarantee that either animals or human moral patients will be treated better by moral agents. But it would seem to be a helpful and possibly an essential precondition of making moral progress in our treatment of them.

Three indirect duty views will be examined. These are (1) rational egoism, as this is set forth by the contemporary Canadian philosopher Jan Narveson, (2) contractarianism, as this is understood by John Rawls, and (3) Kant's position. We will explore these positions in the order just given and assess each on its merits. Later on in this chapter (5.6) an objection fatal to *all* indirect duty views will be explained and defended.

5.3 NARVESON'S VIEW: RATIONAL EGOISM

The position Narveson advocates, which he calls *rational egoism*, is thought by him to support an indirect duty view. According to this position "every rational being attempts to maximize its utilities, whatever they may be, that is, to satisfy its desires, interests, etc."[4] As a consequence of adopting this stance, according to Narveson, the individual rational egoist sees the need to enter into an agreement with other rational egoists on "a set of restrictions on (everyone's) behavior,"[5] because to do so helps the individual egoist maximize his utilities. Narveson would have us believe that this set of restrictions represents what we presently mean by "morality." Rights, too, have their basis in self-interest, according to Narveson. "To talk of rights," he says, " . . . is to talk of the basis of claims which we have self-interested reason to make and do make, to varying degrees."[6] As for why other rational egoists should recognize the claims made by an individual egoist, this is, as one might suspect, because it is supposedly in their rational self-interest to do so: "They have an interest in our respecting them in their case, an interest which rationally induces them to close the deal, as it were, and commit themselves to paying the price of respecting them in our case."[7]

A consequence of Narveson's position is that individuals who are unable to enter into agreements, make self-interested claims and, once having made them, bring appropriate pressure to bear to see that these claims are acknowledged by others, cannot possibly have rights. Now, since animals, according to Narveson, fail to meet these requirements, they fail to qualify as possessors of rights. More than this, Narveson thinks they fail to be directly protected by the restrictions comprising morality. As Narveson states, "This perspective"—that is, rational egoism—"puts animals out of reach of morality without at all denying that they are capable of suffering, etc. Instead, it provides the basis for a frank, and of course heartless, rejection of the relevance of their sufferings."[8]

A superficial reading of Narveson suggests he is denying that animals even qualify as moral patients. But some further things he says make it clear that he allows them this status. He notes that "there is plenty of room within it (that is, within rational egoism) to argue, say, that we would be better people if we did respect animals, or that animals really are quite lovable and we would do better to treat them as pets than as potential meals, and so on."[9] These remarks, including the unpacking of the "and so on"—for example, rational egoists might have aesthetic, scientific, sentimental, or ecological interests in animals—make it clear that Narveson is not denying that we have any duties regarding animals, only that we can have any direct duties to them. In itself, the suffering and, more generally, the harm done to animals is of no moral significance; it is only if or as harming them happens to affect *our* interests that we have a reason, albeit an indirect one, for disapproving of it.

Though Narveson is not as clear as one might wish on this score, his account of our duties with respect to animals is in essential respects the same as the account he gives of our duties with respect to humans who, because they lack the right "rational equipment," also fail to qualify as rational egoists. The humans in question are young children and mental incompetents of all ages. The duties we have in their case are indirect duties, and Narveson sketches his account of the grounds of our duties involving these moral patients. If we can show that his views regarding human moral patients are deficient, we can reach the same verdict in the case of his views regarding animals like these humans in the relevant respects. That is the main strategy used in the critical argument that follows, but I shall also want to raise other objections along the way.

Narveson's reasons for recognizing indirect duties to human children and the mentally enfeebled of all ages are set forth in the following passage:

> There are reasons of a straightforward kind for extending the ambit of morality to infants and morons, etc. We want to extend it to children because most of us want to have our own children protected, etc., and have really nothing to gain from being permitted to invade the children of others; we have an interest in the children of others being properly cared for, because we don't want them growing up criminals or delinquents, etc. (and we do want them to be interesting and useful people). And we shall want the feeble-minded generally respected because we ourselves might become so, as well as out of respect for their rational relatives who have a sentimental interest in these cases.[10]

How adequate is Narveson's position? Not very. One feature of Narveson's account of egoism, we know, is his belief that not all human beings are capable of entering into the sort of agreements the results of which he would have us identify with the rules of morality. A newly born baby, for example, cannot do so. To enter into such agreements requires a degree of physical, mental, and emotional maturity the very young have yet to reach. At what point, exactly, a growing child reaches the requisite degree of maturity may well be impossible to say, but it seems safe to assume that a four-year-old child has not reached it.

Narveson advances a number of reasons why the interests of a normal child of this age should be protected. These are given in the longish quote above. Here, however, let us ask why the interests of a child of this age should be protected, if the child happens to be mentally enfeebled but not so enfeebled that he lacks desires, beliefs, emotions, and the other abilities possessed by animals (2.6). One of the reasons Narveson gives is that "we ourselves might become (mentally enfeebled)," and thus we ourselves will have an interest in insuring that the interests of the mentally enfeebled are protected. But who is this "we" that Narveson refers to? It can only be rational egoists, those human beings, in other words, who have reached a level of maturity enabling them to determine what is in their self-interest, all considered, and thereby enter into advantageous agreements. Suppose we grant that it would not be in the self-interest of a rational egoist to reach an agreement whereby his interests would not be protected, if he should happen to become mentally enfeebled. Then we can ask whether this fact provides us, as rational egoists, with a reason for protecting the interests of others who are similarly enfeebled.

The answer is, no. For no rational egoist could possibly be acting in a way that was contrary to his interest in being treated well if he should end up being mentally enfeebled, if he entered into the following agreement (and if we assume that the agreements egoists reach are kept): Human beings who have reached a level of maturity sufficient to reach agreements based upon one's self-interest shall have their interests protected if they subsequently become enfeebled; but this protection shall not be extended to those human beings who are or become enfeebled *before* they are sufficiently mature to enter into agreements based upon what is in their self-interest. To enter into this agreement cannot possibly be contrary to the rational egoist's interest in having his interests protected if he should happen to become enfeebled (and assuming such agreements are honored), since *his* ability to enter into this agreement insures that *he already is* one of those humans whose interests are to be protected by the terms of the agreement. *He* stands to gain a good deal of insurance, as it were, at very little cost. And the fact that the congenitally enfeebled, for example, stand to lose a great deal need not sway either his reason or his conscience: it need not sway his reason, since there is nothing logically inconsistent, viewed from the perspective of rational egoism, in protecting the interests of those mental incompetents who once were capable of entering into self-interested agreements while failing to protect the interests of those who never were able to do this; and it need not sway his conscience since, given that he is an egoist, what he ought to do is just what he is trying to do—namely, reach an agreement that favors maximizing his interests. If, then, rational egoism is to provide a basis for protecting the interests of all mental incompetents, including those born in this condition, the grounds for this protection must be sought in some place other than in the egoist's interest in seeing that he is treated well, that his interests are protected, if he should happen to become enfeebled at some later date.

This brings us to Narveson's second reason—namely, that, as rational egoists, we will have reason to protect the interests of children, including those who are mentally enfeebled, because their rational relatives will have a "sentimental interest" in their being treated well, and it will be in our self-interest generally to be supportive of whatever is required to show respect for this interest of theirs. Besides (a point Narveson does not make but could have), we would want the interests of these moral patients protected if we happened to be related to them, and, as rational egoists, we could not expect others to do what we are not ourselves willing to do. This latter reason will be examined simultaneously with the examination of the one Narveson does give.

There is a fatal objection to any attempt to ground the protection of the interests of children generally and the enfeebled in particular in the "sentimental interests" of others, which is, after all, what Narveson must do, given the failure of his first reason. Appeal to "sentimental interests" makes the duty to protect these moral patients *wholly contingent* upon other beings having and continuing to have a "sentimental interest" toward them. Where this interest is lacking, there an egoistic basis for this duty will be lacking also. And it is a plain, even if it is a regrettable, matter of fact that this interest not only can be lacking but sometimes actually is noteworthy for its absence. Suppose Smith has no interest in the life and well-being of a child to whom he happens to be related; say he has a retarded son, whom he despises. And suppose Smith would personally gain a great deal if he were to arrange to have his son used as a subject in grossly painful, trivial research. What argument *can* the proponent of egoism give as to why Smith should not volunteer his son, or, if it is in my self-interest to help Smith "close the deal," why I should not assist him? Will he say that to be a party to such grossly immoral conduct cannot possibly be in one's self-interest? Then he is naive. The gears of right conduct are not so finely meshed with those of self-interest that we cannot profit personally by doing what is wrong. Will he say that it is human nature to have a "sentimental interest" in the life and well-being of our children and thus that the sort of case imagined never can occur? Then he flies in the face of the harsh realities of human existence. Even in the case of so-called normal children, not a few are unwanted, unloved, uncared for; the case of the retarded is no different. Will he say, then, that, though this much is true, still one can never be certain it will be to one's advantage to permit children to be treated in ways that harm them? Then he underestimates human cunning and sagacity. Occasions can and do arise where one can be as certain as one can be in such matters, that harming children, or allowing others to do so, will maximize one's utilities. Assuming that neither Smith nor I have any "sentimental interest" toward his son, assuming that to allow him to be harmed would be to our advantage, and recognizing, as argued above, that Narveson's first reason fails to provide a rational basis for protecting the interests of retarded children, then it follows, given the tenets of Narveson's version of egoism, that neither Smith nor I have a duty to protect the interests of his son.

Perhaps it will be objected that no moral theory can itself insure that people will do what is right and avoid doing what is wrong, something which, it might be alleged, the preceding objection assumes. However, this would be to misunderstand the force of what has been argued. What has been argued is that Narveson's attempt to ground our indirect duties to the mentally enfeebled, duties *he* recognizes and attempts to account for, is rationally defective. It is not that his theory fails to do what no theory should be required to do—namely, insure that everyone does what is right and avoids doing what is wrong. Rather, his theory fails to give a satisfactory account of our duties involving mentally enfeebled humans, considered on its own merits (i.e., *even assuming* that these duties are indirect duties). (The same kind of argument can be given against attempts to ground duties to "normal" children in the "sentimental interests" of others.)

There are further problems with a Narvesonian attempt to reduce morality to the dictates of rational egoism, however, problems concerning what his theory could allow in the case of the treatment of moral agents. On Narveson's view, what agreements a given rational egoist should strike with others is contingent on what the former judges to be in his (presumably long-term) self-interest. Imagine such an egoist who happens to have the benefits of wealth, leisure, education, access to the best medical care, and the other goods that characterize upper middle-class existence. Suppose most other rational egoists are similarly advantaged, while a small minority lack these benefits and live in abject poverty. And suppose, finally, that the majority judges that, all considered, the following sort of agreements would serve their interests best: Policies are to be instituted favoring their retention of wealth, access to an education, and the like, while denying these benefits to the minority of egoists who presently lack them. A rigid class or caste system is agreed upon, including the necessary social and legal machinery to further the ends of the advantaged by keeping the disadvantaged in their place. Now, one might question whether such an arrangement could truly be in the long-term self-interest of those rational egoists who now happen to be advantaged. However, there is no reason why this is impossible, even granting that those who are presently advantaged would have to pay a certain price in terms of their security because, for example, a revolt on the part of the disadvantaged is always a possibility. And the advantaged also will have to give up some portion of their time and wealth to insure that a trained and loyal cadre of lawyers, law enforcement officers, and legislators effectively protect the interests of the advantaged rational egoists. Despite these costs, it remains possible, all considered, that such agreements will be in the self-interest of each advantaged rational egoist and judged to be so by each.

The implications of such agreements must surely offend our sense of justice. Although social and political arrangements that favor the interests of the advantaged over the disadvantaged perhaps are not unjust in all cases, social and political arrangements *designed* with the overriding purpose of favoring the advantaged while denying others opportunities to secure the benefits the advantaged enjoy (e.g., wealth and proper medical care) are paradigms of social and political injustice. They arbitrarily discriminate against some in order to further the interests of others and so present us with grossly inequitable, unjust social and political institutions. That a given moral position implies that such arrangements are morally permissible provides the grounds for lodging a most serious moral objection against it.

Narveson's version of rational egoism does imply this. As an advantaged rational egoist, my decision to enter into agreements with other rational egoists, as well as what agreements to make, *can* only be decided on the basis of what is, or what I judge to be, in my self-interest. That being so, no compelling reason can be offered as to why I might not limit my agreements to those rational egoists who happen to be similarly advantaged, agreeing with them on the desirability of keeping a given minority of other rational egoists in their present disadvantaged position and, as a consequence, also agreeing on the desirability of instituting the necessary repressive measures to accomplish this end. Rational egoism, then, at least in the form we find it sketched by Narveson, has unacceptable implications, even if we limit our attention to the implications of that position to how *moral agents* may be treated. An "account of morality" that not only fails adequately to accommodate those human moral patients who are not rational egoists but also fails to insure the equitable treatment of those humans who are, cannot be a satisfactory theory of morality all considered; neither, then, can it be a satisfactory basis on which to "leave out animals."

The most obvious reply to this last objection, and to the earlier criticisms of his views on our duties involving retarded humans, is not available to Narveson. The reply is that our intuitions about what is wrong or unjust should play no role in assessing the adequacy of moral theories. Though some philosophers take this stance, Narveson is not one of them. He is generally sympathetic to the appeal to our intuitions, believing that our intuitions provide us with a reasonable place from which to start our theory construction and a tenable touchstone against which to test a theory once constructed.[11] That much conceded, it follows that Narveson neither would nor could dispute the propriety of assessing his own theory in terms of how well it conforms with these intuitions. Finding that it fails to conform, he should recognize that its failure in this regard is a serious defect.

5.4 RAWLS'S POSITION: CONTRACTARIANISM

The final objection raised against Narveson's version of rational egoism involves recognizing that advantaged rational egoists could agree on arrangements that unfairly redound to their favor, giving them unjust access to certain benefits (e.g., wealth or leisure) while denying access to others. Suppose, however, that we imagine that the rational egoists we are concerned with are not persons in the ordinary world. We might imagine them as disembodied persons existing beyond or before the world comes to be. Imagine, further, that the task they have before them is to choose principles of justice that will govern the basic institutions of the society into which they will someday be "incarnated." And imagine, finally, that, while in their disembodied state, these persons do not know any particular facts about what they will be like, when they are incarnated. Unlike Narveson's rational egoists, this new breed of rational egoists do not know whether they will be, say, black or white, male or female, rich or poor, when the time falls due for them to be born into the society whose basic principles of justice they must select. They do not even know when they will be born, though they do know that the society in which they will one day be citizens will be materially prosperous. Lacking as these rational egoists would be concerning their own eventual possession of the various benefits and limitations that would enhance or detract from their own individual welfare, they could hardly be in a position to do what Narvesonian rational egoists can. The latter can select social and political arrangements that will unfairly further their interests over the equal interests of others who are not presently advantaged. This new breed of rational egoist cannot do this. Since they do not know any particular fact about what they will be like, these rational egoists simply are not in a position to choose principles of justice that arbitrarily favor those who are rich, say, over those who are poor, if they are to act in a self-interested way. Indeed, since they do not know whether they will be rich or poor, it can hardly be wise for them to choose principles favoring members of the one class over those of the other. Thus, this way of viewing rational egoists seems to be immune to the final objection raised against Narveson's version of rational egoism.

Those familiar with John Rawls's *A Theory of Justice* will recognize that the imaginary situation described in the previous paragraph provides one way of interpreting what Rawls refers to as "the original position" and goes some way toward suggesting why Rawls introduces this heuristic device. Underlying Rawls's approach to a general theory of justice is the necessity that the very selection of principles of justice must insure impartiality. If we allow those who select the principles of justice to know that they will be, say, white educated males of the leisured class, then, given that they are to choose these principles on the basis of what is most likely to further their own interests, the principles they should choose are those that will further the members of that particular group. If, however, operating from behind "a veil of ignorance," the individuals in the original position do not know any *particular* facts about their subsequent identity, they cannot be in a position to select principles that arbitrarily favor their particular interests. Thus is the veil of ignorance intended to insure an impartial basis for selecting the basic principles of justice.

The requirement that those in the original position be ignorant of any particular fact about their future identity also extends to their ignorance of how they will fare with respect to the "natural lottery." For all they know, they may be born beautiful or ugly, intellectually gifted or moronic, graced by athletic talents or physically handicapped. Since individuals have not *done* anything to deserve the natural abilities (or lack of them) with which they come into the world, possession (or nonpossession) of such abilities cannot provide a just basis on which to select the basic principles of justice. Ignorance of how each individual will fare with respect to the possession of these abilities, to insure impartiality, must be included in what these individuals do not know when, operating from behind the veil of ignorance, they select these principles. Among the things they *do* know, on Rawls's view, is that they will at some time be a member of the society concerning whose basic principles of justice they are deciding *and* that, as future members of this society, they will be human beings.

One would think, given the preceding, that the principles of justice selected by those in the original position would apply, and direct duties of justice would be owed, to *all* human beings, both human moral agents and human moral patients. In fact, however, Rawls evidently thinks otherwise. In an essay that predates *A Theory of Justice*, Rawls explicitly limits those to whom direct duties of justice are owed to moral agents. "It is," he writes, "a necessary and sufficient condition" to qualify as an object of direct duties of justice that one "be capable, to a certain minimum degree, of a sense of justice."[12] One must, that is, understand what justice is and be able to bring considerations of justice to bear on one's deliberations and act accordingly, at least to a minimum degree, if one is to be owed duties of justice. Or, to put the same point in terms already previously explained, one must be a moral agent to be owed duties of justice by other moral agents. Because not all human beings are moral agents, or "persons" in Rawls's sense, it follows, given the views expressed by Rawls in this earlier essay, that not all human beings are owed duties of justice.

In *A Theory of Justice* Rawls says some things that suggest that he backs away from this earlier position. Most significant in this respect is his claim that he has "not maintained that the capacity for a sense of justice" (or, what comes to the same thing, on the interpretation advanced here, the capacity for moral agency) "is necessary to be owed duties of justice."[13] But this claim must be squared with what Rawls then goes on to say about individuals who lack the sense of justice. "It does *seem,*" he writes, "that we are not required to give strict justice to creatures lacking this capacity."[14] As Edward Johnson, a philosopher at the University of New Orleans, notes in his critical discussion of Rawls, "This is puzzling. Although possession of a sense of justice is not necessary to be owed justice, we are nevertheless 'not required to give strict justice anyway to creatures lacking this capacity.' What then? 'Loose' justice? Or no justice at all?"[15] The suspicion is that, what Rawls takes back with one breath, he reaffirms with the next. For it can only *seem* that we do not owe strict duties of justice to creatures lacking the capacity for a sense of justice if it *seems* that having this capacity is a necessary condition of being owed these duties. Thus, though the Rawls of *A Theory of Justice,* unlike the Rawls of the earlier essay, refrains from explicitly maintaining that having this capacity is necessary for being owed duties of justice, the available evidence indicates that he remains enamored of this view. This suspicion gains additional support when we note that in *A Theory of Justice* Rawls states that the "only contingency which is decisive" (decisive, that is, regarding who is owed direct duties of justice) "is that of having or not having the capacity for a sense of justice."[16] But if this is the *only* contingency that is decisive, then having this capacity cannot be viewed merely as a sufficient condition of being owed these duties; it must also be viewed as necessary as well. Despite some wavering on Rawls's part, therefore, it would not be implausible to interpret him as continuing to suppose that having the capacity for a sense of justice, or for moral agency, is both a necessary and sufficient condition of being the sort of individual to whom duties of justice are owed.

Because Rawls is not unequivocal on this important matter, fairness and caution dictate that we distinguish between two positions he might hold, a strong one and a weak one. The strong position is that being a moral agent is a necessary and sufficient condition of being owed duties of justice. The weak position is that being a moral agent is a sufficient condition but that it only "seems" that it is necessary. On either position, the implications for animals, as they exist in the actual world, are not very promising. Since animals are not moral agents, the strong position implies that we have no duties of justice to them, while the weak position implies that it "seems" that we do not. Neither position, it will be argued in what follows, is consistent with Rawls's own account of what he calls "natural duties," and both rest on an arbitrary denial of the direct moral significance of animals and those humans like them in the relevant respects, when it comes to questions of justice. Before turning to these matters, however, there is a further problem of interpretation that requires our attention.

In Rawls's view, neither the weak nor the strong position characterized above entails that we have no duties regarding moral patients, including animals.[17] What Rawls fails to make clear is whether those duties we have regarding animals are direct or indirect duties. It is therefore unclear whether Rawls should be included among the proponents of indirect duty views. Reasons will be advanced in what follows, however, that show that Rawls is committed to a view of this kind if his overall position, as he understands it,[18] is to be consistent. In order to show this I will initially assume that the duty not to be cruel is supposed by him to be a direct duty.[19] Then it will be shown that this would render his overall position inconsistent, again as he understands it. After this has been shown, I will then go on to diagnose the source of the arbitrariness that infects Rawls's view of the moral status of moral patients generally and of animals in particular.

After having noted, in *A Theory of Justice*, that "it does seem that we are not required to give strict justice" to creatures who are not moral agents, Rawls goes on to state the following:

> It does not follow that there are no requirements at all in regard to them (i.e., animals). . . . Certainly it is wrong to be cruel to animals and the destruction of whole species can be a great evil.[20]

Thus, though animals are not moral agents, and so are not owed—or at least it "seems" that they are not owed—strict justice, we do have duties in their case, including in particular the duty not to be cruel to them. If we assume, for the present, that this latter duty is a duty we have directly to animals, then Rawls's position comes to this: we have some direct duties to animals, despite the fact that they are not moral agents (i.e., persons), but we do not have a duty of justice to them, or at least it "seems" that we do not.

This difference between those to whom we owe the duty of justice, on the one hand, and those to whom we owe the duty not to be cruel, on the other, is at odds with what Rawls says about these duties elsewhere in *A Theory of Justice*. In section 19 of that work ("Principles for Individuals: The Natural Duties") Rawls offers two characteristics of what he calls *natural duties*. First, "they apply to us without regard to our voluntary acts," and second, "they hold between persons irrespective of their institutional arrangements," "obtain(ing) between all as equal moral persons."[21] The first characteristic distinguishes natural duties from those duties, such as the duty to keep a promise, that arise as a result of the performance of a voluntary act; the second distinguishes natural duties from those we have as a result of our occupying a given place in an institutional arrangement, such as the duty of an employee to an employer.

Rawls lists examples of natural duties. Of particular importance for present purposes is that the list includes both "the natural duty not to be cruel"[22] and "the duty of justice."[23] The dilemma Rawls must face should already be apparent. Natural duties, he says, hold between *persons*— "between all as equal moral persons." But animals are not persons, which is why we are not required, or at least "it does *seem* that we are not required," "to give strict justice" to them. If, however, both the duty not to be cruel and the duty of justice are natural duties, if natural duties hold equally between all persons, and if the fact that animals are not persons casts doubt upon or undermines our having the natural duty of justice to them, then the fact that animals are not persons should *also* cast doubt upon or undermine our having the natural duty not to be cruel to them. Yet Rawls allows that we have a duty not to be cruel to animals. If, however, the fact that animals are not persons does *not* by itself show or raise the suspicion that we do not have the natural duty against being cruel to animals, then this same fact cannot by itself show or raise the suspicion that we do not have the natural duty of justice to them. Yet Rawls denies that we have the duty of justice to them (the strong position) or affirms that it at least "seems" that we do not (the weak position). The dilemma that Rawls must face, then, is that he simply cannot have it both ways. *Either* being a person is a decisive consideration for determining those to whom we have, or "seem" to have, natural duties, in which case he cannot believe that we have a direct duty to animals not to be cruel to them, *or* being a person is not a decisive consideration, in which case he cannot advocate either his strong or his weak position regarding animals and the duty of justice. Whichever alternative Rawls should choose, it must be one or the other, not both.

Two replies that seek to defuse this dilemma are worth considering. First, it might be objected that the duty of justice can only obtain between individuals who can have this duty to each other and that this is a relevant difference between this duty and the duty not to be cruel. In the case of this latter duty, this objection holds, we have it to animals despite the fact that they do not have it (or any other duty) to us. In the case of the duty of justice, however, we do not have it to animals because they cannot have this duty to us.

This reply goes no way toward defending a disanalogous understanding of the two natural duties in question. What one wants is an explanation of why the fact that animals cannot owe the duty of justice rules out their being owed this duty (or at least "seems" to) if the fact that they cannot owe the duty not to be cruel does not rule out (or "seem" to rule out) their being owed that duty. The objection just sketched fails to provide such an explanation, and it is difficult to imagine what such an explanation might look like. What might appear to be the two most promising kinds of explanation are not available to Rawls, given his analysis of natural duties. We cannot say that we have no duty of justice to animals because they stand outside certain actual political or other types of institutional arrangements; natural duties do not depend for their binding force on such arrangements. Nor can we say that we have no duty of justice to animals because we have not ourselves, as actual persons, in the actual world, entered into any "agreement" with them; natural duties do not depend for their existence on the performance or nonperformance of any voluntary act on the part of anyone in the actual world. This much granted, it should be clear that no appeal to *our* acts or *our* institutions can provide grounds for disenfranchising animals when it comes to the natural duty of justice or to any other natural duty.

The second reply ignores the contingencies of the actual world and refers instead to the hypothetical situation of the original position. Animals are owed the duty against being cruel, but not the duty of justice, according to this second reply, because this is the judgment that would be reached by those in the original position. After all, since the original contractors are self-interested persons who know they will be human beings when they are "incarnated" in the actual world, they will view the duty of justice in a way that is calculated to forward their self-interest as the human beings they know they will become. Thus, to exclude animals from those to whom the duty of justice is owed can hardly be contrary to the self-interest of the original contractors.

This objection merits two replies at this juncture. First, appeals to the agreements reached by those in the original position, agreements which supposedly affirm that we have the natural duty not to be cruel to animals but deny that we have the natural duty of justice to them—such appeals simply fail to address the dilemma posed earlier. Whatever agreements they reach, the original contractors must at least be consistent regarding the grounds they have for reaching them; and they cannot be consistent in this regard if, without citing any relevant difference, they *affirm* that being a person is a decisive consideration for determining who is owed one natural duty (justice) but *deny* that being a person is a decisive consideration for determining who is owed another natural duty (the duty not to be cruel). Since mere appeals to the hypothetical agreements of those in the original position fail to cite, let alone defend, a relevant difference regarding the scope of the two natural duties in question, such appeals provide no escape from the dilemma raised against Rawls. Second, if, following Rawls, we assume that those in the original position know that they will be human beings when they are "incarnated" in the actual world, we need to ask what possible basis the original contractors can have for agreeing that the natural duty not to be cruel includes a *direct* duty not to be cruel to animals. The duties these contractors will recognize must be contingent upon what duties are in their self-interest to recognize. But if, *ex hypothesi*, those in the original position will never become animals, and know this, then they cannot possibly have any self-interested reason to recognize a *direct* duty not to be cruel to animals—a duty, that is, owed directly to animals *independently* of human interests. Thus, if the duty not to be cruel is a natural duty, which is what Rawls says it is, and if we have this duty directly to animals, which is what we are assuming he believes, then the grounds for our having this duty directly to animals are not to be found by asking about the supposed "outcome of a hypothetical agreement" struck between the self-interested persons in the original position. A contract including direct duties to animals cannot be forthcoming if the only basis for selecting duties is the yardstick of human interest. In view of the two objections raised against the second reply, therefore, Rawls cannot be spared the pain of the dilemma urged against him by having recourse to what does or does not transpire in the original position.

The dilemma posed above thus seems recalcitrant to attempts to amputate or dull its horns, if the duty not to be cruel to animals is viewed by Rawls as a duty we have directly to animals. This dilemma can be avoided, however, if Rawls views this duty as an indirect duty. It is not clear that he does view this duty in this way. At one point in *A Theory of*

Justice, Rawls states that "the capacity for feelings of pleasure and pain and for the forms of life of which animals are capable clearly impose" *some* duties on us, including the duty not to be cruel to them.[24] A natural interpretation of this claim is that *these facts themselves* about animals impose certain duties on us, in which case the duties these facts impose would seem to be direct duties we have to animals themselves. Now, it may be that Rawls *wants* to view some duties regarding animals in this way—that is, as direct duties. For reasons already adduced, however, he cannot do this except at the price of rendering his position, as he understands it, inconsistent. If we assume, then, that when faced with the choice between (1) abandoning his weak or strong positions concerning justice and animals, on the one hand, or (2) abandoning his presumed view that at least some duties regarding animals are direct duties, on the other, Rawls would select the option that is least damaging to his overall position as he understands it, then it is not unreasonable to suppose that he would choose the second alternative. Were Rawls to make this choice one might concede that he at least has an apparently consistent position when it comes to our duties regarding animals and other moral patients. But serious questions remain concerning the adequacy of his position.

To begin with, Rawls's exclusion of *human* moral patients from the class whose members are owed the duty of justice results from his failure to distinguish clearly between (1) the abilities necessary if one is to be able to *select* between alternative principles of justice and (2) the abilities necessary if one is to be *owed* duties of justice. Rawls is certainly correct in believing that those individuals in the original position who are called upon to select principles of justice must have a sense of justice and a conception of their own good as expressed in an overall life plan, though each is ignorant of the specific details of the actual plan they will have when they come to be in the actual world.[25] Even granting this, it does not follow that only moral agents are owed duties of justice, or even that this "seems" to be so. Indeed, not only does this not follow, but there are ample reasons to believe that those in the original position would have self-interested reasons for denying this. For consider: Those in the original position do not know how they will fare as a result of the natural lottery when they are "incarnated." For all they know, they may turn out to be human moral *patients* when they come to be, despite the fact that, in their preincarnated condition, they have the abilities of moral agents. If we assume that those in the original position select principles of justice with a view to what will be in their self-interest *after* they have been "incarnated," they would do well to select principles that recognize a direct duty of justice to human moral patients. Not to do so would be to run the serious risk of not having one's interests adequately protected in one's incarnated state, if one turns out to be, say, a moron. Moreover, those in the original position *will* be children, if they are born humans, whether normal or otherwise, at some point in their life. Rather than permit the protection morality will afford them in their youth to be contingent upon "the sentimental interests" of their elders, as, for example, on Narveson's view they would be, a sensible contractor would select principles imposing duties of justice *even* in the case of how these humans should be treated. While *those who select* these principles must have a sense of justice, *those who are owed* duties of justice need not. A *sufficient* condition of being owed such duties is that one have a welfare—that one be the experiencing subject of a life that fares well or ill for one as an individual—independently of whether one also has a conception of what this is. To recognize this condition as sufficient would be an eminently reasonable position for anyone who, operating as a self-interested contractor from behind the veil of ignorance, was called upon to select principles of justice and to decide who is owed duties of justice. It is only if we allow those in the original position knowledge that they will be human moral *agents*, not human moral *patients*, that they could have self-interested reason to affirm that duties of justice are owed to the former but not the latter. But the veil of ignorance, if it is to insure impartiality in the selection of principles of justice, including who is covered by these principles, will not allow this knowledge.

Once we recognize that those in the original position would have self-interested reasons to require that human moral patients are owed duties of justice, we will also see that animals like these humans in the relevant respects cannot be nonarbitrarily excluded from being owed these same duties. The only apparent reason the original contractors could have for judging the case of animals differently is if we assume, as Rawls does, that those in the original position know that they will be human beings, whether agents or patients. But this is to prejudice the case against recognizing duties of justice to animals from the start. To allow those in the original position to know what *species* they will belong to is to allow them knowledge no different in kind from allowing them to know what race or sex they will be. If knowledge of these latter details must be excluded by the veil of ignorance, in order to insure a fair procedure in the selection of principles of justice, then knowledge of the former detail must be excluded as well. The veil of ignorance cannot be thick enough if, while denying access to many of the particular contingencies of one's life because knowledge of them might prejudice one's selection of principles of justice, it nevertheless allows one to know that one will belong to the species *Homo sapiens*. The fact that on Rawls's understanding of his theory, animals are not, or at least it "seems" that they are not, owed strict justice should hardly be surprising. The cards as dealt in the original position are stacked against them.

Perhaps it will be objected that the supposition that any person in the original position could become a nonhuman animal would render the very point of the original position incoherent. Since persons in that position are being asked to choose basic principles of justice, principles which, among other things, are to lay the foundation of social and political institutions that will govern the distribution of harms and bene- fits to those who can meaningfully be said to be beneficiaries in their own right, animals can be excluded from consideration. Whatever else we might want to say about animals, it might be claimed, they cannot have "a good life" and thus cannot be beneficiaries in the relevant sense. To deny that they are owed duties of justice thus is not arbitrary.

This response has a point, up to a point. It is doubtful at best that we can reasonably view, say, grasshoppers or fleas as themselves either having or not having a life that is better or worse for them, considered as individuals. However, the situation with respect to other animals is importantly different. The case has been made for regarding mammalian animals in particular as being conscious and sentient; as having desires or preferences that may be either satisfied or frustrated; as having various higher-order cognitive capacities, including memory and the ability to form beliefs, including beliefs relating to their own future; as agents in the world, in the sense that they can act intentionally in pursuit of the satisfaction of their desires or preferences; and as individuals who have a psychophysical identity over time. In the case of these animals, therefore, it makes perfectly good sense to view them as having an individual welfare—as faring well or ill during the course of their experimental life, logically independently of whether anyone else happens to value what happens to them. These animals thus *can* have a good life, relative to their nature, and thus *can* be beneficiaries in the relevant sense, even if it is true that because of their limited intellectual capacities they themselves are unable to form a conception of their long-term welfare, or have a sense of justice, or have categorical desires, or adopt a rational life plan. Accord- ingly, assuming that the principles of justice to be selected by those in the original position concern, among other things, the distribution of those harms and benefits essential to an individual's having a good life, the selection would exclude only some animals from being owed duties of justice. Normal mammalian animals, one year of age or older, would, or at least should, be covered by the principles that are chosen. The charge of arbitrariness has not been met.

In reply, perhaps it will be objected that it is not justice but metaphysics that excludes even these animals from being owed duties of justice. To suppose that a person in the original position could be "incarnated" as a dog or chimpanzee, it might be claimed, is to violate standard metaphysical views about identity. Metaphysically, a dog or a chimpanzee just can't be the same individual as one who once occupied a place in the original position. It is not arbitrary to exclude animals from being owed duties of justice, therefore, it could be argued, since even the original contractors may be permitted to know metaphysical truths, including the truth that, whatever else might transpire in the actual world when they are "incarnated," they simply can't turn out to be a (nonhuman) animal.

As remarked at the outset of chapter 3, problems of identity are admittedly serious problems, but their seriousness cuts both ways in the present case. If it is true, as Rawls presumably would allow, that any given person in the original position might turn out to be a human idiot or worse when he comes to be in the actual world, and still be the same individual he was in the original position, then the possession of the central characteristic definitive of moral personality (a sense of justice) cannot be a criterion of personal identity. That being so, what reason can there be against a person in the original position being "incarnated" as a dog or chimpanzee? It would be a palpable double standard to affirm that a human idiot is the same individual as one of the persons in the original position despite the fact that, as an idiot, he lacks a sense of justice, but to deny that a dog or chimpanzee can be the same individual as one of the persons in the original position because, given their cognitive and moral poverty, these animals lack a sense of justice. Moreover, to attempt to avoid this display of arbitrariness by supposing that persons in the original position "just know" that they will be human beings, however handicapped, begs the question rather than answering it. For the question at issue is how animals can be *nonarbitrarily* excluded from those who are owed duties of justice. To attempt to avoid the point of this question by assuming that the original contractors "just know" what species they will belong to when they are "incarnated," is to repeat the problem rather than to resolve it. The charge that the veil of ignorance *arbitrarily* allows those in the original position to know what species they will belong to has not been met.

We may summarize and conclude our examination of Rawls's account of our duties regarding animals as follows: For Rawls to deny that we have a natural duty of justice directly to animals, or to allow that it "seems" that we do not, conflicts with his view that we have a duty not to be cruel to animals, assuming that this duty is a natural duty owed directly to animals. Rawls could escape this inconsistency by claiming that all our duties regarding animals, including even the duty not to be cruel to them, are indirect duties, and he could advance a similar position in the case of our duties regarding human moral patients who are relevantly like these animals. But though his position would be consistent at this level, if he were to advocate an indirect duty view, it is not adequate in other respects. In particular, the approach Rawls relies on as a vehicle for determining who is owed direct duties (the agreements that would be reached by self-interested contractors in the hypothetical "original position") would, or should, yield the result that human moral patients *who have an experiential welfare* are owed the direct duty of justice, since it would be in the self-interest of the original contractors to insure that their interests be protected by justice, should these contractors turn out to be human moral patients in the actual world, as in the case of children they will. However, once this much is acknowledged, the question arises concerning how nonhuman animals who have an experiential welfare can nonarbitrarily be denied being owed this same duty. To allow the original contractors to know that they will be human beings is to prejudice the deliberations in favor of human beings and *should* be excluded by the veil of ignorance. To attempt to meet this objection by denying that persons in the original position could become animals on the grounds that this contravenes metaphysical laws about identity is demonstrably at odds with what Rawls himself implies about identity. Thus, even were we to grant that, by advancing an indirect duty view, Rawls's position is consistent, thereby passing one test that any adequate moral theory must pass, we would still have principled reasons for denying that it passes another crucial test—namely, that of impartiality (see 4.2ff.). Rawls's exclusion of animals from the class of individuals who are owed duties of justice is consistent, if it is, only because the grounds for excluding them are arbitrary. Since no ethical theory can be the most reasonable one, all considered, if it is demonstrably arbitrary, to be satisfied with Rawls's theory, despite its many other merits, would be to be satisfied with less than the best. That it requires, if it is to be consistent, that our duties regarding animals are indirect duties is one of its central weaknesses rather than one of its cardinal strengths.

5.5 KANT'S POSITION: HUMANITY AS END IN ITSELF

Unlike Rawls, whose considered views on our duties regarding animals are unclear at best, Kant provides us with an explicit statement of an indirect duty view. That Kant should hold such a view should not be

surprising; it is a direct consequence of his moral theory, the main outlines of which may be briefly, albeit crudely, summarized for a second
time (see 4.5). On Kant's view, rational beings, by which he means moral
agents, are ends in themselves (have, that is, independent value, or
worth, in their own right, quite apart from how useful they happen to be
to others). As such, no moral agent is ever to be treated *merely* as a means.
This is not to say that we may never make use of the skills or services of
moral agents in their capacities as, say, mechanics, plumbers, or sur-
geons. It is to say that we must never impose our will, by force, coercion,
or deceit, on any moral agent to do what we want them to do *just* because
we stand to benefit as a result. To treat moral agents in this way is to treat
them as if they had no value in their own right or, alternatively, as if they
were things. As Kant remarks, "beings whose existence depends, not on
our will, but on nature, have nonetheless, if they are non-rational only a
relative value and are consequently called things."[26] Moral agents are not
nonrational, do not have "only a relative value," and are not things.
Moral agents (rational beings) are ends in themselves.

What Kant calls the "categorical imperative" is, he believes, the
correct principle for determining how imperfect rational beings ought to
treat themselves or one another. In the case of my interactions with other
moral agents, what the categorical imperative requires of me, as was
noted in the earlier characterization of Kant's views, is that I never make
an exception for myself by acting on reasons I could not will that every
other rational being could act on. For example, I cannot make a deceitful
promise, hoping to benefit from the deceit, and universalize my reasons
(what Kant calls my "subjective maxim"), since if all moral agents were to
do what I aspire to do, then no one would believe such promises when
they were made. If I were to universalize the exception (making a deceitful promise), I would destroy the rule (the making of reliable promises).
Thus am I unable to universalize my reasons for making my deceitful
promise, and thus is it wrong to make it. To insure that I do not do what is
wrong, I must abide by the first formulation of the categorical imperative,
the Formula of Universal Law: "I ought never to act except in such a way
that I can also will that my maxim should become a universal law."[27]

The immorality of making a deceitful promise also can be illuminated,
Kant thinks, by viewing it against the backdrop of the kind of value moral
agents possess. As was mentioned earlier, the worth of rational beings
does not rule out the permissibility of making use of their skills or
services. It does rule out treating them as if they had no value over and
above the use we can make of them. This is something I am guilty of, for
example, whenever I withhold information from moral agents that is

relevant to their making a rational judgment because I stand to gain from their ignorance. For example, if I were to promise Ann that I will return the money I want to borrow from her, but withheld from her my intention not to repay, then I would be keeping from her information that is relevant to her making a rational judgment about whether to lend me the money. And I do this because *I* stand to be the beneficiary of her ignorance. (Were she to know of my intention never to repay, she probably would not lend.) In this way, then, I treat Ann as if she had value merely as a means relative to my goals or purposes, as if she were a mere thing. To treat her in this way, Kant believes, is wrong. For we are always, he writes, "to treat humanity, both in (our) own person and in the person of every other, always as an end, never as a means merely."[28] This, the second formulation Kant gives of the categorical imperative, is referred to as *the Formula of End in Itself*.

Kant believes that the two formulations of the categorical imperative given in the above are equivalent. He is committed to thinking this because he believes that there is *only one* supreme principle of morality, not several. He believes that any act whose maxim fails to pass the test of universalizability (the Formula of Universal Law) also fails the test of End in Itself, and vice versa, *and* that acts whose maxims pass the former test also pass the latter, and vice versa. There is no act, he thinks, that passes (or fails) one of the tests without also passing (or failing) the other. This assumed equivalence between the two formulations of the categorical imperative will occupy our attention at the conclusion of our discussion of Kant's position.

Kant's understanding of the foundation of morality, unlike Narveson's and Rawls's, is not egoistic. We are not to imagine that morality arises from, or consists in abiding by, agreements (contracts) reached by rational, self-interested individuals because it is in their long-term self-interest to do so. Indeed, for Kant, to view morality as grounded in self-interest is to leach the very life blood from it. What morality presupposes, on his view, is that, independently of any consideration of self-gain, individual moral agents can do what is right *because it is the right thing to do*. It is only when individuals do their duty, *because it is their duty*, that what they do has moral worth. To suppose, as Narveson and Rawls do, that the basis of morality is self-interest is to destroy the very possibility of morality, as Kant understands this. Moreover, though on Kant's view moral agents do stand in a relationship of reciprocity, in the sense that the fundamental direct duty I have to any moral agent is the very same duty that any moral agent has to me, the obligatoriness of my treating you with respect, as befits your independent value, is not contingent upon your treating me in a reciprocal way. The direct duties I have to you would not evaporate or diminish if you failed to fulfill your duties as they affect me, or vice versa. Such failure on your part, to fulfill your duties to me, which would destroy the very foundation of our moral relations given a view like Narveson's, would not cause the slightest tremor given Kant's view. Since I am not a participant in the moral game, so to speak, because of what I stand to gain by playing, the rules are not rescinded or eased by your behaving in ways that flaunt them and harm me. For my part, I must continue to act as morality requires, out of respect for what is right, not with a view to my self-interest.

While Kant's moral theory is not a version of egoism, it has affinities with the rational egoism of Narveson and the contractarianism of Rawls, when it comes to specifying those individuals to whom one has direct duties. On the rational egoism model, these are, as we know, those individuals, and only those individuals, who are themselves capable of entering into the "agreements" that are chosen to mutually regulate the behavior of individual rational egoists; moral patients in general and animals in particular are excluded. The same is true, though for different reasons, given Kant's position. Moral agents have direct duties *only* to moral agents, whether themselves or others. This is so, on Kant's view, because beings who exist but are nonrational have "only a relative value" and thus fail to be ends in themselves. Because they fail to have independent value, we have no direct duty to them to treat them, in accordance with the formula of End in Itself, in those ways we are duty-bound to treat those beings (rational beings, moral agents) who are ends in themselves. If we have duties to nonrational beings, they must be indirect duties, or duties having an indirect bearing on our discharging those duties we have directly to moral agents, ourselves or others.

We should expect, therefore, that, when he turns to the question of our duties involving animals, Kant would opt for an indirect duty view. Anything more than this would simply fly in the face of his considered views on the nature and foundation of morality. This is an expectation Kant fulfills. "So far as animals are concerned," he writes,

> we have no direct duties. Animals are not self-conscious and are there merely as a means to an end. That end is man. . . . Our duties to animals are merely indirect duties to mankind. Animal nature has analogies to human nature, and by doing our duties to animals in respect of manifestations of human nature, we indirectly do our duties to humanity. Thus, if a dog has served his master long and faithfully, his service, on the analogy of human service, deserves reward, and when the dog has grown too old to serve, his master ought to keep him until he dies. Such

action helps to support us in our duties towards human beings, where they are bounden duties. If then any acts of animals are analogous to human acts and spring from the same principles, we have duties towards the animals because thus we cultivate the corresponding duties towards human beings. If a man shoots his dog because the animal is no longer capable of service, he does not fail in his duty to the dog, for the dog cannot judge, but his act is inhuman and damages in himself that humanity which it is his duty to show towards mankind. If he is not to stifle his human feelings, he must practice kindness towards animals, for he who is cruel to animals becomes hard also in his dealings with men . . . (whereas) . . . tender feelings towards dumb animals develop humane feelings towards mankind.[29]

Three preliminary criticisms are worth making before moving on to assess Kant's general account of our duties involving animals. First, Kant is mistaken when he claims that "animals are not self-conscious." Arguments have been advanced earlier (2.5) that make ascriptions of self-consciousness to animals both intelligible and confirmable. Second, on one interpretation of what it means to "judge," it is false that a dog and, by implication, similar animals "cannot judge." If to judge that something is a bone requires (a) having a (even our) concept of bone and (b) applying that concept in a given case—that is, judging (believing) 'That is a bone'—then it is false, for reasons given in chapter 2, that "animals cannot judge." If, instead, Kant has some other kind of judgment in mind—in particular, if he means that animals cannot make *moral* judgments by making reference to the categorical imperative—then what he says is doubtless true. The same is true of moral patients generally, however, so that Kant cannot disqualify animals as objects of direct moral concern because they cannot make moral judgments unless he also is willing to disqualify all moral patients. And to disqualify *human* moral patients, as will be argued below, will cause serious problems indeed for Kant's general position. Third, in the passage just quoted Kant fails to support his assertion that animals exist "merely as a means to an end," that end being "man." And it is difficult to see how he could provide a compelling argument in this regard. The plausibility of viewing animals as having value only if or as they serve human ends lessens as we begin to recognize that, like relevantly similar humans, animals have a life of their own that fares better or worse for them, logically independently of their utility value for others. It is thus exceedingly unclear how it could be correct to suppose that *their* value is reducible, without remainder, to their utility to mankind, unless one is willing to make the same judgment in the case of humans like these animals in the relevant respects, which

Kant is not. This line of argument will be developed more fully momentarily.

These matters to one side, what shall we say of Kant's general account of our duties involving animals? Despite well-known exceptions (some Nazis practiced great kindness to animals), Kant's general psychological point may be right: people who are indifferent to the suffering they cause animals may come in time to form a habit of indifference and thus might be equally indifferent to the suffering they visit upon humans, while those who are sensitive in their dealings with animals may develop a habit of sensitivity that is also expressed in their dealings with humans. The point certainly is arguable, and some noted champions of better treatment for animals—George Bernard Shaw, for example—would seem to rest their unqualified opposition to the use of animals in science on a position like Kant's in the relevant respects. "We must," Shaw writes, "apply the test of character, and ask ourselves not merely, 'What will happen if I do this particular (experiment)?' but 'What sort of man will I be if I do it?' "[30] In Shaw's view, as in Kant's, it is the effects that our treating animals in certain ways has upon our character, and for Kant, and perhaps for Shaw as well, the effect our character has on how we treat human beings, that provide the grounds for morally approving or disapproving our treating animals in certain ways.

The contemporary English philosophers Alexander Broadie and Elizabeth M. Pybus dispute Kant's position on two counts, neither of which contests the accuracy of Kant's psychological speculation. (A variation of Kant's psychological argument will be offered in different contexts below, 9.1 and 9.4.) They argue, first, that Kant's position is "radically at odds with a sound ordinary view concerning our treatment of animals, namely, the view that animals, in so far as they have a capacity for suffering, are objects of direct moral concern,"[31] and, second, that Kant's view regarding our duties involving animals leads to absurdity and is internally inconsistent with other principles in his ethical theory. Though the former criticism is well founded, it is doubtful that the latter criticism is. The reasons Broadie and Pybus marshal in support of their second criticism are as follows:

> [Kant's] argument, put briefly, is to the effect that if human beings maltreat animals they will acquire a tendency to use rationality (in themselves or in other people) as a means. But, according to Kant, animals are, in the technical sense, things, and consequently are precisely what we should use as means. His argument therefore is that if we use certain things, viz. animals, as means, we will be led to use human beings as means.[32]

Something has gone wrong here. Kant never maintains that it is wrong to use animals as *means*—for example, as beasts of burden. What he does maintain is that the *maltreatment* of animals is wrong because it leads those who do so to treat persons in a similar way. And it is clear that Kant does not suppose—as, in the passage just quoted, Broadie and Pybus erroneously assume that he does—that the concept of maltreating an animal, on the one hand, and the concept of using an animal as a means, on the other, are the same or logically equivalent concepts. For we can, given Kant's views, use an animal as a means without at the same time necessarily maltreating it, as when, for example, a blind man uses a Seeing Eye dog but treats him with love and devotion.

This same error underlies the charge of absurdity and inconsistency that the authors level against Kant in bringing their argument to a head. They write:

> Thus, if [Kant] is to use the argument that using animals as *means* will lead us to use rationality as means, he must generalize it, and say that because of the effect on our behaviour towards other people, we ought never to use anything as a means, and we have an indirect duty not to do so. This is not merely absurd, but contrary to his imperative of skill (emphasis added).[33]

The point is, however, that Kant does *not* maintain that using animals as *means* will lead to the effects in question; what he does maintain is that *maltreating* them will. So Broadie and Pybus cannot argue that Kant's position leads to the absurd consequence that we have an indirect duty not to use any thing as a means on the ground that Kant holds that we have an indirect duty not to use animals in this way. Nor can they say that his view here is inconsistent with his imperative of skill. For what follows from what Kant says is not that we have an indirect duty not to use any thing as a means; what follows is that we have an indirect duty not to *maltreat* any thing, if, by doing so, we are led to use the rationality in ourselves or in others merely as a means.

Broadie and Pybus have a reply to this attempted defense of Kant. "For Kant," they write,

> whatever is not an end in itself cannot be an object of direct moral concern. But Kant holds that animals are not ends in themselves. If, therefore, we are to speak, as Kant wishes, of maltreating an animal, we are to speak of maltreating something which is not an object of direct moral concern. Now maltreatment is a moral concept, in so far as it refers to a mode of dealing with objects which is unfitting to their nature. But if animals are not objects of direct moral concern, then in what can maltreatment of them consist?[34]

The inference we are to make is that Kant's position will not allow him to give an account of how animals may be maltreated. But is this true? It would seem not.

The issue, it bears emphasizing, is not whether Kant provides us with an acceptable account of how animals may be treated; it is whether his ethical theory allows for the *possibility* of his presenting any account at all. It seems that it does. What Kant could argue is that maltreatment of those things that have value merely as means consists in treating them in ways that reduce their value as means, which, given the sort of value *they* have, *is* "unfitting to *their* nature." And he could then argue that since *things* have value merely as means, no moral wrong is thereby done *to them* when they are treated in ways that are "unfitting to their nature." Rather, the explanation of when and, if so, why maltreating things is morally wrong is that this will in time lead moral agents to maltreat individuals who exist as ends in themselves.

An example might make this clearer. An angry child who breaks his art supplies does not destroy something that exists as an end in itself; he destroys something that has value as a means. Now, the supplies, which have value merely as means, *have* been treated in a way that is "unfitting to their nature" as things to be used for painting. But no moral wrong is thereby done *to them*; the child violates no direct duty owed to the supplies. It does not follow, however, that we either would or must view his conduct as morally indifferent, or that we cannot follow Kant's lead in attempting to explain why his behavior should be nipped in the bud. After all, one ought not to let one's emotions get the best of one, not only because this will lead one to do some foolish things in a fit of rage (e.g., destroy art supplies one will later regret not having) but also because a repetition of such behavior could in time lead one to lash out in morally offensive ways toward those individuals toward whom one does have direct duties. Needlessly to destroy something that has value merely as a means arguably *is* to treat that thing in a way that is "unfitting to its nature"; but the *moral* grounds for objecting to such destruction *could* be viewed as distinctively Kantian in flavor. Despite objections to the contrary, therefore, Kant can have a consistent position regarding the maltreatment of things having value merely as a means. This much granted, it is a small step, given *his* view of animals, to see that his position regarding their maltreatment also is consistent with the general principles of his ethical theory. This is because animals are, in Kant's view, as Broadie and Pybus note, *things* and have "only a relative value." As things, then, we maltreat animals when we treat them in ways that reduce their value as means for those individuals for whom, in Kant's view, they exist in the first place—human beings. To treat animals in ways that diminish their utility for us is indeed to treat them in ways "unfitting to their nature," given Kant's view, since their nature is to exist as means to our purposes. But the grounds Kant has, and those he can consistently have, for objecting to the maltreatment of animals, are not that acting in this way is contrary to any direct duty we have to them; rather, as in the analogous case regarding the gratuitous destruction of the art supplies, the grounds he has, and can consistently have, lie in the (supposed) effects this will have on our character and thus, in his view, on how in time the habit of treating animals cruelly will lead us to fail to fulfill our direct duties to those to whom we have such duties—namely, ourselves and other human beings.

To defend the internal consistency of Kant's position, given his assumptions, is one thing. To defend its adequacy is quite another. That position cannot be any more adequate than the assumption that animals are *things* and, relatedly, that they have value "merely as a means to an end," that end being man. The assumption that animals are things is false at best. For reasons given in chapter 3, it is reasonable to view animals as having a welfare that is not logically tied to their use by humans to promote human ends. Moreover, while it is admittedly true that animals lack the kind of autonomy required for moral agency, it is false that they lack autonomy in any sense. For animals not only have preferences, they can also act, on their own, to satisfy these preferences. To view them, as Kant does, as—like art supplies—*things*, and thus as having, as art supplies have, value only relative to human desires and purposes, is radically to distort what animals are. Even were we to concede, contrary to Broadie and Pybus, that Kant's position is consistent, it does not follow that we should view it as adequate.

That Kant's assumptions are ill founded may perhaps be shown more clearly by considering the moral status of *human* moral patients, given his assumptions. By definition human moral patients are not moral agents and so, on Kant's principles, are not rational beings. Because they are not rational beings, they can have no value in their own right and must, instead, be viewed as things, having value "merely as a means to an end." It follows from this that we can do no direct moral wrong to any human moral patient. All that can be said about our moral dealings with such humans is that our duties involving them are indirect duties to rational beings. Thus, I do no moral wrong *to a child* if I torture her for hours on end. The moral grounds for objecting to what I do must be looked for elsewhere—namely, in the effects doing this will have on my character, causing me, so Kant's view supposes, to become "hard" in my dealings with human moral agents. But suppose I torture only one human moral patient in my life. Though I am squeamish at first, suppose I steel myself against my usual sensitivities and use all my imagination to visit horror upon the child. And suppose that, having satisfied myself of what I had supposed might be true—namely, that I have no taste for torture—I release my captive and never again indulge in torturing any human being again. The habit of cruelty finds no permanent home in my breast. Are we to say that therefore I did nothing wrong to my one and only torture victim? However implausible this must seem, Kant's position does imply that the correct answer is affirmative.

But Kant's position is worse than implausible; it is arbitrary. Let us suppose, for the sake of argument, that, as a result of the pleasure I take in causing human moral patients to suffer, I come in time to develop sadistic habits and that these in turn lead me to cause human moral agents to suffer. It would be quite remarkable, to say the least, if doing the one led me to do the other if there was no resemblance between how the two reacted to what I did to them. If, for example, putting human moral patients on the rack produced no behavioral evidence that this hurt them, then how could I reasonably infer that doing this to human moral agents would produce the suffering which, as a sadist, I enjoy inflicting? In order for the causal story to be at all plausible,[35] we must suppose that human moral patients, like human moral agents, can suffer *and* that they can manifest their anguish behaviorially in ways that resemble the ways human moral agents behave when they are made to suffer. If their behavior is similar, however, as it must be if I am to be led from causing the one to suffer to causing the other to suffer, it is reasonable to believe that their suffering also is similar. But if the suffering is similar, and if causing it in the case of moral agents violates a direct duty owed to them (as Kant allows), then how can we *nonarbitrarily* avoid the conclusion that causing suffering to human moral patients violates a direct duty owed to them? To reply that moral agents can act in accordance with the categorical imperative while human moral patients cannot is true but irrelevant. The issue concerns their *shared* capacity for suffering, not their differing abilities. If the duty not to cause moral agents gratuitous suffering is a duty owed directly to them, the same must be true of the duty not to do the same to human moral patients. Otherwise we flaunt the requirement of formal justice: we allow dissimilar treatment of *relevantly* similar cases. Kant's position does violate this requirement, and the violation of it, as we shall see more fully in a moment, is an unavoidable consequence of the moral arbitrariness of his theory.

A defender of Kant might object that Kant has been misinterpreted. It is, he holds, for *humanity generally, not just for human moral agents*, that things having value merely as a means, including animals, exist. Thus, *all* human beings, *not* just those who are moral agents, exist as ends in themselves, on his view, and the argument of the last paragraph is exposed as unfounded. Now, it may be that Kant *thinks* that all human beings, including human moral patients, exist as ends in themselves, but he cannot *consistently* think this. For since human moral patients lack the rational prerequisites for moral agency, they can have "only a relative value" and must, therefore, given Kant's understanding of these matters, be viewed as things. This attempted defense of Kant misfires, therefore, and only serves to sharpen the dilemma he must face: he must choose between viewing human moral patients as ends in themselves, so that being a moral agent is not a necessary (though it may be a sufficient) condition of being an end in itself, *or* viewing these humans as having "only a relative value" as things. If he chooses the former option, then we can have direct duties to human moral patients; if he chooses the latter, we cannot. Neither alternative is salutary for Kant. If the former is chosen, then he is obliged to surrender a central tenet of his ethical theory—namely, that *only* rational beings (i.e., only those who are moral agents) exist as ends in themselves. If the latter alternative is chosen, he is open to the charge of moral arbitrariness.

Though neither alternative is welcome news for Kantians, the selection of the nonarbitrary one has good sense and reason on its side. Human moral patients *are not things*; they *themselves* are individuals who have an experiential welfare; moral agency is *not* a necessary condition of being of direct moral concern. But logic plays no favorites. This same condition cannot be necessary in the case of other moral patients. If human moral patients are owed direct duties, so are those animals like them in the relevant respects. To deny that we have direct duties to those animals who have an experiential welfare, but to affirm this in the case of human moral patients like these animals in the relevant respects, *would* be symptomatic of an unsupported, and unsupportable, speciesist understanding of morality.

One final point, one that plumbs the depths of Kant's arbitrariness, merits our attention before moving on. As remarked earlier, Kant offers what he regards as alternative, equivalent formulations of the categorical imperative. Any act that passes the test of Universal Law also passes the test of End in Itself, and vice versa; and any act that fails the one also fails the other. This can be shown to be false. Suppose I am considering whether to be a vegetarian, not out of considerations that relate to my health but because I think that the intensive rearing of farm animals is wrong and is wrong because of how the animals are treated. If I make use of the Formula of Universal Law, there is no reason why I cannot universalize the relevant subjective maxim: no one is to support the intensive rearing of farm animals by purchasing meat from these sources. But now suppose I consult the Formula of End in Itself. That formula instructs me always to treat *humanity*, either in my own person or in the person of any other, always as an end, never as a means merely. But *how* am I to assess the morality of my moral objections to factory farming by reference to *that* formulation of the categorical imperative? Since the beings I am concerned about are not human beings, that formula provides me with *no possible guidance*. But if it provides me with no possible guidance, then the two formulae—that of Universal Law *and* End in Itself—are not equivalent after all. For though my subjective maxim about not supporting the intensive rearing of animals passes the test of Universal Law, the morality of supporting the intensive rearing of animals cannot even be tested by, let alone pass, the Formula of the End in Itself. The moral arbitrariness characterizing Kant's position thus makes its presence felt at the most fundamental level—at the level of his interpretation of the fundamental principle of morality. Only undefended prejudice could lead Kant to suppose that an expansive formulation of the fundamental principle of morality (that of Universal Law), one that allows us to test directly our maxims with regard to how animals may be treated, is equivalent to a restrictive formulation (that of End in Itself), one that has no direct bearing on questions relating to how animals may be treated. To limit the direct scope of the supreme principle of morality to how *humans* are to be treated arbitrarily favors these individuals as it arbitrarily excludes others.

5.6 THE MORAL ARBITRARINESS OF ALL INDIRECT DUTY VIEWS

In the past three sections we have considered representative indirect duty views and found them wanting, usually for reasons peculiar to the particular position under examination (e.g., the inequality just noted between Kant's two formulations of the categorical imperative). A common theme that emerged in the discussions of all three positions, however, was that of moral arbitrariness, and it will be useful in this final section to develop this theme more fully, both with a view to bringing our examination of indirect duty views to a close and as a way of preparing for our examination of direct duty views in the next chapter. The argument about to be developed involves making appeals to our intuitions. We know that this procedure is philosophically controversial, which is why the preceding discussions of representative indirect duty views included some criticisms of each view that did not involve such appeals. If these appeals are allowed, however, not only can we contest those indirect duty views we find in Narveson, Rawls and Kant by making such appeals (and we have contested each in places by making them), we can also mount an argument fatal to *any* indirect duty view. This is the argument to which we shall now direct our attention.

A suitable place to begin is with Ross's observation that "if we think we ought to behave in a certain way to animals, it is out of consideration primarily for their feelings that we ought to behave so; we do not think of them as a practicing-ground for virtue."[36] What Ross says here could be enlarged upon to include all moral patients like animals in the relevant respects (i.e., individuals who have beliefs, desires, memory, psycho-physical identity, a welfare, etc.). Neither young children nor the en-feebled, for example, are a "practicing ground" for moral agents in their pursuit of virtue. If we think it wrong to treat these humans in certain ways, we think this "primarily out of consideration for" (here we depart from Ross's way of putting the point) *their welfare*. Both these human beings and animals, Ross implies, are of direct moral concern and are owed some direct duties.

Ross certainly seems to be correct in his description of what some people think about the moral status of animals and, by implication, about humans like these animals in the relevant respects. The problem is, this evidently is not what everyone thinks. In particular, it evidently is not what those who subscribe to indirect duty views believe. To treat any moral patient well or ill, these views imply, is not to discharge any duty we have directly to that individual, and while it may be an exaggeration to say that how we treat moral patients is, on these views, merely a sort of moral warm-up for the really serious moral game played among moral agents, indirect duty views are committed to regarding how we treat moral patients as of no direct moral significance.

But the question is not just who thinks what about the moral status of moral patients. The question is, Which of the alternatives before us—the view that moral patients are of direct moral significance or the view that they are not—is the most reasonable view? This is a question Ross's description of "what we think," considered by itself, fails to answer. Because many, perhaps even most, people happen to think that we have some direct duties to moral patients, it does not follow that we do. Our prereflective intuitions do not wear their reasonableness on their sleeve. But while the reasonableness of our prereflective belief in the present case is not guaranteed just by the fact that we have it, reasons can be adduced in support of its claim to our considered assent.

The procedure for testing our prereflective intuitions, sketched in the previous chapter (4.3), is relevant here. It is to be assumed that we commit ourselves to making a conscientious effort to reach the best judgment we can, and we do this by striving to think about our prereflective beliefs impartially and coolly, against the backdrop of having as much relevant information as we can reasonably acquire, and mindful of the need to think rationally and consistently. We then reflectively review our intuitions with a view to determining which, if any, can withstand the heat of this process of critical assessment. If we make this effort in the present case, the following beliefs can be seen to have the necessary credentials to qualify as considered beliefs: It is wrong, other things being equal, to kill a moral agent, to make moral agents suffer, to deny moral agents access to opportunities for the satisfaction of their desires when it is in their interest to satisfy them (e.g., opportunities to secure basic physical health or access to the acquisition of skills, an education, or needed legal counsel). Now, these beliefs, and others besides, share an important feature. They all involve prohibitions against harming moral agents. For harms, as was argued in an earlier chapter (3.3), may take the form of inflictions or deprivations that diminish an individual's welfare, either by causing that individual gratuitous suffering, as is true of harms that are inflictions, or by denying that individual opportunities to satisfy desires or fulfill purposes that contribute to her welfare. Because these beliefs share this common feature, it is possible to articulate a general principle (*the harm principle*) that unifies them. This principle states that *we have a direct prima facie duty not to harm individuals.* To say that we have a *direct* duty means that we owe it to those individuals themselves, who fall within the scope of this principle, not to harm them, while to say that the duty is prima facie means that though this duty may be overridden in some cases (e.g., in self-defense), the burden of showing why and how it may be justifiably overridden must be borne by those who override it. When and how this principle can be overridden are issues explored at length in a later chapter (8.7ff.). At this juncture our interest lies in exploring how extensive the scope of the harm principle is, in particular whether it applies to all and only moral agents.

This cannot be what we believe if we share Ross's prereflective intuitions. If we share them, we believe that we have a prima facie direct duty not to cause moral patients to suffer or to cause them harm in other ways, *and* that the reason this is wrong is *because of the harm done to these individuals*, not because of how others (e.g., interested relatives of children, or pet-owners) will feel about the harm done. Those who accept indirect duty views must think that our intuitions are mistaken. How

might we rationally adjudicate this disagreement? To begin with, if advocates of indirect duty views could show that moral patients *cannot be
harmed*, then our intuitions, not their views, would have to be abandoned. Certainly we could not rationally hold that the harm principle
applies to our moral dealings with certain individuals if these individuals
cannot be harmed in the first place. However, the case has been made, in
chapter 3, that animals not only can be, they are harmed when, for
example, they are caused gratuitous suffering or are denied the opportunity to exercise their preference autonomy when it is in their interests to
do so. Thus, this attempt to overturn our prereflective intuitions about
the prima facie direct duty owed to these animals and to those humans
like these animals in the relevant respects, fails.

    In reply it might be objected that, though moral patients can be
harmed, their harm is never equal to the harm caused to moral agents. To
deny moral agents opportunities for the exercise of their liberties or to kill
them is to cause far more grievous harm, it might be claimed, than to deny
moral patients the opportunity to exercise their preference autonomy or
to kill them. Thus, it is a mistake to view the moral status of moral patients
as being equal to that of moral agents. The duty not to harm is a duty
owed directly to moral agents. Because the moral status of moral agents
and patients is not equal, this duty is an indirect duty in the case of moral
patients.

    This reply embodies an important confusion. The question at issue is
not whether, say, killing a moral agent and a moral patient are, other
things being equal, equally harmful. The question is whether we have
any direct duties to moral patients. This question is logically distinct from
the question about the *comparative magnitude* of harming a moral agent in a
given way, on the one hand, and harming a moral patient in a similar
way, on the other. For it may be true that harming either is directly wrong
and yet the wrong done when we do some things to a moral agent (e.g.,
kill one) is a greater harm than the harm done when we do the same to a
moral patient. Just because my harming you in one way (say I lock you in
a closet for two days) is, though wrong, *less* wrong than my harming you
in another way (say I torture you to death over a period of many weeks), it
does not follow that *only* in the latter case do I violate a direct duty I have
to you. The comparative harm done by two acts does not settle anything
whatever about whether the duties I violate in the two cases are direct or
indirect duties. That is the truth the reply under discussion fails to
recognize. (The issue of the magnitude of harms done to moral agents and
patients is explored more fully below, in 8.10).

    A different objection to the view that we have direct duties to moral patients does not deny that moral patients can be harmed but denies that they can ever be harmed in the same ways as moral agents. Individuals who are moral agents, this objection holds, can be harmed by denying them opportunities for advanced education or by denying them an equal voice in the affairs of their government. Moral patients cannot be harmed in these ways. Thus, this objection concludes, the harms done to moral agents are wrongs done directly to them, but the harms done to moral patients are not. And the duties in the former case are direct duties, but those in the latter are indirect.

This defense is right, up to a point. Because of our higher-order intellectual and other abilities, we who are moral agents can be harmed in ways moral patients cannot be. But both can be harmed in similar ways. To deny either a moral agent or a moral patient basic nutritional suste-nance, or to inflict gratuitous suffering on either, or to bring about either's untimely death *is* to harm the one just as surely as it is to harm the other. While granting that some of the ways moral agents can be harmed are peculiar to moral agents, we are right to insist that some of the ways they can be harmed are common to moral patients. When these common harms are at issue, to affirm that we have a direct duty to moral agents not to harm them but deny this in the case of moral patients is to flaunt the requirement of formal justice or impartiality, requiring, as it does, that similar cases be treated dissimilarly. And that is to fall far short of making an ideal moral judgment.

In view of the failure of the arguments for the opposite conclusion and assuming that no better arguments are in the offing, we are justified in maintaining that the harm principle's scope includes animals and those human moral patients like these animals in the relevant respects. There is no *nonarbitrary* way to narrow the scope of this principle to exclude moral patients. Accordingly, even were we *not* to share Ross's prereflective intuitions regarding these moral patients, even were we *initially* of the opinion that we have no direct duty to these moral patients not to harm them, critical reflection of the sort we have just engaged in would require us to change our opinion, if we are to be consistent and if we accept the harm principle.

The position favored here—that the duty not to harm moral patients is a duty we owe directly to them—can be strengthened by invoking the requirements of making an ideal moral judgment. Let us consider each in turn. Have we made our assessment of the principle's implications "coolly"? It is difficult to imagine how the opposite charge could be sustained. No wildly emotional claims have been made; the rhetoric of the passions has not been employed. Throughout, the effort has been made to make the case, in a disciplined, noninflammatory style, that the duty not to harm is a direct duty owed to normal mammalian animals, aged one year or more and to those other moral patients like these animals in the relevant respects. So at least one requirement of making an ideal moral judgment has been met.

A second requirement is that we be consistent, that we not assert or imply inconsistent propositions. People are not always the best judge of their rational foibles, including their inconsistencies, and so it is perhaps best to await the judgment of others concerning whether any inconsistencies can be detected in the argument of this last section. As an autobiographical remark, however, it is perhaps worth noting that I can neither see nor imagine how the charge of inconsistency could be sustained.

A third requirement is impartiality, which I have interpreted in terms of conforming to the principle of formal justice, of treating similar cases similarly. This is a requirement that has not been lost sight of. On the contrary, one common failing of the three indirect duty views discussed earlier is that *they* fail to meet this requirement. Indeed, once we have made the case that moral patients can be harmed, and can be harmed in ways that are in some cases similar to the ways moral agents can be harmed, respect for the requirement of impartiality will require that we make similar judgments about the harmful treatment of both. Understood in context, it is those who deny that we have direct duties to moral patients, not those who affirm this, who are guilty of failing to meet this requirement.

Fourth is the requirement of being informed, of having the relevant empirical considerations at hand and understanding them. Ideally, of course, we must have *all* the relevant empirical matters in tow, and no claim could be made that this ideal has been completely realized by the preceding discussion. Nevertheless, it is essential to note that the empirical considerations relevant to viewing animals as having an experiential welfare have been identified and defended in earlier chapters. These animals, and those human moral patients like them in the relevant respects, are conscious and sentient; have desires and preferences; have various cognitive abilities including memory and the ability to form beliefs, including beliefs about their own future; are agents in the world in the sense that they can act intentionally or purposively to bring about the satisfaction of their desires or preferences; are self-aware or self-conscious; have a psychophysical identity over time; and so on. The empirical grounds for viewing animals in these ways have been canvassed, and representative arguments challenging these findings have been considered and found wanting. This by itself does not constitute incontrovertible proof of the view of animals favored here, but it is fair to say that the case made for viewing them in this way has been explored in more depth and with greater care than we find in the case of Kant, for example. Though the ideal of "complete information" has not been fulfilled, it has not gone unnoticed either.

The fifth requirement for making an ideal moral judgment is that of relying on a correct or valid moral principle. In the preceding chapter some of the most important criteria for evaluating moral principles, and the theories of which they form a part, were sketched, and it will be useful to apply these criteria to the harm principle. The first criterion is that a moral principle cannot be adequate if it is inconsistent—if, in particular, it implies that the very same act can be both right and wrong. The harm principle does not have this implication. To inflict gratuitous suffering on anyone who can suffer, be they moral agent or moral patient, is wrong, according to this principle, no matter what morally responsible agent does it, no matter when the act is performed, or where. It is not as if, say, doing this while in England is wrong but doing it in California is quite all right.

The second criterion is that of adequate scope. Does the principle in question unify, by identifying relevant grounds for, a wide range of cases, and may it therefore be appealed to and relied on when we are faced with making decisions in a large number of situations? The wider the scope, the greater the principle's potential use. The harm principle does have considerable scope, applying, as it does, to how we may treat *any* moral agent *or* patient. It does not follow, of course, that it is enough by itself to cover all moral matters, and, for reasons offered in subsequent chapters, there are grounds for denying that it does. Having said this, however, it remains true that the harm principle has considerable scope and so cannot be rejected on the grounds that it is too narrow in its application to be of much use.

Precision is the third criterion relevant to assessing moral principles. This is an essential requirement since, unless we are clear on what a moral principle means, we will have no clear way of determining what it requires. The harm principle has that degree of precision it is reasonable to expect and require of a moral principle. The notion of harm has been explained at length, so that anyone who understands that explanation also understands what the principle rules out as prima facie wrong. Granted, the notion of harm is not as precise as ideas we find in, say, geometry, where a square, for example, can be given an exact definition. But morality is not geometry, and it would be unreasonable, as Aristotle implies when he makes his observation about how much precision an educated person would and should expect in different subjects, to demand that the notion of harm be defined with mathematical precision.

The last criterion identified was that of conforming with our (considered, reflective) intuitions. A good deal has been said on this score already. The harm principle unifies, by identifying the relevant grounds for, a large number of our reflective intuitions. Many of these intuitions involve beliefs about direct duties owed to moral agents (e.g., that it is prima facie wrong to kill them or deprive them of their liberty). So, to give up the harm principle—to reject it—would leave one with the challenge of trying to find *another* principle that is equal to or better than the harm principle in the relevant respects (i.e., in terms of scope, consistency, precision, and conformity with our reflective intuitions). It is not *logically* impossible that there might be such a principle, and to claim that, though this is possible, there is no other equally good or better principle would be unjustified at this stage in the argument. At the same time the onus of proof must be borne by those who think otherwise. Since a strong presumptive case has been made that the harm principle meets the relevant criteria for evaluating a moral principle, the challenge of showing that there is another principle that satisfies these criteria to an equal or better extent must be met by those who would deny or replace it.

The preceding does not constitute a strict proof of the harm principle—proof of the sort one can give in, say, geometry. But just as it is unreasonable to expect definitions in morality that are as precise as those we find in geometry, it is similarly unreasonable to expect proof of the same kind. This does not mean that we must regard this principle as self-evident. Reasons *can* be given for accepting it. This is what has been attempted in the present section. To show that the harm principle meets the criteria appropriate for evaluating moral principles, so far as one ever can "show" this, and to defend, as has been done (4.6), the most controversial criterion we have appealed to—namely, conformity with our reflective intuitions—is as much as can reasonably be expected. Without having to claim that this principle is self-evident, we have *good reasons* to accept the harm principle even though we cannot give, and should not be expected to give, a proof of that principle comparable to proofs in geometry.

To have made the case for acceptance of the harm principle, given all that this case involves and implies, is to undermine the credibility of any indirect duty view. The harm principle's scope cannot be nonarbitrarily limited to all and only moral agents; it must apply to all those whose experiential welfare can be adversely affected by harms, whether inflictions or deprivations. Moral agents can be harmed in these ways, and so we have a direct prima facie duty in their case not to harm them. But animals also can be harmed in these ways, as can human moral patients like these animals in the relevant respects. Thus has the case been made, to the extent any moral case can be made, for acknowledging that we also have a direct prima facie duty in their case not to harm them. To deny this, given the reasonableness of the harm principle, can only be a symptom of moral arbitrariness. Since, by definition, *all* indirect duty views deny that we have any direct duties to moral patients, no indirect duty view can provide us with an adequate moral theory. The theme of arbitrariness that recurred in our earlier discussions of representative indirect duty views thus proves to be illustrative of the moral arbitrariness that must plague them all. (The moral arbitrariness of indirect duty views is diagnosed at a deeper level below, 8.12.)

5.7 SUMMARY AND CONCLUSION

The chapter began by drawing a distinction between direct and indirect duty views (5.1). The former hold that at least some of the duties we have involving animals are duties we owe directly to animals; the latter hold that all those duties we have regarding animals are indirect duties owed to others (e.g., God). Only indirect duty views were discussed. Such views are not speciesist if the reason for denying direct duties to animals is their failing to be moral agents, since many human beings (e.g., children and the retarded) also lack this status. Like animals, these humans are moral patients (5.2); they can neither do what is right nor what is wrong, but they may be on the receiving end, so to speak, of the right and wrong acts performed by others. Indirect duty views attempt to account for our duties involving moral patients while denying that we either do or can do anything right or wrong directly to them.

Representative indirect duty views were considered and rejected, the rational egoism of Jan Narveson (5.3) because, among other reasons, it could sanction grossly unjust institutional arrangements between moral agents; the contractarianism of John Rawls (5.4) because, among other reasons, those in the original position are arbitrarily allowed to know that they will not be animals when they are "incarnated"; and Immanuel Kant's respect for humanity (5.5) because, among other reasons, it rests on an impoverished understanding of what animals are.

The demonstrable arbitrariness of indirect duty views provided a backdrop for identifying a moral principle (the harm principle) that applies to our treatment both of moral agents and moral patients (5.6). That principle lays down a prima facie direct duty not to harm any relevantly similar individual who can be harmed—that is, any individual who has beliefs and desires, is capable of acting intentionally, and so forth, and who has an experiential welfare. The case for accepting this principle was made by making reference to its success in meeting the relevant criteria for evaluating moral principles (consistency, adequate scope, precision, and conformity with our reflective intuitions) and by explaining that our judgment of its validity was made, so far as it is reasonable to hope, in compliance with the relevant conditions of an ideal moral judgment (impartiality, rationality, information, and "coolness"). Though not proven in the way that, say, the Pythagorean Theorem can be proven in Euclidean geometry, the arguments given in support of the harm principle provide good reasons for accepting it. Any ethical theory that fails to account for our prima facie direct duty not to harm *moral agents and moral patients* cannot be an adequate theory, all considered. Necessarily, therefore, no indirect duty view can command our rational assent. Whether any direct duty view passes this test is the central question examined in the chapter that awaits us.

6

Direct Duty Views

U nlike the views examined in the previous chapter, those examined in the present one recognize at least some direct duties to moral patients and thus are not open to the objection of moral arbitrariness fatal to all versions of indirect duty views. Like these latter views, however, direct duty views openly espouse or imply that we can provide an adequate account of our duties regarding moral patients without appealing to their rights. To demonstrate the inadequacy of direct duty views is therefore necessary as a preliminary to making the case for the rights of moral patients. As was true in the previous examination of indirect duty views, not all direct duty views can be examined, but, as in that previous case, those considered are the strongest, not the weakest.

Two views will be examined: (1) act utilitarianism and (2) a position that attempts to account for our duties regarding animals by prohibiting cruelty and enjoining kindness. This latter position has no commonly accepted name, but it will be useful to give it one. Let us refer to it as *the cruelty-kindness view*; the defects of this view will be exposed first.

6.1 THE CRUELTY-KINDNESS VIEW

Especially among those affiliated with organizations that labor for the better treatment of animals, the position is often expressed that we ought not to be cruel to animals and ought rather to be kind to them. Those who express this view are not committed to believing, as, for example, Kant does, that the reason why we ought to be the one and ought not to be the other lies in the effects such treatment will have on how we treat human beings. Proponents of this view may and, in most cases, do believe that these are duties we owe directly to animals, the prohibition against cruelty encapsulating our negative duties to animals (how they are *not* to be treated) and the injunction to be kind encapsulating our positive duties in their case (how they *are* to be treated). It is only when understood in this way that the cruelty-kindness view will concern us.

It is unclear whether those who subscribe to this view would be willing to generalize it to include our treatment of human moral patients like animals in the relevant respects, but it is difficult to see how they could avoid this without being arbitrary. If it is because animals are moral patients, and not because they are animals, that we have the duties against cruelty and for kindness in their case, then we should also have these same duties directly to human moral patients. Granted, we may have other duties to human moral patients—such as, the duty to provide children with opportunities for an education. But however many other duties we may or may not have to human moral patients, it is reasonable to assume that we have some of the same duties in their case as we have in the case of animals *and* that, among these common duties, those who advocate the cruelty-kindness view would recognize the two duties at hand. For the purposes of the discussion below, however, it is not essential that an advocate of this view recognize any of the same direct duties in the case of human moral patients as, on this view, are owed to animals. It is enough that those who advocate this view believe that (a) we have negative and positive duties directly to animals, and (b) these direct duties can be adequately accounted for, respectively, by reference to the prohibition against cruelty and to the injunction to be kind. This view, for reasons that will become apparent as we proceed, fails to provide a satisfactory basis either for our negative or for our positive duties to animals. This can be shown by first exposing the deficiencies of the prohibition against cruelty in this regard.

Cruelty

It would be difficult to find anyone who is in favor of cruelty, and when individuals and organizations champion the cause of animal welfare by denouncing cruelty to animals, they strike a responsive moral chord. Theoretically, however, our negative duties to animals are not adequately grounded if we rest them on the prohibition against cruelty. This becomes clear once we become clearer about the idea of cruelty itself.

Cruelty is manifested in different ways. People can rightly be judged cruel either for what they do or for what they fail to do, and either for what they feel or for what they fail to feel. The central case of cruelty appears to be the case where, in Locke's apt phrase,[1] one takes "a seeming kind of Pleasure" in causing another to suffer. Sadistic torturers provide perhaps the clearest example of cruelty in this sense: they are cruel not just because they cause suffering (so do dentists and doctors, for example) but because they enjoy doing so. Let us term this *sadistic cruelty*.

Not all cruel people are cruel in this sense. Some cruel people do not feel pleasure in making others suffer. Indeed, they seem not to feel anything. Their cruelty is manifested by a lack of what is judged appropriate feeling, as pity or mercy, for the plight of the individual whose suffering they cause, rather than pleasure in causing it; they are, as we say, insensitive to the suffering they inflict, unmoved by it, as if they were unaware of it or failed to appreciate it as *suffering*, in the way that, for example, lions appear to be unaware of, and thus are not sensitive to, the pain they cause their prey. Indeed, precisely because one expects indifference from animals but pity or mercy from human beings, people who are cruel by being insensitive to the suffering they cause often are called "animals" or "brutes," and their character or behavior, "brutal" or "inhuman." Thus, for example, particularly ghastly murders are said to be "the work of animals," the implication being that these are acts that no one moved by the human feelings of pity or mercy could bring themselves to perform. The sense of cruelty that involves indifference to, rather than enjoyment of, suffering caused to others we shall call *brutal cruelty*.

Cruelty of either kind, sadistic or brutal, can be manifested in active or passive behavior. Passive behavior includes acts of omission and negligence; active, acts of commission. A man who, without provocation, beats a dog into unconsciousness is actively cruel, whereas one who, through negligence, fails to feed his pet to the point where the dog's health is impoverished is passively cruel, not because of what he does but because of what he fails to do. Both active and passive cruelty have fuzzy borders. For example, a woman is not cruel if she occasionally fails to feed her cat. She *is* cruel if she fails to do so most of the time. But while there is no exact number of times, no fixed percentage, such that, once it is realized, cruelty is present, otherwise not, there are paradigms nonetheless.

We have, then, at least two kinds of cruelty (or two senses of the word *cruelty*) and two different ways in which cruelty can be manifested. Theoretically, therefore, cruelty admits of at least four possible classifications: (1) active sadistic cruelty; (2) passive sadistic cruelty; (3) active brutal cruelty; and (4) passive brutal cruelty. Let us grant that all varieties of cruelty ought to be condemned and discouraged. The question that remains is, granting this, does anticruelty, in any or all of its forms, provide an adequate basis for our negative duties to animals? It does not. For cruelty, in all of its forms, necessarily involves reference to an individual's mental state—namely, whether one takes pleasure in causing or allowing another to suffer or whether one is indifferent to doing this. Thus, if anticruelty were advanced as a basis for our negative duties to animals, it would follow that we fulfill our negative duties to them so long as we are not cruel to them—that is, so long as we do not enjoy, or are not indifferent to, causing or allowing them to suffer. This is manifestly inadequate. How one *feels* about what one does is logically distinct from the moral assessment of *what* one does. More particularly, how one feels about the suffering one causes an animal is logically distinct from whether it is wrong to make the animal suffer. To make an animal suffer is not justified just on the grounds that one is not indifferent to its suffering, or just on the grounds that one does not enjoy making it suffer. In other words, to make an animal suffer is not justified just on the grounds that the one who makes it suffer is not cruel, in any or all of cruelty's various forms. So, while we can agree that cruelty is to be condemned and ought to be discouraged, we must not agree that the prohibition against cruelty provides a satisfactory basis for our negative duties to animals.

Kindness

Kindness perhaps is an idea second only to cruelty in terms of its currency in discussions about our treatment of animals. "Be kind to animals," we are enjoined, and few, if any, would take exception to the spirit of this injunction. But, like the prohibition against cruelty, the prescription to be kind will not bear the weight some people want to place on it. It simply will not do the job of grounding our positive duties to animals.

Like *cruel, kind* and its cognates are terms of moral appraisal we use to assess and describe a person's acts or character. A kind person is one who is inclined (disposed) to act with the intention of forwarding the interests of others, not for reasons of self-gain, but out of love, affection, or compassion for the individual whose interests are forwarded. Kind people, in a word, are not selfish, not ones who act to forward the interests of another only if or so long as doing so forwards their own interests.

What, then, does the injunction to be kind to animals mean? It means either that, when it comes to this or that individual act, we are to treat animals in such a way that our intention is to forward their interests, not from a selfish motive but out of love, affection, or compassion for them, *or* that we are to cultivate, through such individual actions, the disposition to treat animals in this way for these reasons. And there is no denying the moral worth of the ideal that the injunction to be kind, interpreted in either of these ways, places before us. And yet, for reasons in some cases not unlike those given against the view that the prohibition against cruelty can satisfactorily serve as the basis for our negative duties to animals, the injunction to treat animals kindly fails to provide us with a satisfactory basis for our positive duties.

First, kindness, like cruelty, has conceptual connections with "the mind of the agent"—namely, with the agent's motives and intentions. And this invites the same observation in the case of kindness as was apposite in the earlier case of cruelty: the morality of what persons do (the rightness or wrongness of their actions) is logically distinct from, and should not be confused with, their "mental states," including the motives or intentions from which their acts proceed. While those who act kindly deserve our moral admiration, they deserve this not because they thereby do what is right (possibly they do, but possibly they do not); they deserve this because they exhibit their goodness as people. So, just as the evil that cruelty is must be kept distinct from judging a cruel act wrong, the good that kindness is must be kept distinct from judging a kind act right.

Second, the injunction to be kind to animals must fail to capture or account for the idea that we *owe* it to animals to treat them in certain ways, that treating them thus-and-so is something that is *due* to them. The injunction in question cannot capture or account for this because kindness is not something we *owe* to anybody, is not *anyone's* due. To be the beneficiary of a kind act no doubt generally is to be blessed, but no one has a claim on anyone else's kindness. Kindness is not justice, and to the extent that animals are owed just treatment (see below, 7.6ff.), we cannot look to the injunction that we be kind to animals as a principle that accounts, or even helps to account, for this dimension of our duties to animals. For these reasons, then, the injunction to be kind to animals, like the prohibition not to be cruel to them, cannot serve as a principle on which to rest our direct duties to animals.

There is a lesson to be learned from the cruelty-kindness view's failure to provide an adequate basis for our duties to animals. No view can provide an adequate account of these duties if it requires that we make reference to the mind of the agent (to either the agent's motives or intentions). Whatever else might be said about the second view to be considered in this chapter—utilitarianism—it at least cannot be faulted for this reason.

To speak of *the view* known as utilitarianism, as we know from the earlier sketch of utilitarian theory (4.4), is to speak somewhat loosely. Utilitarians all agree that consequences and consequences alone determine the morality of what we do. And they all agree that it is "the best" consequences for everyone affected by the outcome that we should aim to bring about. But not all utilitarians agree on what makes some consequences better than others or on whether the principle of utility should be directly applied to individual actions or used to validate rules. In order to make my examination more orderly, I will begin by considering the position of the hedonistic utilitarians—Bentham and Mill. Later in this chapter I will discuss a contemporary alternative to this view, the *preference utilitarianism* advanced by Peter Singer (6.3). Though it is not always clear whether the utilitarians in question should be interpreted as act utilitarians or rule utilitarians, I shall limit the examination to the former throughout the present chapter. Whenever the word *utilitarianism* and its cognates occur, therefore, this should be understood as an abbreviation for "act utilitarianism" and its cognates. Rule utilitarianism will be examined in the following chapter (sec. 7.7).

6.2 HEDONISTIC UTILITARIANISM

The classical utilitarians are hedonists. They hold that pleasure and pleasure alone is intrinsically good, and pain and pain alone intrinsically evil. To determine what the best consequences would be in any given case, they think, we must determine which alternative available to us will bring about the optimum balance of pleasure over pain for everyone affected by the outcome. If there is some one alternative that will do this, that is the one we have a duty to select. If there are two options that will produce equally good results, and none that will produce any better, then it does not matter which of the two we choose, only that we morally ought to choose one of them. What we must never do, what is always wrong, is to select an option that will bring about less than the optimal balance of pleasure over pain.

To speak of the optimal balance of pleasure over pain for everyone affected by the outcome illustrates the *aggregative nature* of all forms of utilitarianism. Instead of asking what will bring about the best results for me personally, which is what I should ask given rational egoism, I must ask what will bring about the best results for everyone involved, and selecting an option that brings about the best *aggregative* results for everyone might not be the same as selecting the option that brings about the best results for me personally. This point can be illustrated by means of the following abstract example.[2] Suppose we assign a plus score ("+") to pleasures and a minus score ("−") to pains; suppose there are four individuals who will be affected by what is done (Black, White, Yellow, and Red); suppose that White is the individual who must decide what to do, facing a choice between two alternatives (A_1 and A_2); and suppose the consequences of his selecting A_1 and A_2 are, respectively, as follows:

Consequences of Selecting A_1

Individuals	Pleasures	Pains	Net per individual
Black	+5	−20	−15
White	+30	−10	+20
Yellow	+5	−20	−15
Red	+5	−20	−15

Consequences of Selecting A_2

Individuals	Pleasures	Pains	Net per individual
Black	+15	−10	+5
White	+10	−15	−5
Yellow	+20	−25	−5
Red	+20	−25	−5

The consequences for White would clearly be better if he chose A_1 than if he chose A_2 (+20 if A_1 is chosen, −5 if A_2 is). But that is not the alternative White should choose, given hedonistic utilitarianism. What every moral agent must do is choose that option, if there is one, that will bring about the best aggregative results—the optimal balance of pleasure over pain— for *everyone* affected by the outcome. And that would require that White opt for A_2, as can be seen by totaling the pluses and minuses, not only for White alone but for the four individuals involved. A_1 yields a total of +20 and −45 for a net of −25; A_2 yields a total of +5 and −15, for a net of −10. A better *aggregative* balance of pleasure and pain is thus obtained by choosing A_2, even though White would personally be better off if he chose A_1. What White *morally* ought to do, then, is A_2. He may not want to do it. He may dislike doing it. He may complain. But no one ever said doing what morality requires is always easy, and it is no objection to hedonistic or other forms of utilitarianism to note that they can require that we ought to do something we don't want to do. Morally, it is the best *aggregative* balance we must aim to achieve, not what's best for us personally.

Hedonistic utilitarianism must seem a congenial position to anyone who thinks we have some direct duties to animals. After all, the pleasures and pains of *everyone* affected by the outcome of what we do must be taken into account. The position will not allow us to consider the pleasures or pains of some (e.g., our friends or fellow citizens) and ignore the pleasures and pains of others (e.g., strangers or foreigners). *Everyone's* pains and pleasures count, a position that, given the reasonableness of viewing animals as having pleasant and painful sensations, implies that their pleasures and pains count too. Moreover, impartiality requires that we make similar judgments about relevantly similar cases. If it ever is true that the pains and pleasures of animals are relevantly similar to those of moral agents, then we must count the value of the animals' pleasures and pains as being equal to that of moral agents' pleasures and pains. Since in some cases, most notably the case of acute physical suffering, what is experienced by animals and moral agents is relevantly similar, the value or disvalue of what they experience must not only be counted but *counted equally*. A strong *egalitarianism*, one that knows no species boundaries, characterizes hedonistic utilitarianism. In Bentham's famous words, "Each to count for one, no one for more than one." From the point of view of hedonistic utilitarianism, animals have a vote in the moral affairs of the world equal to the vote of moral agents, when the pleasures or pains of both are equal. Paradigmatic speciesism, latent in Kant's view perhaps, has no foothold in this version of utilitarianism. *All* sentient creatures, whether humans or animals, are members of the moral community and are all directly owed some of the same duties.

Much to their lasting credit, the classical utilitarians championed the cause of animal welfare, something for which all who work for the improved treatment of animals are indebted. Despite their salutary efforts, however, and notwithstanding the initial attractiveness of their egalitarian enfranchisement of animals into the moral community, hedonistic utilitarianism faces insuperable objections. And it is a good thing that it does; for though on its surface this version of utilitarianism seems to provide more than enough protection for the welfare of animals and those human moral patients like animals in the relevant respects, appearances are deceiving. Hedonistic utilitarianism has the appearance of the long-awaited draft of truth only because of the arid landscape animals occupy given indirect duty views. Once we look closely into the cup it offers, we will think twice before we drink.

Killing Moral Agents

I will begin this assessment by first considering the implications for moral agents of hedonistic utilitarianism. We have a prima facie direct duty not to harm moral agents, including not to kill them. That is a position defended in the previous chapter (5.6). Any adequate ethical theory must be able to account for the strictness of this duty. Hedonistic utilitarianism cannot. The argument that shows this follows.

How must the hedonistic utilitarian approach questions about the morality of killing moral agents? The pleasures and pains of the victim must be considered certainly, including the foreseeable pleasures and pains he would have had, had he not been killed. But the victim's pleasures and pains carry no more moral weight than the equal pleasures and pains of anyone else. To count his pleasures or pains more heavily is ruled out by the egalitarianism claimed as one of the virtues of classical utilitarianism. Since "each is to count for one, no one for more than one," the victim cannot have more than one vote, so to speak, in the determination of whether it would be wrong to kill him. Provided that, by killing the agent in question, the optimal *aggregate* balance of pleasure over pain is secured, the hedonistic utilitarian not only cannot find any moral fault with the killing, his theory positively requires that it be done.

Such a result clashes with our reflective intuitions about the wrongness of killing. Killing a moral agent is so grievous a moral wrong, we think, that it can only be justified under very special circumstances (e.g., self-defense; see below, 8.10ff.). The hedonistic utilitarian's position makes killing too easy to justify. It is not only in *exceptional* circumstances that killing is permissible—quite *ordinary* circumstances would allow it.

Hedonistic utilitarians are not unaware that their theory seems to run grossly counter to bedrock moral beliefs, and it is a mark of the seriousness with which they themselves view this problem that they advance arguments which, if nothing else, are ingenious in their attempt to save this theory. Their principal argument is as follows: As moral agents we have a sense of our own mortality. We understand that we are not destined for eternal life, not on this planet at least, and we sometimes worry about this, which is the occasion for some unpleasant or painful mental perturbations. The knowledge we have that moral agents sometimes *kill* other moral agents is one of the things that contributes to our anxiety about our own death. This knowledge causes insecurity in our dealings with others, and this insecurity is detrimental to the hedonistic utilitarian's objective of producing the best balance of pleasure over pain for all concerned. To assess the morality of killing, therefore, we need to take into account more than just the pleasures and pains of those directly involved: the killer and the victim. We also need to take into account the worry, anxiety, and insecurity caused others who live with the knowledge that the killing has occurred. Once we do this, the hedonistic utilitarian argues, we recognize that killing is wrong, when it is, largely because of its *side effects*—because of the anxiety and other unpleasantness caused the survivors who learn of the incident. Paradoxically, that is, the principal reason why killing moral agents is wrong is not because of the harm done to the victims; primarily it is because of the harm done to the survivors.

This reply cannot carry the weight hedonistic utilitarians place on it. Its deficiencies can be highlighted by considering killings done in secrecy. A successful secret killing cannot cause the side effects that figure so prominently in the hedonistic utilitarian's account of the wrongness of killing. Given that the murder is committed in secrecy, the general public has no knowledge of it and so cannot lose sleep over its occurrence. If we imagine that an undetected murder did bring about the optimal balance of pleasure over pain for those affected by its outcome, then the hedonistic utilitarian could have no moral grounds to object to it; indeed, *his* theory *justifies* it. This result also clashes with our reflective intuitions about the wrongness of killing. The secrecy of a murder makes no moral difference to its wrongness, or if it makes any difference it actually compounds the wrong rather than diminishing it. Since those who murder in secrecy deserve to be punished for their offense, and since, because of the secrecy of their act, they never are detected or punished, justice is not done in their case, and this adds to the moral offensiveness of what they do. Hedonistic utilitarianism thus fails on two counts, failing to account *both* for the wrong done by secret killings *and* for the wrong attaching to the unknown criminal's escaping punishment. Because hedonistic utilitarians themselves attempt to show how their theory can illuminate our intuitions about the wrongness of killing, appeals to these intuitions in assessing the adequacy of their theory, even if such appeals could not be independently justified, are entirely appropriate.

Killing Moral Patients

The failure of the hedonistic utilitarian's account of the wrongness of killing moral agents is an important failure for those who believe that serious moral questions also arise in the case of killing moral patients. If the hedonistic utilitarian's account was adequate in the case of killing moral agents, it would be difficult to avoid the implication that it provides a satisfactory account of the morality of killing moral patients, and that would be an unwelcome result for those who want a firm basis for objecting to killing these latter individuals. For consider: If the morality of killing were properly assessed in terms of how much mental anguish the killing of some individuals causes others, then the door would be open to a lot of killing of moral patients, both humans and animals, especially if this is done painlessly. Bentham sees this implication of hedonistic utilitarianism clearly in the case of animals when he writes that "the death they (i.e., animals) suffer in our hands commonly is, and always may be, speedier, and by that means a less painful one, than that which awaits them in the inevitable course of nature."[3] But animals are not the only moral patients of whom this is true. Unloved or unwanted children, or burdensome mental incompetents of any age, could be killed "humanely" by appeal to the same criteria: their painless death would be a "speedier, and by that means a less painful one, that that which awaits them in the inevitable course of nature." Indeed, there is no reason why the same argument might not be extended to the "humane" killing of *any* young child, since, as Bentham recognizes, killing young children is "of a nature not to give the slightest inequitude to the most timid imagination."[4] "Once we are old enough to comprehend the policy," as Peter Singer observes, "we are too old to be threatened by it."[5] But while the killing of human moral patients could be justified along Benthamite lines, the status of animals calls for special note. After all, since humans can have no serious worry that the employees in the nation's slaughterhouses, to use farm animals as a working example, will any day now turn to slaughtering human beings, our knowing that these animals are killed will not occasion "the slightest inequitude" in our breast. Moreover, by the time these animals are slaughtered, the pain caused to *other* animals as a result of physical separation (e.g., when a bobby calf is taken from his mother) has already occurred at a time well in the past; the actual killing of these animals is therefore quite unlikely to cause any (or much) anguish or insecurity to those animals who survive. The *apparent* attractiveness of hedonistic utilitarianism is just that—apparent.

Individuals as Receptacles

If we agree that hedonistic utilitarianism makes killing too easy to justify, we may then go on to ask what there is about this position that leads to this unhappy consequence. One way of diagnosing its fundamental weakness is to note that it assumes that both moral agents and patients are, to use Singer's helpful terminology, *mere receptacles* of what has positive value (pleasure) or negative value (pain). They have no value of their own; what has value is what they contain (i.e., what they experience). An analogy might be helpful. Suppose we think of moral agents and patients as cups into which may be poured either sweet liquids (pleasures) or bitter brews (pains). At any given time, each cup will have a certain hedonic flavor: the liquid it contains will be more or less sweet or bitter. Now, what we are to aim to bring about, according to hedonistic utilitarianism, is not the best-tasting liquid for this or that particular individual; rather, what we must aim to achieve is the best aggregated balance of the sweet and the bitter among all those individuals affected by what we do; it is the *best total balance* of the sweet over the bitter that we aim to realize. That being so, there is no reason why it may not be necessary to redistribute the contents of any given cup among the others or, indeed, why it may not be necessary to destroy a given cup ("receptacle") quite completely. The hedonistic utilitarian cannot object to such redistribution or destruction, if this is necessary to bring about the best balance of sweet over bitter, considered aggregatively, for all the cups involved, assuming, as always, that the sweet and bitter liquids in all the cups have been considered and counted equitably. That is how and why hedonistic utilitarianism can sanction successful secret killings: one receptacle (one "cup") is destroyed, with the result that the cups affected by the outcome obtain a better aggregative balance of the sweet (pleasure) over the bitter (pain) than was otherwise achievable. Fundamentally, then, it is how hedonistic utilitarians view individuals of direct moral concern, together with the utilitarian injunction to bring about the best consequences, that leads to unsavory moral implications. Seen in this light it is easy to understand why someone might think that utilitarianism could avoid these implications if hedonism and, by implication, its view that individuals of direct moral concern are mere receptacles, were renounced. Just such a version of utilitarianism is advanced by Singer, whose positive position we shall now turn to consider.

6.3 PREFERENCE UTILITARIANISM

Singer refers to his position as *preference utilitarianism*. On his view, those consequences we ought to aim to produce, those consequences that are "the best," are those that, on balance, "further the interests (i.e., desires or preferences) of those affected." And this, though it differs from "classical utilitarianism," he states, "is a form of utilitarianism."[6] Suppose that it is. How might this form of utilitarianism be used to explain why killing is wrong? The key to the preference utilitarian account, as Singer sees this, lies in recognizing that some individuals not only prefer things here and now, they also have preferences regarding their future, in particular *a preference to go on living*. Since the preference utilitarian holds that "an action contrary to the preferences of any being, unless this preference is outweighed by stronger contrary preferences, (is) wrong," it follows that killing individuals "who prefer to continue living is therefore wrong, other things being equal. Unlike classical utilitarianism," Singer continues, "preference utilitarianism makes killing *a direct wrong done to the (individual) killed*, because it is an act contrary to his or her preference. That the victim is not around after the act to lament the fact that his or her preferences have been disregarded is irrelevant."[7]

On Singer's view, then, whether the killing of any individual, A, is a direct wrong to A depends on whether A has the desire (prefers) to go on living. Having this *particular* desire, in other words, is both a necessary and a sufficient condition of killing's being a direct wrong. By making this desire a necessary condition Singer fails to account for why we have a direct prima facie duty not to harm, by killing, animals and those human moral patients like these animals in the relevant respects. To desire to continue to live presupposes that one have a conception of one's own mortality—that one can foresee or anticipate one's eventual demise. And it presupposes, further, that, having considered what one's death involves together with one's anticipated life prospects, one desires to continue to live in preference to dying. It is extremely doubtful that the moral patients at issue have the intellectual wherewithal to conceive of their own death or to make the kind of comparative judgment Singer's view requires. That animals "struggle against death," as was noted in our earlier discussion of the prima facie harm that death is (3.5), is insufficient evidence from which to infer that they have a conception of their own mortality, a point Singer concedes when, writing of a fish's attempt to dislodge a barbed hook, he observes that the animal's "struggle against danger and pain does not suggest that the fish is capable of preferring its own future existence to non-existence."[8] But if the *fish's* behavior is insufficient to establish that the fish has *this particular preference*, how can the behavior of *other* animals show that they do? To argue, as we have, that how some animals behave is intelligibly described and parsimoniously explained in ways that imply that they have *some* preferences about their own future is one thing; to hold that they have *the particular preference* Singer thinks is decisive—namely, the preference to go on living rather than dying—is quite another.

Despite these important limitations in what animals may be reasonably viewed as preferring, Singer maintains that killing some animals *is* a direct wrong. Some animals, he maintains, are self-conscious or self-aware. They are aware of themselves as "distinct from other entities in the world," "aware that they exist over a period of time," with "a past and a future."[9] Still other animals, though they are conscious, are not self-conscious. These are claims that have been clarified and defended in earlier chapters of the present work. So Singer is so far right. When he says that killing self-conscious animals is a direct wrong done to them, however, what he says is unsupported by his analysis of the direct wrong of killing. For though self-conscious animals do have some desires that relate to their future, it is extremely unlikely that they also have a conception of their own mortality, in which case they cannot have "a desire to go on living," in the relevant sense. What Singer must do, if he is to hold that killing self-conscious animals is a direct wrong, is modify his requirement. But how? The most obvious and, for reasons offered in the earlier discussion of the prima facie harm that death is (3.5), the most reasonable modification would be as follows: A sufficient condition of killing A's being a direct wrong done to A is that continued life *is in A's interests*—is, that is, a benefit to A, something that, in the case of self-conscious animals, makes possible the satisfaction of those desires that it is in their interests to satisfy. Modified in this way, Singer's position *will* imply that killing self-conscious animals *is* a direct wrong, even though they themselves do not "desire to go on living." (Singer could, it is true, continue to maintain that another sufficient condition of killing's being a direct wrong is that the victim have the particular desire he singles out—namely, the desire to go on living. But unless he alters his position in the way suggested, it fails to provide grounds for viewing the killing of self-conscious animals as a direct wrong.)

Individuals as Replaceable Receptacles

If Singer were to modify his position as suggested, would it then be adequate? Success here depends on whether Singer avoids the fundamental flaw of hedonistic utilitarianism—the view that individuals of direct moral concern are *mere receptacles* of value. Singer explicitly denies that self-conscious individuals are mere receptacles. How well he avoids the implications of hedonistic utilitarianism thus turns on the adequacy of his reasons for viewing self-conscious individuals in the way he does. So let us consider what these reasons are.

Sentient but nonself-conscious beings (hereafter referred to as *conscious beings*), Singer believes, *are* mere receptacles of what is good (pleasure) and evil (pain). They are "cups" that, from moment to moment, contain either the bitter (pain) or the sweet (pleasure), and to destroy them is merely to destroy something that contains (experiences) what is valuable. To illustrate the general point, imagine that a given conscious being, X, will have a total life score of +25 pleasure and −4 pain, for a net of +21. Imagine further that, were we to kill X we would have sufficient interest to bring another being, Y, into existence, whose total life score would be +21 or better. Then, were we to kill X, nothing of value would be lost, the net total of X's pleasures being equalized or bettered by the net total of Y's. It is in this sense, and for these reasons, that Singer regards conscious beings as *replaceable receptacles* of value. The status of self-conscious beings is claimed to differ. Unlike "beings that are conscious, but not self-conscious," beings that "can properly be regarded as receptacles for experiences of pleasure and pain, rather than as individuals leading lives of their own," Singer writes, "rational self-conscious beings are individuals, leading lives of their own . . . (and are) *not* mere receptacles for containing a certain quantity of happiness."[10] Whereas the killing of a conscious being does nothing contrary to that being's preferences (by definition, beings who are merely conscious, on Singer's view, have no preferences), to kill self-conscious beings is to do something that frustrates their preferences, and this is a prima facie wrong done directly to them, even granting that, once dead, they cannot fret over how their preferences have been frustrated. Because self-conscious beings have preferences about their future, *they* are more than receptacles.

There are serious problems here. As the English philosopher H. L. A. Hart was the first to observe, Singer gives no argument to support the view that self-conscious individuals are not mere receptacles. Though having preferences is distinct from experiencing pleasure, Singer's version of utilitarianism—preference utilitarianism—implies, Hart argues, that self-conscious beings "*are* in a sense mere receptacles, not indeed for experiences of pleasure and pain, but for preferences. . . . "[11] To the extent that Singer's position really is a form of utilitarianism—that is, really does enjoin us to act so as to bring about the best consequences (the optimal aggregate balance of the satisfaction of preferences over their frustration, for all concerned)—then, Hart contends, "there is nothing to show that such preferences evaluated for the purposes of Preference Utilitarianism by reference to numbers and intensity cannot be replaced by others as well as outweighed by others."[12] To make Hart's point about replaceability clearer, imagine that a given self-conscious individual, A, would have a total life score of +80 for preferences satisfied and −15 for preferences frustrated, for a net of +65, were A to live out his natural life, whereas his net score would be, say, +50 if we killed him. Imagine, further, that we could bring another self-conscious being into existence whose total life score would exceed either score; say the total would be +93. Other things being equal, the preference utilitarian must hold that we ought to kill A, since, on that view, A *is* replaceable by, and ought to be replaced by, B.

Moreover, despite Singer's protestations to the contrary, self-conscious beings *are*, as Hart alleges, "receptacles," given preference utilitarianism. Granted, one must take such a being's preferences into account, and count them equitably, before deciding what ought to be done. Nevertheless, there is no reason why, having done this, it might not be true that the optimal balance of satisfaction over frustration of preferences, for all concerned, might not be achieved by killing A. This is Hart's point when he says that, according to preference utilitarianism, preferences must be evaluated "by numbers and intensity." And it is also what Singer himself implies when he writes that "an action contrary to the preferences of any other being, unless this preference is outweighed by stronger contrary preferences, (is) wrong, other things being equal." The key phrase here is "unless this preference is outweighed by stronger contrary preferences." *Whose* preferences? It cannot be only the preferences of a particular individual (e.g., A's preference to go on living). Because utilitarianism bids us consider the preferences of *everyone* affected by the outcome, the "contrary preferences" could be the preferences of those whose preferences stand to be optimally satisfied by bringing about A's death. If, having taken everyone's preferences into account, and counted them all equitably, we were to find that killing A would bring about the optimal aggregate balance of satisfaction of preferences, all considered, then that is what we should do, given preference utilitarianism. On that view, in short, A *is* only a receptacle of what has value (i.e., preference satisfaction), lacking any independent value of his own.

The implications of the view that self-conscious individuals are replaceable receptacles, given preference utilitarianism, are not favorable to Singer's attempt to provide a version of utilitarianism preferable to hedonistic utilitarianism. A central problem for this latter view, as we have seen, is that killing a self-conscious being would be justified if this brought about the optimal aggregate balance of pleasure over pain for those affected by the outcome. And *that* makes killing too easy to justify. Singer evidently wants to avoid this, and he thinks he can do so by retaining utilitarianism while scrapping hedonism. But Singer's position does not avoid this. Self-conscious individuals *are* just as much replaceable receptacles given preference utilitarianism as they are given hedonistic utilitarianism. The only difference is that they are replaceable receptacles with preferences in the former case, and replaceable receptacles with pleasures and pains in the latter. In this regard preference utilitarianism marks no improvement over hedonistic utilitarianism. Both fail the test of conformity with our reflective moral intuitions.

Singer, we know, does not believe that ethical theories should be tested by how well they conform to our intuitions, either prereflective or reflective (see 4.3). Consistent with this position, he could simply bite the bullet, so to speak, when it comes to the implications of preference utilitarianism. If we point out that, other things being equal, his position allows killing moral agents if they are replaced by others with equal preference satisfaction scores, or, indeed, so long as the preferences of already existing moral agents are optimally satisfied as a result, and that we think this is wrong, Singer could reply that it is our intuitions that need changing, not his theory. Moreover, even were we to offer an argument, as we have in the preceding chapter (5.6), that moved our intuitions about the wrongness of such killing from the status of pre-reflective to reflective intuitions, Singer might still hold his ground.

Singer's reasons for rejecting appeals to intuitions were considered earlier and judged deficient (4.3). However, rather than merely contest Singer's theory from a vantage point whose validity he is certain to question from the outset, it will be more productive to challenge his position from a perspective whose validity he cannot rationally contest. The perspective is that of consistency, a noncontroversial minimal requirement that must be met by any ethical theory if it is to have any claim on our rational assent (see 4.6). Interpreted strictly, Singer's theory fails to meet this requirement. Interpreted in ways that overcome this deficiency, his theory remains unsupported. That, in brief, is the destination of the argument on which I am about to embark.

Singer's Dilemma

Utilitarianism frequently is attacked on the ground that it can sanction inequitable distributions of harms (evils) and benefits (goods). Since the goal set by the theory is aggregative (we are to act so as to bring about the best total balance of good over bad consequences, all considered, for everyone affected by the outcome) critics argue that following this principle could require that some few individuals be made to suffer a lot so that the rest might individually gain a little, the aggregated gain by the many more than compensating for the grievous losses of the few. The preceding discussion of the wrongness of killing and the problems this raises for utilitarians is a special instance of this general line of attack against utilitarianism. (I shall have more to say on this score in 6.5, 8.10 ff.). But there are other notions and principles of equality in addition to, and more basic than, those that figure in the debate over equal distribution. This latter debate concerns the justice of distributing goods and evils among various individuals, assuming that, before distributive concerns, the affected individuals have been treated equitably. It is this *predistributive* requirement of just treatment that Bentham marks by his famous declaration, "each to count for one, no one for more than one," an understanding of equality, in Singer's words, that "utilitarians, from Jeremy Bentham to J. J. C. Smart, take . . . as axiomatic . . . in deciding moral issues."[13] In their rush to air objections based on the unsavory distributive implications of utilitarianism, utilitarianism's critics have failed to give equal time to the problem this Benthamite notion of equality poses for utilitarian theory in general and for Singer's version of that theory in particular. What these problems are, we shall now begin to see.

The Benthamite notion of equality bulks large in Singer's thought. Our first question concerns how he understands this notion. It is not factual equality. When, for example, we say that humans are equal, we do not mean that they have the same abilities, hair color, or number of arms. If this were what we meant, the declaration of equality would be patently false. Instead, the kind of equality Singer has in mind is expressed by what he refers to as "the basic moral principle of equality,"[14] a principle that is "not a description of an alleged actual equality among humans: it is a prescription of how we should treat humans"[15] and, Singer argues, many nonhuman animals besides. What this principle prescribes is that "the interests of every being affected by an action are to be taken into account and given the same weight as the like interests of any other being."[16] For convenience' sake let us refer to the principle just quoted as *the equality principle*. That principle, then, according to Singer, is (a) prescriptive, not descriptive; (b) basic; (c) moral; (d) concerns the range of interests to be considered ("the interests of every being affected by an action are to be taken into account"); and (e) prescribes that equal interests be counted equally.

Two options are available to Singer, given his view that the equality principle is a basic moral principle. Either he may regard it as a basic moral principle in the logical sense of 'basic,' meaning that it cannot be derived from any other moral principle,[17] or he may regard it as basic in a nonlogical sense, meaning that though it is derivable it is of especially crucial moral importance. Surprisingly, some of what Singer writes strongly suggests that he inclines toward the former option, as witness the following:

> The only principle of equality I hold is the principle that the interests of
> every being affected by an action are to be taken into account and given

the same weight as the like interests of any other being. . . . Utilitarianism presupposes this principle.[18]

This last sentence commits Singer to the view that a logical relationship holds between the principles of equality and utility. When he says that utilitarianism *presupposes* the equality principle, he implies that unless we assume the validity of the equality principle utilitarianism has no moral or logical footing. What the quoted passage implies, in short, is that rather than the moral principle of equality depending on that of utility, the reverse is true: the principle of utility depends on the more basic moral principle of equality.

No consistent utilitarian can believe this. If utility is, as it must be for the utilitarian, and as Singer says it is, "the *sole* (moral) basis of morality,"[19] then all other moral principles must be derivable from it, and it in turn cannot presuppose any other more or equally basic moral principle. For a utilitarian to argue otherwise is to render utilitarianism incoherent. Singer must, therefore, avoid the first option at all costs.

The second option promises to be more attractive.[20] If, as this option maintains, the equality principle, like all other moral principles save that of utility itself, is derivable from the principle of utility, then selecting this alternative at least permits one to advance what appears to be a coherent version of utilitarianism. But the attractiveness of this second option is illusory. The attempt to ground the equality principle in that of utility involves a gross distortion of the notion of equality as it applies to interests. The equality or inequality of the interests of two individuals, A and B, depends on how important their respective interests are *to them*, A's interest being equal to B's if their interests have like importance to A and B, respectively, A's and B's interests being unequal if the case is otherwise. The equality or inequality of their interests cannot depend on how the interests of others will be affected if A's and B's interests are considered as equal or unequal. If this were so, we would be free to regard the *same* interests of A and B as equal at one time and as unequal at another, because the interests of others happened to be affected differently by regarding A's and B's interests differently at these different times. This is to make a shambles of the notion of equality as it applies to interests. And yet this is precisely where we are led in our understanding of equal interests, if the obligation to respect the equality principle is derived from the principle of utility. For the *utility* of counting A's and B's interests as equal can vary from case to case, even if their interests themselves do not. Thus, if utility is our guide, we are permitted to count the same interests as equal in one case and as unequal in another. This is to distort the concept of equal interests beyond recognition.

The upshot of the foregoing does not bode well for a position like Singer's. The dilemma that must be faced is that of either setting forth a view of the relationship between the moral principles of utility and equality that renders utilitarianism inconsistent (the argument given against the first option) or setting forth an account of the relationship between these two principles that avoids the charge of inconsistency but only at the price of grossly distorting the concept of equal interests (the argument given against the second option). It should be emphasized that the choice between these two alternatives cannot be avoided by a utilitarian who, like Singer, maintains that the equality principle is a *moral* principle. For then that principle must either be conceived to be underived, in which case the charge of inconsistency will apply, or derived, in which case the charge of distortion will prevail. In either case, therefore, the equality principle can find no home within utilitarianism, if, like Singer, utilitarians view the equality principle as a moral principle.

Equality as a Formal Principle

There is an obvious way for utilitarians, including Singer, to try to avoid this outcome. This is to regard the equality principle as a *formal* moral principle rather than as a substantive one—as a principle, that is, that does not itself lay down a moral obligation concerning what we ought to do but instead sets forth a condition that must be met by any substantive moral principle that does lay down such an obligation. On this view of the equality principle, in other words, this principle incorporates at least a partial test for determining when a principle is a moral as distinct from a nonmoral principle. Principles that pass this test to that extent qualify as moral principles; those that fail it lack that status. Thus, the principle of utility qualifies, but rational egoism, at least as Narveson seems to understand it (5.3), fails to quality as a moral principle, properly conceived.

To regard the equality principle as a formal moral principle does avoid the dilemma fatal to those utilitarians who, like Singer, view that principle as a substantive moral principle. The trouble for this defense of utilitarianism is that it is false that the equality principle is a formal moral principle, in the sense explained. Recall that that principle (i) concerns the range of interests to be considered ("the interests of every being affected by an action are to be taken into account") and (ii) prescribes that equal interests be counted equally. If the equality principle is said to be a formal moral principle, then any principle that fails to comply with (i) and (ii) fails to qualify as a moral principle. This is false. Kant, for example, who arguably thinks that considerations about the interests Singer has in mind—namely, preference-interests (see 3.2)—are irrelevant to the determination of where our moral duty lies, may advance a defective vision of morality. But not even Kant's harshest critics will maintain that the categorical imperative does not have the status of a moral principle: mistaken it may be, but at least it must be found to be mistaken *as a moral principle*. (In the following chapter a nonutilitarian moral principle, the respect principle, will be explained and defended; this principle does not meet the equality principle as this is interpreted by utilitarians.) Since, then, principles that fail to comply with (i) and (ii) might nonetheless be moral principles, it is false that the equality principle is a formal moral principle, in the sense explained.

Equality as a Conditional Formal Principle

If the equality principle is not a formal moral principle, and if, for the reasons given in the earlier discussion of Singer's views, this principle cannot reasonably be viewed as a substantive moral principle within utilitarian theory, then what is a utilitarian to do? The Benthamite proviso, "each to count for one, no one for more than one," allegedly "axiomatic" for utilitarianism, paradoxically seems not to be able to find a place within that theory.

Short of abandoning utilitarianism, there remains one final alternative. This is for the utilitarian to regard the equality principle as a conditional formal principle. To say it is conditional is to say that it becomes operative only if certain conditions are met. Singer provides a clue as to what these conditions might be when he observes that each of us has a "very natural concern that (our) own interests are to be looked after."[21] Suppose we acknowledge this natural propensity. Then we shall surely want others to take note of our interests and weigh them equitably—that is, not to discount the importance of our interests just because they are not their interests. If my interest in x is the same as yours, then I shall want you to give the same weight to my interest as you give to yours. If you do not, then you will have lapsed back into egoism, which is tantamount to saying that you are not taking the moral point of view. For to take that point of view requires that one be willing to universalize one's judgments of value. This requirement falls to me, however, not just to others. If I place a certain value on my interest in x, I must recognize the like value of anyone's similar interest; and if I would have others take note of my interests, because they are important to me, then I must take note of theirs, recognizing that they are important to them. In this way, then, we arrive at the equality principle, only now viewed as a conditional formal principle.

Let us refer to this way of viewing equality as *conditional equality* and express this principle as follows: If I would have others consider my interests and count them equitably, and if I am to take the moral point of view, then I commit myself to considering the interests of all those affected and to counting equal interests equally. Those who, like Kant, think that an individual's preference-interests are irrelevant to the determination of where our duty lies, are likely to look with disfavor even on this way of viewing the equality principle, arguing that we ought not to mix considerations about such interests with taking the moral point of view. But suppose we bypass this line of debate for the present and assume that some individual (A) not only understands but actually accepts conditional equality; that is, assume that A *would* have others consider his interests and weigh them equitably, that A *would* take the moral point of view, and that, as a consequence of both these assumptions, A *does* agree that he, too, must canvass the interests of others and count equal interests equally. Granting all this, we may then go on to ask about how A may view the principle of utility.

Two options are at hand. The first is that acceptance of conditional equality is *consistent* with utilitarianism. This is a weak option because on its face it provides no reason for selecting utilitarianism in preference to other substantive views of morality that also are consistent with acceptance of conditional equality—such as, Ross's view that there are many rules of prima facie duty. The second, strong option is that acceptance of the conditional equality principle *logically commits one to* the principle of utility. This strong option can itself take two forms, SO_1 maintaining that acceptance of conditional equality commits one to accepting the principle of utility *to the exclusion* of any other substantive moral principle, SO_2 maintaining that acceptance of conditional equality commits one to accepting utility as a minimal moral principle while leaving open the possibility that *there may be other* moral principles besides that of utility that one may also consistently accept. Hare possibly accepts SO_1. One must say "possibly" because it is not altogether clear what Hare's considered view is in this regard.[22] Singer, however, evidently accepts SO_2, since he states the following:

> The utilitarian position is a minimal one, a first base which we reach by universalizing self-interested decision making. We cannot, if we are to think ethically, refuse to take this first step.[23]

Here Singer allows that there *may* be other moral principles in addition to utility, while maintaining that we *must* accept utility if, starting with our individual interests, we take the moral point of view. For to take that point of view, starting with our self-interest, commits us to the conditional equality principle, and this in turn commits us to utilitarianism. At least this appears to be both a natural and fair interpretation of the crucial argument for accepting utilitarianism in the following passage:

> Suppose I begin to think ethically, to the extent of recognizing that my own interests cannot count for more, simply because they are mine, than the interests of others. In place of my own interests, I now have to take account of the interests of all those affected by my decision. This requires me to weigh up these interests and adopt the course of action most likely to maximize the interests of those affected. Thus I must choose the course of action which has the best consequences, on balance, for all affected. This is a form of utilitarianism. It differs from classical utilitarianism in that 'best consequences' is understood as meaning what, on balance, furthers the interests of those affected, rather than merely what increases pleasure and pain.[24]

It is by means of the argument just quoted, then, that Singer evidently believes we are able to support SO_2—the view, again, that acceptance of the principle of conditional equality commits one to accepting utility at least as a minimal, though not necessarily as the only substantive, moral principle.

Suppose this is true. Where have we got to? At the very most we have arrived at *a* consequentialist principle: *one* moral principle we should recognize is that of acting in ways that, on balance, further the interests (desires, etc.) of those affected. Logically, this is a far piece indeed from utilitarianism, the view that, in Singer's words, utility is "the *sole* (moral) basis of morality." For all we know, and as Singer himself concedes, there might be other moral theories, distinct from utilitarianism, that could accept the consequentialist principle at which he arrives. Moreover, all that this argument *could* show is that *if* we begin to do our moral thinking from the point of view of furthering our own interests, and *if* we take the moral point of view, then we commit ourselves to the consequentialist principle Singer identifies.[25] What this argument fails to show is that we *should* begin to do our moral thinking starting with the point of view of individual self-interest. Why suppose that a moral principle we commit ourselves to, starting from this point of view, is a *valid* moral principle? Where is the argument that shows this? In all fairness to Singer, it must be said that he fails to give one *and* that he should make good this omission. There are other places to begin our moral thinking and other principles we will reach if we begin in other ways. Kant provides us with an alternative approach and an alternative principle; a second will be advanced in the chapter that follows.

The situation, then, is this. No consistent utilitarian can regard the equality principle as a moral principle, and those who are not already committed to favoring consequentialist moral principles will not accept the utilitarian's interpretation of the equality principle as a formal principle that any and all moral principles must satisfy. Moreover, even if we concede that we commit ourselves to the consequentialist principle Singer articulates, if we would have others consider our preferences and count them equitably, and if we take the moral point of view, it does not follow that we commit ourselves to utilitarianism—the view, again, that the principle of utility is "the *sole* (moral) basis of morality," *or* that we should begin to do our ethical thinking from this point of view, *or* that the principle we reach if we do start in this way is a valid moral principle. For these reasons, then, preference utilitarianism, as a full-blooded version of utilitarianism, remains lacking in convincing support. Why this should be good news to those who labor for the better treatment of animals is a topic I will now begin to address.

6.4 SINGER'S GROUNDS FOR VEGETARIANISM

Throughout this chapter I have been interpreting Singer's position as an example of a direct duty view, a position that holds that we have some direct duties to animals but denies that they have any rights. Readers familiar with some of Singer's earlier writings on animals might think he has been misinterpreted. For example, in his well-known essay "All Animals Are Equal," Singer quotes Bentham's famous passage: "the question is not, Can they (that is, animals) reason? nor Can they *talk?* but, Can *they suffer?*" Singer then comments:

> In this passage Bentham points to the capacity for suffering as the vital characteristic that gives a being the right to equal consideration.[26]

Here, it might be objected against the present interpretation, Singer points to a particular capacity—namely, the capacity for suffering or, as he says a few lines later, the capacity for "suffering and/or enjoyment"—as the basis for the right to equal consideration. No mention is made of utilitarian considerations. On the contrary, it would not be an unnatural interpretation to say that Singer thinks that certain beings have *the right* to equal consideration of interests *because of their nature*— because, as a matter of their nature, they have the capacity to suffer or to enjoy or both. Arguably, Singer could be interpreted as thinking that sentient animals have one basic moral right: the right to equal consideration of their interests.

Nor is this right the only right Singer mentions. To avoid the preju- dice of speciesism, we must "allow that beings which are similar (to humans) in all relevant respects have a similar right to life."[27] At least some animals *are* sufficiently similar to humans in "all relevant respects"; thus, at least some animals have a right to life, Singer implies. But if we ask what those respects are by virtue of which the humans and animals in question have an equal claim to the right to life, these are the natural capacities of the beings in question, which, it might be alleged, further supports interpreting Singer as believing that at least some animals have, as all or at least most humans do, certain natural or basic rights—in this case, the right to life.

Natural though this interpretation appears, Singer has stated clearly that it fails to capture his considered position. In response to a critic's complaint that he has little to say about the nature of rights, Singer writes as follows:

Why is it surprising that I have little to say about the nature of rights? It would only be surprising to one who assumes that my case for animal liberation is based upon rights and, in particular, upon the idea of extending rights to animals. But this is not my position at all. I have little to say about rights because rights are not important to my argument. My argument is based on the principle of equality, which I do have quite a lot to say about. My basic moral position (as my emphasis on pleasure and pain and my quoting Bentham might have led [readers] to suspect) is utilitarian. I make very little use of the word "rights" in *Animal Liberation*, and I could easily have dispensed with it altogether. I think that the only right I ever attribute to animals is the "right" to equal consideration of interests, and anything that is expressed by talking of such a right could equally well be expressed by the assertion that animals' interests ought to be given equal consideration with the like interests of humans. (With the benefit of hindsight, I regret that I did allow the concept of a right to intrude into my work so unnecessarily at this point; it would have avoided misunderstanding if I had not made this concession to popular moral rhetoric.)

To the charge of having embroiled the animal liberation debate in the issue of animals' rights, then, I plead not guilty. As to who the real culprit might be . . .[28]

This passage leaves little room for doubt as to what Singer thinks. His previous references to "animal rights," he thinks, not only were unneces- sary for his utilitarian position but were lamentable, something he now "regrets," a "concession to popular moral rhetoric" rather than a rea- soned appeal.

Perhaps this is so. Perhaps appeals to "the rights of animals" must bear the diagnosis Singer gives of his earlier work. It would be premature to make a judgment at this juncture. The positive argument for recognizing the rights of animals remains to be considered. Our present task is restricted to asking how well Singer defends his views about our duties to animals, once this is shorn of his "rhetorical" excesses. The inadequacy of his utilitarian position can be illustrated by concentrating on one obligation he claims we have—namely, the obligation to be vegetarians. Once the inadequacy of his position is recognized in relation to this issue, one can easily see how it is similarly inadequate when applied to others— for example, the use of animals in science, a use of animals to which Singer also takes moral exception.

Anyone writing on the topic of the treatment of animals must acknowledge an enormous debt to Singer. The growing public awareness of the gruesome details of factory farming is in no small measure due to the wide readership his work, especially *Animal Liberation*, has rightfully commanded. All of us by now know, or at least have had the opportunity to find out, that chickens are raised in incredibly crowded, unnatural environments; that veal calves are intentionally raised on an anemic diet, are unable to move enough even to clean themselves, and are kept in the dark most of their lives; that other animals, including pigs and cattle, are being raised intensively in increasing numbers. But this debt to Singer's work does not imply that his moral argument for vegetarianism is adequate. Here is the way he brings that argument to its moral destination:

> Since, as I have said, none of these practices (of raising animals intensively) cater for anything more than our pleasures of taste, our practice of rearing and killing other animals in order to eat them is a clear instance of the sacrifice of the most important interests of other beings in order to satisfy trivial interests of our own . . . we must stop this practice, and each of us has a moral obligation to cease supporting the practice.[29]

There are several problems here. The first concerns the grounds Singer has for judging that "our pleasures of taste" are "trivial interests." Many people, including many quite thoughtful persons, do not regard the situation in this way. Many go to a great deal of trouble to prepare tasty food or to find "the best restaurants" where such food is prepared. Singer might say that people who place so much importance on the taste of food have a warped sense of values. And maybe they do. But that they do, if they do, is something that stands in need of rather elaborate argument, one not found in any of Singer's published writings. This is not to say that the interest we have in eating tasty food is as important an interest as we (or animals) have in avoiding pain or death. It is just to say that it is unclear, and that Singer has given no argument to show that our interest in eating tasty food is, in his words, "trivial."

Second—and now granting to Singer his assumption that our interest in eating pleasant tasting food is trivial—it is unclear how, as a utilitarian, he can argue that we have a moral obligation to stop supporting the practice of raising animals intensively (this practice is henceforth symbolized as *p*) because of some statement about the *purpose of p*. The question the utilitarian must answer is not, (a) What is the purpose of *p*? It is, (b) All things considered, what are the consequences of *p*, and how do they compare to the value of the consequences that would result if alternatives to *p* were adopted and supported? When, therefore, Singer objects to *p* on the ground that it does not "cater for anything more than our pleasures of taste," he gives us an answer to (a), not, as we should expect from a utilitarian, an answer to (b). The difference between the two questions and their respective answers is not unimportant. For though the purpose of *p* might be correctly described as that of catering to our (trivial) pleasures of taste, it does not follow *either* that this is a utilitarian objection one might raise against *p*—it is not—*or* that, when a distinctively utilitarian objection is forthcoming, it will dwell on Singer's characterization of *p*'s purpose. His characterization also leaves out much that, from a utilitarian point of view, must be judged to be highly relevant to determining the morality of *p*.

The animal industry is big business. It is uncertain exactly how many people are involved in it, directly or indirectly, but certainly the number must easily run into the many tens of thousands. There are, first and most obviously, those who actually raise and sell the animals; but there are many others besides, including feed producers and retailers; cage manufacturers and designers; the producers of growth stimulants and other chemicals (for example, those designed to ward off or to control disease); those who butcher, package, and ship the meat or eggs or other animal products to which Singer might (and does, as in the case of eggs from battery-hens) take moral exception; and the extension personnel and veterinarians whose lives revolve around the success or failure of the animal industry. Also consider all the members of the families who are the dependents of these employees or employers. The interests these persons have in "business-as-usual," in raising animals intensively, go well beyond pleasures of taste and are far from trivial. These people have a stake in the animal industry as rudimentary and important as having a job, feeding a family, or laying aside money for their children's education or their own retirement. What do these people do about a job, a means of supporting themselves or their dependents, if we or they see the error of their or our ways and become vegetarians? Certainly it is no defense of an immoral practice to plead that some people profit from it. In the case of slavery, for example, we would not cease to condemn it merely because we were apprised that plantation owners found it beneficial. But Singer, we know, is disdainful of appeals to our moral intuitions, so this appeal is not available to him. In the particular case of the morality of raising animals intensively, moreover, Singer, *as a preference utilitarian*, cannot say that the interests of those humans involved in this practice, those whose quality of life presently is bound up in it, are irrelevant. If preference satisfaction is the yardstick of what is right and wrong, then *everyone's* preference satisfaction must count and be counted equitably, which means that the preferences of those involved in, and supportive of, the animal industry, not just those who oppose it, must find their place in the calculations. Since there are many more humans who prefer a continuation of this industry than who oppose it, it is quite unclear how the preferences of the latter can outweigh those of the former. If the preferences of farm animals are added, the situation remains cloudy at best. It is not just for trivial reasons that those humans involved in the animal industry want to see it continue and prosper. Interests *important to them* are at stake, and it is just at this point that *the significant conservative bias* of preference utilitarianism, alluded to in an earlier context (4.3), comes into view, blunting the efforts of its advocates when they call upon people to make significant changes in how they live. Preference utilitarians might think they can show that people have a duty to become vegetarians without denying the relevance of people's present dietary and other preferences in the determination of where their duty lies; but no preference utilitarian, it seems fair to say, has shown this.

The difficulties faced by a preference utilitarian such as Singer actually are more complicated than the preceding suggests. Because of his version of utilitarianism, Singer must insist on the relevance of *side effects*—that is, the interests of *everyone* affected by the consequences of altering the animal industry, not just those who happen to be directly involved in it. For example, the short- and long-term global economic implications of a sudden or gradual transition to vegetarianism, by large numbers of persons, must seriously be investigated by any utilitarian. It is not enough to point out, as vegetarians sometimes do, that grains not used to feed intensively raised animals *could* be used to feed the starving masses of humanity; a utilitarian must have the hard data to show that this possibility is at least probable and, judged on utilitarian grounds, desirable. The debate between Singer and Garrett Hardin over the desirability of famine relief, judged on utilitarian principles, is relevant here and points to the enormity of the task that confronts anyone who would rest vegetarianism on utilitarianism.[30] Though the issues involved are very complicated and cannot receive anything approaching even a modest airing on this occasion, one thing is certain: it is not *obviously* true that the aggregated consequences for everyone affected would be better, all considered, if intensive rearing methods were abandoned and we all (or most of us) became (all at once or gradually) vegetarians. Some nice calculations are necessary to show this. Without them, a utilitarian-based vegetarianism cannot command our rational assent. Even the most sympathetic reader, even "fellow travelers" in the vegetarian movement, will fail to find the necessary calculations in Singer's work. They simply are not there.

Singer, or a defender of his position, can be expected to protest at this point by noting that utilitarianism, as he understands it, involves acceptance of the equality of interests principle, the principle that "the interests of every being affected by an action are to be taken into account and given the same weight as the like interests of any other being." We have already seen the difficulties Singer faces in finding a place for this principle in his preference utilitarianism. These difficulties haunt him here. One problem with this principle is that it does not tell us what we ought to do, once we have taken the interests of all affected parties into account and counted equal interests equally. All that it tells us is that this is something we must do. Even if, in addition to this principle, we are also supplied with the principle of utility, we are still some distance from the obligation to be vegetarian; for what we would have to be shown, and what Singer fails to show, as argued in the above, is that the consequences of all or most persons adopting a vegetarian way of life would be better, all considered, than if they did not. That is not shown merely by insisting that equal interests are equal.

A defender of Singer might object that an important argument has been overlooked. On a number of occasions Singer argues that we would not allow to be done to human imbeciles what we allow to be done to more intelligent, more self-conscious animals; for example, we would not allow trivial, painful experiments to be conducted upon these humans, whereas we do allow them to be conducted on primates.[31] In this and analogous ways, we are guilty of a gross form of prejudice (speciesism): we are grossly inconsistent from the moral point of view.

This view of Singer's is not without considerable moral weight, but it does not strengthen his avowedly *utilitarian* basis for vegetarianism or, more generally, for more humane treatment of animals. (A nonutilitarian critique of speciesism is offered below, 8.11). In order for this argument for moral consistency to provide a *utilitarian* basis for more humane treatment of animals, Singer would have to show that it would be just as wrong, *on utilitarian grounds*, to treat animals in certain ways as it is to treat humans in comparable ways. Singer, however, does not show, first, that, on utilitarian grounds, it would be wrong to treat humans in the ways described (here he merely appeals to our settled conviction that it would be wrong to do this, an unusual move, given his own criticisms of making such appeals) and, second, that it would be just as wrong, on utilitarian grounds, to treat animals as these humans would be. In short, Singer fails to give a utilitarian basis, one that judges matters on known or probable consequences, for the argument he deploys to challenge speciesist practices.

Nor will it do, as a defense of Singer, merely to assume that the equality of interests principle must be violated by the differential treatment of the humans and animals in question. That would have to be shown, not assumed, on utilitarian grounds, since there is no reason why the following is not possible: The interests of animals raised intensively are counted as equal to the interests of humans like them in the relevant respects who might be raised as a food source under similar circumstances, but the consequences of treating the animals in this way are optimific (i.e., produce the best aggregate balance of good over evil) whereas those resulting from raising these humans intensively would not be. More generally, *dissimilar treatment* of beings with equal interests might well have greatly varying consequences. So, even granting that we would not approve of treating these humans in the ways animals are routinely treated, and even assuming that the humans and animals themselves have an equal interest in avoiding pain and death, it does not follow that we have been given a utilitarian basis for vegetarianism or the cause of more humane treatment of animals generally. The requirement that, in certain settings (e.g., scientific research), animals and human moral patients be *treated similarly*, over and above counting their like interests equally, is a requirement Singer implicitly accepts but fails to justify.

Singer's Paradox

So far the discussion has been limited to noting that Singer fails to provide an adequate utilitarian basis for the obligation to be a vegetarian. It now remains to show that his attempt to do so leads to a highly paradoxical consequence, one that, on reflection, dooms the enterprise from the start. In responding to various critics' accusations that being a vegetarian must be a largely symbolic gesture for the individual utilitarian, since one person's boycotting meat will fail to make any difference in the way animals are treated in factory farming, Singer replies that in the case of chickens, for example, "there must be some point at which the number of vegetarians makes a difference to the size of the poultry industry. There must be a series of thresholds, hidden by the market system of distribution, which determine how many factory farms will be in existence. In this case one more person becoming a vegetarian will make no difference at all, unless that individual, added to the others who are already vegetarians, reduces demand below the threshold level at which a new factory farm would have started up (or an existing one would have remained in production, if industry is declining)."[32] Whether we now know what these "thresholds" are is a moot point for present purposes. The point to be stressed now is the paradoxical nature of this aspect of Singer's utilitarian basis of the obligation to be vegetarian. What it comes to is that in being a vegetarian I am doing what I ought to do *only if* it happens to be true that enough other people happen also to be vegetarians so that, when the effects of their boycotting meat are joined with the effects of my boycott, it happens to be the case that some number of chickens that would have been raised in a factory farm are spared that fate. If, on the other hand, the effects of our collective boycott happen not to make any difference in the number of chickens raised intensively, then, in being vegetarians, we are not doing what we ought to do, not because of any failing on our part (assume we work very hard to persuade others but fail to do so), but because of the effects of the decisions of others (i.e., nonvegetarians), whose demand for meat more than offsets the effect of our boycott. But to make the rightness of what vegetarians do contingent upon the decisions of those very persons who are doing what vegetarians deplore—and Singer's view does imply this—is paradoxical at best, all the more so when we pause to observe that, on this view, all that nonvegetarians need do, in order to insure that they personally escape the obligation to be vegetarian, as this is determined by the vegetarian's impact on factory farming, is to continue doing precisely what it is that they are presently doing—namely, eating meat! For there is, on this view, no obligation to abstain from eating meat if too few people do abstain, so that those who do eat meat do nothing wrong. And if, perchance, the ranks of vegetarians were to swell to such an extent that their collective impact on factory farming could, other things being equal, close this or that intensive rearing operation, the nonvegetarians, given Singer's position, could still take steps to escape the obligatoriness of vegetarianism, as this is assessed by the impact of vegetarians on factory farming. All that nonvegetarians would need do is *eat more meat*, thereby negating the collective effect of the vegetarians and so, on Singer's view, thereby negating the meat eater's obligation to be vegetarian. One should not say that the meat eaters would be doing what is right in this case. Quite the contrary. What should be said is that Singer cannot argue that what they are doing is wrong, by appeal to the impact of alternative diets on factory farming. Granted, the number of persons who are vegetarians does bear on the number of animals raised in factory farms; and granted, vegetarians must profoundly wish that their individual and collective efforts will ultimately reduce the number of animals so raised; nevertheless, the obligation to be vegetarian cannot be grounded in these considerations, except at the price of the paradox Singer's view is heir to. How this obligation is to be grounded is explained and defended below (9.1).

6.5 UTILITARIANISM AND SPECIESISM

Earlier in this chapter (6.3) it was observed that utilitarianism frequently is attacked on the grounds that it can sanction highly inequitable distributions of goods and evils. Since the end set by the theory is aggregative, requiring that we act to bring about the best balance of goods over evils for all affected by the outcome, critics argue that some individuals might be required to shoulder an inequitable share of the evils so that others may collectively maximize intrinsic goods. The challenge raised against both hedonistic and preference utilitarianism concerning the morality of killing is an example of this kind of objection. One individual is killed and, as a consequence, optimal aggregate consequences are obtained, all considered. The survivors reap the benefits; the victim loses everything. The situation must strike us as radically unfair, and yet, if the consequences, including the side effects, are optimific, the act utilitarian (the version of utilitarianism we have been concerned with throughout this chapter) must concede that his position is powerless to lodge a moral complaint. There are many other examples of act utilitarianism's allowing similar inequalities in treatment (e.g., allowing that an innocent person might be punished to secure optimal results, all considered). We shall not rehearse all these objections again. Here it is relevant to note that a position like Singer's can allow the very thing it ostensibly rules out—namely, speciesism.

On its face, utilitarianism seems to be the fairest, least prejudicial view around. Everyone's interests count, and no one's interests count for any more than the like interests of anyone else. The trouble is, as we have seen, there is no necessary connection, no pre-established harmony between everybody's abiding by the equality principle and everybody's having their interests forwarded equally. On the contrary, reliance on the principle of utility could sanction acting in ways where some individuals have their interests affected in significantly adverse ways—for example, they are killed because this brings about optimal aggregated results. Critics of utilitarianism argue that the utilitarian principle's potential for allowing inequitable distribution of goods and evils could even allow institutionalized injustices such as racism and sexism and that respect for the equality principle will not preclude this possibility. These prejudices can take different forms and find expression in different ways. One form would even deny the relevance of considering the interests of members of a given race or sex; another would consider them but not count their interests as equal in importance to the like interests of the members of the "superior" race or sex. Utilitarianism, with its reliance on the equality principle (assuming this reliance could be justified), would not sanction either of these views, and Singer powerfully denounces them. There is, however, a third form these prejudices might take. In this form the interests of the members of the "inferior" race or sex are considered and are counted equitably; it just so happens that, all considered, the overall aggregated good is maximally promoted if we distribute goods in ways that favor the members of a particular race or sex, ways that are detrimental to those who belong to the "inferior" race or sex. Forms of racism or sexism, prejudices that seem to be ruled out by the utilitarian's reliance on the equality principle, could well be resurrected and, if the facts turn out a certain way—that is, if distributing goods and evils in ways that favor the "superior" over the "inferior" races or sexes did bring about the best consequences, all considered—would be justified. If the utilitarian were here to reply that distributing goods and evils in this way must violate the equality of interests principle and so, on his view, would be forbidden, we must remind him that differential treatment is not the same as, and does not entail, violating that principle. Theoretically, it is quite possible, for example, to count the interests of blacks and whites the same (and thus to honor the equality principle) and still discriminate between the races when it comes to who gets what, the whites getting the lion's share of the goods and the blacks the leftovers, on the grounds that such discrimination in the *distribution* of goods promotes the utilitarian objective. Whether utilitarians can show that the facts are against this sort of thing ever being justified, in the actual world, is an open question at this point, one we will examine in a somewhat different context in the following chapter (7.7). The modest point being urged here is that, for all its emphasis on equality, utilitarianism would sanction recognizable forms of sexism and racism, if the facts happened to turn out a certain way.

The situation regarding speciesism is the same, only worse. As utilitarians, we must consider the interests of animals and count their interests equitably; thus, certain kinds of speciesism (e.g., one where we don't even regard the interests of animals as relevant) are ruled out. But respect for the equality principle is no guarantee that animals will be treated equitably, given the principle of utility, when it comes to distributive questions. That animals are raised intensively, for example, while human beings are not, provides no distinctively *utilitarian* argument against raising animals in this way. For it may be that treating animals in these ways brings about the best consequences, all considered, while comparable treatment of human beings would not. Theoretically, therefore, utilitarianism could provide a basis on which to defend recognizable speciesist practices. Whether it actually does must depend on whether the consequences of treating animals in these ways are better, all considered. Since Singer, for example, fails to provide us with the necessary empirical data showing that the consequences would be better, all considered, taking the interests of *everyone* involved into account, if we ceased to raise animals intensively, it follows that, for all we know, this treatment, which does reflect *a* kind of speciesism—as will be explained more fully later (8.11)—might actually be justified, given a version of utilitarianism like Singer's. A position like his, all considered, is some distance from providing a foundation for genuine "animal liberation." I shall return to this theme, in the examination of rule utilitarianism (7.7).

6.6 SUMMARY AND CONCLUSION

In this chapter we have examined representative direct duty views. Though far from complete, those views reviewed seem to hold the most promise of accounting for our direct duties to moral patients generally and animals in particular without relying on appeals to their rights. The cruelty-kindness view fails, it was argued (6.1), because it confuses considerations about the worth of moral agents with considerations about the morality of their acts, supposing that the mental states or dispositions of agents (their motives or intentions) determine the rightness or wrongness of what they do. Act utilitarianism, whether hedonistic or preference, avoids this confusion but fails to provide an adequate basis for the stringency of the prima facie direct duty not to harm (6.2–6.3). Among the many problems any form of act utilitarianism must face, one in particular was highlighted—namely, that of secret killings. Because of the secrecy of the killing, the side effects known killings give rise to (the anxiety and insecurity in the minds of the living) cannot be appealed to, and the act utilitarian is therefore forced to account for the immorality of secret killings independently of such considerations. Hedonistic utilitarianism fails in this regard because the pleasures lost by the victims can be more than made up for by the pleasures gained by the criminals; and preference utilitarianism is similarly unable to explain why such killings are wrong since the loss of preference satisfaction on the part of the victims can again be more than compensated for by the gains of others, including the increased satisfactions of the criminals.

A second major line of argument sought to show that both the cruelty-kindness view and the various forms of act utilitarianism examined would, if accepted, fail to provide the solid basis sought by those who labor for the better treatment of animals and those human moral patients like animals in the relevant respects. If, as the cruelty-kindness view supposes, our direct negative duties to these moral patients require only that we not be sadistically or brutally cruel to them, then persons who harm these individuals but who feel empathy with or sympathy for them would be above moral reproach: their *deeds* could not be morally faulted. In the case of all those forms of utilitarianism examined, moreover, the harm done to these moral patients could not be morally criticized so long as harming them was causally related to bringing about the optimal aggregate balance of good (e.g., pleasure) over evil (e.g., pain) for everyone affected by the outcome, a wheel of justification that is greased by the absence of foreboding anxiety in some cases (e.g., infanticide and the slaughter of farm animals for food). Neither cruelty-kindness nor utilitarianism, therefore, provide a satisfactory basis for the direct duties we owe to these individuals.

Utilitarianism frequently is applauded for its egalitarianism: each is to count for one, no one for more than one. In this way, so its advocates assume, utilitarianism avoids the pernicious prejudices of sexism, racism, and speciesism. All this sounds very good indeed. The problem arises when we ask *how* the utilitarian obtains the principle rooted in this notion of equality and what status it can have within utilitarian theory. No utilitarian can regard it as *obligatory* to consider the interests (preferences, pleasures) of those involved and count equal interests, and the like, equally since this obligation will be either (a) basic (underived) or (b) nonbasic (derived). If it is said to be the former, then utilitarianism is rendered inconsistent, since utility *and utility alone* is basic for utilitarians; if it is said to be the latter, then the notion of equality is distorted since the equality or inequality of any two interests (or pleasures, etc.) must depend on these pleasures or interests themselves, not on the utility of counting them as equal or unequal. Similarly deficient is the claim that the equality principle is a formal principle, since those who are not utilitarians can advance moral principles without first accepting the utilitarian interpretation of equality. At the very most the equality principle, as understood by utilitarians, can be viewed as a conditional formal principle: *if* one wants others to give equal consideration to one's own interests, and *if* one takes the moral point of view, *then*, it may be alleged, one is committed to the consequentialist principle to act so as to further the interests of those affected by the outcome. However, even if we concede that one is committed to this principle, given the fulfillment of the conditions just sketched, it does not follow that one is committed to *utilitarianism* (the view that utility is the *sole* basis of morality), *or* that the principle one is committed to is a valid moral principle, *or* that this approach to identifying moral principles (starting with one's own desires, etc.) is a valid approach. There are more questions that go begging than are answered when utilitarianism is argued for on the basis of accepting the conditional equality principle.

Finally, Peter Singer's attempt to base the obligation to be vegetarian on utilitarianism was examined (6.4). It was noted that the equality principle (assuming it fits his preference utilitarianism), since it is a *pre*distributive principle, is consistent with treating individuals radically differently when it comes to deciding how to bring about the best aggregate balance of good over evil, which is a distributive concern. One cannot assume, therefore, that the equality principle is violated if people are willing to treat animals and relevantly similar human moral patients differently. As a utilitarian, Singer must acknowledge that questions about the differential treatment of various individuals, even those who are relevantly similar in terms of their interests, must depend on the consequences. In the particular case of the intensive rearing of farm animals, therefore, it is an open moral question for any utilitarian, Singer included, whether such treatment is wrong, and it cannot be assumed that the treatment these animals receive is wrong if those people who are willing to tolerate it are not willing to tolerate similar treatment of human moral patients who are like these animals in the relevant respects. For there is no reason why the *consequences* in the two cases must be the same, and it is consequences that, for any utilitarian, are morally decisive, assuming the equality principle has been satisfied.

To show that, viewed from the perspective of preference utilitarianism, we have a moral obligation to be vegetarians, Singer must therefore show that the consequences for all concerned would be better if we were vegetarians than if we were not. Singer fails to show this for the simple reason that he fails to adduce the necessary empirical details. Moreover, despite his powerful denunciations of speciesism (and sexism and racism), his position could sanction recognizable versions of these prejudices (6.5). It is not enough to count the equal interests of, say, pigs and children equally, if we are to avoid speciesism; it is also essential that we treat both fairly *after* we have done this, something that is not guaranteed merely by respecting the equality principle. Finally, Singer's reply to the charge that, when viewed against his preference utilitarian position, an individual's deciding to be a vegetarian is a largely symbolic gesture was shown to lead to the paradoxical consequence that meat eaters can avoid the obligation to be vegetarian by the simple expedient of eating more meat. If the criticisms raised against Singer are fair and on target, neither those who seek a solid foundation for the obligation to be vegetarian nor those who seek a sound theory will find it in his preference utilitarianism.

7

Justice and Equality

One condition of the ideal moral judgment (see 4.2) is impartiality, understood as compliance with the formal principle of justice. That principle requires that all individuals be given their due, something we fail to do if similar individuals are treated dissimilarly. The principle is said to be a formal principle because by itself it does not specify what individuals *are* due. The principle implies only that, whatever this is, justice will not be done if, without being able to cite a morally relevant difference, individuals are treated differently.

Justice, understood as a formal principle, obviously is not enough. Unless we have some reasonable basis for determining what individuals are due, we will lack principled grounds for deciding when two or more individuals are *morally relevantly* similar or dissimilar, and, lacking this, we will also lack a principled basis for deciding what each is due as a matter of strict justice. Thus arises the need to give a normative interpretation of justice.[1]

Not surprisingly, there is no single interpretation or theory of justice. Such is the nature of competing theories in any discipline; it is not peculiar to moral philosophy. The disagreements that exist should not encourage us to believe that there is no rational way to separate the wheat from the chaff. Indeed, the overarching objective of the present chapter is to do just that. I shall proceed as follows. Three interpretations of justice will be explained and critically assessed (7.1–7.2). Two of the three (perfectionism and utilitarianism) will be rejected and the third (the equality of individuals) will be defended. This latter interpretation rests on postulating that certain individuals have a distinctive kind of value (inherent value), and both the nature of this value and the criteria for its attribution will be explained (7.2–7.5). These considerations will provide the basis for acceptance of the respect principle (7.6), a principle that stipulates a direct duty of justice owed to all those individuals who have inherent value. That principle, it will be argued, applies to our dealings with moral agents *and* moral patients, and applies equally, since, for reasons offered in the sequel, moral agents and patients must be viewed as possessing equal inherent value. Attempts to dispense with the respect principle and the postulate of inherent value on which it rests, in particular the option offered by rule utilitarianism, will be considered and refuted (7.7). The respect principle will be defended as a valid moral principle (7.8), and the connection between that principle and the harm principle will be explained (7.9).

7.1 UTILITARIAN AND PERFECTIONIST THEORIES OF JUSTICE

Though they were not called by this name, the previous chapter brought us in touch with alternative utilitarian interpretations of formal justice. Recall the importance utilitarians place on counting each for one, no one for more than one. That seems eminently just in spirit and intent, eminently *egalitarian*: no one individual is viewed as being more or less entitled to the same consideration accorded other relevantly similar individuals. Now, it is fundamentally important to emphasize that equal consideration, for utilitarians, is a *predistributive* requirement. For hedonistic utilitarians, for example, individuals are treated equally, are treated as justice requires, if their pleasures and pains are considered and counted as equal in importance to the like pleasures and pains of any other(s). That is what every individual is due, as a matter of justice, and those who are denied equal consideration and weighting of their equal pleasures, given hedonistic utilitarianism, may validly claim, or have claimed on their behalf, that they have been treated unjustly. I shall have a good deal more to say about utilitarian interpretations of justice in the present chapter (see, especially, 7.7).

Utilitarianism is not the only normative interpretation of justice, and not all theories are as egalitarian as utilitarianism aspires to be. The ancient Greek philosopher Aristotle and the nineteenth-century German philosopher Friedrich Nietzsche, for example, advance *perfectionist theories of justice*, according to which what individuals are due, as a matter of justice, depends on the degree to which they possess a certain cluster of virtues or excellences, including intellectual and artistic talents and a character that expresses itself in the performance of heroic or magnificent deeds. Those who possess such virtues abundantly are due more, as a matter of justice, than those who possess them to a limited degree or not at all. It is, therefore, a short step from accepting a perfectionist theory of justice to allowing highly differential treatment of individuals who differ in the extent to which they possess the virtues favored by such a theory; and it should come as no surprise that, enamored as he was by such a conception of justice, Aristotle, for example, thinks that some human beings are slaves by nature—are, as it were, born to be slaves, so bereft are they of even the minimum capacity for artistic, intellectual, and other virtues. *Their* function is to serve the higher, more deserving interests of the virtuous—for example, by carrying out such tasks as growing food and collecting refuse, tasks for which they are naturally suited by their intellectual and aesthetic poverty, work that relieves the virtuous of the need to spend their time in such low-level pursuits and thus provides them with the leisure necessary to develop their artistic and intellectual virtues optimally. Nor can those consigned to serve their natural masters complain of a lack of justice. They get exactly what is their due. Since a just society calls for arrangements that further the perfection of the virtuous, those lacking the preferred virtues cannot complain of any injustice in being required to serve the needs of the artistic and intellectual elite.

Perfectionist theories of justice are morally pernicious, providing, as they do, the foundation of the most objectionable forms of social, political, and legal discrimination—chattel slavery, rigid caste systems, and gross disparities in the quality of life available to citizens in the same state, for example. But perfectionist theories are objectionable at a deeper level. Whether individuals have the talent necessary to acquire the favored virtues (e.g., ability to do higher mathematics) is beyond their control. What natural talents individuals have, to hearken back to a helpful phrase of Rawls's, is the result of "the natural lottery." Those who are born with intellectual or artistic gifts have not themselves done anything to deserve preferred treatment, any more than those who are born lacking these gifts have done anything to deserve being denied those benefits essential to their welfare. No theory of justice can be adequate that builds justice on so fortuitous a foundation, one that could sanction forwarding the "higher" interests of some over the vital interests of others, even to the point where the latter could be enslaved by the former, thereby having their liberty and other benefits acutely diminished, *in the name of justice*. Though consensus is a rare thing in the cloakrooms of philosophy, few, if any, philosophers today would defend a perfectionist theory of justice, for the reasons given (though not only for these). We shall have occasion to remind ourselves of the perils of perfectionism and the need to avoid them in the argument that follows. But it will also be suggested, in a different context, that considerations about the number and variety of one's abilities are morally relevant considerations in some unusual cases (see 8.13).

Viewed against the backdrop of perfectionist theories of justice, Bentham's declaration about each counting for one, no one for more than one must be perceived as a breath of fresh egalitarian air, and it is small wonder that this aspect of utilitarian philosophy was highly instrumental in bringing about many of the most important political, legal, and economic changes in the direction of a more egalitarian society, especially during the nineteenth century, especially in England. Though the actual consequences of the utilitarian push for equality are today viewed as commendable, the status of the equality principle in utilitarian theory is quite another matter, as was explained in the preceding chapter (6.3). Those arguments will not be aired here, though they will concern us later (7.7). Here I shall embark on offering an alternative interpretation of formal justice, one that is distinctly nonperfectionist and, though egalitarian, nonutilitarian. The ways in which the interpretation of justice favored here differs both from perfectionist and utilitarian theories of justice will be explained as we proceed. A defense of that interpretation must await its clear statement (see 7.8).

7.2 INDIVIDUALS AS EQUAL IN VALUE

The interpretation of formal justice favored here, which will be referred to as *equality of individuals*, involves viewing certain individuals as having value in themselves. I shall refer to this kind of value as *inherent value* and begin the discussion of it by first concentrating on the inherent value attributed to moral agents.

The inherent value of individual moral agents is to be understood as being conceptually distinct from the intrinsic value that attaches to the experiences they have (e.g., their pleasures or preference satisfactions), as not being reducible to values of this latter kind, and as being incommensurate with these values. To say that inherent value is not reducible to the intrinsic values of an individual's experiences means that we cannot determine the inherent value of individual moral agents by totaling the intrinsic values of their experiences. Those who have a more pleasant or happier life do not therefore have greater inherent value than those whose lives are less pleasant or happy. Nor do those who have more "cultivated" preferences (say, for arts and letters) therefore have greater inherent value. To say that the inherent value of individual moral agents is incommensurate with the intrinsic value of their (or anyone else's) experiences means that the two kinds of value are not comparable and cannot be exchanged one for the other. Like proverbial apples and oranges, the two kinds of value do not fall within the same scale of comparison. One cannot ask, How much intrinsic value is the inherent value of this individual worth—how much is it equal to? The inherent value of any given moral agent isn't equal to any sum of intrinsic values, neither the intrinsic value of that individual's experiences nor the total of the intrinsic value of the experiences of all other moral agents. To view moral agents as having inherent value is thus to view them as something different from, and something more than, mere receptacles of what has intrinsic value. They have value in their own right, a value that is distinct from, not reducible to, and incommensurate with the values of those experiences which, as receptacles, they have or undergo.

The difference between the utilitarian-receptacle view of value regarding moral agents and the postulate of inherent value might be made clearer by recalling the cup analogy (see 6.2). On the receptacle view of value, it is *what goes into the cup* (the pleasures or preference-satisfactions, for example) that has value; what does not have value is the cup itself (i.e., the individual himself or herself). The postulate of inherent value offers an alternative. The cup (that is, the individual) has value *and* a kind that is not reducible to, and is incommensurate with, what goes into the cup (e.g., pleasure). The cup (the individual) does "contain" (experience) things that are valuable (e.g., pleasures), but the value of the cup (individual) is not the same as any one or any sum of the valuable things the cup contains. *Individual moral agents themselves have a distinctive kind of value,* according to the postulate of inherent value, but not according to the receptacle view to which utilitarians are committed. It's the cup, not just what goes into it, that is valuable.

Two options present themselves concerning the possession by moral agents of inherent value. First, moral agents might be viewed as having this value to varying degrees, so that some may have more of it than others. Second, moral agents might be viewed as having this value equally. The latter view is rationally preferable. If moral agents are viewed as having inherent value to varying degrees, then there would have to be some basis for determining how much inherent value any given moral agent has. Theoretically, the basis could be claimed to be anything—such as wealth or belonging to the "right" race or sex. More likely, the basis might be claimed to be possession of certain virtues or excellences, such as those favored by Aristotle. On this latter (perfectionist) account of inherent value, those who have abundant intellectual or artistic skills would have more inherent value than those who have some, and these latter individuals would have more than those who lack these virtues completely. To accept this view of the inherent value of moral agents is to pave the way for a perfectionist theory of justice: those with less inherent value could *justly* be required to serve the needs and interests of those with more, even if it is not in the interests of those who serve to do so. And the subjugated could have no grounds to complain of the injustice of the treatment they receive. Because they have less inherent value, *they* would get what they deserve. Such an interpretation of justice is unacceptable. Equally unacceptable, therefore, is any view of the inherent value of moral agents that could serve as the basis of such a theory. We must reject the view that moral agents have inherent value in varying degrees. All moral agents are equal in inherent value, if moral agents have inherent value.

Three corollaries of the conclusion just reached are worth noting. First, the inherent value of moral agents cannot be viewed as something they can earn by dint of their efforts or as something they can lose by what they do or fail to do. A criminal is no less inherently valuable than a saint, if both are moral agents and if moral agents have inherent value. Second, the inherent value of moral agents cannot wax or wane depending upon the degree to which they have utility with respect to the interests of others. The most beneficent philanthropist is neither more nor less inherently valuable than, say, an unscrupulous used-car salesman. Third, the inherent value of moral agents is independent of their being the object of anyone else's interests. When it comes to inherent value, it matters not whether one is liked, admired, respected, or in other ways valued by others. The lonely, forsaken, unwanted, and unloved are no more nor less inherently valuable than those who enjoy a more hospitable relationship with others. To view all moral agents as equal in inherent value is thus decidedly egalitarian and nonperfectionist.

"But why," it might be asked, "should we prefer the view that all moral agents have equal inherent value over the egalitarianism associated with utilitarianism? Since both are equally egalitarian, why choose *the postulate of inherent value*, to give a name to the view being championed here, in preference to utilitarianism?" This question concedes more to utilitarianism than is its due, since, for reasons advanced in the previous chapter (6.3), it is unclear how, if at all, utilitarian theory *can* find room within itself to account for its version of equality. But there is a further difference between the implications of utilitarian theory and the postulate of inherent value, one that strengthens the latter as it weakens the former. Recall the unsavory moral implications of act utilitarianism, including in particular the utilitarian justification of secret killings of moral agents. For the act utilitarian, we are guilty of no injustice if we kill a moral agent in order to bring about the best aggregate balance of good over evil for all concerned, assuming that everyone's interests were counted and weighted equitably. This approach to ethical judgment assumes that the only kind of value that falls within the scope of a concern for justice is the kind that, so to speak, "goes into" receptacles (e.g., pleasant experiences). Given the postulate of inherent value, however, concern for justice must look to a different kind of value. If moral agents have inherent value, we cannot ignore that value when attempting to determine what treatment is just or unjust. In particular, since this kind of value is not the same as, is not reducible to, and is incommensurate with the kind of value that "goes into" receptacles, we cannot be treating a moral agent as justice requires if the justification is claimed to reside merely in the instrumentality of the act in bringing about the best aggregate balance of, say, pleasures over pains for all those affected by the outcome. No killing of a moral agent, then, whether done in secrecy or not, can be just if its justification assumes that moral agents are mere receptacles. This does not mean that it must always be wrong to kill a moral agent. What it means is that killing a moral agent cannot be in keeping with the requirements of justice, *if* moral agents have inherent value and *if* the defense is an act utilitarian defense. A defense of that kind assumes that moral agents are mere receptacles, which, given the postulate of inherent value, they are not. That this postulate enables us to avoid the counterintuitive implications of act utilitarianism in the case of secret killings of moral agents must surely count as a point in favor of, rather than a point against, viewing moral agents as inherently valuable.

Similar remarks apply to the possible justification of other harms done to moral agents by moral agents. To cause moral agents to suffer or to deprive them of their liberty, for example, cannot be defended merely by appealing to the better balance of, say, pleasure over pain for all concerned. To suppose otherwise is again to assume that moral agents are *merely* receptacles of valuable experiences and so may be treated in ways that optimize these values without the victims being treated unjustly. All that is required to insure just treatment, on utilitarian grounds, is that the preferences (pleasures, etc.) of all affected by the outcome be considered and that equal preferences (pleasures, etc.) be counted equally. But if moral agents have a value that is *not* reducible to or commensurate with the value of their own or everyone else's valuable experiences, then how moral agents are to be treated, if they are to be treated justly, cannot be determined *merely* by considering the desires, and the like, of all involved, weighting them equitably, and then favoring that option that will bring about the optimal balance of goods over evils for all involved. To suppose otherwise is to assume that questions of just treatment can be answered by ignoring the value of the individual moral agent, which, if moral agents are viewed as equal in inherent value, simply is not true. Moreover, because all moral agents are viewed as equal in inherent value, if any have such value, what applies to how some may be justly treated applies to all, whatever their race, say, or sex. Given the postulate of inherent value, no harm done to *any* moral agent can possibly be justified merely on the grounds of its producing the best consequences for all affected by the outcome. Thus are we able to avoid the counterintuitive implications of act utilitarianism if we deny the receptacle view of moral agents and postulate their equal inherent value.

7.3 "ALL ANIMALS ARE EQUAL"

To this point I have restricted my comments on inherent value to the inherent value of moral agents. It might be thought—and it is thought by some, most notably Kant, for reasons explained in an earlier chapter (5.5)—that the notion of inherent value or some related idea (e.g., conceiving of moral agents as "ends in themselves") applies to all moral agents and only to moral agents. But the attempt to restrict inherent value to moral agents is arbitrary. As we saw in the previous discussion of indirect duty views (5.6), any position that denies that we have direct duties to those moral patients with whom we have been and will continue to be concerned (normal mammalian animals, aged one or more, and those human moral patients like these animals in the relevant respects) is rationally defective. Some of our duties regarding animals are duties we owe directly to them. Moreover, as was argued above (5.6), some of the harms done to these moral patients are harms of the same kind as harms done to moral agents. We cannot consistently hold, therefore, that moral agents and patients can never be harmed in relevantly similar ways. They can. Thus, if we view all moral agents as having equal inherent value, if we rely on this account of the value of these individuals to avoid the counterintuitive implications of act utilitarianism, denying that the harm done to some moral agents can be justified merely on the grounds that harming them brings about optimal consequences for all concerned, if some of these harms done to moral agents are harms of the same kind as harms done to moral patients, and if the duties not to harm either moral agents or moral patients in these ways are prima facie duties owed directly to each, then it would be arbitrary to regard moral patients as lacking inherent value or to suppose that they have the status of mere receptacles. If, in short, we postulate inherent value in the case of moral agents, then we cannot nonarbitrarily deny it of moral patients.

Some might concede that moral patients must be viewed as having *some* inherent value, if we postulate inherent value in the case of moral agents, but deny that the inherent value of moral patients is equal to that possessed by moral agents. But the grounds on which this could be argued will inevitably confuse the inherent value of individuals with (a) the comparative value of their experiences, (b) their possession of certain favored virtues (e.g., intellectual or artistic excellences), (c) their utility relative to the interests of others, or (d) their being the object of another's interests. And this confusion will prove fatal to any attempt to defend the view that moral patients have less inherent value than moral agents. Since the inherent value of moral agents does not wax or wane depending on *their* comparative happiness or *their* total of pleasures-over-pains, it would be arbitrary to maintain that moral patients have less inherent value than moral agents because *they* (i.e., moral patients) have less happy lives or because *their* total of pleasures-over-pains is less than that of moral agents—even if this were true, which it may not be in some cases. Moreover, since one cannot suppose that moral agents have varying degrees of inherent value depending on the extent to which they possess some favored virtues or have varying utility with respect to the interests of others, without paving the way for the unjust treatment of those who have less by those who have more—treatment that would be allowed by discredited perfectionist theories of justice—one cannot *non-arbitrarily* maintain that how much inherent value moral patients have depends on the degrees to which they possess the virtues in question or on how much utility for others they have. Morality will not tolerate the use of double standards when cases are relevantly similar. If we postulate inherent value in the case of moral agents and recognize the need to view *their* possession of it as being equal, then we will be rationally obliged to do the same in the case of moral patients. *All* who have inherent value thus have it equally, whether they be moral agents or moral patients. All animals *are* equal, when the notions of 'animal' and 'equality' are properly understood, 'animal' referring to all (terrestrial, at least) moral agents and patients, and 'equality' referring to their equal possession of inherent value.[2] Inherent value is thus a *categorical* concept. One either has it, or one does not. There are no in-betweens. Moreover, all those who have it, have it equally. It does not come in degrees.[3]

7.4 INHERENT VALUE AND REVERENCE FOR LIFE

Those who, like Kant, restrict inherent value to moral agents limit this value to those individuals who have those abilities essential for moral agency, in particular the ability to bring impartial reasons to bear on one's decision making. The conception of inherent value involved in the postulate of inherent value is more catholic, applying to individuals (e.g., human moral patients) who lack the abilities necessary for moral agency. If moral agents and moral patients, despite their differences, are viewed as having equal inherent value, then it is not unreasonable to demand that we cite some relevant similarity between them that makes attributing inherent value to them intelligible and nonarbitrary. In the nature of the case this similarity cannot be something that varies from individual to individual, since that would allow their inherent value to vary accordingly. Thus, no physical characteristic (e.g., having two eyes or five fingers) can mark the relevant similarity; nor will species membership suffice (e.g., belonging to the species *Canus lupus* or *Homo sapiens*); nor will still more general biological classifications do (e.g., being an animal). One characteristic shared by all moral agents and those moral patients with whom we are concerned is that they are *alive*, and some thinkers evidently believe that it is the possession of this characteristic that marks off the class of individuals who have inherent value from those who do not. Albert Schweitzer is perhaps the most famous thinker whose position invites this interpretation, and his famous ethic of "reverence for life" enjoys wide currency in many public discussions of how we ought to live, not only regarding how we ought to treat one another, in our reciprocal relationships as moral agents, but also regarding how we ought to treat other living things, including moral patients. But there are problems concerning both the scope and precision of Schweitzer's principle, some of which Schweitzer himself, perhaps unwittingly, exposes without resolving in the following passage:

> True philosophy must commence with the most immediate and compre-
> hensive facts of consciousness. And this may be formulated as follows: "I
> am life which wills to live, and I exist in the midst of life which wills to
> live". . . . Just as in my own will-to-live there is a yearning for more life,
> and for that mysterious exaltation of the will which is called pleasure, and
> terror in face of annihilation and that injury to the will-to-live which is

called pain; so the same obtains in all the will-to-live around me, equally whether it can express itself to my comprehension of whether it remains unvoiced.

Ethics thus consists in this, that I experience the necessity of practising the same reverence for life toward all will-to-live, as toward my own. Therein I have already the needed fundamental principle of morality. It is *good* to maintain and cherish life; it is *evil* to destroy and to check life. . . . A man is really ethical only when he obeys the constraint laid on him to help all life which he is able to succour, and when he goes out of his way to avoid injuring anything living. He does not ask how far this or that life deserves sympathy as valuable in itself, nor how far it is capable of feeling. To him life as such is sacred. He shatters no ice crystal that sparkles in the sun, tears no leaf from its tree, breaks off no flower, and is careful not to crush any insect as he walks. If he works by lamplight on a summer evening he prefers to keep the window shut and to breathe stifling air, rather than to see insect after insect fall on his table with singed and sinking wings.[4]

Among the many things that are unclear in this passage is why those who are enjoined to have reverence for all *life* should take care not to shatter an ice crystal, since there is no clear sense in which ice crystals are "alive" or exhibit "will to live." That ice crystals may be beautiful, and that conscientious sojourners would not needlessly destroy their beauty or the beauty of nonliving nature generally, is arguable—though not easily! But *if* we are enjoined not to destroy the beauty of the natural order, even when the object of beauty is not alive, then we are in need of a more general principle than that of "reverence for (all) life." More importantly, reliance on a more general principle will imply that *being-alive* is not a necessary condition of something's having inherent value, with the result that "the ethic of reverence for life" will not be the *sole* fundamental principle its champions imply that it is.

In reply to these difficulties it might be suggested that *being-alive* is a *sufficient* condition of an individual's having inherent value. This position would avoid the problems indigenous to the view that being-alive is a necessary condition, but it stands in need of quite considerable analysis and argument if it is to win the day. It is not clear why we have, or how we reasonably could be said to have, direct duties to, say, individual blades of grass, potatoes, or cancer cells. Yet all are alive, and so all should be owed direct duties if all have inherent value. Nor is it clear why we have, or how we reasonably could be said to have, direct duties to collections of such individuals—to lawns, potato fields, or cancerous tumors. If, in reply to these difficulties, we are told that we have direct duties only to some, but not to all, living things, and that it is this subclass of living things whose members have inherent value, then not only will we stand in need of a way to distinguish those living things that have this value from those that do not but more importantly for present purposes, the view that being-alive is a sufficient condition of having such value will have to be abandoned. Because of the difficulties endemic both to the view that being-alive is a necessary condition of having inherent value and to the view that this is a sufficient condition, and granting that moral agents and moral patients share the important characteristic of being alive, it is extremely doubtful that the case could be made for viewing this similarity as the relevant similarity they share, by virtue of which all moral agents and patients have equal inherent value.

7.5 INHERENT VALUE AND THE SUBJECT-OF-A LIFE CRITERION

An alternative to viewing being-alive as the relevant similarity is what will be termed *the subject-of-a-life criterion*. To be the subject-of-a-life, in the sense in which this expression will be used, involves more than merely being alive and more than merely being conscious. To be the subject-of-a-life is to be an individual whose life is characterized by those features explored in the opening chapters of the present work: that is, individuals are subjects-of-a-life if they have beliefs and desires; perception, memory, and a sense of the future, including their own future; an emotional life together with feelings of pleasure and pain; preference- and welfare-interests; the ability to initiate action in pursuit of their desires and goals; a psychophysical identity over time; and an individual welfare in the sense that their experiental life fares well or ill for them, logically independently of their utility for others and logically independently of their being the object of anyone else's interests. Those who satisfy the subject-of-a-life criterion themselves have a distinctive kind of value—inherent value—and are not to be viewed or treated as mere receptacles.

The claim that the value of those individuals who satisfy this criterion is *logically* independent of their utility for, and the interests of, others must be kept distinct from, and not confused with, the obvious fact that the welfare of those who satisfy this criterion is *causally* related to their perceived utility and the interests of others. Actively to harm either a moral agent or patient (e.g., to cause either gratuitous suffering) is to do something that causally detracts from their individual welfare, just as actively to benefit either (e.g., by providing either with the opportunity to pursue their desires, when it is in their interests to do so) is prima facie to contribute to their welfare. Especially in the case of human moral patients, individuals who, because of a variety of conditions, are incapable to varying degrees of taking care of themselves, how they fare in life is to a very considerable degree causally dependent on what we do to them or for them. For example, young children and the mentally enfeebled of all ages lack the requisite knowledge and sometimes even the requisite physical abilities to satisfy even their most basic needs and correlative desires. If we do not act on their behalf, they will fare ill. But even in the case of these individuals, their having a welfare, their being the experiencing subject of a life that fares well or ill *for them*, logically independently of their utility for us or of our taking an interest in them—this fact about them is not causally dependent on what we do to or for them. Indeed, the very possibility of our doing anything that affects their experiential welfare, for good or ill, *presupposes* that they are the experiencing subjects of such a life, on their own, as it were. And the same is true both of those moral patients (e.g., animals in the wild) who can take care of themselves without the need of human intervention and of those humans who are moral agents. Though what we, as moral agents, do to each other causally affects how we fare during the course of our individual lives, that we are the subjects of such a life is not similarly causally dependent on what others do to or for us. We have this status in the world, as do moral patients, whether human or animal, on our own; having this status is *logically* part of what it is for us or them *to be* in the world.

The subject-of-a-life criterion identifies a similarity that holds between moral agents and patients. Is this similarity a relevant similarity, one that makes viewing them as inherently valuable intelligible and nonarbitrary? The grounds for replying affirmatively are as follows: (1) A relevant similarity among all those who are postulated to have equal inherent value must mark a characteristic shared by all those moral agents and patients who are here viewed as having such value. The subject-of-a-life criterion satisfies this requirement. *All* moral agents and *all* those moral patients with whom we are concerned *are* subjects of a life that is better or worse for them, in the sense explained, logically independently of the utility they have for others and logically independently of their being the object of the interests of others. (2) Since inherent value is conceived to be a categorical value, admitting of no degrees, any supposed relevant similarity must itself be categorical. The subject-of-a-life criterion satisfies this requirement. This criterion does not assert or imply that those who meet it have the status of subject of a life to a greater or lesser degree, depending on the degree to which they have or lack some favored ability or virtue (e.g., the ability for higher mathematics or those virtues associated with artistic excellence). One either *is* a subject of a life, in the sense explained, or one *is not*. All those who are, are so equally. The subject-of-a-life criterion thus demarcates a categorical status shared by all moral agents and those moral patients with whom we are concerned. (3) A relevant similarity between moral agents and patients must go some way toward illuminating why we have direct duties to both and why we have less reason to believe that we have direct duties to individuals who are neither moral agents nor patients, even including those who, like moral agents and those patients we have in mind, are alive. This requirement also is satisfied by the subject-of-a-life criterion. Not all living things are subjects of a life, in the sense explained; thus not all living things are to be viewed as having the same moral status, given this criterion, and the differences concerning our confidence about having direct duties to some (those who are subjects) and our not having direct duties to others (those who are not subjects) can be at least partially illuminated because the former meet, while the latter fail to meet, the subject-of-a-life criterion. For these reasons, the subject-of-a-life criterion can be defended as citing a relevant similarity between moral agents and patients, one that makes the attribution of equal inherent value to them both intelligible and nonarbitrary.

Three further points require our attention before turning to the task of articulating and defending the principle of justice grounded in the notion of inherent value. First, though satisfying the subject-of-a-life criterion marks a relevant similarity, one that makes the attribution of inherent value to moral agents and patients both intelligible and nonarbitrary, the claim has not been made, nor does anything said in the above imply, that satisfying this criterion is a *necessary* condition of having inherent value. It *may* be that there are individuals, or possibly collections of individuals, that, though they are not subjects of a life in the sense explained, nevertheless have inherent value—have, that is, a kind of value that is conceptually distinct from, is not reducible to, and is incommensurate with such values as pleasure or preference satisfaction. The issues here are extremely complicated. As I have argued elsewhere, the very possibility of developing a genuine ethic *of* the environment, as distinct from an ethic *for its use*, turns on the possibility of making the case that natural objects, though they do not meet the subject-of-a-life criterion, can nonetheless have inherent value.[5] Attempts to show that this is conceptually absurd are inconclusive at best, while attempts to show that postulating inherent value in natural objects or collections of such objects, though intelligible, is unnecessary, suffer from a similar fate. Nevertheless, it is extraordinarily difficult to give an intelligible account of inherent value in this connection. For example, though criteria can be given regarding when, say, an oak tree is good of its kind (i.e., good as an oak tree), and though these criteria are not dependent on a good oak tree's having utility for others or being the object of anybody's interests,[6] an oak tree's being good of its kind by itself has no more moral significance than, say, a cancer cell's or a murderer's being good of their kind.[7] And the same applies to collections of oak trees (or cancer cells, or murderers). Those who would work out a genuine ethic of the environment in terms of the inherent value of natural objects (trees, rivers, rocks, etc.) or of collections of such objects are not logically debarred from undertaking the task by anything said or implied in these pages, since the subject-of-a-life criterion is set forth as a sufficient, not as a necessary, condition of making the attribution of inherent value intelligible and nonarbitrary. While no one is denied the possibility of working out such an ethic, however, those who aspire to do it certainly have their work cut out for them. (For further remarks on environmental ethics, see 9.3.)

Second, and relatedly, the argument of the present section does not logically preclude the possibility that those humans and animals who fail to meet the subject-of-a-life criterion nonetheless have inherent value. Since the claim is made only that meeting this criterion is a sufficient condition of making the attribution of inherent value intelligible and nonarbitrary, it remains possible that animals that are conscious but not capable of acting intentionally, or, say, permanently comatose human beings might nonetheless be viewed as having inherent value. As in the case of nonconscious natural objects or collections of such objects, however, it must be said that it is radically unclear how the attribution of inherent value to these individuals can be made intelligible and nonarbitrary. The difficulties alluded to in the earlier discussion of viewing being-alive as either a necessary or sufficient condition of having such value may be taken as illustrative of the kind of difficulty one is likely to encounter in this quarter (see 7.5). It may be that animals, for example— which, though conscious and sentient (i.e., capable of experiencing pleasure and pain), lack the ability to remember, to act purposively, or to have desires or form beliefs—can only properly be viewed as receptacles of what has intrinsic value, lacking any value in their own right. One should avoid being doctrinaire on this point. In any event, the attempt to resolve these issues is well beyond the scope of the present work and so, as in the case of exploring the foundations of an environmental ethic, marks a point at which it is incomplete. (For further observations on this matter, see 9.3.) This incompleteness does not infect the adequacy of the subject-of-a-life criterion, however, when this is understood as a sufficient condition in the sense explained, nor does it undermine the claim that normal mammalian animals, aged one or more, as well as humans like these animals in the relevant respects, can intelligibly and nonarbitrarily be viewed as having inherent value.

Third, it is important to emphasize that the preceding argument in support of the subject-of-a-life criterion does not commit "the naturalistic fallacy"—the view, *very* roughly speaking, that it is a fallacy to infer values from facts. The position argued for in the above cannot fairly be reduced to the following:

> Premise (1) Some individuals are the subjects of a life that fares well or ill for them, logically independently of their utility for others or of their being the object of another's interests (a fact).
>
> Conclusion (2) Therefore, these individuals have inherent value (a value).

The present work is not the proper occasion to address the question, Is the naturalistic fallacy a fallacy? Whether it is or not, the argument of the preceding pages is considerably more complicated than the movement from premise (1) to conclusion (2) would suggest. To view certain individuals (e.g., moral agents) as having equal inherent value is a *postulate*— that is, a theoretical assumption. As befits any theoretical assumption, however, it is not one made without reason. On the contrary, it is an assumption that vies with alternative theories about the value of moral agents, in particular the views that they lack value in their own right and are only receptacles of experiences that are valuable in themselves (the utilitarian view) or that they have value in their own right but a kind of value that varies from individual to individual, depending upon the possession of favored virtues (the perfectionist view). And there *are* reasons for accepting this postulate. To postulate that moral agents have equal inherent value provides a theoretical basis for avoiding the wildly inegalitarian implications of perfectionist theories, on the one hand, and, on the other, the counterintuitive implications of all forms of act utilitarianism (e.g., that secret killings that optimize the aggregate consequences for all affected by the outcome are justified). The role of the subject-of-a-life criterion must be viewed, if it is to be viewed fairly, against this larger background. The reasons we have for postulating equal inherent value for all moral agents and patients are logically distinct from that criterion. That criterion is introduced *after* we have indicated the reasons for postulating that moral agents and patients have equal inherent value, not before; thus, its role is not to "derive" the equal inherent value of moral agents *or* of moral patients; rather, its role is to specify a relevant similarity among all those individuals who, by force of argument, are to be viewed as having equal inherent value, if we postulate it in the case of all moral agents, a similarity that makes the attribution of inherent value to them intelligible and nonarbitrary. Reasons have been advanced in the preceding for regarding the subject-of-a-life criterion as equal to this task. To characterize the argument of the previous pages as amounting to the inference from premise (1) to conclusion (2), therefore, is not to characterize that argument. It is to caricature it.

7.6 JUSTICE: THE PRINCIPLE OF RESPECT FOR INDIVIDUALS

The view that moral agents and moral patients have equal inherent value is not itself a moral principle since it does not itself enjoin us to treat these individuals in one way or another. In particular, the postulate of inherent value does not itself provide us with an interpretation of the formal principle of justice, the principle, it will be recalled, that requires that we give each individual his or her due. Still, that postulate does provide us with a basis for offering such an interpretation. If individuals have equal inherent value, then any principle that declares what treatment is due them as a matter of justice must take their equal value into account. The following principle (*the respect principle*) does this: *We are to treat those individuals who have inherent value in ways that respect their inherent value.* Now, the respect principle sets forth an egalitarian, nonperfectionist interpretation of formal justice. The principle does not apply only to how we are to treat some individuals having inherent value (e.g., those with artistic or intellectual virtues). It enjoins us to treat *all* those individuals having inherent value in ways that respect their value, and thus it requires respectful treatment of all who satisfy the subject-of-a-life criterion. Whether they are moral agents or patients, we must treat them in ways that respect their equal inherent value. In its present form, however, the respect principle lacks the precision it is reasonable to require of a moral principle. It does not specify *what* respect for such value requires. Some general comments in this regard may now be offered.

To put matters in their most general negative form first, we may say that we fail to treat individuals who have inherent value with the respect they are due, as a matter of strict justice, whenever we treat them *as if they lacked* inherent value, and we treat them in this way whenever we treat them *as if they were mere receptacles* of valuable experiences (e.g., pleasure or preference satisfaction) or *as if their value depended upon their utility* relative to the interests of others. In particular, therefore, we fail to display proper respect for those who have inherent value whenever we harm them so that we may bring about the best aggregate consequences for everyone affected by the outcome of such treatment. The grounds for claiming that such treatment is disrespectful and unjust should be apparent. It can hardly be just or respectful to harm individuals who have inherent value merely in order to secure the best aggregate consequences for everyone affected by the outcome. This cannot be respectful of inherent value because it is to view the individual who is harmed *merely* as a receptacle of what has value (e.g., pleasure), so that the losses of such value credited to the harmed individual can be made up for, or more than compensated, by the sum of the gains in such values by others, *without any wrong having been done to the loser.* Individuals who have inherent value, however, have a kind of value that is distinct from, is not reducible to, and is incommensurate with such values as pleasure or preference satisfaction, either their own or those of others. To harm such individuals *merely* in order to produce the best consequences for all involved *is* to do what is wrong—*is* to treat them unjustly—because it fails to respect their inherent value. To borrow part of a phrase from Kant, individuals who have inherent value must never be treated *merely as means* to securing the best aggregate consequences.

The respect principle, as a principle of justice, requires more than that we not harm some so that optimific results may be produced for all affected by the outcome; it also imposes the prima facie duty to assist those who are the victims of injustice at the hands of others. This is not peculiar to the present interpretation of formal justice. All initially plausible ethical theories recognize both the duty not to act unjustly oneself as well as the duty to assist those who are the victims of injustice at the hands of others. Justice, that is, not only imposes duties of nonharm; it also imposes duties of assistance, understood as the duty to aid those who suffer from injustice. All individuals who have inherent value are to be given their due, and sometimes what they are due is our assistance. I shall return to this topic in the sequel (9.1).

Like utilitarian interpretations of formal justice, the interpretation provided by the respect principle is not a principle of distributive justice; neither it nor they lay down conditions that must be met if the distribution of benefits (goods) and harms (evils) arising as the result of a given act or rule are just distributions. In opposition to utilitarian interpretations, however, the interpretation of justice in terms of respect for individuals having inherent value *rules out, in advance, the permissibility of arriving at any distribution in certain ways.* No individual who has inherent value may justly be treated as a mere receptacle in order to secure optimal consequences for all affected by the outcome. How the benefits are distributed among the beneficiaries is irrelevant to assessing the injustice involved in securing them. Thus, while both utilitarian interpretations of equality and the respect principle are predistributive principles, the two differ fundamentally in what they can allow, something that will become increasingly clear as we proceed (see, especially, 8.12).

7.7 RULE UTILITARIANISM AND JUSTICE

The objections raised against utilitarianism in the previous chapter and the contrast drawn between utilitarianism and the interpretation of formal justice favored in the present one have focused on act utilitarianism. As was mentioned in the initial survey of utilitarian theory (4.4), not all utilitarians are act utilitarians; some are rule utilitarians. The latter hold that the rightness or wrongness of a given act is to be determined by its conforming or failing to conform to a valid moral rule, and rules are said to be valid, according to rule utilitarianism, if (roughly speaking) general observance of them promotes the overreaching utilitarian goal of bringing about the best aggregate consequences for all affected by the outcome. The same kind of dispute about what counts as "the best consequences" that divide act utilitarians plays a similarly divisive role among rule utilitarians, so that there are rule utilitarians who are hedonists, some who are preference utilitarians, and so forth. As important as this dispute is, the differences that separate rule utilitarians from one another go beyond what does or does not have intrinsic value. Some rule utilitarians argue for 'ideal rule utilitarianism,' a position that regards rules as valid *if* everybody's following them *would* yield the best consequences, even though there is little chance that many people will. Others argue for nonideal utilitarian visions of morality, contenting themselves with asking what rules it is reasonable to believe that most people will (normally) follow or at least will (normally) think should be followed. And still others offer yet different interpretations of the rules that, as utilitarians, they seek to validate. For reasons too apparent to need reciting, it will not be possible to assess all varieties of rule utilitarianism. It must be sufficient for now to indicate why rule utilitarianism, of whatever form, has seemed to some utilitarians to be preferable to act utilitarianism, how a rule utilitarian might respond to the objections I have raised against act utilitarianism, and how a rule utilitarian could dispute the necessity of postulating inherent value and of formulating a principle of justice that relies on this postulate. Then I shall indicate why, despite the apparent strengths of rule utilitarianism, its claims to adequacy are more shadow than substance.

Consider the case of killings done in secret. The act utilitarian, it has been argued, is committed to permitting such killings if they bring about a better total balance of intrinsic good over evil for those affected by the outcome. That the victim loses a lot—indeed, loses everything!—is no cause for moral alarm, nor can it be the occasion for cries of injustice, *if* his interests (pleasures, etc.) were considered and counted equally with the like interests (pleasures, etc.) of others. The rule utilitarian will protest. The rule against killing ("Thou shalt not kill" or "It is wrong to kill") is a valid moral rule, and its validity does not mysteriously vanish when killings are done in secrecy or when the killers reap a harvest of intrinsic values for themselves, goods that more than compensate for the loss on the victim's part. Since this rule is valid, and since killing in secrecy, even if it brings about the best consequences for all those affected by the outcome, is not a valid exception to it (killing in self-defense, for example, might be), those who kill in such circumstances do what is wrong, the rule utilitarian will aver, and the wrongness of their act can be accounted for by utilitarianism after all—by rule utilitarianism, that is.

Now, the grounds for denying the permissibility of such acts, the rule utilitarian can contend, do not require that we either postulate that certain individuals have 'inherent value' or offer interpretations of justice in terms of giving those who have such value the 'respect' they are due. The immorality of harming any moral agent, for example, whether by killing her or by making her suffer, merely to optimize the best aggregate consequences, is nicely accommodated for by appeal to valid moral rules against harming anyone in these ways, the validity of these rules resting on the utility of having them. Rule utilitarianism, therefore, is a simpler theory than any theory that postulates that certain individuals have inherent value, its advocates will claim, since it can account for what its competitor accounts for without making the additional, unnecessary assumption that some individuals have inherent value. And since, other things being equal, the simpler theory should be chosen (see 5.6), utilitarianism wins the day.

There are familiar objections to rule utilitarianism—for example, whether, in its nonideal forms, it is at bottom indistinguishable from act utilitarianism and so heir to all the objections that confront that version, and whether, in its ideal forms, it really is a form of utilitarianism at all. We will bypass these objections on the present occasion.[8] There are other, less familiar but no less damaging, criticisms of rule utilitarianism that will concern us.

The view that we have *direct* duties to moral patients has been defended in an earlier chapter (5.6). If a moral theory is to be adequate, it must provide a credible account of these duties. Rule utilitarianism fails in this regard. Granted, if we concede the equality principle to rule utilitarians—a large assumption, it should be noted—they will be in a position to hold that the interests (pleasures, etc.) of moral patients must be considered and counted equally with the like interests (pleasures, etc.) of any other individual, including moral agents. But this, as we have seen, is a *pre*distributive requirement that *by itself* in no way guarantees that we will have any of the same direct duties to moral patients that we have to moral agents, over and above considering their respective interests and counting them equally. Whether we are obliged on rule utilitarian grounds not to harm moral patients—as we are on that view, let us grant, not to harm moral agents—must depend on whether there are distinctively utilitarian grounds for recognizing a rule setting forth a direct duty against harming the former. The rule utilitarian fails to show that we have such duties to moral patients. In the case of the rule against harming moral *agents,* what the rule utilitarian can argue is the following: If we were to accept rules that allowed that some moral agents could be harmed in certain ways while other moral agents would be protected in this respect, then those persons who belonged to the victimized group would naturally feel resentful and envious, feelings that, Hare remarks, are "disagreeable state(s) of mind (which) lead people to do disagreeable things."[9] To allow rules that foster and encourage envy and resentment and the "disagreeable things" these feelings give rise to, is hardly conducive to promoting the best consequences for all involved, and it is arguable (though not easily!) that a rule utilitarian could object to the adoption of rules that permit harming some moral agents but not others because of the consequences for, and brought into being by, those moral agents not covered by the rule.

This kind of argument (let us call this *the argument from envy*) simply is not available to the rule utilitarian, when the individuals at issue are moral patients, whether animals or human moral patients like these animals in the relevant respects. To feel envy over how some are treated or resentment about one's own situation, because moral rules sanction preferred treatment for others, presupposes that one is able to take stock of how the parties involved are treated, recognize the differences in the treatment they receive as a result of the rules, and, as a consequence of this realization, feel envious or resentful. Moral agents can do this. Moral patients cannot. The latter simply lack the intellectual sophistication to do so. They may be *treated* wrongly as a result of certain rules, but no one will claim that they can or will *recognize* their treatment as wrong because of these rules. Neither, then, is it plausible to maintain that they will feel the envy or resentment attending this recognition in the case of moral agents.

Similarly deficient are appeals to so-called diminishing marginal utility. "Almost always," Hare writes, "if money or goods are taken away from someone who has a lot of them already, and given to someone who has little, total utility is increased, other things being equal."[10] In the case of the distribution of money to moral patients, what Hare claims is, strictly speaking, false. If we give money or other comparable goods to moral patients, there is no reason to believe that total utility will be increased and very good reason to believe that just the reverse will transpire. Lacking as these individuals are in those capacities that would enable them to appreciate the use they can make of money, relative to their own interests, there is no reason to believe that they would, and good reason to believe that they would not, make use of their financial windfall in ways that increase their own interests and thereby increase total utility. To put money and other comparable goods in the hands of a chimpanzee or a young child won't serve the cause of maximizing utility.

In response it can be said that of course we are not to give money and other comparable goods *directly* to moral patients; rather, we are to distribute these goods to other, competent humans in whose care moral patients are entrusted. It is in this way, we may be asked to believe, that we can optimize total utility and thereby provide the needed basis for a rule against harming moral patients. The money used to provide them with the opportunities to satisfy their desires or fulfill their purposes is of greater utility than the comparable sums we might spend in pursuit of other desires or purposes.

This response begs all the important empirical questions that, in the nature of the case, rule utilitarians must answer. What would be the consequences, all considered, if money and other comparable goods were distributed in this way, and how would these consequences fare in comparison with the total consequences that would result if we decided against such a distribution? Unless we know this, it is arbitrary to assume that a rule against harming moral patients, many of whom permanently lack the ability to promote utility by what they do (what contribution to "the general welfare" can the senile make?), can be defended by appeal to declining marginal utility. For it might be that the harms done to these individuals, if we decided not to recognize a rule against harming all or some of them, would be more than offset by the benefits others could thereby obtain. For example, might not the consequences be better, all considered, if we allowed scientific research on morons? In order to take a principled position on this matter, when one's position turns on considerations about the comparative total consequences of our recognizing or not recognizing such a rule, one needs the relevant empirical questions answered, and answered in detail. As is "almost always" the case (recall the earlier criticism of Singer on a similar point, 6.4), the utilitarian does not have the necessary details at hand. And this serves his position ill. Appeals to declining marginal utility can only be as forceful as knowledge of the facts allows. Where knowledge gives way to speculation, these appeals lose their force. Even allowing that appeals to declining marginal utility may carry the day for the utilitarian in some contexts, they are weak and ineffective in the present one.

How, then, can the rule utilitarian account for our having a direct prima facie duty not to harm moral patients? One reply that, as it were, has always been in the wings might now be thrust to center stage: though moral patients cannot feel envy or resentment as a result of discriminatory rules, which makes the argument from envy inapplicable in their case, *other* individuals, it might be argued, *will most certainly* be angered and outraged were we not to recognize a rule against harming moral patients. The parents, relatives, and friends of human moral patients, for example, will certainly feel this way, and those who labor for the better treatment of animals will have comparable feelings in response to those speciesist practices the absence of this rule would allow. Now, these feelings, like those of envy and resentment, are disagreeable, and are likely to lead these people to do disagreeable things, things that, were they to become common—as they would (let us assume) if we failed to recognize the rule in question—would most certainly be detrimental to optimizing overall aggregate utility. In this way, then, it might be argued, the necessary utilitarian backing for recognizing a rule against harming moral patients is provided and is supported by as much empirical certainty as it is reasonable to require on the part of the utilitarian. Moral agents *will* behave badly, because they *will* be angered and outraged if we fail to protect moral patients by having a rule against harming them. We know this. It is not mere speculation.

This response, however plausible it may seem, simply will not do. It has the effect of transforming our *direct* prima facie duty not to harm moral patients into an *indirect* duty. We are to recognize a rule against harming moral patients, according to this reply, not because of the harm done directly to them, nor because of the harm they will do to others as a result, but because of the adverse consequences that would obtain for, and as a result of the actions of, *others* (parents, friends, etc.) if we did not recognize such a rule. For reasons advanced at length in the critical discussion of indirect duty views in chapter 5, *the duty not to harm moral patients is a direct duty we have to them,* and the adequacy of any theory stands or falls depending on whether and, if so, how well it can account for this direct duty. The rule utilitarian's having recourse to the last reply is symptomatic of that theory's failure to meet this requirement.

The critical discussion of rule utilitarianism to this point can be summed up by posing the following dilemma: (1) If rule utilitarians affirm that there is a moral rule against harming moral patients, a rule that generates a direct duty not to harm them, then they fail to ground this rule *either* by appealing to the argument from envy (moral patients cannot feel envious or resentful because of rules that discriminate against them and favor others) *or* by appealing to declining marginal utility (an appeal that will beg all the essential empirical questions). Nor can they ground this rule merely by appealing to the harms moral patients endure (e.g., suffering), since the very question at issue is whether we ought to recognize a direct duty not to harm these individuals, *judged on rule utilitarian grounds,* and it is an open question, so far as rule utilitarianism is concerned, whether having such a rule would or would not serve to bring about gains on the part of others that more than compensate for the losses on the part of the moral patients who are harmed. What *other* fact, then, *about moral patients themselves,* if not their envy and the disagreeable deeds this would give rise to on their part, *could* provide a utilitarian reason for recognizing a direct duty against harming them? None comes readily to mind, and though the preceding discussion does not conclusively prove that no such fact can be found, the onus of proof is certainly on the rule utilitarian to find one. Unless or until he does—and it is fair to say that it is most unlikely that he will—the attempt to ground a rule against harming moral patients on the disutility that results from what *they* will feel or what *they* will do, as a result of being harmed, seems certain to prove inefficacious.

That is the first horn of the rule utilitarian's dilemma. The second one is this: (2) If, in the face of the grave difficulties just summarized, rule utilitarians have recourse to the "disagreeable" mental states that would be produced in the minds of *others* (e.g., parents) if we were not to recognize a rule that generated a duty not to harm moral patients (e.g., children), then the rule utilitarian would have *a* utilitarian reason for having such a rule, but the duty that the rule generated could no longer be regarded as a *direct* duty owed to moral patients. Now, since the case has been made that we have direct duties to moral patients, the rule utilitarian must avoid (2) at all costs. Accordingly, the adequacy of rule utilitarianism stands or falls on how well it can account for our having a *direct* prima facie duty not to harm moral patients. In view of the reasons offered in (1), we have very strong reasons indeed for denying that it can pass this test. Rule utilitarianism lacks the wherewithal to ground direct duties owed to moral patients.

Rule utilitarians might reply to this dilemma by contesting our earlier arguments against indirect duty views, especially those parts of that argument that involve appeals to our intuitions. What one wants, these utilitarians might say, echoing Singer's words, is a "sound theory" against which to test our intuitions, not a proliferation of appeals to our intuitions as a way to test the soundness of a theory. This *sounds* very well and good, but the burden of proof, it will be recalled, is on those who proclaim it to show that what they want done, can be done. *Can* we get a "sound theory" without appealing to our reflective intuitions? This brings us to a final set of objections to rule utilitarianism, when that theory is assumed to stand on its own, as it were, immune to criticisms of it based on appeals to reflective intuitions.

Recall the difficulties posed for utilitarians in the previous chapter (6.3), when they are asked to explain the status of the equality principle. Depending on the theory of value advanced by any given utilitarian, the equality principle will require that intrinsic goods (e.g., preference satisfactions, or pleasures) be considered, no matter whose they are, and that equal weighting be observed (i.e., equal pleasures, or preferences, are to be counted equally). But what can be the *status* of the equality principle within any version of *rule* utilitarianism? It cannot be a fundamental moral principle, since the principle of utility, and that principle alone, is supposed to have this status. Nor can it be a derivative moral principle, a "valid rule," since the equality or inequality of pleasures, preferences, interests, etc. cannot depend on the utility of weighing them as equal or unequal. The equality principle, in short, cannot have the status of a *moral* principle (or rule) within rule utilitarian theory. Neither can it have the status of a *formal* principle, a principle that must be met if any putative moral principle is to qualify as a genuine moral principle. The respect principle has the status of a moral principle, and yet it does not enjoin us to count equal preferences, pleasures, and so forth, equally. At the very most the equality principle, as understood by rule utilitarians, can have the status of a *conditional formal principle*, one that we must accept if, starting with our own individual interests, pleasures, and so on, we then take the moral point of view.

As was noted in the earlier discussion (6.3), however, this argument could at most establish that those who begin to do their ethical thinking from the point of view of their own self-interest would commit themselves to *a* consequentialist principle; the validity of utilitarianism—the view that the principle of utility is the *sole* moral basis of morality—does not follow. Rule utilitarians, therefore, cannot rely on our (assumed) acceptance of the conditional equality principle, as they understand it, to secure our commitment to utilitarianism. Moreover—and for present purposes more fundamentally—some *reason* must be given as to why we should begin thinking about what is moral or immoral from the vantage point of our individual self-interest. *Why* begin there, after all? Certainly a compelling reason would be at hand if it could be shown that, starting from this point, we reach a sound moral theory. But, for reasons just adduced for a second time, if one starts from one's own self-interest, one does not reach (i.e., one is not committed to) the principle of utility as *the one and only* valid moral principle. So the burden of showing why we should, not simply that we might, begin to do our ethical thinking by starting with our own self-interest must be shouldered by those who advocate this as the place to begin. That burden has not been adequately borne by those who would have us start there, not by Narvesonian rational egoists, not by Rawlsian original contractors, and not by preference or other utilitarians. Just as in our earlier discussion of the equality principle and act utilitarianism, therefore, my present finding is that rule utilitarians cannot extract a commitment from us to accept utilitarianism even were we to accept the conditional equality principle (more on this point in a moment). To claim that, when compared with any theory that involves postulating inherent value, rule utilitarianism is simpler and therefore preferable, is to assume the greater part of what rule utilitarians must show—namely, that their theory is at least equal to its theoretical competitors in illuminating why we have those duties we have (rule utilitarianism is not equal to this task since, among other reasons, it cannot adequately account for our direct duty not to harm moral patients) *or* that, apart from testing the theory against our intuitions about such duties, there are *independent* grounds for recognizing the theory as sound (rule utilitarians fail to show this since, among many reasons, they fail to show that acceptance of conditional equality commits one to the theory of utilitarianism). Rule utilitarians, in short, have yet to provide compelling reasons to accept their theory, and we have good reasons to reject it. That theory may be simpler than a theory that involves postulating inherent value, but simplicity isn't everything. (As to why we should not accept the conditional equality principle, see below, 8.13.)

7.8 DEFENDING THE RESPECT PRINCIPLE

In the earlier chapter on ethical theory a procedure was sketched for testing the validity of alternative ethical principles. We begin with our unexamined moral beliefs (our prereflective intuitions) and initiate the process of critical assessment by making a conscientious effort to make an ideal judgment in their case. We strive to be impartial, "cool," rational, conceptually clear, and as informed as we can be. Those beliefs that withstand this process of critical evaluation cannot be fairly described as beliefs we "just happen" to have or summarily dismissed as prejudices. They are considered beliefs, or intuitions in the reflective sense, beliefs that may then be used as a basis for identifying general moral principles that systematize these intuitions and as a touchstone against which competing ethical principles can be tested, subject, it will be recalled, to the proviso that some of these beliefs may themselves stand in need of revision or abandonment if they cannot be accounted for by principles shown to be valid in other respects. If we engage in this process of critical reflection, the case can be made for rational acceptance of the respect principle.

Among our prereflective intuitions are those that concern when it is wrong to harm a moral agent. It is, we believe (unless we have already pledged our allegiance to utilitarianism), wrong to kill a moral agent just so that an optimal balance of intrinsic goods over evils may be secured by all those affected by the outcome. And it is similarly wrong to harm a moral agent in other ways for similar reasons—for example, to cause a moral agent gross suffering or to deny her the satisfaction of her basic needs or the opportunities to acquire essential skills on the grounds that this will optimize the balance of good over evil for all affected by the outcome. These are beliefs we hold, not only before, but after we have begun to reflect critically on them, not because of excessive emotional involvement, *or* because we arbitrarily favor some moral agents (say, women or Americans) over others, *or* because we are fuzzy-minded about the concepts of 'moral agency' or 'harm,' *or* because we are ill informed about the relevant facts; nor can it be claimed that the beliefs are irrational because they lead to inconsistent consequences. These beliefs qualify as *considered* beliefs, and they should therefore play a legitimate role in the reflective formulation and assessment of alternative ethical principles.

Now, the respect principle illuminates and unifies, by identifying relevant grounds for, these beliefs. That principle requires that we not treat moral agents as if they were mere receptacles of value, lacking any value in their own right. This is what we would be doing if we supposed that the harms done to one moral agent could be justified merely by appealing to the optimal aggregate balance of intrinsic good over intrinsic evil secured by all those affected by the outcome. The respect principle will not allow this. Those who have inherent value have a kind of value that is distinct from, is not reducible to, and is incommensurate with intrinsic values, either their own intrinsically valuable experiences or those of others. We must treat such individuals with the respect due them, as possessors of such value, and this we will manifestly fail to do if we treat them in ways that could only be justified if moral agents were viewed as something that, given the postulate of inherent value, they are not—namely, as mere receptacles of value, lacking any value in themselves. The respect principle thus both matches and goes some way toward the goal of systematizing our considered beliefs about the wrongness of harming moral agents.

One wants more from a moral principle than this, however. There are other relevant criteria, set forth and defended in the earlier chapter on ethical theory, that a valid ethical principle must meet. The respect principle meets them. That principle is *consistent* certainly. It does not assert or imply that we can treat some moral agents (e.g., Jews) as if they were mere receptacles while denying that we can do this in the case of others (e.g., white Anglo-Saxon Protestants). It lays down a requirement concerning how any and all moral agents must be treated, as a matter of strict justice. Every moral agent is to be given his or her due, and what each is due, as a matter of strict justice, is the same respectful treatment due any other. The respect principle, therefore, is eminently egalitarian, providing an alternative interpretation of Bentham's declaration that each is to count for one, no one for more than one. Moreover, because this principle applies to our treatment of all moral agents, it has *adequate scope*. There are literally billions of cases where it daily applies. It does not become operative only, say, when bridge is being played or at high table. As for *precision*, the respect principle makes clear, intelligible requirements: We are *not* to treat any moral agent in ways whose possible justification consists *merely* in appealing to the optimal aggregate consequences that result for all those affected by the outcome. In its present form, it is true, the respect principle provides negative direction only and, by itself, it fails to provide the needed guidance concerning when, and if so why, it is justifiable to harm a moral agent. These are matters that will concern us in the following chapter (see 8.7ff.). Even in its present form, however, the respect principle meets the relevant criteria for evaluating a moral principle: it is consistent, has adequate scope and precision, and matches a broad range of our reflective intuitions. What its logical status is (that is, whether it is a fundamental or derivative moral principle) remains an open question at this point (on this question, see 8.12). What is not open to serious question is whether, having identified this principle, having explained how it unifies and illuminates our considered beliefs about when it is wrong to harm moral agents in a broad range of cases, having satisfied the legitimate requirements of scope, precision, and consistency, and having done all this in an unemotional, disciplined fashion, in deference to the requirements of impartiality, rationality, and the other conditions that give content to the ideal moral judgment—what is not open to serious question is whether, having done all this, we have failed to take any steps in the direction of justifying acceptance of the respect principle. If the foregoing considerations do not provide good reasons to accept that principle, one can only ask what *could* provide good reasons for accepting any principle.

Respect For Moral Patients

The interplay between our pretheoretical beliefs and principles, such as the respect principle, is a two-way street, and we must, therefore, consider the implications of accepting this principle. This requires asking how other unconsidered beliefs we may happen to have match this principle. In particular, it requires asking whether the scope of the respect principle can be nonarbitrarily limited only to how moral agents may be treated. The arguments of the past three chapters provide the grounds for claiming that any and all attempts to limit the scope of the respect principle to moral agents must be deficient. Against indirect duty views, it was argued that we have a direct prima facie duty not to harm moral patients; thus, we cannot maintain that the respect principle applies only to our dealings with moral agents on the grounds that (a) this principle applies only to how we may treat those individuals to whom we have direct duties and that (b) we have no direct duties to moral patients. Nor can we avoid recognizing that moral patients fall within the principle's scope on the grounds that they have no inherent value or less inherent value than moral agents; this will not do because attempts to disenfranchise moral patients in this way will lay the groundwork for a perfectionist theory of justice, a theory that will either sanction unjust treatment of some moral *agents* or avoid this—but only at the price of arbitrariness. To accept the respect principle, in short, commits us to recognizing that it applies also to our dealings with moral patients. *They* are not to be treated as if they are mere receptacles. We cannot justify harming *them* merely on the grounds that this will produce an optimal aggregate balance of intrinsic goods over intrinsic evils for all concerned. *We owe them* respectful treatment, not out of kindness, nor because of the "sentimental interests" of others, but because justice requires it. If our prereflective intuitions about how all or some moral patients may be treated happen to differ from how they must be treated, if the respect principle is accepted, then these beliefs will have to be changed. Not to change them, given the arguments most recently advanced, and assuming the respect principle is accepted, is to expose oneself to the charge of being prejudiced, and rightly so.

These implications of the respect principle—that moral patients generally, and animals in particular, are to be treated with respect *and* that respectful treatment is their due, as a matter of strict justice—may strike some people as so bizarre that they will want to avoid accepting the respect principle and the postulate of inherent value on which it rests. The cumulative force of the arguments presented in the last three chapters is that there is no rational, nonarbitrary way to avoid this principle and this postulate so long as it is reasonable to believe (and reasons have been given to support believing) that it is prima facie wrong to harm moral agents *and* that harming them cannot be justified merely on the grounds that this is necessary to bring about optimal aggregate consequences for all concerned. If just this much is accepted, there is no rational, nonarbitrary way to avoid viewing harm done to moral patients in the same way. And once this has been shown, it can then be shown (and has been shown) that the leading attempts to account for this duty without postulating inherent value and without relying on the respect principle must be inadequate either because they will fail adequately to account for this duty in the case of moral agents (a cardinal failure of act utilitarianism and rational egoism) or because they will fail adequately to account for this duty in the case of moral patients (a singular failure of rule utilitarianism and Rawls's and Kant's positions). And if, finally, we are told to abandon the attempt to validate ethical principles or test ethical theories by having recourse to our reflective intuitions because they are prejudices or because we can construct a sound ethical theory without relying on them, our reply should be that the former claim simply is untrue and the latter demonstrably unsubstantiated. For these reasons, then—all of them taken in concert, no one of them taken in isolation from the rest—we have good reason to accept the respect principle, the postulate of inherent value on which it is based, and the full range of implications that flow from their acceptance.

7.9 THE DERIVATION OF THE HARM PRINCIPLE

Although its logical status remains an open question at this point, the respect principle clearly is more fundamental than the harm principle since this latter principle can be derived from the former (on the logical status of the respect principle, see 8.12). The derivation proceeds as follows: The respect principle rests on the postulate of inherent value, and the case has been made for intelligibly and nonarbitrarily viewing all those who satisfy the subject-of-a-life criterion as having value of this kind. Now, those who satisfy this criterion are the subjects of a life that is experientially better or worse for them, logically independently of their utility for others and their being the object of another's interests. Those who satisfy this condition, in short, are individuals *who have an experiential welfare*—whose experiential life fares well or ill, depending on what happens to, or is done to or for, them. The notions of benefit and harm thus apply to our thought and talk about these individuals, benefits consisting of opportunities for the satisfaction of desires and the fulfill-ment of purposes that are in the interests of these individuals, and harms being what detract from their individual welfare. Because those who have a welfare, in the sense explained, have inherent value, and because those who have inherent value are owed treatment respectful of this value, those who have a welfare are owed treatment respectful of their distinc-tive kind of value. Prima facie, therefore, we fail to treat such individuals in ways that respect their value if we treat them in ways that detract from their welfare—that is, in ways that harm them. We have, in short, a prima facie direct duty not to harm those individuals who have an experiential welfare, which is precisely what the harm principle declares. The respect principle, then, not only succeeds in matching our considered beliefs about when it is wrong to harm moral agents but also provides the basis from which a second moral principle (the harm principle)—a principle of direct duty whose validity was defended in an earlier context (5.6)—can be derived. And that must surely count as an additional point in favor of rational acceptance of the respect principle.

To show that the harm principle is derivable from the respect princi-ple is not to show that no matter what the circumstances, it is always wrong to harm another, either a moral agent or a moral patient. This issue will be explored at length in the following chapter (8.7ff). Even at this juncture, however, the following should be clear. Those cases, if any, in which individuals may justifiably be harmed must not contravene the requirement of just treatment set forth by the respect principle. For example, the justification of the harm done cannot rest on the assumption that the harmed individual is a mere receptacle of value, lacking any value in his own right. That would be to treat the harmed individual unjustly because disrespectfully, and no harm done to a moral agent or patient can be justified if it is unjust.

7.10 SUMMARY AND CONCLUSION

The formal principle of justice stipulates that each individual is to be given his or her due. This much is uncontroversial. The controversy begins when we ask what individuals *are* due. Answers to this question offer normative interpretations or theories of justice. Three such interpretations were considered: (1) perfectionism, which holds that what individuals are due depends on the degree to which they possess certain virtues (e.g., intellectual skills); (2) utilitarianism, which holds that what individuals are due is equal consideration of their interests (or pleasures, etc.); and (3) the equality of individuals view, which holds that what individuals are due is equal respect for their equal inherent value. Perfectionism was rejected (7.1) because it would justify the unjust exploitation of the less virtuous (e.g., the less intelligent) by the more virtuous; and utilitarian interpretations were rejected because they either fail to account for the full range of the wrongful acts that may be done to moral agents (a central defect urged against act utilitarianism in an earlier chapter, 6.2) or because (7.7) they fail to account for the full range of our direct duties to moral patients (a central defect of rule utilitarianism). The equality of individuals interpretation overcomes these defects, first, because all those individuals who have inherent value have it equally (thus the unsavory implications of perfectionism are avoided) and because, second, we would fail to show respect for the inherent value individuals possess if we were to treat them in the ways that act utilitarianism and rule utilitarianism would sanction or require.

The notion of inherent value was explained (7.2). Those who have value of this kind are more than receptacles of the value that attaches to their experiences, the view of individuals and their value (or lack of value) common to all forms of utilitarianism. Inherent value is distinct from, not reducible to, and incommensurate with intrinsic values (e.g., pleasure). The postulate of inherent value must be defended on theoretical grounds, and the attempt was made to offer such a justification. If we do not make this postulate, it was argued, we will be unable to account for our considered beliefs (our reflective intuitions) about when it is wrong to harm either moral agents or moral patients. Though this postulate will oblige us to construct a less simple theory than some (e.g., utilitarianism), that is a price we must be willing to pay if we are to have the most adequate theory, all considered.

To deny that moral patients have inherent value, or to affirm that they have less inherent value than moral agents, it was argued (7.3), is arbitrary. "All animals are equal" is true, when understood in context. The question of the relevant similarity shared by all those who have equal inherent value was addressed. This similarity cannot be, say, some physical characteristic or some biological fact (e.g., species membership). The view that it is being-alive was considered and rejected (7.4), and the subject-of-a-life criterion was clarified and defended (7.5). Individuals are subjects of a life if they are able to perceive and remember; if they have beliefs, desires, and preferences; if they are able to act intentionally in pursuit of their desires or goals; if they are sentient and have an emotional life; if they have a sense of the future, including a sense of their own future; if they have a psychophysical identity over time; and if they have an individual experiential welfare that is logically independent of their utility for, and the interests of, others. This criterion is a sufficient condition for making attributions of inherent value intelligible and nonarbitrary. Whether it is a necessary condition was left an open question.

As a matter of strict justice, then (7.6), we are required to give equal respect to those individuals who have equal inherent value, whether they be moral agents or moral patients, and, if the latter, whether they be humans or animals. That is something each is due (7.8). Injustice arises when we treat those who have such value in ways that fail to display proper respect (for example, by treating them as if their value was reducible to their utility for others).

The harm principle, a principle that sets forth a prima facie direct duty not to harm either moral agents or patients, is derivable from the respect principle (7.9), when we note that (1) those individuals who satisfy the subject-of-a-life criterion are individuals who are intelligibly and nonarbitrarily viewed as meriting respect because they are intelligibly and nonarbitrarily viewed as possessing inherent value, and that (2) as subjects-of-a-life, all have an experiential welfare. Prima facie, therefore, we fail to show respect for these individuals when we do anything that harms them. Whether and, if so, how the duty not to harm these individuals may be justifiably overridden are issues that remain to be examined, but no harm done to moral agents or patients can be justified if it is unjust. No harm can be justified, accordingly, if it contravenes the respect principle, treating the harmed individuals as mere receptacles of value or as things whose value is reducible to their utility relative to the interests of others.

8

The Rights View

I n this chapter the case for recognizing the rights of moral agents and patients is brought to a head. The statement and defense of the rights view requires making use of the conclusions reached in the preceding; but it also involves exploring ideas conspicuous for their absence to this point, most notably the idea of rights. I shall proceed as follows. Moral and legal rights will be distinguished (8.1); the former are analyzed in terms of valid claims that have correlative duties (8.2–8.3). Since the respect principle sets forth an unacquired duty of justice, calling for the respectful treatment of all who have inherent value, it is argued that those who have this kind of value have a valid claim, and thus a right, to treatment respectful of their value (8.4). Because both moral agents and patients have value of this kind, and have it equally, both are shown to have an equal moral right to treatment respectful of their value (8.5). A number of objections against the arguments of the first five sections are then considered (8.6), and, in the next section (8.7), two principles that imply that all or some of those individuals who have inherent value may never justifiably be harmed are explored and found to be deficient. A further objection, one that contests the meaningfulness of regarding moral patients as innocent, is disputed (8.8), and a final objection, raised against the permissibility of counting the number of innocent individuals to determine what ought to be done, is refuted (8.9). Having thus prepared the way for recognizing the equal prima facie moral right of moral agents and patients not to be harmed, the next section (8.10) turns to the task of identifying and validating those principles that justify overriding this right. The radical difference between the rights view and utilitarianism is then explained (8.11), and a number of objections to, and implications of, the rights view are considered (8.11). Before the final section's summary and conclusion, two issues broached but not resolved in earlier chapters are considered (8.12).

8.1 MORAL AND LEGAL RIGHTS

Whether individuals have legal rights depends on the laws and other legal background (e.g., the constitution) of the society in which they live. In some countries (e.g., the United States) citizens meeting certain requirements have the legal right to vote or run for elected office; in other countries (e.g., Libya) citizens do not have these rights. Moreover, even in those countries that give this right to its citizens, the requirements are not always the same and are subject to change. In the United States, for example, citizens once had to be twenty-one years of age to vote in federal elections; now they must be eighteen. At one time one could not vote if one were black or female or illiterate; now one has this right regardless of race or sex or educational achievement. Legal rights thus are subject to great variation, not only among different countries at the same time but also in the same country at different times. When it comes to legal rights, not all individuals are equal. This should not be surprising. The legal rights individuals have arise as the result of the creative activity of human beings. Those rights set forth in the Bill of Rights, for example, were not rights that citizens of the United States could claim as legal rights before these rights were drawn up and the legal machinery necessary for their enforcement was in place.

The concept of moral rights differs in important ways from that of legal rights. First, moral rights, if there are any, are universal. This means that if any individual (A) has such a right, then any other individual like A in the relevant respects also has this right. What counts as the relevant respects is controversial, something we will have to come to terms with in what follows (8.4). What is not controversial is the exclusion of some characteristics as relevant. An individual's race, sex, religion, place of birth, or country of domicile are not relevant characteristics for the possession of moral rights. We cannot deny that individuals possess moral rights, as we can in the case of the possession of legal rights, because of, for example, where they live.

A second feature of moral rights is that they are equal. This means that if any two individuals have the same moral right (e.g., the right to liberty), then they have this right equally. Possession of moral rights does not come in degrees. All who possess them possess them equally, whether they are, say, white or black, male or female, Americans or Iranians.

Third, moral rights, unlike legal rights, do not arise as a result of the creative acts of any one individual (e.g., a despot) or any group (e.g., a legislative assembly). Theoretically, one could, it is true, create legal rights that accord with or protect moral rights, but that is not the same as creating these moral rights in the first place. If there are moral rights, they do not "come to be" in the way legal rights do.

Few issues divide philosophers as deeply as the debate over moral rights. When, for example, Singer expresses his regrets over referring to rights in the course of his argument for animal liberation (see 6.4), what he says is illustrative of the tendency on the part of some thinkers to disparage appeals to rights in moral philosophy, appeals that are, in the words of the nineteenth-century English philosopher D. G. Ritchie, "a rhetorical device for gaining a point without the trouble of proving it" (a "device" that, Ritchie goes on to observe, "may be left to the stump-orator or party journalist but which should be discredited in all serious writing").[1] An even more caustic accusation about the use of "the rhetoric of rights" is offered by Hare, who laments the frequency with which people ask the question, What rights do I have? "For people who ask this . . . question," he writes, "will, being human, nearly always answer that they have those rights, whatever they are, which will promote a distribution of goods which is in the interest of their own social group. The rhetoric of rights, which is engendered by this question, is a recipe for class war, and civil war. In pursuit of these rights, people will, because they have convinced themselves that justice demands it, inflict almost any harms on the rest of society and on themselves."[2] Worse than being a mere "rhetorical device," appeals to and beliefs about rights, on Hare's view, can be positively harmful.

It is no accident that Hare and Singer, for example, who we know are advocates of utilitarianism, should disassociate themselves from reliance on moral rights. In doing so they follow in Bentham's well-known footsteps. "Rights are," he writes,

> . . . the fruits of the law, and of the law alone. There are no rights without law—no rights contrary to the law—no rights anterior to the law. . . . There are no other than legal rights;—no natural rights—no rights of man, anterior or superior to those created by the laws. The assertion of such rights, absurd in logic, is pernicious in morals.[3]

Worse than "nonsense"—Bentham actually characterizes talk of rights other than legal rights as "nonsense upon stilts"[4]—invocations of "the rights of man" are *dangerous* nonsense. How much the repudiation of moral rights by these utilitarians is itself a "rhetorical device" may be left to the reader to decide.

It is relevant to note that not all utilitarians have been theoretically ill disposed to moral rights. Mill provides a clear counterinstance to the prevailing utilitarian tendency, believing that utilitarian theory is adequate to the task of accommodating moral rights. Whether he is correct in thinking this is a matter I will postpone examining at this juncture (see 8.6). Here it will be useful to review what he says about rights and contrast this with Bentham's view. Moreover, by endorsing, as I shall, the analysis Mill gives of moral rights, the way will be blocked to the objection that I rely on an analysis for which no utilitarian can have any sympathy. The strategy is to play to the strength of those utilitarians who acknowledge moral rights, rather than to play to their weakness.

"When we call anything a person's right," Mill writes,

we mean that he has a valid claim upon society to protect him in the possession of it, either by the force of law or by that of education or opinion. If he has what we consider to be a sufficient claim, on whatever account, to have something guaranteed him by society, we say he has a right to it. . . . To have a right, then, is, I conceive, to have something society ought to defend me in the possession of.[5]

Unlike Bentham's view of rights, Mill's does not restrict rights to those that are recognized by the existing laws of a given society and suitably enforced. It is quite possible, given Mill's analysis of rights, for someone to have a valid claim to something (and thus a right to it) and yet for society not to recognize the validity of this claim and thus to fail to protect the individual in his possession of it. While on Bentham's view there can be no rights except those recognized by law (i.e., legal rights), on Mill's view there can be socially unacknowledged and legally unenforced rights (i.e., moral rights). And this is a virtue of Mill's position. One of the roles appeals to rights play, as the American philosopher David Lyons notes, is their use "to argue for changes in the social order."[6] Bentham's analysis of rights makes this literally meaningless—that is, nonsense—since where there is no socially acknowledged and enforced right (i.e., no legal right), there can be no right period. Mill's analysis allows for the meaningfulness of appeals to rights in such cases, while implying that such appeals are not self-authenticating: just because we *claim* to have a right to so and so, it does not follow that our claim is a valid one nor, therefore, that we have the right in question. If the validity of the claim is not shown or, worse still, if we fail seriously even to address the task of showing its validity, then Ritchie's remark is apt: our appeal to "our rights" *is* "a rhetorical device," a device we use "for gaining a point without the trouble of proving it." There is no reason why this *must* be so, however, or why, because some (perhaps even most) "appeals to rights" are rhetorical, in the sense Singer and Hare bemoan, all appeals to rights should be summarily dismissed. Mill, for all his insistence on utility as the sole (moral) basis of morality, is not ill disposed to all appeals to moral rights. That is an example of theoretical tolerance we might all do well to emulate.

Two further features of Mill's analysis of moral rights warrant comment. First, moral rights, understood as valid claims, have correlative duties. If I have the right to liberty, for example, then you and society generally have a duty, in Mill's words, "to protect me in the possession of it." My liberty is something "society ought to defend me in the possession of." Recognition of my moral rights therefore carries implications concerning both what you, as a moral agent, must and must not do. What you must not do is violate my rights, and what you must do, other things being equal, is protect me against any others who would violate them. Your recognition of my moral rights thus both imposes certain limits on your liberty and grounds obligations of assistance you have to me. It is because the moral rights individuals have carry these implications that recognition of these rights is the serious business it is. Indiscriminate invocation of "our rights" can cheapen the notion as it irritates those who are called upon to bear the burdens of duties of assistance and forbearance, if the rights are recognized.

Second, to characterize moral rights as Mill does—as valid claims—leaves it an open question how these claims are to be validated. Bentham's disenchantment with the idea of moral rights can be partly explained by his impatience with the method of validation some have favored—for example, that moral (natural) rights are conferred by nature itself, or that they are "self evident," or, relatedly, that they are there to be discovered by "the pure light of natural reason." One can agree that these are unreliable procedures for validating rights and still allow that rights *can* be validated—that is, that good reasons can be given to recognize some claims to rights as valid claims. Mill once again provides us with guidance concerning how this may be done. The validity of a right, he believes, must depend on its compliance with moral principles whose validity have been independently established. In Mill's case the validating moral principle is that of utility. It should not be surprising, therefore, that he should write as follows:

> To have a right, then, is, I conceive, to have something society ought to defend me in the possession of. If the objector goes on to ask why it ought, I can give him no other reason than general utility.[7]

There is, however, nothing in Mill's analysis of rights as valid claims that logically ties validation of these claims to the utility of recognizing them. As Lyons remarks, "someone who rejected the general welfare standard could consistently accept Mill's analysis of rights (or something like it) and use a different basis for validating the relevant claims. This is because his analysis of rights . . . is independent of the general welfare standard."[8] What moral principles validate rights, in other words, is left open by Mill's analysis of what rights are. An alternative to Mill's utilitarian validation will be offered below (8.4).

8.2 CLAIMS AND VALID CLAIMS

The view that moral rights are valid claims has a high degree of initial plausibility. To have a right is to be in a position to claim, or to have claimed on one's behalf, that something is due or owed, and the claim that is made is a claim made against somebody, to do or forbear what is claimed as due. Mill has little to say about the nature of claims. The distinguished American philosopher Joel Feinberg does. Like Mill, Feinberg analyzes rights as claims that are validated ("called for") by reference to valid moral principles or "the principles of an enlightened conscience."[9] Unlike Mill, Feinberg explores the notion of a claim at length, distinguishing between (1) making a claim, (2) having a valid claim-to, (3) having a valid claim-against, and (4) having a valid claim all considered. Only in the last case does one have a right, on his analysis, yet the other considerations have a role to play in explicating both what rights are and how they are to be validated. How these several ideas are related may be explained as follows:

To make a claim is a performance; it is to assert that one is oneself entitled, or that someone else is entitled, to treatment of a certain kind and that the treatment is due or owed directly to the individual(s) in question. To make a claim thus involves both claims-to and claims-against. It involves claims-against a given individual, or many individuals, to do or forbear doing what is claimed is due, and it involves a claim-to what one is claiming is owed. Both these features of making a claim are crucial to the process of validating a claim that has been made. I cannot have a valid claim (i.e., a right) if I do not have a valid claim-against someone, and I cannot have a valid claim-against someone if that individual does not have a duty to me to do or forbear doing the act I claim is owed me. This is why no one has a valid claim (i.e., a right) to the charitable acts of others. Duties of charity allow considerable individual discretion concerning how they may be discharged. I might give my money to Oxfam and Sisters of the Poor, you might give yours to CARE and the Sierra Club, and we both might thereby fulfill our duty of charity, more or less. But though we have a duty to be charitable, charitable organizations themselves have no right to our contributions, and they have no right to this because they have no valid claim-against us in this regard. A representative of the United Way, for example, has no valid grounds on which to argue that we have a duty of charity to contribute money to that organization in particular. And since neither the United Way nor any other charitable organization has a valid claim-against us in this respect, no such organization has a right to our charitable acts. For similar reasons, we have no rights with respect to the natural order. Individuals are everyday affected, for good or ill, by what happens as a result of nature's running its course, but no one can reasonably complain that nature violates his or her rights. Nature *could* violate our rights only if we could validate our claims-against it, and we could validate our claims-against it only if we could make the case that nature has direct duties to us to do or forbear doing certain acts that are our due. But nature has no duties; only moral agents do. When we, as we sometimes do, speak of nature or its consequences as "unjust" or "unfair," we speak metaphorically. What happens as a result of natural laws happens; it is neither just nor unjust, fair nor unfair, though it can be, and frequently is, beneficial or harmful. Nature no more violates our rights than it respects them.

The claims-to feature of making and validating claims also is important. To make a claim is to assert that treatment is due. Whether the treatment claimed as due *is* due depends in part on whether it is within the powers and capacities of those against whom the claim is made to do or forbear doing what is claimed as due. It is no good your claiming to be owed a vacation in Acapulco or a retreat in Vail from me. To make claims to something against someone cannot be valid if they cannot be satisfied.

To fully validate a claim (i.e., to establish a right) therefore clearly involves more than making a claim. The claim that is made must be validated both as a claim-to and as a claim-against. To satisfy the former requirement one must show that the treatment claimed as due makes requirements of those against whom the claim is made that they can meet;

to satisfy the latter requirement one must show that the treatment claimed as due is owed by those individuals against whom the claim is made. Now, to meet this latter requirement will involve appeals to valid moral principles that set forth direct duties. This should come as no surprise. Since to make a claim-to something against others is to assert that they are required to act in certain ways, one must show that this treatment is owed or is due, and to show this one must show that the treatment in question is required by valid moral principles of direct duty. This is why moral rights have correlative moral duties. If I have a right to, say, life and liberty, then others have direct duties to me with respect to these rights. It is only when claims-to and claims-against are coupled with appeals to appropriate, valid moral principles that we have a valid claim, all considered (i.e., a moral right). It is because many claims to rights are not validated in this way that appeals to rights have gotten a bad name. But, again, just because this is sometimes, even frequently, true, there is no reason why this must be true of all appeals to rights.

To establish one's rights is not by itself enough to establish anyone's duty in any actual situation. This is clearest in cases where rights themselves come into conflict. I may have a right to free speech, for example, but it does not follow that others have a duty in each and every circumstance to allow me to say anything I please. Others have rights, too, and what I do in the name of my right to free speech might conflict with their rights, as when, in the proverbial case, I shout "Fire!" (when there is none) in a crowded theater. To establish one's rights is to establish *their moral relevance* in the determination of what, in any actual case, morally ought to be done. Whatever ought to be done, in other words, cannot be determined independently of considering the rights of those involved, even though what ought to be done cannot be determined just by citing this or that right possessed by this or that individual.

8.3 ACQUIRED AND UNACQUIRED DUTIES

The merits of the analysis of rights in terms of valid claims might be clearer if we apply it to both acquired and unacquired duties. Unacquired duties (what Rawls calls "natural duties"), to use Rawls's characterization, "apply to us without regard to our voluntary acts" and hold "irrespective of institutional arrangements."[10] Acquired duties are the reverse: we have them because of our voluntary acts or our place in institutional arrangements. The duties to keep a promise and to honor a contract are acquired duties. The duty to treat others justly is an unacquired duty. The analysis of rights in terms of valid claims applies to duties of both kinds. In the case of promising, for example, the person to whom the promise is made (the promisee) can have a valid claim-to fulfillment of the promise and a valid claim-against the promisor to do so; the promisee will have a valid claim-to in this case if it is within the powers of the promisor to carry out his end of the bargain, and the promisee will have a valid claim-against the promisor if, as is true in this case, the claim is made against an assignable individual (namely, the promisor) and if the moral rule, "Keep your promises" is valid. Why this rule is valid will be explained below (8.12). For present purposes the example of promising should suffice to illustrate how the analysis of rights in terms of valid claims is applicable to the analysis of acquired duties and how, once it is applied, the existence of correlative rights can be established. Our primary interest, for reasons that will become clearer as we proceed, concerns the application of this analysis to unacquired duties.

Paramount among our unacquired duties is the duty of justice—the duty not to treat individuals differently in the absence of a relevant dissimilarity. Of course, how this formal principle of justice should be normatively interpreted occasions heated disputes, as we saw in the preceding chapter. Questions about how this principle should be interpreted to one side, it should be clear that the duty to be just differs in kind from, say, the duty to keep a promise. I come to have this latter duty as a result of my voluntary acts; not so in the case of the duty of justice. That is a duty we have, in Rawls's words, "without regard to our voluntary acts" and "irrespective of institutional arrangements." Some would dispute this. Given his version of rational egoism, for example, Jan Narveson evidently would deny that we have an unacquired or natural duty of justice. If morality consists of "the arrangements" struck by rational egoists, it is difficult to see how the duty of justice could be otherwise; we *would* acquire that duty, given this position, if or as we reached the agreement to treat one another justly, however such treatment is interpreted, in which case our duty of justice *would* arise as a result of "our voluntary acts." Reasons have been advanced against this vision of morality in the earlier discussion of Narveson's views (5.3); they will not be repeated here. The inadequacy of a Narvesonian account of morality in general, especially its arbitrary exclusion of moral patients as individuals who are owed direct duties, casts sufficient doubt on its adequacy in the particular case of our direct duty of justice.

Rawls's contractarianism is less clear on this issue. Rawls does assert that the duty of justice is a natural duty, but what he then goes on to say about "the principles of justice" makes it less clear whether the duty of justice does not after all depend on the "voluntary acts" of *some* persons—namely, the hypothetical acts of those in the original position. Here is what he says:

> From the standpoint of justice as fairness, a fundamental natural duty is the duty of justice. This duty requires us to support and comply with just institutions that exist and apply to us. It also constrains us to further just arrangements not yet established, at least when this can be done without too much cost to ourselves. Thus if the basic structure of society is just, or as just as it is reasonable to expect in such circumstances, everyone has his duty to do his part in the existing scheme. Each is bound to these institutions independent of his voluntary acts, performative or otherwise. Thus even though the principles of duty are derived from a contractarian point of view, they do not presuppose an act of consent, express or tacit, or indeed any voluntary act, in order to apply. The principles that hold for individuals, just as the principles for institutions, are those that would be acknowledged in the original position. These principles are understood as the outcome of a hypothetical agreement.[11]

This passage poses difficult problems of interpretation. It begins with a claim about the kind of duty the duty of justice is—namely, it is a natural duty and, as such, does not depend on any of *our* voluntary acts. About halfway through the quoted passage, however, we are told that "the principles of duty" are similarly independent of any voluntary act on our part. And then, at the passage's conclusion, Rawls states that "these principles are understood as the outcome of a hypothetical agreement." What is unclear is whether what Rawls says about the *principles* of justice also applies to what he says about the *duty* of justice. If it does, some unhappy consequences result. For consider: We have the natural duty of justice, unlike the duty to keep a promise, independently of any of our voluntary acts. The principles of justice, however, are to be understood as "the outcome of a hypothetical agreement." Now, if what is said about these principles also applies to the duty of justice, what we have is the view that *our* having the duty of justice, although it is not contingent on any of *our* voluntary acts, *is* contingent upon the acts of those who reach the hypothetical agreements in the original position. This is eminently unsatisfactory. Just as our having the duty of justice cannot depend on our voluntary acts, so our having this duty cannot depend on the "hypothetical acts" of others. Presumably, therefore, Rawls's view is not that *our having this duty* is contingent on what those in the original position decide; rather, it is that the *principles* of justice—that is, what duties justice requires one to do or forbear—are what are decided upon by those in the original position. Interpreted in this way, Rawls's position does not have the air of paradox it would have if he were interpreted to hold *both* that our having duties of justice does not depend on our voluntary acts *and* that our having these duties does depend on the hypothetical acts of others. However, even when interpreted in this way, Rawls's position, at least as he understands it, fails to provide an adequate account of those to whom we have these duties. Like Narveson's account, Rawls's is demonstrably arbitrary when it excludes moral patients from the class of individuals to whom duties of justice are owed (see 5.4).

Now, at least some acquired duties (e.g., the duty to keep a promise) arguably have correlative rights (e.g., the right of the promisee against the promisor). Whether this is true in the case of all acquired duties can remain an open question, given the purposes of the present study. (This question is pursued further in 8.9, in the discussion of "special considerations.") One question that is not open is whether all duties are acquired duties—that is, duties that arise as a result of our voluntary acts or because of our place in an institutional arrangement. Some duties do not belong in this category, and among those duties that do not the most important, for present purposes, are those that involve the just treatment of all those who are morally relevantly similar. Of course, what treatment is due those who are morally relevantly similar depends on how the formal principle of justice is interpreted, an issue I shall explore momentarily. The central point worth noting here is that since the duty of justice is not an acquired duty, the right to just treatment, if there is such a right (i.e., if the claim to just treatment is a valid claim), must be viewed as an unacquired right—what I shall term *a basic right*. Like its correlative duty, this right cannot reasonably be viewed as one we have as a result of our voluntary acts or because of our place in an institutional arrangement. No attempt to validate this right can be adequate if it miscategorizes this right—that is, if it treats this basic right as an acquired right. The validation of this right offered in the next section cannot be disputed on this ground.

8.4 THE RESPECT PRINCIPLE AND
THE RIGHT TO RESPECTFUL TREATMENT

In the previous chapter a normative interpretation of the formal principle of justice was given and defended. That interpretation rests on the postulate of inherent value, the view that all those individuals who satisfy the subject-of-a-life criterion (7.5) are intelligibly and nonarbitrarily viewed as having a kind of value (inherent value) that is distinct from, is not reducible to, and is incommensurate with the intrinsic value of their own or anyone else's experiences·(e.g., their pleasures or preference satisfactions) and that all who have this kind of value have it equally. These individuals, it was argued, are therefore due, as a matter of strict justice, treatment that is respectful of the kind of value they have, and all are owed this treatment equally; in particular, individuals who have inherent value are not to be treated as if they were mere "receptacles" of valuable experiences (e.g., pleasures), a view that opens the door to allowing that some moral agents or patients may be harmed (e.g., made to suffer) because the aggregate balance of pleasure over pain for all those affected by the outcome would yield "the best" aggregate consequences. The validity of the respect principle, interpreted as a predistributive normative principle of justice, was supported (7.8) by showing that the arguments for it meet the requirements of making an ideal moral judgment, to the extent that this is reasonable to require, and by showing that this principle itself meets the appropriate criteria for evaluating moral principles (adequacy of scope and precision, consistency, and conformity with our reflective intuitions). The case has been made, in short, to the extent to which the case can be made, for rational acceptance of the respect principle, as a valid normative principle of just treatment. It now remains to be asked whether, given the preceding analysis of rights as valid claims and the requirements of validating claims, the case can be made for recognizing the basic right of those who have inherent value to the respectful treatment the respect principle requires of us. The argument for the recognition of this right may be set forth as follows:

First, justice—unlike charity, for example—*is* something one can intelligibly claim as one's due, something that one is owed. Though a representative of the United Way has no valid basis on which to claim that I owe it to his organization in particular to make a financial contribution, he does have a moral basis on which to claim that I owe it to him to treat him as justice requires. This is true regardless of how justice is interpreted; it is not peculiar to the interpretation favored here. Even a perfectionist theory (see 7.1) allows that justice *is* owed to anyone who can be treated justly or unjustly; it just so happens that, on perfectionist theories, what is due varies considerably, depending upon how much or how little different individuals happen to possess certain virtues (e.g., artistic talents). There is, therefore, nothing conceptually odd in maintaining that individuals who have inherent value can claim just treatment as their due, or have this claimed on their behalf, because they have a right to such treatment. Since what is being claimed as their right is something claimed as their due, since justice is due them, and since the duty of justice is an unacquired duty, there is nothing logically untoward in correlating a basic right to just treatment with the unacquired duty of justice.

Second, if one's making a claim to just treatment is to be valid, then both the claim-to and claim-against aspects of such a claim must be valid. Demands for just treatment, when these are informed by the notion of respect central to the respect principle, can be validated on both counts. Such claims are valid claims-to. I can specify *what* it is that I am claiming as my due (namely, treatment that accords with the respect principle) and the treatment I claim as my due is within the powers or capacities of those against whom I make the claim. Moreover, the claim I make is a valid claim-against, first, because I can identify those individuals against whom I make it—namely, all those moral agents who do or might have any moral dealings with me—and, second, because the claim I make against them is, in Feinberg's words, "called for" by a valid moral principle, the respect principle. My claim to respectful treatment, therefore, is a valid claim, all considered, and thus, given the analysis of moral rights as valid claims, I have the moral right to be treated with respect.

Third, the moral right to respectful treatment is not mine alone. All individuals like me in the relevant respects must also have this right, have it equally, and have it independently of its recognition by the laws of this or that nation. This is part of what it means to speak of moral rights (see 8.1), and no account of moral rights or their validation can be adequate if it fails to meet these requirements. The analysis of rights as valid claims and the procedure outlined for validating them pass these tests, when it comes to possession of this right by *moral agents.* Since all moral agents are like me in the relevant respects (all have inherent value and all have it equally), all have the same right to respectful treatment that I do and all have this right equally. Moreover, since the basis for this right is independent of the legislative acts of any individual(s), our having this right is independent of its recognition by the laws of this or that nation. Indeed, precisely because the basis for this right is independent of the laws of any nation, appeals to this right can be used in the way Lyons recognizes—as a way "to argue for changes in the social order," including changes in the law itself.

To avoid the conclusions reached in the present section one would have to show *either* that the respect principle is not a valid moral principle, *or* that the analysis of rights as valid claims is unsatisfactory,[12] *or* that the argument just given in support of recognizing the validity of, and thus the right to, respectful treatment in the case of all moral agents is deficient. The defense of the respect principle was given in the previous chapter and will not be repeated here. The argument just given in support of the right to respectful treatment will have to stand on its own as given; nothing further will be offered in direct support. As for the correctness of the analysis of rights in terms of valid claims, some objections to it will be considered but only after the full implications of recognizing the right to respectful treatment have been set forth. Here it will suffice to remind those utilitarian critics of "the rhetoric of rights" that, in analyzing rights as valid claims, we have not seized upon an analysis that finds no home in the literature of utilitarianism. It is, after all, the very analysis Mill favors.

8.5 THE RIGHTS OF MORAL PATIENTS

The case for recognizing the moral right of *moral patients* to respectful treatment parallels the argument given in the preceding section. *The validity of the claim to respectful treatment, and thus the case for recognition of the right to such treatment, cannot be any stronger or weaker in the case of moral patients than it is in the case of moral agents.* Both have inherent value, and both have it equally; thus, both are owed respectful treatment, as a matter of justice. Moreover, since the validity of the claim-to such treatment in the case of moral agents has been shown, the same is true in the case of the validity of the claim-to such treatment in the case of moral patients. It lies within the power of all moral agents to treat all those moral patients with whom they do or might have any dealings with the respect that, as possessors of inherent value, they are due. Similarly in the case of moral patients having valid claims-against moral agents: the individuals against whom the claim holds are all those moral agents who do or might interact with moral patients, and the claims made against moral agents in this regard are validated by appeal to the respect principle and the postulate of inherent value on which it rests. Because moral patients have inherent value and have neither more nor less inherent value than that possessed by moral agents, they have the same right to respectful treatment possessed by moral agents *and* they possess this right equally—that is, moral agents and moral patients have an equal right to respectful treatment. Moreover, because moral agents have this right independently of the legislative acts (the laws) of this or that nation, the same is true in the case of moral patients. In the case of animals, in particular, therefore, one cannot argue against their having the basic moral right in question on the grounds that it is not recognized as a legal right by any nation.

It would be arbitrary in the extreme, therefore, to accept the postulate of inherent value, the respect principle, the analysis of rights as valid claims, and the argument for the right to respectful treatment in the case of moral agents, and then to deny that moral patients have this right. If the arguments used to validate this right in the case of moral agents are sound, then moral patients, including animals, have this right also. That is the destination toward which this work has been moving from the outset. It is not an act of kindness to treat animals respectfully. It is an act of justice. It is not "the sentimental interests" of moral agents that grounds our duties of justice to children, the retarded, the senile, or other moral patients, including animals. It is respect for their inherent value. The myth of the privileged moral status of moral agents has no clothes.

It is of more than passing interest to note that the argument for recognition of the basic moral rights of moral agents and patients does not depend on appeals to the utility of recognizing these rights. As was observed in the original characterization of the rights view (4.5), certain individuals are viewed as having certain rights, according to this view, independently of considerations about the value of the consequences that result from recognizing that they have them. For the rights position, basic moral rights are more basic than utility and independent of it, so that the principal reason why, say, killing a moral agent or patient is wrong, if and when it is, lies in the violation of the individual's moral rights, and not in considerations about all those others who will or who will not receive pleasure or pain or who will or who will not have their preferences satisfied or frustrated. The argument of the present section should make it clear how those who favor the rights view can argue for their position independently of appeals to utility. Certain individuals have the basic right to respectful treatment because of the kind of value they have (inherent value), a kind of value that is itself independent of utility, and the criterion that makes its attribution to certain individuals both intelligible and nonarbitrary (the subject-of-a-life criterion) also makes no reference to, and thus is independent of appeals to, the utility of recognizing it. It is not, then, for utilitarian reasons that we recognize and validate the basic rights of moral agents and patients—not by appeal to "the *general* welfare." Their basic rights are validated by appeals to the respect that, as *individuals* who possess inherent value, they are due as a matter of strict justice.

8.6 A MISCELLANY OF OBJECTIONS

A number of objections can be anticipated and deserve an airing. Some challenge the analysis of rights as valid claims; others dispute the necessity of recognizing rights, however they are analyzed. The objections, in short, do not all belong to the same family of ideas. But let us consider each in its turn with the hope that, by meeting the challenge each poses, the position they challenge will itself be clearer and its reasonableness more evident.

There are alternatives to analyzing rights in terms of valid claims. H. J. McCloskey, an Australian moral philosopher, subscribes to the entitlement theory of rights and is critical of viewing rights as valid claims. We will have to be content with considering McCloskey's main criticism, where, by denying that all rights are claims-against, he disputes the view that all moral rights are valid claims.

> Special rights are sometimes against specific individuals or institutions— e.g., rights created by promises, contracts, etc. . . . but these differ from . . . characteristic . . . general rights where the right is simply a right to . . .[13]

What McCloskey calls "special rights" are those rights that arise as a result of our voluntary acts. They are acquired rights correlated with acquired duties. If I make a promise to you, I acquire the duty to keep the promise, and you acquire the right to hold me to it. In the case of unacquired duties (e.g., the duty of justice), there are also correlative unacquired (basic) rights: I have the duty to treat you justly but not because of my voluntary acts, and you have a right to be treated justly. What McCloskey thus seems to be denying is that, unlike acquired (or special) rights, unacquired (basic) rights are not rights we have *against* anyone.

This objection fails. It is true that, in the case of acquired duties and rights, the right is characteristically a right-against someone in particular—for example, your right *against me* to keep my promise. But there is no reason why all rights must be rights-against *an* individual or against *a few* individuals, if they are to be rights-against others. The right I have to respectful treatment is a right I have to be treated respectfully, a right I have against not just this or that individual but against all moral agents with whom I do or might have moral dealings. The sheer number of those against whom I have this right is no reason to deny that I have it against anyone. There is, it is a true, a paradoxical sounding implication of this view—namely, that I have this right against literally hundreds of millions of people. And some might find this odd at least. Feinberg, however, has a reply that removes the air of oddness and the sound of paradox; but it also has problems of its own. There is, he writes, "nothing troublesome" in the idea that I have rights against and duties to legions of moral agents.

> If a general moral rule gives me a right of noninterference (for example) in a certain respect against everybody, then there are literally hundreds of millions of people who have a duty toward me in that respect; and if the

same general rule gives the same right to everyone else, then it imposes on me hundreds of millions of duties—or duties towards hundreds of millions of people. I see nothing paradoxical about this, however. The duties, after all, are negative; and I can discharge all of them at a stroke simply by minding my own business. And if all human beings make up one moral community and there are hundreds of millions of human beings, we should expect there to be hundreds of millions of moral relations holding between them.[14]

In his reply Feinberg assumes that there are purely negative duties and negative rights. My right to noninterference is a negative right correlated with your negative duty not to interfere in my affairs. If you do not interfere, you have, Feinberg implies, fulfilled your duty to me in this regard; indeed, since the duty is negative, you can fulfill it to literally millions of people "at a stroke simply by minding [your] own business." In saying this Feinberg overlooks the other side of rights, even so-called negative rights, something to which Mill was wisely sensitive—namely, the duty of assistance (see 8.1). If you have a right to noninterference, then my duty to you in this regard does not consist merely in my minding my own business; I also have a prima facie duty to assist you if others deny you the exercise of this right. The duty of assistance is a prima facie duty certainly; there may be other, more pressing moral demands that override this duty in particular cases. But to suppose that I automatically do all that I am duty-bound to do with respect to your right merely by "minding my own business" is to mistake half the picture for the whole.

Having said this, Feinberg's reply to McCloskey still stands. The sheer number of those to whom I have duties or who have rights against me cannot militate against the adequacy of analyzing rights in terms of valid claims. Those who have a right to noninterference have a valid claim against literally millions, and literally millions have a duty of noninterference in this case. But these latter also have a prima facie duty of assistance.

Feinberg limits his remarks to human beings, but there is no reason why what he says should be less true if we add our duties to animals or their rights against us. The principal negative duty we have in their case is not to treat them disrespectfully, and the correlative negative right they have against us is not to be treated in ways that ignore their equal inherent value. But just as our negative duty not to interfere in the lives of others does not consist merely in our minding our own business, so our duty regarding the respectful treatment of animals involves more than our taking care to treat them with respect. Since they have a valid claim to respectful treatment, we have a prima facie duty to assist them when others treat them in ways that violate their rights. We shall have occasion to remind ourselves of this "other side" of rights in what follows.

It is possible to accept the analysis of moral rights as valid claims and deny that animals and, by implication, moral patients generally have moral rights. An objection of Ross's takes this form.

> On the whole, since we mean by a right something that can be justly claimed, we should probably say that animals have no rights, not because the claim to humane treatment would not be just if it were made, but because they cannot make it.[15]

Now, to deny that animals have rights or to hold that "we should probably say" that they lack them because *they* cannot justly claim anything is to disqualify more than animals. All moral patients are similarly deficient in this respect, and thus all must be disqualified. Once this is recognized, Ross's objection can be seen to involve a number of confusions. There are some rights that it is not unreasonable to deny that moral patients have. For example, the acquired right that persons have to their doctoral degree, once they have satisfactorily completed the requirements for obtaining it, is such a right. Moral patients do not have this right, but not because they cannot claim it; they do not have it because they have not fulfilled the appropriate requirements to acquire this right. Lacking as they are in this respect, they do not have the right that successful candidates acquire, to use Rawls's words, as a result of their "voluntary acts" or because of their place in "an institutional arrangement." In the case of unacquired (i.e., *basic*) rights in general, and of the basic right to respectful treatment in particular, however, no similar basis for excluding moral patients is at hand. Individuals can have valid claims and not make claims or even lack the ability to make them. To make a claim, we have said, is a performance, and no account of moral rights can be adequate that makes the existence of basic moral rights contingent upon the performance of this or that voluntary act. To have a valid claim, as distinct from making a claim, is to have a certain sort of moral status, and one can have this status without claiming it or even being able to do so. Whether one has this status depends not on whether one can claim one's rights but on whether one has them, and this depends on whether sound arguments can be given for the recognition of these rights *independently* of the ability on the part of the individual who possesses them to claim them. American jurisprudence, for example, recognizes this possibility in the case of the legal rights of children and the retarded. Though they lack the ability to claim their legal rights or even to understand that they have them, the law recognizes that others (e.g., legal guardians), acting in their behalf, can claim the rights of these moral patients. There is no reason why the case of the basic *moral* rights of moral patients must or should be judged any differently. Just as these individuals can have legal rights that they neither understand nor can claim on their own, so these same individuals can have basic moral rights that they fail to understand but that can be claimed for them by others acting in their behalf. In the particular case of animals, therefore, they have the right to respectful treatment despite their inability to understand this and notwithstanding their powerlessness to make or press their claims in this or any regard. That burden falls to those who would act for them.

In saying this we say nothing that departs from Mill's important insight, when he notes that "to have a right . . . is . . . to have something society ought to defend me in the possession of." When, as in the case of moral patients, they have rights but are themselves incapable of claiming or defending them, then the duty "society" has to do this for these individuals is, one might say, all the greater. The less cognizant individuals are of their rights, the less power they have to defend them, the more we who understand and recognize their rights must do for them in defense of their rights. With this observation we again remind ourselves that respect for the basic rights of others involves prima facie duties of assistance. Because those who have the right to respectful treatment have a *right* to this treatment, my duty to them is not restricted *just* to *my* avoiding treating them unjustly; I am also duty-bound to "defend (them) in the possession of" this right and what possession of this right entitles them to. Thus if, for example, animals are used in scientific research in ways that violate their right to respectful treatment, and assuming that I myself am not engaged in such research, it does not follow that I have thereby done all that morality requires of me. There is also my prima facie duty to assist those who are the victims of injustice, and the powerlessness of animals to insure that their rights are respected arguably makes my duty to assist them, if anything, greater, not lesser.

It is sometimes claimed, more in discussions than in print,[16] that recognition of the rights of animals leads to absurd consequences. If sheep have rights, it is claimed, then these are violated by wolves and other predatory animals, who harm their prey in a variety of ways (e.g., by causing them acute suffering). But if we have a duty of assistance to animals to stop those who violate their rights, then are we not duty-bound to stop the wolf in his tracks, so to speak, and protect the sheep?

However, were we to do this, the wolf could hardly be the beneficiary, since he would be denied necessary sustenance. Were we to carry out our duty to assist the sheep against the wolf's violations of the sheep's rights, we could only succeed in violating the wolf's rights, whereas if we allow the wolf to violate the sheep's rights, we fail to do what we should to assist the sheep. *Whatever* we do, therefore, we stand to be morally condemned, which is absurd. And since it is the attribution of rights to animals that leads to these absurd consequences, we have rational, principled grounds to refrain from attributing rights to them.

This argument is open to the very charge of absurdity it levels against attributing rights to animals. In the earlier discussion of moral agency and patiency (5.2), the point was made and defended that moral patients have *no* duties and thus do not have the particular duty to respect the rights of others. *Only moral agents can have duties*, and this because only these individuals have the cognitive and other abilities necessary for being held morally accountable for what they do or fail to do. Wolves are not moral agents. They cannot bring impartial reasons to bear on their decision making—cannot, that is, apply the formal principle of justice or any of its normative interpretations. That being so, wolves in particular and moral patients generally cannot *themselves* meaningfully be said to have duties to anyone, nor, therefore, the particular duty to respect the rights possessed by other animals. In claiming that we have a prima facie duty to assist those animals *whose rights are violated*, therefore, we are not claiming that we have a duty to assist the sheep against the attack of the wolf, since the wolf neither can nor does violate anyone's rights. The absurd results leveled against the attribution of rights to animals simply do not materialize.

Another common attempt to refute the rights view is to argue that it fails radically to match some of our considered beliefs.[17] Imagine five survivors are on a lifeboat. Because of limits of size, the boat can only support four. All weigh approximately the same and would take up approximately the same amount of space. Four of the five are normal adult human beings. The fifth is a dog. One must be thrown overboard or else all will perish. Whom should it be? If all have an equal right to be treated respectfully, must we draw straws? Would it not be unjust, given the rights view, to choose to sacrifice the dog in preference to one of the humans? And doesn't this show that the rights view, because it authorizes appeals to considered beliefs as a legitimate way to test moral principles, dies at its own hands, so to speak? For no reasonable person would suppose that the dog has a "right to life" that is equal to the humans' or that the animal should be given an equal chance in the lottery for survival. This objection can be adequately addressed only after the grounds for overriding the right not to be harmed have been explored (8.7ff.) and must await its proper time (8.13).

One final objection attempts to resurrect utilitarianism as a theory that can account for all moral rights without our having to postulate inherent value and without validating rights by reference to the respect principle. This is Mill's position, and there is much to be said for it. Society does have the duty to protect individual rights, and at least part of this challenge can be effected by "the force of law or by that of education or opinion." But it does not follow from this that the only reason one can give to support this effort is the one Mill gives—namely, "general utility." Indeed, this cannot be the sole reason, cannot even be an adequate reason, in the case of the basic rights possessed by moral patients. As was argued in the earlier discussion of rule utilitarianism (7.7), that position fails to provide a satisfactory justification of unacquired *direct* duties owed to moral patients, whether these be humans or animals. That theory, therefore, cannot adequately ground rules by reference to which the rights of moral patients can be validated. At the very most (and it is highly questionable that rule utilitarianism is equal to this task) that theory could ground rights possessed by moral agents, rights that are validated in *their* case by appeal to valid moral rules. However, since no theory can be adequate, all considered, if it fails to account for the unacquired direct duties owed to, and the correlative rights of, moral patients, rule utilitarianism cannot be the adequate theory we seek. As for act utilitarianism, moral rights, conceived as valid claims, can find no place in the thought of those who view appeals to rights as "rhetoric."

8.7 OVERRIDING THE RIGHT NOT TO BE HARMED

Individuals who have inherent value have an equal basic right to be treated with respect. According to the rights view, this is a right that we can never be justified in ignoring or overriding. In all our moral dealings with moral agents and patients, we must always treat them with that respect to which, as possessors of inherent value, they are due. This is the fundamental precept of the rights view. From it, it follows that we must never harm individuals who have inherent value on the grounds that all those affected by the outcome will thereby secure "the best" aggregate balance of intrinsic values (e.g., pleasures) over intrinsic disvalues (e.g., pains). To harm some *for these reasons* is to treat them as if they were mere receptacles of value, lacking any value in their own right, which is, therefore, to treat them in ways that fail to display the respect they are due as a matter of strict justice. (Other ways of failing to show respect are discussed below, 8.11—8.12, 9.1ff.) Because individuals who have inherent value have a valid claim, and thus, in this case, a basic right to respectful treatment, because their having this kind of value can be used to derive the unacquired prima facie direct duty not to harm them (see 7.8), because *basic* rights are validated by appeals to valid moral principles of *unacquired* duty, and because the claim made against being harmed is a valid claim-to and a valid claim-against, it follows that individuals who have inherent value also have a valid claim, and thus, in this case, a basic prima facie right not to be harmed, the validation of *this* right resting ultimately on the respect principle and the postulate of inherent value on which it rests. To say this right is a prima facie right is to say that (1) consideration of this right is always a morally relevant consideration, and (2) anyone who would harm another, or allow others to do so, must be able to justify doing so by (a) appealing to other valid moral principles and by (b) showing that these principles morally outweigh the right not to be harmed in a given case.

It is possible to deny that this right is prima facie only. Some assert or imply that some individuals have an *absolute* right not to be harmed, a right, that is, that may *never* justifiably be overridden. One principle that implies this is *the pacifist principle* (we ought never to use harmful violence, no matter what the circumstances). A second principle (*the innocence principle*) is more restrictive. It allows that causing harm to some may be justified, but it is never justified when those who are harmed are innocent. We ought never, this principle declares, do anything that harms the innocent, no matter what the circumstances. Neither principle is valid. To show this we will first consider four different situations where what causes harm[18] can be justified by appeal to our considered beliefs. These are (1) self-defense by the innocent, (2) punishment of the guilty, (3) innocent shields, and (4) innocent threats. A fifth type of case (prevention cases) will be explored later (8.10). This initial survey will be limited to situations involving only human beings.

Self-Defense by the Innocent

The most obvious case where the right not to be harmed may be justifiably overridden, if appeals to our considered beliefs are allowed, involves self-defense by the innocent. To illustrate this, suppose you are attacked by a violent assailant. Can you be justified in using violence to defend yourself, even though, in doing so, you are certain to harm your attacker? Those who accept the pacifist principle say you cannot. Since the use of harmful violence is always wrong, no matter what the circumstances, its use in self-defense, even when the defender is innocent, is not morally permitted.

Jan Narveson argues that the pacifist's position is incoherent.[19] If the use of harmful violence is wrong, he argues, it must be wrong *not* to use it if this is the only way to prevent greater violence in the future; but if it is wrong not to use it in such circumstances, then its use must be justified in such circumstances. And if it is *justified* in such circumstances, then its use cannot be wrong, no matter what the circumstances. The pacifist's position is thereby exposed as inadequate because inconsistent.

Narveson's critique of pacifism assumes that all pacifists are *consequentialists*, persons who prohibit the use of violence now because of the consequences its use will bring about in the future. Against such a position, Narveson's critique is successful, *if* those who advance it are willing to concede that the use of harmful violence sometimes does reduce the amount of violence in the future *and* that we can know that this is true in a given case. It is not clear that Narveson's adversaries would concede this. They might claim that the use of harmful violence *always* leads to more violence in the future, or that we can *never know* that it will not. These are bold empirical claims, to say the least, and, like any other such claim, stand in need of careful, thorough, well-documented support. No pacifist of the consequentialist variety has to date succeeded in meeting this challenge, and it is unclear that any could. For example, to cite this or that case where the use of harmful violence led to more violence in the future, either large-scale uses of violence (e.g., wars) or less-grand uses (e.g., fist fights between children), simply will not do, first, because even if one could point to *some* cases in which we knew that the use of violence led to more violence, it would not follow that this is true in *all* cases, and, second, because *just* establishing that the use of violence now will lead to the use of more violence in the future is not to establish enough for this brand of pacifism. The possibility remains that not using violence now will *also* lead to the use of violence in the future *and* that the amount of future violence brought about by nonviolent behavior now would exceed, perhaps greatly exceed, the amount of harmful violence brought about by the use of violence now. All of which is to say that pacifists, in all fairness to them and their position, more than have their work cut out for them, if they regard the pacifist principle as a consequentialist principle and if they are to avoid Narveson's charge of incoherence. Since it cannot be reasonable to regard a principle as valid if it stands in need of extensive empirical backing and lacks it, and since the pacifist principle, interpreted as a consequentialist principle, stands in need of, and lacks, such backing, we are justified in denying the claims made on its behalf by this brand of pacifist.

The pacifist has an option. He could maintain that the use of harmful violence is wrong *in itself*, and *irredeemably* so, apart from its future consequences. The pacifist, that is, could subscribe to a *non*consequentialist version of pacifism. Now, to dispute this version of pacifism by arguing, as Narveson does, that the use of harmful violence in some cases might actually reduce the amount of violence in the future, would be judged strictly irrelevant by those who are nonconsequentialist pacifists. Since they do not rest their opposition to violence on its consequences, objections that rely on appeals to consequences will simply slip by their position rather than engaging it head-on.[20] Recognizable forms of pacifism thus seem immune to Narveson's attempt to demonstrate the incoherence of all forms of pacifism.[21] If we are to have reasons for rejecting the nonconsequentialist version of pacifism, therefore, we must look elsewhere than to the test of consistency.

Among the grounds for rejecting the pacifist principle, the most telling involve appeals to our reflective intuitions. Included in our considered beliefs are those that concern the right of the innocent to defend themselves against their aggressors, even if this defense involves violence and even if its use will result in harm being done to the assailant. Granted, we do not believe that one is morally entitled to use just any violent means, in any amount, to repel an attack. As in the law, so in morality, a principle of proportionality commends itself: we are entitled to use force, but not excessive force, to defend ourselves, while allowing for the difficulty, in conditions of stress and emergency, of determining what force is excessive. For example, use of a lethal gas is prima facie disproportionately harmful as a defense against a thief who snatches a purse; use of a temporarily disabling device (e.g., mace) is not. While we may concede that some pacifists hold a consistent position, very little else can be said in its favor. Because this position is so at odds with our considered beliefs, in a broad range of cases, and because the reasonableness of appealing to our reflective intuitions to test moral principles has been defended earlier (4.3), we have principled reasons to reject the pacifist principle in its nonconsequentialist form. Of course, if the pacifist could show that, independently of appeals to our considered beliefs, he has a "sound theory," then it is our intuitions, not his theory, that would have to be changed. In all fairness to pacifism, however, it must be said that no pacifist has shown this, that the onus of doing so must be borne by those who believe in this position, and that the mere sincerity and intensity with which the belief is held go no way toward meeting this challenge. After all, many Nazis evidently sincerely believed in their position with great intensity.

Punishment of the Guilty

A second and, in some respects, related kind of case involves punishment of the guilty. Punishment is not punishment unless it involves some loss or diminution in the quality of the life of (i.e., some harm done to) the person being punished, as when, for example, individuals lose some portion of their wealth by being fined or lose their liberty, in varying degrees, by being imprisoned. A principle of proportionality applies here too. The punishment, we say, must fit the crime; the harm done to the offender must be "proportionate" to the harm done to the victim, if justice is to be done. This leaves open the question of whether punishment has any *further* purpose (e.g., to reform the offender or to deter others from committing comparable offenses). Whatever further purposes punishment may have, there is no punishment, and thus nothing to have a further purpose, if the offender is not harmed, most notably in the form of deprivations. Though the justice of how we punish, and the fairness of the means by which we select who to punish, are matters of increasing moral consternation, the belief that mentally competent adult criminals merit punishment is a conviction most are likely to count as one among their considered beliefs. How reasonable we are in believing this, if we do, fortunately is a matter we will be able to avoid exploring in the present work, since even if we are justified in punishing (and, thus, harming) those who are guilty, overriding the right of animals not to be harmed cannot be defended on these grounds, since animals, because they are not moral agents, cannot be guilty.

Though this is not the occasion to work out the full implications, it is worth noting in passing that the rights view could not sanction any form of punishment that failed to treat the convicted criminal with that respect to which he or she is due as one who possesses inherent value. For no one can gain or lose this value by anything that person does or fails to do. In particular, therefore, we cannot justify punishing the criminal on the grounds that this will bring about a better aggregate balance of goods over evils for all those affected by the outcome. That would be to treat the criminal as a mere receptacle, and that is contrary to what justice requires, according to the rights view. Regarded in this light, the rights view is sympathetic to the recognition of "the rights of the criminal," although it is also sympathetic to the view that some people deserve to be punished—that is, harmed—because of the harm they have done.

Innocent Shields

Tragically, situations arise in the world where innocent individuals are used as "shields" to protect those engaged in unlawful activities. A bank robber takes a teller for his protection, for example, or terrorists take hostages; in both cases the innocent are used in the interests of those who operate outside the law, in the belief that, so long as those who are innocent are held captive, those who would attack their captors will think twice before doing so. Granted that the hostages are innocent, and granted that to do anything that will foreseeably cause harm to the innocent is certainly prima facie wrong, are there adequate reasons for believing that this is always wrong, no matter what the circumstances? If pacifism in any of its forms (consequentialist or nonconsequentialist) was a reasonable position, then we would know how to answer this question straightaway: we ought never to use violent means that will foreseeably result in harm being done to the captives—or to their captors! But pacifism is not a reasonable position. An alternative to pacifism allows harm in some cases but disallows it in all cases where those who are harmed are innocent. Those who hold this position subscribe to *the innocence principle*: it is always wrong to harm the innocent, no matter what the circumstances. The right *of the innocent* not to be harmed, in other words, is absolute, a right never to be overridden.

The innocence principle faces the same kind of objections as the pacifist principle. Those who advocate this principle may do so either as consequentialists or as nonconsequentialists. If the former, they are likely to argue that the right of the innocent not to be harmed ought never to be overridden because to do so will always lead to harm being done to a greater number of innocents in the future. As in the case of the pacifist principle, the innocence principle, when interpreted consequentially, can only be as compelling as the empirical claim on which it rests, and it is radically unclear that overriding the right of the innocent will *always* lead to more innocents being harmed. Imagine this case.[22] A terrorist has taken possession of a tank and has commenced to kill, one by one, the twenty-six innocent hostages he has bound to a wall. All attempts to negotiate release of the hostages are flatly rejected, and there is every reason to believe that the terrorist will kill all the hostages if nothing is done. Under the circumstances the only reasonable way to save these hostages is to blow up the tank. Suppose the means to blow it up are at hand. Only suppose the terrorist has taken the precaution of strapping another innocent hostage to the tank. Any means used to blow up the tank will kill that hostage. What ought we to do? On the consequentialist interpretation of the innocence principle, we ought not to blow up the tank because (a) this will harm the one innocent hostage and because (b) overriding the right of the innocent not to be harmed will always lead to harm being done to more innocents in the future. This latter claim lacks credibility in the present case. At least in the foreseeable short-run, overriding the right of the one hostage (the innocent shield) will prevent harm being done to the remaining hostages. There is, that is, a strong epistemic presumption, in the terrorist case, against the empirical claim made on behalf of the consequentialist interpretation of the innocence principle. Granted, one who subscribes to this version of the innocence principle could maintain that, whatever might be true in the short-run, more innocents will be harmed *in the long-run* if we override the right of the innocent shield in this case. But the burden of proof must surely fall to those who claim this. It is not enough that they express this belief as an article of faith, however sincerely or passionately held it might be. One wants detailed empirical backing for so sweeping a claim, and unless one has it there is more than ample reason to contest the validity of the innocence principle in its consequentialist interpretation, on the grounds that those who advance it fall far short of the ideal of having the relevant information.

If, in the face of these difficulties, harming the innocent is claimed to be irredeemably wrong, apart from the consequences, then, as was true in the case of the analogous interpretation of the pacifist principle, this interpretation of the innocence principle can be dismissed on the grounds that it is radically at odds with our considered beliefs in a broad range of cases. Since the innocent have a right not to be harmed, since their having this right grounds a duty on our part to "defend them in the possession of their right," since the twenty-six hostages are innocent, since they cannot defend themselves, since they *will* be harmed if we do nothing, and since all our options are such that, whatever we choose, some of the innocents directly involved will be harmed, what we ought to do is act so as to prevent the deaths of the twenty-six. Not to do so would be to fail to do what we must, if we are to insure that *their* right not to be harmed is not overridden when steps could be taken to prevent this. That the lone hostage is an innocent shield adds to the tragic circumstances of the case; it does not make doing what will harm him irredeemably wrong.

Innocent Threats

A final type of case involves *innocent threats*. This sort of case can be illustrated by considering an example where a young child poses a serious threat to others. Imagine the child has come into possession of a loaded revolver and has begun to fire it at us. Since the child is not a moral agent, we cannot view his moral status in the same way as ordinary adults. The child, that is, is not guilty; hence, the aptness of referring to the child as "an *innocent* threat." Is it ever permissible in such cases to use means to prevent the child from seriously endangering our lives, even if the means used will, or are likely to, harm the child? It is difficult to imagine how a negative answer could be defended short of making an appeal to either pacifism or the innocence principle, positions we have already rejected. Since we are innocent of any relevant wrongdoing, how can it be wrong to do what we must to defend ourselves? Granted, we ought not use excessive force, since this will, or is likely to, cause excessive harm to the innocent threat. Nevertheless, since we are innocent of any relevant wrongdoing, since we *are* seriously threatened by the gun-wielding child, and assuming nonviolent options have been conscientiously explored (we assume that attempts to reason with the child have failed), it cannot be wrong to do what will harm the child, even though the child is innocent and so does no wrong.

Now, two of the four kinds of case—namely, punishment of, and defense against, the guilty—do not cover human moral patients. Since human moral patients can do nothing that is wrong, they can do nothing that merits punishment. Unlike competent human adults who break the law, human moral patients do not deserve to be punished and so cannot be justifiably punished on these grounds. Similarly, though we can justifiably defend against the threats posed by human moral patients, it would be a gross distortion to view our defense as a case of the defense of the innocent against the guilty. If we are justified in doing what will foreseeably harm human moral patients because of the threat of harm they pose, it must be a case of our defending ourselves against *innocent threats*. Moreover, since human moral patients are innocent, there is no reason why they cannot occupy the unenviable position of *innocent shields;* and since there are some cases where it is permissible to harm an innocent shield, there is no reason why our judgment must be different in cases where the innocent shield in question is a human moral patient.

8.8 THE INNOCENCE OF MORAL PATIENTS

An objection to the foregoing worthy of consideration does not rest on the pacifist or innocence principles. Objections based on those principles imply that the innocent, including human moral patients, are *not protected enough* if we allow any exceptions to these principles. The objection about to be considered implies that human moral patients are *protected too much* if restrictions are placed on what may be done to them because they are claimed to be innocent. Human moral patients are *not innocent*, this objection holds, at least not in any morally relevant sense of 'innocent,' and so should not be covered by principles that specify how the innocent may be treated.

The grounds on which this objection can be raised are as follows. It makes perfectly good sense to view moral agents as innocent (i.e., as not having done anything wrong) in this or that particular case; but this is because it also makes perfectly good sense to view them as capable of doing what is wrong. In saying that they are innocent, we are saying that they have done no wrong *though they might have.* In the case of human moral patients, however, the same cannot be said. Since they lack the ability to do what is wrong, to say that they are "innocent" cannot mean that they have done no wrong though they might have. 'Innocent' makes sense only when 'guilty' does; and as human moral patients are by definition incapable of being guilty, they are also incapable of being innocent. Granted, this objection continues, we may and sometimes do say that they are "innocent" in the sense that they are inexperienced in the ways of the world, as when we say of a newborn baby, "She is (or looks) so innocent." Still, this sense of 'innocent' is not the morally relevant sense, not the sense in which 'innocent' is used when we appeal to the principle that it is prima facie wrong to harm the innocent. That sense applies only to those who can do what is wrong, not to those who, like human moral patients, cannot. To suppose that these human beings are covered by that principle is therefore to be taken in by an equivocation, harmless enough if we do not take it seriously, morally crazed if we do.

This objection has a point, up to a point. Human moral agents and patients do differ with respect to their ability to do what is wrong (or right). Beyond that, the objection misfires. That someone is innocent is an idea that finds a *moral* place in contexts outside our assessment of moral agents. Those individuals can be properly viewed as innocent who can be treated unjustly, and those individuals who can be treated unjustly are those to whom we owe duties of justice and who have a right to just treatment against us. Accordingly, since duties of justice are directly owed both to human moral agents and patients, and since both possess the right to be treated as justice requires, it would be arbitrary in the extreme stipulatively to confine talk of who is "innocent" only to moral agents. Whether those who *can* be innocent *are* innocent depends on (a) whether they have a given right, (b) whether they receive treatment that is prima facie violative of that right, and (c) whether they have done anything to merit this treatment. If they have acted in a way that merits this treatment, they are not innocent; if they have not, they are. Thus, the inability of human moral patients to do anything that *merits* treatment prima facie violative of their rights does not show that they cannot be innocent. On the contrary, what this shows is that, unlike human moral agents, *they cannot be anything but innocent.* Even in those cases in which we can justifiably override a human moral patient's right not to be harmed, as in some cases where such a human is used as an innocent shield or poses a threat, their moral status as innocent individuals remains intact. Moral principles that make requirements concerning how the innocent may be treated demonstrably include how we may treat human moral patients.[23]

The Moral Status of Animals

A parallel argument is at hand in the case of animals. Because they are not moral agents, they can neither do what is right nor what is wrong; like human moral patients, therefore, animals can do nothing that merits treatment that is prima facie violative of their rights. But because the case has been made for the recognition of animal rights (8.5), their inability to do what is wrong does not entail that they are not to be protected by principles that specify how the innocent are to be treated. On the contrary, as in the case of human moral patients, the inability of animals in this regard shows that they cannot be anything but innocent. The principle that it is prima facie wrong to harm the innocent demonstrably applies to our dealings with animals.

Now, reasons have been advanced in the preceding that dispute regarding prohibitions against harming the innocent as absolute, allowing of no justified exceptions, and it would be arbitrary to suppose that the status of animals somehow differs from other innocents in this regard.

Since there are circumstances that justify harming human beings, despite their innocence, it would be perverse to deny this possibility in the case of animals. In particular, if human moral patients may be justifiably harmed because they pose innocent threats or because they are made to serve as innocent shields, there is no reason why animals might not also be justifiably harmed in such cases—though, as in the case of justifying harm done to human moral patients, we shall be unable to justify harming animals on the grounds of punishing, or defending against, the guilty. Of the two relevant kinds of cases at hand (innocent threats and innocent shields), the former is the more likely to arise. A rabid dog is guilty of no moral offense when he attacks us in our backyard; yet he poses a distinct threat, and we do no wrong if we harm the animal in the course of defending ourselves. As for animals viewed as innocent shields, some might regard this as impossible. For example, if the terrorist in our earlier example had strapped a heifer to the tank, few would view the cow's presence as constituting the slightest deterrent to blowing up the tank. But it would be a mistake to infer from this that the cow is not, or cannot be, an innocent shield. Obviously, what will work as a deterrent in such cases varies with the beliefs and attitude of those one hopes to deter; but what works does not determine the moral status of those made to serve as shields. One can imagine a case where a bank robber coerced a black man into serving as an innocent shield and where, because of the racist beliefs and attitudes of the law enforcement officer involved, both were gunned down without the slightest hesitation. That would not show that the black hostage was not an innocent shield, only that the bank robber's selection was not prudential, from his point of view. Similarly in the case of the cow strapped to the tank: that most people wouldn't think twice before blowing up the tank shows not that the animal is not an innocent shield but that she is not a very effective one. Of course, one can imagine circumstances in which the use of an animal as an innocent shield would be efficacious. If the animal is especially rare (e.g., the last surviving male bald eagle) or especially treasured by those involved (e.g., a much-loved pet), the animal might prove to be an effective shield, possibly even more effective than would a normal, adult human being in some cases. But, again, it would be a mistake to infer that *these* animals, *just because they serve the purpose of the offender, are* innocent shields, otherwise not. Their moral status as innocent shields is independent of their deterrent effect. Even when animals are used as innocent shields, however, it does not follow that it must be wrong to do what will harm them. That will depend on the circumstances of the case. Though, because of their innocence, animals fall within the scope of the principle against harming the innocent, they cannot be protected by this principle more than other innocents. Morality does not tolerate double standards, either those that, if accepted, would work to the disadvantage of animals, nor those that, once accepted, will work to their advantage.

A final objection to viewing moral patients as innocent holds that, on this view of things, *anything* that cannot do what is either right or wrong is innocent and must be included in the scope of principles concerning how the innocent may be treated. Thus do we have, so this objection urges, duties to mud, hair, and dirt, which is absurd. This objection misses the mark. Moral patients are intelligibly viewed as innocent because they may be treated in ways that are prima facie violative of *their moral rights* and because they cannot do anything that merits treatment that violates them. The case of mud, hair, and dirt is dissimilar, since we have no reason to believe—at least the rights view itself does not aspire to offer any reason to believe—that these objects have any moral rights that may or may not be violated.

8.9 SHOULD THE NUMBERS COUNT?

Though deficient, the innocence principle contains an important element of truth. The prima facie right not to be harmed may be justifiably overridden in the case of the guilty because of the wrong they have done, but not so in the case of the innocent. Moreover, precisely because doing what will foreseeably harm the innocent is so serious a moral matter, we should allow the right of the innocent not to be harmed to be overridden only in exceptional circumstances, and then only when we have done all that we can reasonably be expected to do before overriding it (e.g., by first attempting to negotiate with the terrorist in the tank example or by first trying to reason with the child who poses an innocent threat by firing the gun). To provide a clear, helpful statement of when this right can justifiably be overridden is difficult certainly. An attempt will be made in this regard below (8.11–8.12). First, though, there is an important objection to consider.

A common theme of some of the examples discussed in the preceding is that one innocent individual must be harmed if harm is to be prevented for a greater number of innocents. In this sense, the discussion assumed that numbers count—not just numbers, to be sure, but the numbers of those who are innocent. Is this a reasonable assumption to make? The American philosopher John M. Taurek thinks not. In his provocative essay, "Should the Numbers Count?"[24] Taurek lodges a series of objections against the view that we may justifiably harm one innocent in order to save the many. To make his position clearer, imagine the following case (an example of what will be referred to as *prevention cases* in the sequel). Fifty-one miners are trapped in a mine cave-in and are certain to die in a very short time if nothing is done. Suppose there is only one way to reach fifty of the trapped men in the allotted time. An explosive charge, deftly placed, will open a parallel shaft through which the trapped men can then escape. But suppose there is this complication: If the explosive is used, the remaining miner, who, as it happens, is trapped in that shaft, is certain to be killed. This one miner could be saved, however, if we placed a similar charge in the shaft where the other miners are trapped; but doing this will have the foreseeable consequence of killing all fifty miners in that shaft. What ought we do? If "the numbers count," then it is difficult to see why we ought not to act to save the fifty even if this means foreseeably harming the one. Taurek challenges this response. In circumstances like the mine example, what we should do, Taurek thinks, is flip a coin to decide who to save. Heads, the fifty; tails, the one. "I would," he writes, "flip a coin in such a case, special considerations apart. I cannot see how or why the mere addition of numbers should change anything."[25]

What counts as "special considerations" is left somewhat vague by Taurek, but at least part of what he has in mind is the possibility of there being *acquired duties* in such cases, duties, that is, that moral agents have as a result of their voluntary acts or because of their place in an institutional arrangement. We can illustrate this point in the following way. Suppose that, prior to the cave-in, the miners had instructed those in charge of rescue operations that, in the event of a cave-in, every effort should be directed at saving the maximum number of miners. This agreement, assuming it was reached voluntarily, would impose an acquired duty on the part of those in charge of rescue operations to save the fifty rather than the one and would count as a "special consideration" in Taurek's view, a consideration that would tip the scales in favor of saving the fifty rather than the one. But it would tip the scales in this direction not because the fifty are fifty times more than one; it would do so because all had voluntarily entered into the agreement in question. When there are no "special considerations" that favor the one option rather than the other in prevention cases, Taurek's view is that the numbers don't count. (We shall return to the issue of "special considerations" below, 8.12.)

But why don't the numbers count? Commenting on cases like the mine case, Taurek writes that "my way of thinking about (such cases) consists, essentially, in seriously considering what will be lost or suffered by this one person (e.g., the lone miner) if I did not prevent it (i.e., in this case, his death), and in considering the significance of that *for him* with what would be lost or suffered by anyone else if I did not prevent it. This reflects a refusal to take seriously in these situations the notion of the sum of two persons' separate losses."[26] In other words, the loss of one miner's life cannot be added to the loss of another miner's life, and another's, and so on, to arrive at some aggregate or total of losses or harms. There is, on Taurek's view, only the loss suffered by this or that individual miner; there is no "aggregate" of their separate losses. And it is this fact—the fact that such losses cannot be totaled—that, on Taurek's view, leads to the conclusion that "numbers don't count" in such cases. Since there is no way to add the separate losses of the involved individuals, there is, special considerations apart, no reason to regard saving the fifty as preferable to saving the one.

Taurek offers an example intended to move us toward recognizing the reasonableness of his position. We are to imagine that were you, a total stranger, to agree to undergo "some pain of significant intensity," I would be spared a lesser pain. It is difficult to imagine how I could reasonably bid you to consent. But now imagine that we introduce many more persons who will be spared relatively trivial pain if you will but agree to suffer in our stead. This changes nothing, in Taurek's view. "If not one of us can give you a good reason why you should be willing to undergo a greater suffering so that he might be spared a lesser one, then there is simply no good reason why you should be asked to suffer so that the group may be spared. Suffering is not additive in this way. The discomfort of each of a large number of individuals experiencing a minor headache does not add up to anyone's experiencing a migraine. In such a trade-off situation as this we are to compare your pain or your loss, not to our collective or total pain, whatever exactly that is supposed to be, but to what will be suffered or lost by *any single one of us*."[27]

What Taurek says about pain is correct, but it adds nothing to his case. *The aggregate of trivial pain experienced by many harms no one*, while the pain you are asked to endure ("some pain of significant intensity") prima facie will harm you. This is what makes the pain example radically disanalogous to the mine cave-in case. In the latter, in contrast to the pain example, we are not being asked to choose between options one of which will harm an innocent, the other of which won't; rather, we are being asked to choose between options *all* of which will harm some innocents *and* harm each in a prima facie comparable way—namely, by causing his death. What reasons, then, are there for "refusing to take seriously in (such a situation) any notion of the sum of two persons' separate losses"? One can see what reasons there are when the "losses" don't all involve harms, as in Taurek's pain example. But when all the options will involve harming the innocent in prima facie comparable ways? Why can we not intelligibly aggregate the harms that will result if, say, we were to choose the option that brought about the deaths of the fifty miners? It is not clear that Taurek has given any reason against the intelligibility of doing so.

Possibly Taurek thinks something like the following: Even if we could aggregate harms or losses, the aggregate *harms no one*. There is, that is, no aggregate individual, a composite, as it were, of the fifty individual miners, who will be harmed if we choose the option that causes the fifty miners to die, an individual who will suffer harm fifty times as great as the harm suffered by the solitary miner, if we were to choose the option that resulted in his death. There are only the fifty-one individual miners, and the loss each will suffer is as great a loss for that individual as the loss that would be suffered by any of the others. To "let the numbers count," Taurek might think, is to assume that there is this aggregate individual who will suffer fifty times as great a loss as the single miner. But since there is no such individual, we cannot let the numbers count, which is why we ought not to count them.

If this is what Taurek thinks, he is confused. Aggregated losses make sense without assuming that there is a particular individual who has lost the total sum. If Bert, Don, and Charley have all invested in Chrysler Corporation, and if all have lost varying sums of money, it does not follow that we can make sense of the total of their losses only by assuming that there is some fourth individual, some aggregate of the three, who has lost the total sum of their separate losses. Their separate losses can be intelligibly summed without assuming this, just as the average of their total losses can be computed without assuming that there is a fifth person (the one who has lost the average) aborning. There is no reason why the case of aggregating harms must be different in this respect. We can intelligibly ask how much Bert, Don, and Charley have been harmed by their financial losses, and we can make sense of the claim that the aggregate of their harms is equal to, or greater or lesser than, the aggregate of the harms of other groups of investors, without our having to assume that there is some other individual, the composite of the three of them, who has experienced the aggregate harm.

Perhaps Taurek might concede that it is possible to aggregate harms in the way suggested but deny that we should do this. The prohibition against doing this is a second thread in his argument, albeit one that is not always kept distinct from his implying that we can't. His position in this regard comes to this: to treat all the miners equally, we must have an equal concern for the survival of each of them. But to have an equal concern for each miner requires that we not let the numbers count. If my concern for the one miner's survival is equal to my concern for each of the fifty, then I must treat them all equitably; and to treat them all equitably requires that I give all an equal chance in the lottery of survival, so to speak, which, in Taurek's view, requires flipping a coin.

This approach is unsatisfactory for at least three different reasons. First, to flip a coin *just once* in such cases is manifestly not to treat all the affected individuals equitably. The odds are stacked unfairly in favor of the one and against the fifty. To make recourse to coin tossing equitable, one would have to flip a coin at least fifty times, one toss *for each* of the fifty miners over and against the single miner. Indeed, to treat the several members of the group of fifty *as if* they constituted a single individual, which is what we would be doing if we allowed a single coin toss to decide their collective fate, is itself dramatically at odds with Taurek's injunction to take their *individual* prospective losses seriously.

Second, the circumstances of the mine case are such that, even were we to flip the coin so as to treat all involved equitably, there would be no reasonable way to carry out the results. Suppose that, after we have tossed the coin fifty times, the results are as chance would predict. The solitary miner wins fifty percent of the tosses, while twenty-five of the fifty miners win the rest. What shall we do? The nature of the case prohibits our saving the twenty-five without killing the one, and if we were to save the one on the grounds that he won fifty percent of the tosses we could not do this without taking steps that are certain to kill the twenty-five miners who beat the solitary miner in head-to-head competition, so to speak. Shall we flip a coin again, with everything riding on the outcome: heads the solitary miner is saved, tails the others perish? But this response will be open to the same objections raised against the initial arrangement. It is *not* to treat all involved equitably because it gives an unfair advantage to the lone miner.

But, third, it is false that, by opting to save the fifty rather than the one, we fail to treat the trapped men equitably, when equality of treatment is interpreted in terms of the respect principle. What each of the miners is entitled to is the same respect due to each as a possessor of inherent value. And this is something we succeed in doing, for reasons soon to be set forth, by saving the fifty at the expense of the one.

8.10 THE MINIRIDE AND WORSE-OFF PRINCIPLES

Despite the criticisms lodged against Taurek's view, there is an important insight contained in it. One way to decide if and when it is permissible to harm those who are innocent is as follows: What we must do is act so as to minimize the total aggregate of harm of the innocent (*the minimize harm principle*). Thus, whenever we find ourselves in a situation where all of the options at hand will produce some harm to those who are innocent, we must choose that option that will result in the least total sum of harm.

The minimize harm principle runs afoul of our considered beliefs. Imagine this prevention case. We may harm A quite radically, *or* we may harm a thousand others in a modest way, *or* we may do nothing, in which case both A and the thousand will be harmed as described. Suppose we could place numerical values on the harms in question. A's harm equals, say, -125; the aggregate of the thousand, each of whom will be harmed at a value of -1, is $-1,000$; and the aggregate of both, then, is $-1,125$. All are innocent. Which alternative ought we to choose? If we are to decide these matters on the basis recommended by the minimize harm principle, what we ought to do is harm A. And that seems grossly unfair. The quality of his life, after all, would be in a shambles, if we chose that option, whereas the welfare of the others, considered as individuals, would only be modestly diminished. What we ought to do is spare A gross harm and spread the harm around by choosing the second option.

Now, if that is what we ought to do, we must resist the minimize harm principle. But because appeals to our considered beliefs are controversial, one would like to be able to invalidate this principle without making such appeals. Taurek's argument against the possibility of aggregating harms can be understood (it is not clear that he intended it in this way) as an attempt to unseat that principle without appealing to our intuitions. If harms *cannot* be aggregated, then we have solid reasons to reject the minimize harm principle.

But it is possible to reject this principle without accepting Taurek's arguments for doing so and without merely appealing to our considered beliefs. The grounds for rejecting it are to be found by working out the implications of the respect principle and the postulate of inherent value on which it rests. The minimize harm principle is a consequentialist principle, one that instructs us to act so as to avoid the worst consequences, where "the worst consequences" are understood as the greatest sum of harm done to all the innocents affected by the outcome. To accept the minimize harm principle thus is to assume that moral agents or patients *are mere receptacles after all*, not of, say, pleasures and pains, but of harms and benefits, so that the harm done to any one individual can be more than compensated for by the greater sum of harm that is thereby spared others. The rights view refuses to regard moral agents and patients in this way. Individuals who have inherent values are *not to be viewed as mere receptacles of anything* and so may never be treated in ways that assume that they are. To treat them so is to fail to treat them with that respect to which, as possessors of inherent value, they are entitled as a matter of strict justice, treatment to which they have a basic moral right. The fundamental error of the minimize harm principle, then, is not that it assumes that the separate harms of different individuals can be aggregated (they can, Taurek's objections to the contrary notwithstanding) *or* that it has implications that clash with our considered beliefs (though it does). Its fundamental error lies in assuming that moral agents and patients are mere receptacles of value, having no distinctive value in their own right. *That is why* this principle has implications that fail to match our considered beliefs.

To reject the minimize harm principle is not enough. If the rights view is to have any claim on our rational assent, it must be able to provide guidance in precisely those sorts of cases where one might be tempted to rely on the minimize harm principle—prevention cases, that is, where, for example, we are required to choose between harming the few or harming the many who are innocent. The rights view recognizes two principles that apply to such cases, both of which are derivable from the respect principle. To prepare the grounds for this derivation requires recalling some of the results of the earlier analysis of harm (see 3.4).

Comparable Harm

In that earlier analysis a distinction was drawn between those harms that are inflictions and those that are deprivations. Harms that are deprivations deny an individual opportunities for doing what will bring satisfaction, when it is in that individual's interest to do this. Harms that are inflictions diminish the quality of an individual's life, not just if or as they deprive that individual of opportunities for satisfaction, though they usually will do this, but because they detract directly from the individual's overall welfare. Debilitating suffering is the paradigm of a harm that is an infliction; harms that are deprivations include limitations on one's autonomy. Whatever the category, not all harms are equal. An untimely death, for example, is a prima facie greater harm than a temporary loss of freedom, and it is a prima facie greater harm because it marks a prima facie greater loss. But harms can be unequal not only when the same individual is harmed in different ways; they may also be unequal when different individuals are harmed in the same way. The untimely death of a woman in the prime of her life is prima facie a greater harm than the death of her senile mother. Though both lose their life, the magnitude of the loss, and thus the harm, suffered by the younger woman is prima facie greater.

It is a virtue of the earlier discussion of harm that it allows us to make distinctions between the magnitude or severity of harms. A related virtue is that it enables us to give content to the notion of comparable harm. Two harms are comparable when they detract equally from an individual's welfare, or from the welfare of two or more individuals. For example, separate episodes of suffering of a certain kind and intensity are comparable harms if they cause an equal diminution in the welfare of the same individual at different times, or in two different individuals at the same or different times. And death is a comparable harm if the loss of opportunities it marks are equal in any two cases. Because of individual variability, however, some things that harm some may not harm others or may not harm them equally. In the case of physical pain, for example, some people can endure more than others, and some people who suffer can in time come to see this as "a blessing in disguise," while others have their lives shattered as a result. We cannot, therefore, automatically assume that prima facie harms of the same kind will necessarily constitute comparable harm in any two cases. What we *may* assume is that there is a strong presumption that they will. Other things being equal, that is, it is reasonable to assume that like harms have like effects—that is, detract equally from individual welfare and so are to be counted as comparable. Moreover, there is a limit to how much harm suffered by someone may be morally attributable to others. If you have grown accustomed to walking through a neighboring field on your way to work, and if I purchase the field and fence it, thereby requiring you to walk around it, which in turn requires that you rise earlier and take longer to go to work, then you are no doubt inconvenienced by what I do and, let us agree, prima facie harmed by it. But *how much you make* of this modest inconvenience is your affair, not mine. If you are driven to distraction by the extra time, lose sleep over it, divorce your wife, and burn down my house, ruining your career and spending time in prison in the bargain, then it is preposterous to hold *me* morally responsible for the heavy dose of harm that has fallen your way. My decision to erect the fence is *causally* linked to your downfall, and I must take moral responsibility for making the decision I've made; but it does not follow that I should be held accountable for your making a greater harm out of a lesser one. When, therefore, the rights view speaks of harming individuals in prima facie comparable ways and of the agent's having to take responsibility for doing this, it does not imply that the agent must also take responsibility for another's making that harm, as a result of his own volition, into something greater than it is.

The Miniride Principle

By making use of the notion of comparable harm, the rights view can formulate two principles that can be appealed to in order to make decisions in prevention cases. The first principle (*the minimize overriding principle*, or *the miniride principle*) states the following:

> Special considerations aside, when we must choose between overriding the rights of many who are innocent or the rights of few who are innocent, and when each affected individual will be harmed in a prima facie comparable way,[28] then we ought to choose to override the rights of the few in preference to overriding the rights of the many.

This principle is derivable from the respect principle. This latter principle entails that all moral agents and patients are directly owed the prima facie duty not to be harmed (5.6) and that all those who are owed this duty have an equally valid claim, and thus an equal prima facie moral right, against being harmed (7.9). Now, *precisely because* this right is equal, no one individual's right can count for any more than any other's, when the harm that might befall either is prima facie comparable. Thus, A's right cannot count for more than B's, or C's, or D's. However, when we are faced with choosing between options, one of which will harm A, the other of which will harm B, C, and D, and the third of which will harm them all, and when the foreseeable harm involved for each individual is prima facie comparable, then numbers count. *Precisely because* each is to count for one, no one for more than one, we cannot count choosing to override the rights of B, C, and D as neither better nor worse than choosing to override A's right alone. Three are more than one, and when the four individuals have an equal prima facie right not to be harmed, when the harm they face is prima facie comparable, and when there are no special considerations at hand, then showing equal respect for the equal rights of the individuals involved requires that we override the right of A (the few) rather than the rights of the many (B, C, D). To choose to override the rights of the many in this case would be to override an equal right three times (i.e., in the case of three different individuals) when we could choose to override such a right only once, and *that* cannot be consistent with showing equal respect for the equal rights of all the individuals involved.

To favor overriding the rights of the few in no way contravenes the requirement that each is to count for one, no one for more than one; on the contrary, special considerations apart, to choose to override the rights of the many rather than those of the few would be to count A's right for more than one—that is, as being equal to overriding the rights of three relevantly similar individuals. Accordingly, because we must not allow any one individual a greater voice in the determination of what ought to be done than any other relevantly similar individual, what we ought to do in prevention cases of the sort under consideration is choose to override the rights of the fewest innocents rather than override the rights of the many. And since this is precisely what the miniride principle enjoins, that principle is derivable from the respect principle.

Two objections to this derivation can be anticipated. Since A's right is equal to B's, and to C's, and to D's, it might be claimed, then A's right must be equal to the rights of A, B, and C taken together. Therefore, this objection contends, to favor doing what will harm A in preference to what will harm B, C, and D is not to let each count for one, no one more for one. The reply to this objection is in some ways reminiscent of earlier criticisms lodged against Taurek. The essential point is a simple one. There is no aggregate individual—no composite of B, C, and D—who has a right not to be harmed, and this for the quite simple reason that there is no aggregate individual in the first place. There are only the separate, distinct individuals—B, C, D—and each of these individuals has a right equal to the right of A. What we are faced with, then, is having to choose not between overriding A's right *or* overriding the equal right of this composite individual, but between overriding A's right or overriding the equal rights of three other, separate, distinct individuals. To treat the three as one—as if they constituted a single, conglomerate individual, with the same (equal) right as A—not only is not required in order to give significance to the idea that each individual has an individual right not to be harmed but is also contrary to the requirement to treat each of the affected individuals equally.

The second objection takes a different tack. It claims that the miniride principle is at odds with the respect principle because it allows us to treat the few who are innocent merely as receptacles, something the respect principle will not tolerate. Since by choosing to override A's right we thereby prevent a much greater aggregate of harm befalling B, C, and D, it is claimed, to allow A's right to be overriden is to imply that A's losses are not as bad as this aggregate, which is why A's right may be overriden. And this, so this objection urges, is to treat A as a mere receptacle in just the same way and for just the same reasons as A is treated as a mere receptacle according to the minimize harm principle—a principle which, it was argued in the above, must be rejected if one accepts the respect principle. Thus, if one accepts the respect principle, one must reject the miniride principle.

This objection confuses considerations about the foreseeable consequences of acting in compliance with the miniride principle with the rights view's grounds for accepting this principle. It is true that the aggregate of harm that will result when the rights of the few who are innocent are overridden in preference to those of the many is foreseeably less bad (i.e., constitutes a less aggregate sum of harm) than that that would result if the rights of the many were overridden in preference to those of the few. But the reason for choosing the former option, according to the rights view, is not that the aggregated consequences of making this choice would be better (i.e., less bad); that *would* be to view the individuals involved as mere receptacles. The reason the rights view gives for choosing to override the rights of the few is that this is what we must do if we are to show equal respect for the equal inherent value, *and* the equal prima facie rights, of the individuals involved. It is, in a word, not the aggregate consequences for all affected by the outcome that matter; it is respect for the equality of the involved individuals that does.

The miniride principle illuminates why, on the rights view, we ought to act to save the fifty miners rather than the one. Earlier discussions of that example tacitly assumed that the harm each of the miners would suffer, if he died, is comparable to the harm that any other miner would suffer. That is a reasonable assumption to make, given that their losses are prima facie comparable. This much granted, and assuming that no special considerations are at hand, the miniride principle requires doing what must be done to save the many even if this means overriding the rights of the few. And it requires this not because the aggregate of the harms that would result from this choice would be less bad than if we chose to act otherwise; it requires this because this is the choice we must make if we are to show equal respect for the inherent value of the individuals involved and if we are to count their equal rights equally.

The Worse-off Principle

The fundamental difference between the rights view and the minimize harm principle comes into sharper focus when we turn to consider prevention cases where harms are not comparable. Recall the earlier prevention case where we are called upon to choose between harming A quite radically (-125), or harming a thousand individuals modestly (-1 each), or doing nothing. If the only consideration relevant to deciding such cases is to minimize the number of rights that are overriden, then what we ought to do is harm A, since one individual is fewer than a thousand and a thousand-and-one. But the miniride principle does not enjoin us *simply* to minimize the number of rights that are overridden; it enjoins us to do this on the assumption that, special considerations aside, the harms faced by all the innocents *are prima facie comparable*. In the example just given, however, the harms are not prima facie comparable. The harm A faces greatly exceeds the harm faced by any one of the thousand, and the aggregate of the harm that would befall the thousand harms no one individual and thus cannot be construed as constituting harm that is comparable to (or more than comparable to) the harm that would befall A. The minimize harm principle would require choosing the option that harms A. The miniride principle, since it applies *only* in prevention cases where harms are prima facie comparable, cannot be relied on in cases, such as this one, where the harm all the innocents face is not prima facie comparable. The rights view thus requires a second principle, distinct from but consistent with the miniride principle, and one that is distinct from and not reducible to the minimize harm principle. The following principle (*the worse-off principle*) meets these requirements. (The following formulation is given in terms of "the rights of the many" and "the rights of the few." However, unequal numbers [the few, the many] are not essential to the worse-off principle; it applies in cases where we must choose between harming one innocent *or* harming another. Such cases are considered in the next section. It also applies when we act to prevent ourselves from being made worse-off. On this, see 9.11.)

> Special considerations aside, when we must decide to override the rights of the many or the rights of the few who are innocent, and when the harm faced by the few would make them worse-off than any of the many would be if any other option were chosen, then we ought to override the rights of the many.

Unlike the miniride principle, the worse-off principle applies to the type of prevention case illustrated by the example at hand, and unlike the minimize harm principle the worse-off principle would not sanction overriding A's right because doing so brought about a lesser aggregate of harm. The worse-off principle sanctions overriding the rights of the thousand even though each is innocent and even though, by overriding their individual rights, we override the right of a thousand innocent individuals not to be harmed in preference to overriding the right of one individual. In this kind of case, in short, numbers don't count.

The worse-off principle, like the miniride principle, is derivable from the respect principle. Notice, first, that the respect principle cannot allow harming A on the grounds that the thousand will be spared *a greater aggregate amount* of harm. To suppose that the harm done to A can be justified in this way is to treat A as a mere receptacle—is to assume, that is, that A's losses can be outweighed by the sum of the losses of the others. The respect principle will not allow this. If we are to treat A with the respect A is due as a matter of strict justice, we cannot simply sum A's losses and then compare them with the aggregate total of the losses of the thousand except at the price of ignoring the distinctive kind of value (inherent value) A has. The approach to decision making affirmed by the minimize harm principle is denied by the respect principle. Appeal to the respect principle will not justify choosing an option that makes the few individuals involved worse-off than any other involved individual would be, if any other option were chosen.

Appeal to the respect principle justifies overriding the rights of the many in prevention cases of the type at hand. This is shown by considering a simple case first. To say that two individuals, M and N, have an equal right not to be harmed, based on the equal respect each is owed, does not imply that each and every harm either may suffer is equally harmful. Other things being equal, M's death is a greater harm than N's migraine. If we are to show equal respect for the value and rights of individuals, therefore, we cannot count a lesser harm to N as equal to or greater than a greater harm to M. To show equal respect for the equal rights of the two, one must count their equal harms equally, not their unequal harms equally, a requirement that entails, other things being equal in prevention cases, that M's right override N's when the harm done to M would be greater if one choice were made than the harm done to N would be if another option were chosen. To assess the matter otherwise—to flip a coin or to override M's right—would be to give to N *more* than N is due. *Precisely because* M and N are *equal* in inherent value, *because* the two have an *equal* prima facie right not to be harmed, and *because* the harm M faces is *greater* than the harm N faces, equal respect for the two requires that we not choose to override M's right but choose to override N's instead.

Now, adding numbers makes no difference in such a case. If, as in our earlier example, A would be made worse-off than any one of the thousand individuals if we chose to harm A and spare the others, then aggregating the harms of the thousand can make no difference. No one *else* is harmed by summing the harms of the thousand; there is, that is, no aggregate individual whose harm can be placed at −1,000 and who can be viewed as having a right not to be harmed that justifiably overrides A's. There are just the thousand, each one of whom will be harmed less than A will and no one of whom will be made worse-off than A would be, if we chose to harm A. For *each* of the thousand, then, A's right overrides his, just as, in the previous paragraph, M's right justifiably overrides N's. *It is the magnitude of the harm done to A and each individual member of the thousand, not the sum of A's harm compared with the sum of the thousands', that deter-mines whose right overrides whose.* Since, *ex hypothesi,* the harm done to A would be greater than that done to, and would make A worse-off than, any other involved individual, respect for the equal rights and value of all those involved requires overriding the rights of the many rather than the right of the individual. In the absence of special considerations, and assuming the few who are innocent would be made worse-off than any of the many who are innocent if we chose to override the rights of the few, the respect principle requires that we override the rights of the many. And since this is what the worse-off principle requires, that principle is derivable from the respect principle.

An objection to this derivation and to the earlier derivation of the miniride principle argues that the rights view is inconsistent. On the one hand, the rights view denies the moral relevance of consequences, as witness its steady attack on utilitarianism and its rejection of the minimize harm principle; and yet, on the other hand, it relies on the notion of comparable harm and invokes considerations about who will be harmed most, as witness its miniride and worse-off principles. And this, so this objection goes, is inconsistent.

This objection is a product of confusion. What the rights view denies is that moral right and wrong can be determined *merely* by determining which alternative act or, as in the case of rule utilitarianism, the adoption of which rules, will bring about "the best" aggregate consequences for all those affected by the outcome, even when "the best" consequences are "the least bad," as, according to the minimize harm principle, they are. The rights view rejects any and all consequentialist theories because any and all assume that consequences and consequences alone determine moral right, wrong, and duty (see above, 4.5). But the rights view does not hold that considerations about consequences are *morally irrelevant*; in particular, it does not claim that we can dispense with such considera-tions in determining *how much* those directly involved will be harmed. However, to insist on the relevance of such considerations is not the same as, and does not entail, the belief that *aggregating* consequences for all those affected by the outcome determines moral right, wrong, and duty. Consequences are relevant because we cannot fix the magnitude of harm for those directly involved without attention to them. Even so, the moral relevance of these consequences is parasitic on moral principles whose validity is *not* argued for on the grounds that their adoption will bring about better consequences for all those affected by the outcome (utilitar-ianism), or for those individuals who enter into certain agreements (rational egoism). The validity of the respect principle and those principles derivable from it—the harm principle (7.9) and the miniride and the worse-off principles (8.10)—rests on the postulate of inherent value, *not* on the principle of utility, *or* on the agreements reached by rational egoists, *or* on any other consequentialist ethical principle. Indeed, to insist, as the rights view does, that considerations about *how much each* of those directly involved will be harmed are *relevant* considerations in prevention cases is precisely what one would expect and should require of a view that advocates *the equal rights of the individuals* involved. How else are we to show equal respect toward each of these individuals except by considering how well their *individual* prima facie right not to be harmed stacks up against the equal prima facie right of the other individuals involved? And how are we to determine this without considering which of those individuals directly involved will be harmed, how much each will be harmed, and so forth? To insist on the relevance of these considerations is simply to insist on the necessity of treating all those directly involved with the equal respect they are due. What we must not do—what would be contrary to the letter and the spirit of the rights view—is to sanction overriding an individual's right *merely* on the grounds that this brings about a better aggregate balance of good over evil for all those affected by the outcome. That would be to authorize treating those who have inherent value merely as a means to this collective goal, and that is prohibited, given the rights view, since it is to treat right-bearers as if they were mere receptacles. Mistaken the rights view may be—only future challenges can decide this—but certainly it is not mistaken because it is inconsistent, at least not for the reasons alleged.

The rights view is antagonistic to utilitarianism, even to those utilitarians, such as Mill, who are not acrimonious to appeals to moral rights; it is, in some respects, sympathetic to Taurek's position, especially in denying, in concert with him, the validity of the minimize harm principle. But one can deny the validity of that principle without denying that harms can be aggregated and without denying that "the numbers" ever count. The miniride and worse-off principles provide an alternative basis to Taurek's position of denying the minimize harm principle and the general utilitarian inclination with which that principle is naturally allied,[29] an alternative that is decidedly nonutilitarian and can only mistakenly be regarded as consequentialist. Moreover, these principles, for the reasons given above, are not independent or disconnected principles—not "self-evident moral axioms," not "self-evident moral laws," not "self-evident moral absolutes." They are principles that can be derived from a still more fundamental principle (the respect principle), a principle that itself can be defended by means of argument rather than by appeals to what is claimed to be "self-evident." None of these principles, including miniride and worse-off, are ad hoc devices tailor made to fit some favored set of considered beliefs. To dispute the rights view just on these grounds would be as unfair as it would be unfounded.

8.11 WHY SIDE-EFFECTS DON'T COUNT

The rights view categorically denies that side effects are relevant considerations for determining when it is justifiable to override the right of the innocent not to be harmed. In denying the moral relevance of side effects the rights view differs fundamentally from all consequentialist theories. For act utilitarians, for example, whether it is wrong to kill or otherwise harm an innocent individual must depend on the consequences of doing so, not only for the individual who is killed but for everyone affected by the outcome (see 6.2). Since the side effects of any given action (that is, how others who are not directly involved are affected by the outcome) *are* part of the consequences of the action, side effects are relevant to the moral assessment of the action, according to act utilitarianism, and are just as relevant as the effects the action has on the individuals directly involved. Since each is to count for one, no one for more than one, directly involved individuals have no privileged moral position within utilitarian theory. And this is so regardless of the kind of act utilitarian theory we are presented (e.g., hedonistic utilitarianism, preference utilitarianism, etc.).

The rights view will not allow this. To suppose that we can justify harming an innocent individual merely by aggregating the consequences for all those affected by the outcome is to treat that individual as if he were a receptacle and thus is contrary to the respect to which, as a possessor of inherent value, he is due as a matter of strict justice. If his right not to be harmed is to be overridden, it cannot be overridden merely on the grounds that doing so is necessary to produce optimal consequences for everyone. This is why the *secrecy* of the killing of a moral agent makes no difference to its justifiability for the rights view, though it does for the act utilitarian.

The radical difference between the rights view and consequentialist theories (e.g., act utilitarianism) can be illustrated in the following way. Imagine we are in a situation where we must choose between doing what will harm one innocent individual, A, or doing what will harm another innocent individual, B. Imagine further that were we to choose the first option, A would be harmed *much* more severely than B would be harmed were we to choose the latter option. Suppose A would be paralyzed for life, B for a day. And imagine, finally, that it so happens that there are interested parties in B's case but not in A's; that is, there are individuals who care about what happens to B but none who care about A, so that if the choice is made to do what will harm B, these interested parties will not like it. How shall we decide what we ought to do? On act utilitarian grounds, we cannot ignore the side effects harming B will have on these interested parties; on the contrary, we must consider their interests and count them equitably. That much conceded, it could well be that, when *all* the consequences are counted and weighed, the *aggregate* of the consequences that would result from choosing to do what harms A could be less bad than those that would result from choosing to harm B. And if that were true, harming A is what we ought to do, given act utilitarianism.

The rights view will not allow this. If, as we assume, the harm done to A makes A worse-off than B, then, special considerations aside, it is wrong to override A's right not to be harmed. The *aggregate* of the harms of others harms no one in particular in a way comparable to the way A would be harmed, and to suppose that A's harm could be justified by totaling the harms of B and those interested in B is to view A as a mere receptacle, something that, on the rights view, he is not. In general, when we must choose among options, all of which will cause harm to some who are innocent and one of which will make a given individual worse-off than the others, then, special considerations aside, we must not choose this latter option. That is what the worse-off principle requires when applied to cases where we must choose which one of two different individuals to harm.

When properly understood, it is the rights view, not utilitarianism, that provides the philosophical basis for principled objections to the worst forms of moral prejudice—such as racism. In their paradigmatic form, moral prejudices consist in supposing that making certain individuals worse-off than others can be justified by appealing to side effects— for example, to the interests of others affected by the outcome. The racist, for example, is more than willing to allow that blacks be made worse-off because *he* and his ilk like whites more than they like blacks. Because, given utilitarian theory, the racist's pleasures, preferences, and so forth, count *and* must be counted equitably, and because, given this theory, we must aim to bring about the best aggregate result, utilitarianism is not *in principle* inhospitable to racism. The rights view bars its entrance. It will not allow the aggregate balance of goods over evils for all affected by the outcome to justify harming anyone, least of all making any individual worse-off than others. Let the racists aggregate their collective gains and losses to their hearts' content; that will go no way toward justifying what they do to individual members of the victimized group, when these individuals are made worse-off than any other individual affected by the outcome.

The same is true of speciesism. Those harms done to animals cannot be justified by appeals to the optimal aggregate balance of goods over evils obtained by others. To suppose otherwise is to assume that those animals who, as individuals, are made worse-off can have their harmful inflictions or deprivations morally offset by summing the goods and evils others obtain or avoid. And this is something that cannot be done unless we view these animals as mere receptacles, an erroneous assumption given the rights view and the postulate of inherent value on which it rests. Thus do we have, on the rights view, the basis utilitarians lack (see 6.4) for protesting against, for example, those who would use animals in terminal research, but not humans, when the death caused these animals marks a greater loss, and thus a greater harm, than it would in the case of some humans who might be used in their place. For the magnitude of the harm that death is, is a function of the number and variety of opportunities for satisfaction it forecloses, and there is no credible basis on which to claim that the death of a normal, adult animal is not a greater loss, and thus a greater harm, than the death of a less aware, retarded human, one who possesses fewer desires, less competence to act intentionally, and is less responsive to others and to the environment generally. Utilitarians, because they insist on the relevance of side effects, imply that it is permissible to override the rights of the animal rather than the human in such cases if the aggregate total consequences for everyone affected by the outcome would be better than those that would result if the human's rights were overridden. That being so, utilitarians cannot lodge a moral complaint, justified by reference to the principle of utility, against using the animal in research unless they are in possession of facts that show that the use of the animal is not optimific, all considered. Significantly, utilitarians are not in possession of the relevant facts (see, above, 6.4; the argument given there, which applies to the utilitarian basis for the obligatoriness of vegetarianism, applies with equal force to the question of the use of animals in science).

The rights view does not need these facts to lodge its moral protest against speciesist practices. It is not the *aggregate* balance of goods and evils for all those affected by the outcome that is decisive; it is the magnitude of the harm done to the individuals directly involved that is. Special considerations aside, to persist in using animals in terminal research, when the magnitude of the harm that death is for them is greater than it would be for a retarded human, *is* speciesist, and it is a variety of speciesism, ironically, that could be supported by the very theory that has been appealed to to denounce this prejudice—namely, utilitarianism. But lest it be thought that the rights view's position on the use of animals and humans in terminal or other research is an invitation to begin to use less fortunate human beings in lieu of animals, let it be clear that the use of human beings, like the use of animals, *cannot be defended merely by appealing to aggregate consequences.* As moral patients, these human beings are to be protected by the very same principles that apply to our dealings with all who are innocent.

The initial attractiveness of utilitarianism as a moral theory on which to rest the call for the better treatment of animals was noted in an earlier context (6.2). Because animals are sentient (i.e., can experience pleasure and pain) and because they not only have but can act on their preferences, any view that holds that pleasures or pains, or preference-satisfactions or frustrations matter morally is bound to seem attractive to those in search of the moral basis for the animal rights movement. Especially because animals are made to suffer in the pursuit of human purposes—in the name of "efficient" factory farming, for example, or in pursuit of scientific knowledge—the utilitarian injunction to count their suffering *and* to count it equitably must strike a responsive moral chord. But utilitarianism is not the theory its initial reception by the animal rights movement may have suggested. It provides no basis for the rights of animals and instead contains within itself the grounds for perpetuating the very speciesist practices it was supposed to overthrow. To secure the philosophical foundation for animal rights requires abandoning utilitarianism.

8.12 MORE OBJECTIONS ANSWERED

Three important criticisms can be anticipated. First, a critic might object that the rights view has implications that clash with our considered beliefs. Imagine that A is a total stranger and B is a family member or friend. And imagine that you must choose between doing something that will harm A, or doing something that will harm B, or doing nothing, in which case both will be harmed. Suppose that the harm A faces is of slightly greater magnitude than the harm B faces, though both harms are significant. Then the rights view, it might be claimed, implies that you ought to act to spare the stranger at the expense of your loved one. And that is counterintuitive.

Now, that result *is* counterintuitive, and any view would do well to avoid it. But it is critical to avoid it for the right reasons. In particular, appeals to side effects are again inappropriate. It would be a mistake to argue as follows: The reason why you ought not to harm your loved one is because, if you do, the aggregate of his harm plus the harm that would befall you (e.g., your mental anguish, doubt, and guilt) if you chose to harm him would be greater than the sum of the harm that would result if you chose to harm the stranger. It would be a mistake to make the decision in this case turn on such considerations because (1) it would be to treat all the parties involved—the stranger, your loved one, and your-self—as if all were mere receptacles of value, and because (2) to let side effects count in this case would open the door to letting them count in *any* case where others have an interest in the outcome. And that would be to allow *any* interested third party to add his losses to the losses of the one he likes and then appeal to this greater aggregate to justify making the one he does not like worse-off. This would give the bigot and the fanatic, for example, the very opening they need to justify their bigotry and fanaticism.

An alternative to this aggregate approach is to view the moral bonds between family members and friends as a *special consideration* that justi-fiably can override the otherwise binding application of the miniride and worse-off principles. This is not a case of a theory's grasping at straws to save itself. It is preposterous to suppose that the reason why I have special obligations to my wife, children, other family members, and friends is because of the salutary side effects this has for others, least of all for society generally. I stand in a special moral relationship to friends and family because I stand in a special personal relationship to them, and though neither relationship quite fits the model of an explicit contract (we don't, that is, actually sit down and write out the terms of our relation-ship), the relationship between loved ones is not totally disanalogous to contractual arrangements either. Like contracts, relationships between loved ones are built on mutual trust, interdependence, and the perfor-mance of mutually beneficial acts. Normally, it is those closest to us whom we stand to help or harm most, and they, us. It would therefore be morally otiose to require that we suspend the moral bonds that character-ize these relationships whenever someone who stands *outside* these rela-tionships will be made slightly worse-off if we decide to prevent harm to someone who occupies a position *within* such a relationship—for exam-ple, a friend. To say this is not to say that there are no possible circum-stances in which we ought to be willing to do what will harm a loved one in order to prevent harm befalling a stranger. If the magnitude of the harms in question vary greatly (say it is a question of preventing the death of a stranger or a minor injury to a friend) then loyalty to one's friend (i.e., that type of special consideration) ought to be set aside and the normal application of the worse-off principle honored. Were one's friend not to understand this, claiming that duties to one's friends override *everything else*, then one would do well to look elsewhere for one's friends. The issues obviously admit of indefinite degrees and call for judgment in some cases where it would be unreasonable to hope for an iron-clad, exceptionless rule on which to base them. The rights view has no such rule, and in this it shares its limitations with all theories vying for our informed assent. Having said this, however, the central point remains: the relationships between friends and loved ones *are* special, and so should be counted among those "special considerations" that can validly suspend the normal application of the miniride and worse-off principles. That is the reason why, in most cases at least, we are justified in sparing significant harm to our friends even when doing so will make a stranger worse-off. The justification of our acting as we do does not consist in totaling our friends' and our own losses.

These remarks on acquired duties provide the occasion for resolving an issue that was raised in passing in an earlier context (8.3). The issue concerns when, and if so how, the validity of putative acquired duties, and their correlative rights, is to be decided. The rights view's position is as follows. Those who reach unjust voluntary agreements or who take part in unjust institutions (e.g., the slave trade) acquire no duties, nor does anyone acquire moral rights, as a result of voluntary participation in such an institution or as a result of the agreements reached by those who perpetuate the institution. As those affected by these agreements and the institution (in this case, the slaves) are not treated with the respect they are due, according to the rights view, the institution is unjust and the putative duties and rights acquired by those who perpetuate it lack moral validity. Lacking this validity, they fail to qualify as valid moral considerations that would justify suspending the normal application of the miniride or worse-off principles. If the choice faced by a slave trader in a prevention case was between either harming a slave significantly or harming a fellow trader less so, then it is the fellow trader who ought to be harmed, not the slave, the appeal to any "contract" made between the slave-traders as constituting a "special consideration" lacking any claim to validity in this case. Since the institution of which the contract is a part is unjust to the core, the contract has no valid moral status. On the rights view, then, appeals to acquired duties *can* play a legitimate role in the determination of what ought to be done *if and only if* these putative duties qualify as valid duties, and these are those duties that meet the requirement of just treatment as specified by the respect principle. *If* this requirement is met, *then* one's voluntary acts and one's place in an institution are the basis for acquiring both duties and rights. A promise voluntarily made thus creates both the acquired duty on the part of the promisor to perform as promised and the correlative right on the part of the one to whom the promise is made to claim performance as being due, if both those who enter into the agreement and those affected by it are treated with the respect that is their due. One has no moral duty to do what violates the rights of another, in other words, even if one promises to do so, and the one to whom the promise is made has no acquired moral right to require performance (as when, for example, a professional killer "contracts" to murder a public-spirited special prosecutor). Only when the agreements reached as a result of a promise or a contract satisfy the respect principle do the participants acquire moral duties and correlative moral rights. When that condition is met, the rights and duties are validated. This is how, according to the rights view, the duty to keep a promise, for example, is validated (see 8.3).

The requirement that voluntary acts and institutions conform with the respect principle, if they are to give rise to valid moral duties and correlative rights, explains why, on the rights view, all attempts to base morality on the agreements reached by self-interested individuals (e.g., Narvesonian rational egoism or Rawlsian contractarianism) *must* prove to be deficient. Agreements or contracts are morally valid, according to the rights view, if and only if they satisfy the requirement of just treatment, as specified by the respect principle, and the validity of that principle is not itself dependent on who reaches what agreements or under what conditions they reach them (e.g., from behind the veil of ignorance). To put the point alternatively, *the moral validity of the agreements or contracts reached must be shown by appeal to a principle that is not itself a product of the contract or agreement*. In this way the arbitrary exclusion of moral patients from those who are owed direct duties—including the unacquired duty of just treatment, an exclusion that characterizes all contractarian theories (5.6)—is traced to its ultimate source. For since, on such views, the principles of just treatment are themselves the "outcome" of the contract, and since only those capable of contracting can be owed "strict" justice, these theories imply that those who are themselves incapable of contracting may be nonarbitrarily excluded from those to whom strict justice is owed. Thus are moral patients, whether humans or animals, excluded. The rights view denies this. The validity of the respect principle, as a principle of just treatment, is independent of contractarian considerations, and the scope of this principle includes all those who may reasonably be viewed as possessing inherent value, including animals and those human moral patients like them in the relevant respects.

Abortion and Infanticide

A second objection contests the rights view because of its alleged implications regarding abortion and infanticide. Since individuals who are not subjects-of-a-life are not recognized as having rights, according to the rights view, and since neither human fetuses nor newborn infants are subjects-of-a-life, it follows, so this objection urges, that neither fetuses nor infants have rights. And from this it follows, so it is alleged, that the rights view implies that we may do anything we please to human fetuses and infants. Since no moral theory can be adequate if it has this implication, however, the rights view is not the adequate theory its advocates suppose.

A number of replies deserve mention. Recall, first, that the rights view advances the subject-of-a-life criterion as a sufficient, not a necessary, condition for possessing inherent value and, by implication, basic moral rights (7.5). Even assuming, then, that neither human fetuses nor infants satisfy this criterion, it does not follow that they *must* lack moral rights. Whether they do remains an open question, given the rights view, just as whether natural objects (trees or sagebrush, for example) possess rights remains an open question, given this view. Second, recall that the rights view does not deny that human fetuses and infants fail to satisfy the subject-of-a-life criterion. At an earlier point (2.6) the decision was made to limit the use of the word *human* to *Homo Sapiens* of one year or more who are not *very* seriously mentally impoverished. That decision was made so that the discussion could proceed without our first having to decide where to draw the line concerning when individual humans acquire or lose the family of mental abilities that makes one the subject-of-a-life, in the sense explained. It was acknowledged at that point that the status of human fetuses and infants in this regard is controversial. It is not *obviously true* that the newly born or the soon-to-be-born have beliefs, desires, and the like, and neither is it *obviously true* that they lack these mental attributes.[30] Whether they do or do not, in short, is an open and much debated question. Though it is beyond the scope of the present work to enter into this debate, it should be clear that the rights view leaves the question central to this debate an open question. And that is a virtue, not a vice, of this view.

Third, even assuming that human fetuses and infants, despite our abundant ignorance concerning their relative mental development, in fact are not subjects-of-a-life and, let us suppose, also lack moral rights, it would not follow that the rights view implies that we are at liberty to do anything we please to them. The rights view advocates taking steps that foster the creation of a moral climate where the rights of the individual are taken seriously indeed. Better, then, to adopt a policy that errs on the side of caution when the recognition of moral rights is at issue. Precisely because it is unclear where we should draw the line between those humans who are, and those who are not, subjects-of-a-life, and in view of our profound ignorance about the comparative mental sophistication of newly born and soon-to-be-born human beings, the rights view would advocate giving infants and viable human fetuses the benefit of the doubt, viewing them *as if* they are subjects-of-a-life, *as if* they have basic moral rights, even while conceding that, in viewing them in these ways, we may be giving them more than is their due.

This argument for enfranchising newly born and soon-to-be-born human beings into the class of right-holders does not appeal to the "sentimental interests" of parents, relatives, or other third parties. (For a critique of the appeal to "sentimental interests" in this connection, see the earlier discussion of Narveson, 5.3.) It is the importance of fostering an environment in which individual rights are respected, whatever people's "sentiments," that underpins the serious moral protection extended to newly born and soon-to-be-born human beings. To specify the implications of the rights view regarding the full range of cases involving abortion and infanticide—in particular, to explore the *possible conflicts* between the rights of fetuses, infants, and others—is well beyond the limited reach of the present work. But what has been said here is enough to indicate why, contrary to the criticism under review, the rights view does not imply that we may do anything we please to human fetuses and infants.

Obligatory and Supererogatory Acts

The third and final objection to be considered in the present section challenges the rights view from a different quarter, arguing that this view, in particular the worse-off principle, implies that supererogatory acts are strict duties. This objection takes the following form: Suppose a race-car driver has been involved in a terrible accident and is certain to die if the available medical personnel are not used to save him. Suppose that four other patients need the services of the personnel, that all could be adequately treated only if none of the staff is diverted to the driver, and that all four will be significantly harmed (e.g., one will lose an arm, a second will be partially paralyzed, etc.) though none will die, if efforts are made to save the driver. Since the rights view will not allow aggregating harms of different individuals as a way of deciding what to do, one who accepts this view cannot claim that the four should be treated because the sum of their harms would exceed the harm borne by the lone driver. Indeed, since the worse-off principle directs us to prevent making the individual worse-off, special considerations aside, that principle, it might be claimed, requires that we override the rights of the four and administer to the needs of the driver, and that the four, recognizing the valid application of this principle in this case, ought to concur, agreeing to endure their respective harms so that the driver might be spared his. And this, so this objection alleges, is the rights view's undoing. For though it would be a remarkable show of self-sacrifice for the four to agree to bear their respective harms so that the driver might be spared his, it is preposterous to claim or imply that the four *ought* to do so—that each has a *duty* in this regard. For them voluntarily to endure their significant harms would be above and beyond the call of duty—would, that is, be supererogatory. Yet the rights view implies otherwise. It implies that each has a duty to do so.

The rights view's reply again turns on taking due note of the "special considerations aside" proviso incorporated in both the miniride and worse-off principles. That proviso does make a difference in many cases, including the present one. The essential point to notice is that those who voluntarily engage in high-risk behavior, including auto racing, obviously choose to expose themselves to certain risks that those who abstain from such activities choose to forgo, and it is part of the unspoken rules that apply to those embarked on such behavior that those who abstain cannot reasonably be *required* to suffer appreciable harm, in the name of justice, so that those who take additional risks might be rescued from their plight when the risk materializes. Those who voluntarily engage in high-risk behavior, in other words, waive their right not to be made worse-off if the means used to save them appreciably harms others who are not engaged in such activity. This is not to deny that those who are uninvolved are free to make the sacrifice to save the risk-taker. It is only to deny that the risk-taker has a valid claim, and thus a right, against them to do so, or that they have a correlative duty to make this sacrifice. If they should decide to make the sacrifice, they would act above and beyond what duty requires, whereas if they decide not to, they could not be faulted for failing to discharge their duty.

The rights view is able to account for supererogatory acts without abandoning either the miniride or the worse-off principle. And it can do so without having recourse to aggregating harms for different individuals and thus without violating the respect principle. The reason why the rights of those who are not involved in high-risk behavior should not be overriden to spare those engaged in such behavior from being made worse-off is not because the sum of their harm would exceed the harm done to the risk-takers who find themselves in perilous circumstances. It is because those who voluntarily engage in such activity *must understand that one of the risks they run is just this*—that if or as they find themselves in perilous circumstances as a result of their engaging in such behavior, their right not to be made worse-off no longer automatically outweighs the rights of those who choose not to run such risks.

Special Considerations

The replies given to the first and third objections raised in the present section illustrate two kinds of special consideration recognized by the rights view. First are those that involve acquired duties and rights, both of which arise as a result of either voluntary agreements (e.g., promises or contracts) or as a result of one's voluntarily assuming a position within a given institutional structure (e.g., taking a job or joining the army). The second class of special considerations involves those who voluntarily engage in certain kinds of activities, including high-risk activity (e.g., mountain climbing) and competitive activities (e.g., long-distance races). Considerations of the first kind are special, according to the rights view, because they involve valid claims, and thus rights, possessed by specific individuals, rights *in addition to* the basic moral rights shared by everyone; to treat those who have these special or acquired rights equitably, there- fore, requires taking their *additional* rights into account. Considerations of the second kind are special because those who voluntarily participate in high-risk or competitive activities voluntarily place themselves outside the normal protection afforded by the miniride and worse-off principles. Considerations of the first kind, in short, are considerations that *add to the strength* of the claims of certain individuals (namely, those who have acquired rights), while those of the second kind are special because they *subtract from the strength* of the claims possessed by others (for example, those who voluntarily participate in high-risk or competitive activities). Both types of considerations will prove to be important when we examine the moral implications of recognizing the rights of animals (9.1ff.).

A third kind of special consideration involves the historical back- ground leading up to situations where we are called upon to decide whose right not to be harmed should be overridden. If some of those involved are in their present predicament because other involved indi- viduals have violated their basic rights in the past, then these past viola- tions make a moral difference in the application of the miniride and worse-off principles. For example, if the solitary person trapped in the mine shaft was forced into the mine by the fifty because they believed they might reap some benefits from his forced labor, the fifty have lost their claim to be protected by the application of the miniride principle, assuming all involved face prima facie comparable harm. Or, again, if the lone miner happened to be an orphaned, unloved, retarded slave, while the fifty were highly intelligent, loved, and respected slave-owners, the fifty would have no valid claim to the protection afforded by the worse-off principle, despite the greater prima facie harm death would be for each of them when compared to the harm death would be for the enslaved miner. Those who forge, as well as those who perpetuate injustice are not on the same moral footing as their innocent victims. To put the same point in different words, unless we recognize that one kind of special consideration concerns the past injustice some have had to bear, the miniride and the worse-off principles would allow the rights of those who perpetuate injustice to override the rights of their victims *in the name of justice*. No account of justice and individual rights that allows this can be sound. No one has a right to profit from violating the basic rights of others. Those who are parties to such injustice lose the protection the miniride and worse-off principles provide and have no just grounds to complain if we override their right not to be harmed and spare the victims of their past injustice.

No claim is here made regarding the completeness of the preceding account of special considerations. Even so, it should be clear that side effects can find no place on the list of special considerations. To allow them a place is to assume that individuals who have inherent value are mere receptacles, something the rights view categorically denies. That is why side effects don't count. When there are cases (e.g., when family members are involved) where the normal application of the miniride or worse-off principle can be justifiably suspended, the rights view will seek to show that the grounds for doing so are to be found among those considerations that are plausibly and consistently viewed as special considerations. If those who advocate the rights view are unable to show this in a broad range of cases, if it can be shown that the implications of the rights view in these cases fail to match our considered judgments, and if an alternative to the rights view, one that is equal to the rights view in other respects, can be shown to systematize and illuminate these convictions, then the rights view will be faced with a serious problem indeed. Whether those who advocate the rights view are equal to the task of defending it against the challenges raised by others obviously must await receipt of the challenges themselves. The outcome cannot be determined in advance. What can be said in advance is that, on the rights view, no consideration can qualify as a special consideration if it assumes or implies that we may sum the pleasures and pains, preference-satisfactions and frustrations, and the like of all those who will be affected by the outcome of alternative acts as a way to determine when the miniride or worse-off principle may be overridden.

8.13 UNFINISHED BUSINESS

Two issues deferred in earlier discussions may now be addressed. The first is the lifeboat case (8.6). Recall the situation. There are five survivors: four normal adults and a dog. The boat has room enough only for four. Someone must go or else all will perish. Who should it be? Our initial belief is: the dog. Can the rights view illuminate and justify this prereflective intuition? The preceding discussion of prevention cases shows how it can. All on board have equal inherent value and an equal prima facie right not to be harmed. Now, the harm that death is, is a function of the opportunities for satisfaction it forecloses, and no reasonable person would deny that the death of any of the four humans would be a greater prima facie loss, and thus a greater prima facie harm, than would be true in the case of the dog. Death for the dog, in short, though a harm, is not comparable to the harm that death would be for any of the humans. To throw any one of the humans overboard, to face certain death, would be to make that individual worse-off (i.e., would cause *that* individual a greater harm) than the harm that would be done to the dog if the animal was thrown overboard. Our belief that it is the dog who should be killed is justified by appeal to the worse-off principle.

The selection of the dog does not conflict with recognizing the animal's equal inherent value or the dog's equal prima facie right not to be harmed. It does not conflict with the former because the animal is not harmed on the grounds that the aggregate of the harm spared the four humans, as a group, outweighs the individual animal's losses. And it does not conflict with the latter because recognition of the equal prima facie right not to be harmed requires that we not count unequal harms equally. To save the dog and to throw any one of the humans overboard would be to give to the dog more than is his due. It would be to count the lesser harm done to the dog as equal to or greater than the greater harm that would be done to any of the humans if one of them was cast overboard. Respect for their equal prima facie rights will not allow this. Any one of the humans who volunteered to give his life to save the dog's would be doing more—indeed, *much* more—than duty strictly requires.

The lifeboat case would not be *morally* any different if we supposed that the choice had to be made, not between a single dog and the four humans, but between these humans and any number of dogs. Let the number of dogs be as large as one likes; suppose they number a million; and suppose the lifeboat will support only four survivors. Then the rights view still implies that, special considerations apart, the million dogs should be thrown overboard and the four humans saved. To attempt to reach a contrary judgment will inevitably involve one in aggregative considerations—the sum of the losses of the million dogs over and against the losses for one of the humans—an approach that cannot be sanctioned by those who accept the respect principle.

To decide matters against the one or the million dogs is not speciesist. The decision to sacrifice the one or the million is not based on species membership. It is based on assessing the losses *each individual* faces *and* assessing these losses *equitably*, an approach that is at once consistent with and required by the recognition of the equal inherent value and the equal prima facie right not to be harmed possessed by all those involved. For similar reasons, deciding against the one dog or the million does not commit one to a perfectionist theory of justice (for a discussion of theories of this type, see above, 7.1). Perfectionist theories sanction the *routine* subordination of the less virtuous by those who are more virtuous, so that the latter may develop their virtues optimally. The rights view disallows such subordination. What the rights view implies should be done in *exceptional* cases—and prevention cases, including lifeboat cases, *are* exceptional cases—cannot fairly be generalized to unexceptional cases. Moreover, lifeboat and other prevention cases, including those discussed earlier, are not decided by appeal to perfectionist principles, according to the rights view. They are decided by appeal to principles that acknowledge and respect the equality of the individuals involved, both their equal inherent value (no one individual's losses are to be outweighed by summing the losses of any group of individuals) and their equal prima facie right not to be harmed (no one individual's lesser harm can count for more than another's greater harm). This is not perfectionism.

A second point deferred in earlier discussions (6.3, 7.7) concerns the argument for utilitarianism based on acceptance of conditional equality. That argument, roughly, claims that (1) *if* we would have others consider our preferences and count them equitably, and (2) *if* we take the moral point of view, *then* (3) we will be obliged to favor that outcome that maximizes the balance of preference-satisfaction over preference-frustration for all those affected by the outcome. In the earlier discussions of this argument it was noted that it fails to show that anyone who accepts (1) and (2) is committed to utilitarianism—the view that the principle of utility is the *sole* moral basis of morality. At the very most, it was argued, acceptance of (1) and (2) would commit one to accepting *a* consequentialist principle. As was also remarked, there are good reasons to resist accepting (1) and (2) in the first place, if one thereby commits oneself to (3). For to accept (3) is to commit oneself to an *aggregative* principle, a principle whose acceptance would sanction harming some who are innocent if the sum of the consequences for all those affected by the outcome, including all the side effects, happened to constitute a better balance of preference-satisfaction over preference-frustration than was otherwise obtainable. This view of moral decision-making is pernicious, according to the rights view. It assumes and perpetuates the view that moral agents and patients are mere receptacles of value, having no inherent value of their own. No one who "takes rights seriously" should accept this aggregative view of moral decision making, or the view of the value of individuals (or, rather, their lack of value) it tacitly assumes without defending. To accept this view is to undermine the very possibility of giving a credible account of the rights of moral agents and patients, for reasons offered at length in the preceding, and it should come as no surprise that those who advance this argument for utilitarianism should disparage appeals to rights as "rhetoric." Their starting point predestines that outcome. To show that, rationally considered, we ought not to start our moral thinking where these thinkers do (that is, with our personal preferences) or end where they end (with a principle that allows or requires us to *aggregate* everyone's benefits and harms, pleasures and pains, etc.) has been one of the principal aims of the arguments of the last four chapters.

Third, and finally, there is the question of the logical status of the respect principle (see 7.8–7.9). That principle certainly is more basic than the harm principle, the miniride principle, or the worse-off principle, since these latter principles are derivable from it, not vice versa. By itself, however, this does not establish that the respect principle cannot be derived from some other, more fundamental principle, and it is difficult to say how this could be proven one way or the other. One does not show that a principle *cannot* be derived because it *has not* been. Though the rights view regards the respect principle as fundamental, it is prepared to leave the question of its possible derivation open, insisting only that (a) no ethical theory can be adequate that fails to include the respect principle and (b) no consequentialist derivation of this principle is possible in principle. To attempt to derive the respect principle by appealing to the optimal consequences that would result from its acceptance is neither more nor less intelligent than attempting to derive the second law of thermodynamics in a similar way. Just as the grounds for rational acceptance of this law are and must be kept distinct from considerations about the beneficial consequences that will or might flow from accepting it, so the grounds for rational acceptance of the respect principle, including its possible derivation from a still more fundamental principle, can only mistakenly be supposed to involve consequentialist considerations.

8.14 SUMMARY AND CONCLUSION

The principal conclusion reached in the present chapter is that all moral agents and patients have certain basic moral rights. To say that these individuals possess basic (or unacquired) moral rights means that (1) they possess certain rights independently of anyone's voluntary acts, either their own or those of others, and independently of the position they happen to occupy in any given institutional arrangement; (2) these rights are universal—that is, they are possessed by all relevantly similar individuals, independently of those considerations mentioned in (1); and (3) all who possess these rights possess them equally. Basic moral rights thus differ *both* from acquired moral rights (e.g., the right of the promisee against the promisor) because one acquires these rights as a result of someone's voluntary acts or one's place in an institutional arrangement *and* from legal rights (e.g., the right to vote) since legal rights, unlike basic moral rights, are not equal or universal (8.1).

Moral rights, whether basic or acquired, were analyzed as valid claims (8.2—8.3). To make a claim is to affirm that certain treatment is owed or is due, either to oneself or to another (or others). A claim is valid if and only if (a) it is a valid claim-against assignable individuals and (b) it is a valid claim-to treatment owed by these individuals, the validity of any claim-to resting ultimately on the validity of principles of direct duty. Because the primary concern of the present chapter was the question of basic moral rights, major emphasis was placed on validating rights of this kind.

The principal basic moral right possessed by all moral agents and patients is the right to respectful treatment (8.4, 8.5). For reasons offered in chapter 7, all moral agents and patients are intelligibly and nonarbitrarily viewed as having a distinctive kind of value (inherent value) and as having this value equally. All moral agents and patients must always be treated in ways that are consistent with the recognition of their equal possession of value of this kind. These individuals have a basic moral right to respectful treatment because the claim made to it is (a) a valid claim-against assignable individuals (namely, all moral agents) and (b) a valid claim-to, the validity of the claim-to resting on appeal to the respect principle, the case for that principle's validity having been made in an earlier context (7.8). The basic moral right to respectful treatment prohibits treating moral agents or patients as if they were mere receptacles of intrinsic values (e.g., pleasure), lacking any value of their own, since such a view of these individuals would allow harming some (e.g., by making them suffer) on the grounds that the aggregate consequences for all those other "receptacles" affected by the outcome would be "the best." It was also argued that all moral agents and patients have a prima facie basic moral right not to be harmed.

To say that this latter right is a prima facie right means that (1) there are circumstances in which it is permissible to override it but (2) anyone who would override it must justify doing so by appeal to valid moral principles that can be shown to override this right in a given case. Two challenges to regarding this right as prima facie—first, the view that we ought never to use harmful violence (the pacifist principle) and, second, the view that we ought never to harm the innocent (the innocence principle)—were considered (8.7) and shown to be deficient, and two moral principles (the miniride and the worse-off principles) were identified as valid principles, derivable from the respect principle, that can justify overriding the right of the innocent not to be harmed (8.10). The miniride principle implies that, special considerations aside, numbers count. When we are faced with choosing between harming the few who are innocent or harming the many, and when all those who will be harmed face prima facie comparable harm, then we ought to choose to override the rights of the few. The worse-off principle implies that, special considerations aside, numbers don't count. Special considerations aside, when we are faced with choosing to harm the many or the few who are innocent, and when the harm faced by the few would make them worse-off than any of the many, then we ought to override the rights of the many rather than the few. (The worse-off principle also applies to cases where only two individuals are involved, as was illustrated.)

Both the miniride and worse-off principles are logically distinct from and should not be confused with the minimize harm principle, the principle that we are to act so as to minimize the aggregate amount of harm done to all those affected by the outcome, including all the side effects. The rights view rejects such an aggregative principle as a basis for overriding individual rights, since all such principles assume that moral agents and patients are mere receptacles of value. For similar reasons, therefore, the rights view rejects, and at the same time provides an option to, utilitarian approaches to deciding when and, if so, why the innocent may be justifiably harmed (8.11).

Various objections were considered (8.6, 8.10), ranging from those that challenge the analysis of rights as valid claims to those that assert that the rights view has implications that are at odds with our considered beliefs. Though not all the objections the rights view must face have or could be considered, those that were addressed are among the most important. To have shown that they fail to mount a serious attack on that view is to have gone some distance toward the goal of providing it with an adequate defense.

Thus has the case for animal rights been offered. If it is sound, then, like us, animals have certain basic moral rights, including in particular the fundamental right to be treated with the respect that, as possessors of inherent value, they are due as a matter of strict justice. Like us, therefore—assuming the soundness of the arguments that have gone before—they must never be treated as mere receptacles of intrinsic values (e.g., pleasure, or preference-satisfaction), and any harm that is done to them must be consistent with the recognition of their equal inherent value and their equal prima facie right not to be harmed. It remains to be asked whether our institutions or practices give animals the justice they are due. That is the central issue explored in the next and final chapter.[31]

9

Implications of the Rights View

*I*n this final chapter some of the implications of the rights view, as these relate to our treatment of animals, are explained and defended. It will not be possible to examine the enormous variety of ways in which human acts and institutions affect animals. In particular, such activities as rodeos, bullfights, horse and dog racing, and other public "sports" involving animals will go unexamined, as will petting zoos, roadside zoos, and zoological parks, including aquaria, and the use of animals in circuses and in the film industry. These uses of animals are not examined, not because they are unimportant, but because others, which are either more common or more celebrated, require pride of place. By making it clear what the rights view's position is regarding those activities and institutions that are examined, it should be clear what its view would be regarding many of those that are not.

The four areas that will concern us are raising and consuming farm animals (9.1), hunting and trapping wild animals (9.2), saving endangered species of animals (9.3), and using animals in science (9.4). The discussion of endangered species will provide the occasion for some further remarks on environmental ethics and concerns.

9.1 WHY VEGETARIANISM IS OBLIGATORY

The right of animals not to be harmed is a prima facie, not an absolute, right. In saying this we concede that there are circumstances in which this right may justifiably be overridden. Because animals are not moral agents, their rights cannot be overridden on the grounds of punishment of, or defense against, the guilty; however, because they may pose innocent threats and may be used as innocent shields, and because the rights of any innocent may sometimes be overridden in such cases, the rights of animals prove no exception (see 8.7). But the harm done to farm animals (e.g., the deprivations they are caused in intensive rearing systems) cannot be defended on the grounds that these animals pose innocent threats or occupy the unenviable position of innocent shields. In order to inquire into the moral acceptability of the harm done to farm animals, therefore, we must first ask how one could most plausibly attempt to defend this harm, given that these animals pose no threat and are not innocent shields.

The Liberty Principle

The rights view recognizes the right of the individual, subject to certain qualifications, to do what is necessary to avoid being made worse-off relative to other innocents, even if this involves harming innocents. The need for certain qualifications should be apparent. For example, just because I would be made worse-off relative to my neighbor if I do not take possession of his Mercedes, it does not follow that I have a right to take possession of his car. Indeed, without appropriate qualifications, the proclamation of this right of the individual would be a license to moral anarchy. The following statement of this right (*the liberty principle*) adds the necessary qualifications:

> Provided that all those involved are treated with respect, and assuming that no special considerations obtain, any innocent individual has the right to act to avoid being made worse-off even if doing so harms other innocents.

The "special considerations" proviso explains why I am not at liberty to take my neighbor's Mercedes just because not having it would make me worse-off relative to him. For since it is his car, he has a right, assuming the car was acquired justly, *in addition to* our mutual right not to be harmed, and the possession of this additional property right is a special consideration that limits my liberty. The second proviso—namely, "provided that all those involved are treated with respect"—rules out other cases. If, for example, I would be made worse-off relative to my Uncle John if I were to forgo the pleasure of torturing him of an evening, I may not do so in the name of exercising the right in question, since to harm him merely on the grounds of the pleasure I would derive would be to fail to treat him with the respect he is due. So the right in question is not a license to moral anarchy but is instead one that has important qualifications, qualifications that are recognized and justified by the rights view.

To say that we have this right is to say that we are at liberty to act in the way the right authorizes, and to say that we are at liberty so to act is to say that it is morally permissible to do so. We may refuse to do so, but were we to refuse we would be doing more than duty strictly requires (i.e., we would be acting supererogatorily). Were I to refuse to do what is necessary to avoid being made worse-off, subject to the provisos listed, I would be acting in a self-sacrificial manner, voluntarily arranging it so that I am the one who is made worse-off, relative to the others involved. This I may do, certainly, but I have no duty to do it, nor does anyone else have a right against me to do so.

The liberty principle is derivable from the respect principle. As an individual with inherent value, I am always to be treated with respect and thus am never to be viewed or treated as a mere receptacle or as one who has value merely relative to the interests of others. Moreover, since, like other such individuals, I have a welfare, I may do whatever is necessary to advance it, subject to the same moral constraints that apply to all moral agents. To deny me the liberty to pursue my welfare simply because others will be less well-off if I do is to fail to treat me with the respect I am due. It is to assume that the treatment I am due as a matter of justice is contingent upon how others will be affected as a result, either individually or collectively. But the treatment I am due is not contingent upon these considerations. It is not contingent upon collective (or aggregative) considerations since such a view assumes that I have value merely as a receptacle, and it is not contingent upon the interests of any other particular individual since, as one who has inherent value, the respectful treatment *I* have a right to is not contingent upon *anyone else's* interests. To claim, then, that I may not do what is necessary to avoid being made worse-off, assuming all involved are treated with respect and in the absence of special considerations, because of how another (or others) will fare as a result of my efforts, is to fail to treat me with that respect I am due. And the same is true of all those individuals who are intelligibly and nonarbitrarily viewed as being the subjects-of-a-life: none may have his/her liberty limited on grounds that assume that the individual is a mere receptacle or has value merely relative to the interests of others. All who have inherent value, therefore, have the equal right to do what is necessary to avoid being made worse-off, subject to the provisos of the liberty principle, even if this requires doing what will harm other innocents.

It should be clear that an individual's liberty right is not restricted only to cases where individuals who exercise this right themselves directly harm others. If the A's harm the B's, and if I would be made worse-off relative to the B's if the A's did not harm the B's, then I act within my rights when I support the A's, provided the other conditions of the liberty principle are met. I may choose not to act within my rights, with the result that I am made worse-off; but I have no duty to do this, and those who are harmed (the B's) have no valid claim against me to allow myself to be made worse-off by choosing not to exercise my right to support the A's.

In addition to the respect, the harm, the miniride, and the worse-off principles, then, the rights view recognizes a fifth principle, *the liberty principle*. It is this principle, it seems, that is most likely to figure in attempts to defend raising farm animals for human consumption—and consuming them. For since both farmers and meat-eaters are authorized to act as the liberty principle allows, they may claim that they are at liberty to raise and eat animals, respectively, even though this involves harming animals or supporting those who do, since *not* to do so would make them worse-off relative to any of those individuals who are harmed in the process—that is, relative to any farm animal. Moreover, to attempt to deny farmers and meat-eaters their exercise of this right in the present case by *aggregating* the harms done to the many animals involved would be to treat the farmers and meat-eaters as if they were mere receptacles, something that, on the rights view, we must never do. So while both the farmers who raise animals for human consumption and those who consume them could concede that others may elect not to eat meat, they could argue that they are within their rights, that they do nothing wrong, in producing meat or eating it.

The rights view denies this conclusion while at the same time conceding the validity of the principle from which it is supposedly derived. The argument just given is sound only if the case can be made that raising animals to eat and eating them satisfies all the requirements of the liberty principle. Once we examine the matter more closely, we shall see that it fails to do so.

What could be the grounds for claiming that the harm done to farm animals can be justified by appeal to the liberty principle? Some of the relevant considerations concern the putative harms that would be done to consumers if they did not eat meat. Among these, the following are the most frequently cited:

1. Animal flesh is tasty and to abstain from eating it is to forgo certain pleasures of the palate.

2. It is personally rewarding to prepare good-tasting dishes, a benefit we would have to deny ourselves if we chose not to eat meat.
3. It is our habit, both (perhaps) as individuals and as a culture, to eat meat, and eating it is convenient; to abstain would be to endure the pains of withdrawal and the loss of convenience.
4. Meat is nutritious, and to cease eating it is to ruin one's health, or at least to run the very serious risk of doing so.

Among the considerations that relate to those associated with the meat industry, the following are the main ones:

5. Some people (e.g., farmers, meat packers, wholesalers) have a strong economic interest in continuing to raise farm animals, and the quality of their life, as well as that of their dependents, is materially tied to a continuation of the present market in food animals.
6. Not only those who are directly associated with the farm animal industry, but the nation generally has an economic interest in the maintenance and growth of this industry.
7. Farm animals are legal property, owned by farmers, and that gives farmers the right to treat their livestock as they wish, even if this is harmful to these animals.
8. Some farm animals, most notably chickens and turkeys, are not directly covered by the principles prescribed by the rights view, so farmers are at liberty to treat these animals without regard to these principles (and, for similar reasons, consumers are at liberty to eat them).

Let us consider each of these considerations with a view to determining how well or ill they can justify the harm done to farm animals.

Taste and Culinary Challenge

Neither (1) nor (2), nor both together, can justify overriding the right of animals not to be harmed. This is clear for several reasons. First, and most obviously, no one has a right to eat something just because they happen to find it tasty or just because they happen to derive satisfaction from cooking it well. If Heather just loves the taste of ghetto children, it hardly follows that Heather has a right to cook them. Nor will it do for Heather to protest that we violate her rights when we put a stop to her culinary adventures. If Heather violates the rights of those she cooks and eats when she cooks and eats them, then she has no grounds to complain that we violate her rights by stopping her. To suppose, then, that the issue at hand concerns whether *our* right to eat animals outweighs *their* right not to be harmed is to beg the essential question. It assumes that we have this right in the first place. That we do, if we do, needs to be argued, not taken for granted. Second, there are many other tasty foods besides those that include meat, and the rewards we can achieve from our culinary accomplishments can be achieved just as well without using meat as by using it. So we are not being asked to choose between two mutually exclusive options: *either* eat tasty food and take satisfaction in creating tasty dishes *or* eat tasteless food and forgo the satisfaction of cooking tasty dishes. Put another way, we are not being asked to choose between eating and cooking with meat *or* harming ourselves by depriving ourselves of opportunities for the pleasures of the palate and the pride of having prepared good food well. And if *we* are not being asked *to harm ourselves* by depriving ourselves in these ways, then we cannot justify supporting those who harm animals because of any harm we would have to endure, as a result of loss of taste or culinary rewards, if we stopped supporting them.

Third, even supposing we were harmed by forgoing eating and preparing meat, the harms we would be called upon to endure could not reasonably be viewed as prima facie comparable to the harm visited upon farm animals. Those animals raised in modern factory farms, for example, are daily harmed, both because of the suffering they are caused and the deprivations imposed on them. In comparison to any "harms" we would be called upon to bear if we were to forgo eating them, the harm routinely done to these animals is prima facie much greater and thus makes these animals prima facie worse-off. Appeal to the liberty principle, therefore, would not justify our continued support of those who harm farm animals, on the grounds that forgoing our culinary interests in meat would make us worse-off.

Three objections are worth considering at this point. First, it might be objected that the foregoing shows only that we cannot justify harming those animals who are raised in close confinement systems by appealing to the harms that would be done to us if we refused to buy and cook meat that originates from these animals. The situation of animals who are raised "humanely," it might be claimed, is quite another matter. If we would take the pains to insure that we eat and cook only these animals, this objection holds, then our gustatory and culinary pleasures rightfully prevail. This objection conveniently overlooks the prima facie harm that death is, not only for us but for the animals in question. An animal whose life is brought to an untimely end, before killing can be viewed as a merciful act, defensible on paternalistic or preference-respecting grounds

(3.7), *is* prima facie harmed, even if raised and slaughtered "humanely." *All* that animal's future prospects for satisfaction are denied. We, on the other hand, were we to forgo eating their flesh, would be called upon to give up a pittance of satisfaction in comparison. It is these animals, then, not us, who are prima facie made worse-off, when the harm done to them is compared with the "harm" we would be called upon to endure if we were to forgo the pleasant taste of meat and the challenge to cook it well.

Second, it might be objected that the foregoing shows only that, stationed in the world as we are, we should eat less meat, not that we should eat none at all. We should, that is, reach a (grudging) compromise between our culinary preferences and respect for the rights of animals. We'll eat less of them, thereby forgoing some of our pleasures, and they, well, they ought to be willing to meet us halfway, so to speak, by acknowledging that the harm done to them isn't everything. Isn't that an equitable middle ground? The answer, according to the rights view, is negative. Fundamentally, it is not the number of animals that matters (though the numbers involved compound the wrong). Fundamentally, what matters is that animals, whether raised in close confinement or "humanely," have their life brought to an untimely end for purposes of human consumption and, as a result, *are caused prima facie greater harm* than any of us would be if we gave up the pleasant taste of meat or the joys of cooking it well. If a *single* animal was slaughtered merely on the grounds of human gustatory preferences and culinary challenges that would not change the moral case one iota. To kill many billions of these animals, on these grounds, is to allow the performance of many billions of acts that cause unjustified harm to many billions of animals. But the wrongness of killing a single animal does not depend on the wrongness of killing many.

The third objection claims that a crucial factor has been systematically ignored. There are a lot of hamburgers, steaks, roasts, and so on, that come out of a single cow, for example, so there are a lot of people, not just a single individual, who will be called upon to forgo a lot of "good eating" and culinary rewards if we give up eating and cooking meat. Add up their total of harms and that total greatly exceeds anything the cow has been made to endure. So, the objection concludes, the cow loses after all. That single animal is not being made worse-off. This objection assumes that people would be harmed by forgoing the pleasant taste of meat and the challenge to cook it well, assumptions that, for reasons offered earlier, are dubious at best. More fundamentally, the objection assumes that we can justify imposing a prima facie greater harm on a given individual if the aggregate of the lesser harms done to others happens to outweigh the total harm done to that individual. The rights view categorically denies the propriety of this approach. To override the rights of individuals on the grounds of such aggregative computations is to treat that individual as a mere receptacle of value, something that, on the rights view, such individuals as cows are not. The totem of utilitarian theory (summing the consequences for all those affected by the outcome) is the taboo of the rights view.

Nutrition and Habit

There is no question that meat is a nutritious food. In particular, it is a source of complete protein, containing all the amino acids essential for human health and vitality. If it were true that these nutrients were not otherwise obtainable, then the case for eating meat, even given the rights view, would be on solid ground. If we were certain to ruin our health by being vegetarians, or run a serious risk of doing so, as (4) (above) contends, and given that the deterioration of our health would deprive us of a greater variety and number of opportunities for satisfaction than those within the range of farm animals, then we would be making ourselves, not the animals, worse-off if we became vegetarians. Thus might we appeal to the liberty principle as a basis for eating meat, assuming the other provisos of that principle were satisfied.

To concede the necessity of meat in a healthy diet is to concede more than is meat's due. The essential amino acids are essential, that is true; but there are alternative ways to obtain them, ways that do not rely on meat. To protest that the kind of knowledge required to combine incomplete proteins to yield complete proteins exceeds the grasp of the consumer's limited intelligence and that, therefore, the meat industry "serves the interests of public health," is patronizing in the extreme. It should be especially demeaning to any female homemaker with the slightest feminist tendencies, since such an attitude helps perpetuate and intensify the myth of the "dumb housewife," someone who not only doesn't now know but lacks the intellect to learn the difference between, say, a fat and a carbohydrate. Certain amino acids are essential for our health. Meat isn't. We cannot, therefore, defend meat-eating on the grounds that we will ruin our health if we don't eat it, or even that we will run a very serious risk of doing so if we abstain. Any "risk" we run can be easily overcome by taking the modest trouble required to do so.[1]

Habit and Convenience

The defense of meat-eating based on habit and convenience ((3) above) is glaringly deficient. That we are in the habit of doing something, or that we find it convenient to do it, goes no way toward justifying the morality of what we do, when our habits or the convenience of indulging them support a practice that harms other innocent individuals. Singer's observations about racism, sexism, and speciesism have a place in this regard. That certain people once were or, for that matter, still are in the habit of discounting the equal moral standing of women or the members of minority races tells us something about the psyches of these people; it does not tell us anything about the justice of their acting from the habits that they have. If, in response to arguments that challenge the justice of racial or sexual discrimination, we are told that it is convenient for the racist or sexist to discount the relevance or importance of the harm done to those who belong to the "wrong" race or sex, our reply should be that questions of just treatment are not decided by the criterion of personal or group convenience. According to the rights view, the treatment of animals should not, and cannot reasonably, be assessed any differently. Valid appeals to the liberty principle assume that all involved are treated with respect, something we would fail to do if we overrode the rights of farm animals by appeals to our habits concerning what we eat or the convenience of doing so. Besides, there already are many convenience items that are both nutritious and meatless—*and* tasty.

Economic Considerations

When we turn to economic considerations, critics may claim that the case against vegetarianism comes into plain view, given two of the principles the rights view advances—first, the worse-off principle and, second, the liberty principle. Let us postpone examining the putative role of this latter principle until the conclusion of the present section and concentrate initially on the worse-off principle.

The farmer, it might be claimed ((5) above), will be made worse-off, relative to the animals he raises, if we, the consumers, became vegetarians and thereby failed to support him. After all, he would lose his financial shirt and, with this loss, the harm done to him would outweigh any harm any one animal raised by farmers, even one raised in close confinement, is called upon to endure. Moreover, since the rights view prohibits aggregating the lesser prima facie harms of the many as a way to justify causing greater prima facie harm to the few, the rights view cannot allow aggregating the lesser prima facie harms of the animals in this case. We *ought* to continue eating meat, it might be claimed, not, to be sure, because we happen to like its taste or because we are in the habit of eating it, but because *we owe it to the farmer* not to make him worse-off, which is what we would do if we stopped buying his products. We will, it is true, continue to have the benefits of pleasant tasting meat dishes as well as the convenience associated with eating meat. But far from resting the defense of meat-eating on anything so flimsy as our personal preferences or habits, we may now take the moral high road: those who eat meat are merely fulfilling their duty to the farmer to do so.

How adequate is this defense of meat-eating? Does it, that is, succeed in offering a defense validated by the worse-off principle? It does not. Recall that the worse-off principle includes the proviso about "special considerations" (8.10). As was explained in an earlier discussion of this notion (8.12), some special considerations involve acquired duties (e.g., the duty to keep a promise), while others involve voluntary participation in activities wherein the participants waive their right not to be made worse-off as a result of participating in these activities. For example, those who voluntarily participate in a high-risk activity, such as hang-gliding or mountain climbing, waive this right, in the ways explained earlier; and that is one of the risks they run. Voluntary participation in competitive activities is similar. In a marathon, the victory goes to the one who runs the full course and crosses the finish line first; justice is done when *that* runner is awarded the prize, assuming that the other runners were not themselves unfairly hindered in their progress on the course. The victor is not to be decided by asking which runner would be made worse-off if he did not win. That would make running the race pointless. Indeed, it would make the event something other than a competitive race. The runner who would be made worse-off if he fails to win deserves no more consideration than any other competitor—nor any less. He cannot claim the prize as being *his* due by appeal to how not getting it will affect his welfare. Voluntarily to enter the competition is to acknowledge that considerations about who will be made worse-off are suspended in this case, and anyone who entered the race and did not understand or acknowledge this would not understand what a competitive race is and would not belong in one.

What is true of road racing is true of any competitive activity, including voluntary participation in any business activity, including raising animals as a business venture. To enter this or any other business not only is to run the risk of not "winning" (of not making a financial success of one's undertaking), it is also tacitly to acknowledge *both* that no one, whether business competitor or consumer, has a duty to purchase one's products or services *and* that such purchase cannot be claimed as one's due. A businessperson who would be made worse-off if her products or services were not purchased has no valid claim on anyone to make the necessary purchases to keep her business afloat. Like road-racing, competitive business is an activity where those who voluntarily participate must understand that the worse-off principle is suspended, and anyone who professes not to understand this does not understand what being in business is.

We do not, therefore, *owe it to any farmer* who sells meat to purchase his products, and neither do we *owe it to anyone else* in the animal industry—those who run the packing houses, the processors and packagers, the wholesalers, deliverers, the retailers, and the like—to buy anything they produce or sell; and none of them has a valid claim against us to do so. What we do owe them is the same equal respect we owe to others. We do not owe them more than this. And it would be to give them more than is their due if we supposed that we owed it to them to purchase their products so that they will not be made worse-off relative to the animals they harm. The worse-off principle is suspended when persons voluntarily engage in competitive activities, something any businessman or woman should well understand.

On the rights view, numbers make no difference in such a case, and neither does the sum of the harms of those who lose out in the competition. If not one farmer but thousands would be made worse-off by our refusing to buy their products, that would not make any moral difference. And if not just these farmers but the others mentioned earlier (e.g., meat processors) would join the farmers in their failure, that, too, would not alter the moral assessment, on the rights view. The sum of their losses, however great, would not give rise to any obligation to buy any of their products.

Perhaps it will be objected that the *dependents* of those in the meat industry will be made worse-off than any animal is made by that industry, if we all became vegetarians. Moreover, since these dependents have not themselves chosen to take a competitive place in this business, their right not to be made worse-off is not suspended in the way that the right of those who voluntarily choose to compete is. Thus, it might be argued, we have a duty to continue to purchase meat, not because we happen to enjoy its taste or find its use convenient, and not because we owe it to those in the business to buy it, but because we owe it to the dependents of those involved in the animal industry to do what we must to insure that they are not the ones who are made worse-off.

Now, it is true that some individuals do have the responsibility to protect the dependents of those in this industry from being made worse-off, if that industry should happen to collapse in general or if this or that farm, packing house, or butcher shop should fail. But it is not the consumers, in their capacity as consumers, who have this responsibility. Fundamentally, it is those very persons on whom these dependents are dependent—namely, those who voluntarily choose to compete in the market in meat—who are responsible to their dependents to do all that justice allows to protect them in the event that the business fails. Since having acquired duties is a legitimate special consideration for choosing to spare causing significant harm to those to whom one has these duties, even though someone else will thereby be made worse-off (see 8.12), someone's having these duties to others makes *that person's* moral responsibility to these individuals greater than those who lack these acquired duties. Those to whom one has acquired duties, after all, acquire additional rights. To allow acquired duties to count as special considerations in some cases, but to deny that those who have these duties have greater moral responsibility to those to whom they have them than do others, would be palpably inequitable. It is those in the meat industry, not consumers, then, who must bear greater responsibility to insure that their dependents (e.g., their children) are not made worse-off if this industry, or some part of it, fails. Consumers do not owe it to any animal farmer, meat packer, and the like, to buy the products of their labor so that his kith and kin will not be made worse-off than any animal harmed by the animal industry; *he* owes it to them to do what must be done to prevent this from happening, in the event that his business fails or his job is lost, assuming that the steps he takes are just and that he is not himself unjustly prevented from taking them. Those who must bear the principal responsibility for the personal losses associated with a business's failure are those whose business it is.

The rights view is not antagonistic to business, free enterprise, the market mechanism, and the like. What the rights view is antagonistic to is the view that consumers owe it to any business to purchase that business's goods or services. The animal industry is no exception. Nor is the rights view antagonistic to respecting and enforcing just agreements voluntarily reached that would serve to protect those whose businesses fail, or those who lose their jobs because of this, or the dependents in either case. Insurance policies that protect those who own and run a business, unemployment benefits due union members, programs designed to equip persons with new skills, and kindred measures are permissible, according to the rights view, so long as they do not violate the rights of others. Moreover, because everyone who runs a business or assumes a job runs some risk of losing it, and because some who have acquired duties to their dependents are woefully lax in discharging them, everyone, including those involved in the meat industry and those who oppose it, ought to recognize the reasonableness of joining in common cause to help those who will be most directly affected—small farmers and meat packers, for example—as advocates of the rights view increase in numbers and influence. Granted, the threat to the animal industry posed by this movement may today be viewed as the least of that industry's worries. Nevertheless, for those involved in that industry to minimize the potential of this threat would be for them to run the risk of not preparing for the impact of an idea whose time has come.

A common argument urged against recognition of the rights of farm animals takes the following form. Since these animals would not exist except for the economic interest the farmer has in raising them, his economic interests should determine how they ought to be treated. If, then, the intensive rearing of farm animals serves the farmer's economic interests, factory farming is justified. The harm done to these animals is, as it were, the price they pay for having that share of existence that falls their way because of the decisions and interests of the farmer.

This argument assumes that those agents who are causally responsible for bringing about a given individual's existence are sovereigns over that individual, once that individual exists, the treatment due that individual to be determined by the interests of those who arrange for his or her existence in the first place. This assumption lacks any claim to credibility. My son would not now exist except for the past decisions and acts of my wife and myself. In that sense, he "owes" his existence to us. But it does not follow from this that, once he has come to be, we, his parents, are thereby entitled to do just anything to him we like. Once he has himself become the subject-of-a-life that fares better or worse for him, logically independently of us, there are strict moral restrictions, grounded in the recognition of his inherent value, that we must respect if we are to treat him as justice requires. We are not his moral sovereigns. The case of farm animals does not differ in any morally relevant way. Once any given animal has become the subject-of-a-life that fares better or worse for her, the same principles of just treatment apply. If the farmer were to protest that it was not for the purpose of just treatment that he brought the animal into existence in the first place, we would be entitled to reply that that makes no moral differences. Once he has such an animal in his care, his past motives and intentions for arranging for the animal to come to be simply do not override the right of the animal to treatment consistent with, and required by, the respect to which she is due. Voluntarily to arrange for the coming to be of farm animals is voluntarily to acquire duties to these animals one would not otherwise have, whether that was one's intention or motive for arranging for their coming-to-be or not. Viewed from the perspective of the rights view, farmers assume moral burdens when they allow their animals to breed, or purchase animals from others who do, just as, analogously, parents assume moral burdens by having or adopting children. One's intentions or motives for having or adopting children, whatever they might be, no more give one a moral license to harm them than the motives and intentions of farmers give them a license to harm the animals in their care. That the farmer is of a different opinion shows only how far he is from the recognition of the rights of animals, not that these animals have no rights to be recognized. (This argument, as well as the one below that addresses the idea of animals as legal property, can be used to respond to popular defenses of "the human right" to use laboratory animals as we choose. I shall not repeat it in the later discussion [9.4] of that use of animals.)

A final consideration relates the farmer's economic interests to the liberty principle. Even if it is true that we have no duty to purchase the farmer's products, and even granting that we cannot defend our own consumption of meat by appeal to the worse-off principle, still, it might be claimed, the farmer operates within his rights by raising animals for food. Since he would be worse-off if he did not raise them, it is permissible for him to do so, despite the harm done to animals. This appeal to the liberty principle neglects a crucial proviso of that principle—namely, "provided that all those involved are treated with respect." This is a requirement that the present practice of raising farm animals for human consumption, whether this is done in factory farms or "humanely," fails to meet.

A practice, institution, enterprise, or similar undertaking is unjust if it permits or requires treating individuals with inherent value as if they were *renewable resources*, and such individuals are treated as if they were such resources if, before they have reached a state or condition where terminating their life can be defended on grounds of preference-respecting or paternalistic euthanasia (3.7), they are killed, their "place" to be filled by another, similar individual whose life will be similarly terminated, and so on. Such an institution is unjust, according to the rights view, because it requires treatment that violates the respect principle, requiring, as it does, that individuals with inherent value are to be treated as if they lacked any independent value of their own and instead had value only relative to the interests of those who engage in the practice or to the preferences of those who support it. Such a practice treats these individuals as *renewable* because it treats them as replaceable without any prima facie wrong having been done to those who are killed, and as *resources* because what value they are assumed to have is viewed as being contingent upon their utility relative to the interests of others. But individuals who have inherent value are not renewable resources and are not to be treated as if they were. They have a kind of value that is distinct from, and is not reducible to, their utility relative to the interests of others, and they are always to be treated in ways that show respect for their independent value, not out of kindness or compassion but as a matter of strict justice. Any practice, institution, or other undertaking that permits or requires treating individuals with inherent value as if they were renewable resources, therefore, permits or requires treatment of these individuals that violates the respect principle. As such, the treatment the practice sanctions, and the practice itself, are unjust.

This verdict of the rights view is reached independently of considerations of the pain or suffering caused to those individuals who are treated as renewable resources, though what pain or suffering they are caused compounds the wrong. *It is the impoverished view of the value of these individuals, not only the pain or suffering they are made to endure, that exposes the practice as fundamentally unjust.* Even were the individuals who were treated as renewable resources, in the sense explained, "treated well" (e.g., not caused unnecessary suffering), that would not alter the basic injustice of the practice; it would only eliminate the further wrong of harming these individuals in this way. It would make the implementation of the practice *less* wrong; but it would not remove the fundamental injustice endemic to the practice.

The grounds for finding unjust any practice that treats individuals who have inherent value as renewable resources are distinct from considerations about the consequences of such a practice. The rights view's position is not that such a practice must, or is likely to, lead to less than the best aggregate consequences for all those affected by the outcome. The value of the consequences that such a practice will, or is likely to, give rise to is irrelevant to finding such a practice unjust. Even were the consequences "the best" that could be obtained, such a practice remains unjust because it continues to permit or require treating individuals with inherent value in ways that are inconsistent with the respect they are due.

The grounds for judging such a practice unjust also are distinct from judging acts or practices wrong because they treat individuals with inherent value as mere receptacles. To treat such individuals as mere receptacles is wrong because unjust, and it is unjust because it fails to treat them with the respect they are due. But to treat such individuals as mere receptacles at least has one advantage over treating them as renewable resources: when treated as mere receptacles, *their* goods (e.g., their pleasures) and *their* harms (e.g., pains) are viewed as being *directly morally relevant* to the determination of what ought to be done; it just so happens that, when viewed in this way, the harm done to them can be justified by appeals to "the best" aggregate consequences. When individuals are treated as renewable resources, however, *their* goods and *their* harms can have no *direct* moral significance. What significance they have, if they have any, is contingent upon what is in the interests of those who treat them as renewable resources. To view individuals with inherent value as renewable resources thus is to view them as *even less than mere receptacles.* Since, on the rights view, it is unjust, because disrespectful, to treat them as if they were mere receptacles, it is an even greater injustice to treat them as if they were even less than this.

Farm animals raised for human consumption are today treated as renewable resources, and this is a verdict we reach whether these animals are raised in close confinement or "humanely." These animals are routinely killed well in advance of their having reached a state or condition where taking their life could plausibly be viewed as an act of mercy; their place in the production line is taken by other animals, who will in time be killed well in advance of their having reached a state or condition where taking their life could plausibly be viewed as an act of mercy; and then others will replace them; and so on, as the system perpetuates itself. Beyond any question, these animals are viewed and treated as renewable or replaceable. That they are viewed and treated as resources, having value only relative to the interests of others, also is true. The moral significance of what harms or benefits these animals is measured by the interests of those who raise them. If hogs are harmed when raised in close confinement, that does not compute morally if a close confinement system advances the interests of the farmer; if beef cattle are harmed by having their life brought to an untimely end, that does not register morally if this practice furthers the interests of the cattle rancher. In saying this one is not saying that those involved in animal agriculture are cruel people, who like nothing better than to torture their animals (for why this is inappropriate, see above, 6.1). It is to make the simple point that these animals are treated as resources, their harms and benefits acquiring moral significance only if or as these relate to the interests of the farmer. If keeping animals unhealthy were economically advantageous, modern agriculture would doubtless find a way to do this. Indeed, it already has: witness the veal calf.

To treat farm animals as renewable resources is to fail to treat them with the respect they are due as possessors of inherent value. It is, then, to treat them unjustly, and this finding makes all the moral difference in the world when, as we are supposing, the farmer claims that he is "within his rights" in raising these animals for human consumption. He *would* be "within his rights," given the liberty principle, *only if* those who are harmed by what he does (namely, the animals he raises) *were treated with respect*. But they are not treated with respect, and cannot be, so long as they are treated as if they are renewable resources. This is why, on the rights view, farmers who raise animals for human consumption are engaged in an unjust practice. Morally, they *exceed* their rights. Morally, this practice ought to cease, and consumers ought to cease to support it. Even if it were true, which it is not, that consumers would be made worse-off relative to the condition of farm animals if they stopped buying meat, it would not follow that consumers "act within *their* rights" when, by choosing to buy meat, they choose to support the practice that allows and requires this treatment. Consumers would be acting within their rights only if this practice treated animals with the respect they are due. Since, for the reasons given, the current practice of raising farm animals for human consumption fails to treat these animals with respect, those who support this practice by buying meat exceed their rights. Their purchase makes them a party to the perpetuation of an unjust practice. Vegetarianism is not supererogatory; it is obligatory.

Here it will be protested (point (6) above) that it is not just the economic interests of the farmers, meat packers, wholesalers, and the like, that are at stake; the economy of the nation is directly tied to the maintenance and growth of the meat industry. To cease purchasing the products of this industry would bring about economic calamity, affecting the welfare of millions upon millions of people, many of whom, through no fault of their own, and without having voluntarily run the risks associated with participation in the meat industry, will be made worse-off. It is in order to avoid this catastrophe that we ought to continue to buy meat.

The rights view denies this defense of support of the meat industry. Just as the benefits others obtain as a result of an unjust institution or practice is no moral defense of that practice or institution, so the harms others might face as a result of the dissolution of this practice or institution is no defense of allowing it to continue. Put alternatively, no one has a right to be protected against being harmed if the protection in question involves violating the rights of others. Since, for reasons given in the preceding, the practice of raising farm animals, as presently conducted, routinely treats these animals in ways that are contrary to the respect they are due as a matter of strict justice, that practice violates the rights of these animals. As such, no one, neither those directly involved in the meat industry nor those who would be affected by its collapse, has a right to be protected against being harmed by allowing that industry to continue. In this sense and for these reasons, the rights view implies that justice *must* be done, though the (economic) heavens fall.

It is, of course, extremely unlikely that the economic heavens will fall. We are not likely to awake tomorrow to discover that, overnight, everyone has been converted to vegetarianism, a development that precipitates the total and instantaneous collapse of the meat industry and the economic gloom such a collapse conceivably might bring. The scenario sketched two paragraphs back, therefore, is most improbable. The dissolution of the meat industry, as we know it, will come incrementally, not all at once, and the economy of the nation and the world will have time to adjust to the change in dietary life-styles. Nevertheless, the essential moral point remains. No one has a right to be protected by the continuation of an unjust practice, one that violates the rights of others. And this is true whether one actively participates in this practice or, though not an active participant, benefits from it and would be harmed by its discontinuance. Vegetarians who would be harmed by the total and instantaneous collapse of the meat industry would have no more right to complain of the "injustice" done to them than would meat-eaters. Since no injustice would be done to them, were that industry to dissolve, even "the veggies" could have no grounds for complaint.

Animals as Legal Property

At this point, if not before, the charge (point (7) above) will be made that farmers *own* animals—that farm animals are their *legal property*—and that this makes all the difference. Just as the color I paint the walls of my house or my decision to sell it are my own affairs because the house is my property, so, it may be argued, what the farmer does to his animals is his own affair, since they are his property. And just as anyone who would deny me the right to paint my walls or to sell my house if I am so inclined would be unjustifiably overriding my property rights, so the attempt to limit how the farmer treats his animals is unjustifiably to override his property rights.

Two responses to this line of argument will have to suffice. First, granted that the present legal status of farm animals is that they are property, and even assuming that their legal status as property is not changed, it does not follow that legal constraints placed on how animals may be treated necessarily violate farmers' property rights. Property rights are not absolute. While what color I choose to paint my walls is my affair, what I choose to do with my property is not my affair alone if what I do with it will have an adverse affect on others. Living as I do in a suburban subdivision, I am not at liberty to turn my house into an adult book store, a gambling casino, a house of ill repute, or even a 7–11. The property rights—not to mention the other rights—my neighbors have impose limits on what I may do with my property. There is no reason why the treatment of animals, even assuming that they are and will continue to be, viewed as legal property, should be otherwise. If, as has been argued at length in the preceding, animals have basic moral rights, then these rights ought to be recognized as imposing strict constraints on what any farmer may be allowed to do to them in the name of exercising his "property rights." That is one reform in the law, on the rights view, that must come and that, assuming enough are committed to the cause, will come.

Second, and more fundamentally, the very notion that farm animals should continue to be viewed as legal property must be challenged. To view them in this way implies that we cannot make sense of viewing them as legal persons. But the history of the law shows only too well, and too painfully, how arbitrary the law can be on this crucial matter. Those humans who were slaves were not recognized as legal persons in pre–Civil War America. There is no reason to assume that because animals are not presently accorded this status that they cannot intelligibly be viewed in this way or that they should not be. If our predecessors had made this same assumption in the case of human slaves, the legal status of these human beings would have remained unchanged.

Only one response to the call to recognize animals as legal persons will be considered here.[2] One can anticipate the following, said by those whose present livelihood is tied to the animal industry. They might argue that if farm animals were no longer viewed as property, farmers would no longer have sufficient economic incentive or legal protection to raise them; and if that were so, these farmers would look elsewhere than the animal industry as a source of reliable income, with the result that there would be fewer farm animals. And this, it might be claimed, shows how counterproductive the rights view is. That view, it may be argued, aspires to protect farm animals; but its ultimate result, if it were to succeed, is that there would no longer be farms where animals are raised for commercial profit. And what kind of protection can that be, if the very creatures one aspires to protect are no longer around to be protected?

This response assumes that the ultimate goal of the rights view, when applied to farm animals, is somehow self-defeating. But this is a product of confusion. It is true—and the point bears emphasis—that *the ultimate objective of the rights view is the total dissolution of the animal industry as we know it*, an objective that should hardly be surprising, given the rights view's verdict that, as presently conducted, this industry violates the rights of farm animals. But this view does not call for the extinction of farm animals, only that those there are be treated as justice requires. If no economically profitable venture could meet this requirement, then that incentive for continuing to have these animals on this earth will be missing. But since it is this very incentive that lies behind viewing these animals as renewable resources and that gives rise to the violation of their rights, its absence should be a cause for celebration rather than regret. Moreover, despite depressing evidence to the contrary, human beings sometimes are motivated to act for other than economic reasons, and there is no reason to assume that, if the day comes when people no longer have an economic interest in raising farm animals, none of these animals will be around. There will be fewer, that much is certain; but that will be an index of our moral progress, not our moral failure. The rights view never claims, and does not imply, that the quality of the life of individual farm animals is logically or causally tied to there being vast numbers of them. This is not true in the case of the quality of the life of individual human beings. There is no reason to judge the case of animals any differently.

Finally, it will be protested (point [8] above) that some farm animals, most notably chickens and turkeys, are not mammals and so, given the rights view's position regarding those animals who are subject-of-a-life, fall outside the scope of the principles prescribed by this view. Poultry farmers, then, so it may be alleged, avoid the condemnation of the rights view, even if it is true that other farmers do not. This defense of the poultry industry fails to take into account how difficult it is to draw the line between animals who do, and those who do not, satisfy the subject-of-a-life criterion, and fails, moreover, to place the justification of poultry farming within the larger context of our culture's habits of treating all farm animals as renewable resources. These are common deficiencies shared by those who, for example, defend the use of nonmammalian animals in science or their harvest in hunting. In order to avoid repeating the main tenets of the rights view's response to arguments of this kind, a reply to this defense of poultry farming will be deferred until an analogous response is given to those who defend using nonmammalian animals in science (9.4).

Vegetarianism, Utilitarianism, and Animal Rights

The fundamental difference between the moral basis of vegetarianism offered by the rights view and the one offered by utilitarianism should now be clear. Assuming that the interests (the preferences or pleasures) of all those affected by the outcome of an action or rule have been taken into account, and assuming that equal interests have been counted equally, justice has been done, according to utilitarianism, and the significant harm done to any one individual is not unjust if causing it is necessary to bring about the optimal aggregate balance of goods (e.g., pleasures) over evils (e.g., pains) for all those affected by the outcome. For the utilitarian, therefore, *it is an open moral question* whether the harm done to farm animals, even the harm they are made to bear in factory farms, is justifiable. *If* the aggregated consequences turn out to be optimal, *then* the harm is justified. The utilitarian's case against the harm done to farm animals cannot be any stronger than how convincingly he shows that the facts are against allowing it. To meet this challenge the utilitarian must have the relevant facts at hand, and this means he must tell us (1) what the consequences *are*, all considered, for all those affected by the outcome of the harm done to farm animals, as well as what the balance of goods (e.g., preference satisfactions) over evils (e.g., preference frustrations) are; (2) what the consequences *would be*, all considered, for all those affected by the outcome, if we were all to become vegetarians, either all at once or gradually; and (3) whether, when everything is taken into account, these latter consequences *would be* better than the former. It is not unfair to the utilitarian basis for the obligatoriness of vegetarianism to remind ourselves that the facts necessary for resting this obligation on utilitarian considerations simply are not at hand. Judged by its own standards, in short, the utilitarian basis for vegetarianism is far from compelling. Recall (see 6.4), finally, that the rightness of *my* refusal to buy meat depends, for the utilitarian, not on what I do, but on how many others do the same thing; for it is only if enough others abstain, and only if this number reduces how many farm animals are harmed or how much harm is done to them, that, according to utilitarian thought, I do what is right. Though it is impossible to know the minds of all, it is unlikely that those who are not already committed to utilitarianism believe that the principle of utility does justice to their thought about why vegetarianism is obligatory.

The rights view succeeds where utilitarianism fails. My acting as duty requires does not depend on how many others act similarly, and no vegetarian should be deterred from his or her course because of the many who continue to support the animal industry or because it is uncertain whether and, if so, when and how one individual's abstention makes a difference—for example, to how many animals are thereby spared the abuse of factory farming. *The individual is right not to purchase the products of an industry that violates the rights of others, independently of how many others act similarly,* and the case against the animal industry does not stand or fall, according to the rights view, on that individual's knowing, or on any individual's knowing, the aggregate balance of goods over evil for all those affected by allowing factory farming or by not allowing it. Since this industry routinely violates the rights of these animals, for the reasons given, it is wrong to purchase its products. That is why, on the rights view, vegetarianism is morally obligatory, and why, on that view, we should not be satisfied with anything less than the total dissolution of commercial animal agriculture as we know it, whether modern factory farms or otherwise.

Life on the Lifeboat

A critic of the rights view might challenge this view by deploying a variant of the lifeboat case discussed earlier (8.13). Recall the situation: There are five survivors, four normal adult human beings and a dog. The boat will support only four. All will perish if one is not sacrificed. Which one ought to be cast overboard? The rights view's answer is: the dog. The magnitude of the harm that death is, it has been argued, is a function of the number and variety of opportunities for satisfaction it forecloses for a given individual, and it is not speciesist to claim that the death of any of these humans would be a prima facie greater harm in their case than the harm death would be in the case of the dog. Indeed, numbers make no difference in this case. A million dogs ought to be cast overboard if that is necessary to save the four normal humans, the aggregate of the lesser harms of the individual animals harming no one in a way that is prima facie comparable to the harm death would be to any of these humans. But suppose, a critic may conjecture, it is not a question of having enough room on the boat. Imagine it is a question of which individual to eat if four others are to survive. Who should be eaten? The rights view's answer, once again, is: the dog. And it is the dog who should be eaten because the harm that death is in the case of that animal is not as great a harm as the harm that death would be in the case of any of these humans. In lifeboat cases, in short, the obligation to be vegetarian can be justifiably over- ridden, according to the rights view. The survivors would be acting within their rights, justified by appeal to the liberty principle, if they chose to kill and eat the dog in these dire circumstances. Any one of them might, it is true, choose not to do this, choosing to sacrifice his own life rather than to be a party to killing the animal. But that would be some- thing that, on the rights view, is not obligatory; that would be supererogatory.

Our imagined critic might suppose that the rights view's assessment of the lifeboat case undermines that view's case against the current practice of animal agriculture. But this is not true, for at least three different reasons. First, stationed in the world as we are, we are not in the situation of the survivors in the lifeboat. They have, we are assuming, no other option than to eat meat if they are to stay alive and well. We do. To concede that the obligation to be vegetarian is overridable in dire circumstances, such as those on the lifeboat, therefore, is not to imply that its obligatoriness wanes for us in our day-to-day existence. Second, and relatedly, what a theory implies ought to be done in exceptional cases (and the lifeboat case *is* an exceptional case) cannot be fairly generalized to apply to unexceptional cases. One cannot, then, argue that since the rights view implies that those humans on the lifeboat would be justified in eating the dog, the rights view implies that we are justified in gorging ourselves at the neighborhood pig-pickin'. That would be analogous to supposing that if a view allows that we would be justified in killing someone intent upon killing us, it must also imply that we would be justified in killing just anyone we had a mind to. No one would, or should, be tempted to suppose that a view that allows one to kill in self-defense must imply this. It is to be hoped that no one would, or should, suppose that the rights view's verdict concerning who should be eaten on the lifeboat is a license to give in to a Big Mac attack. Third, what a view implies may be done in isolated, exceptional circumstances does not commit it to taking a similar view of practices or institutions. Granted, the survivors on the lifeboat would be justified in eating the dog in order to avoid being made worse-off; still, it does not follow that hog farmers, for example, do no wrong in raising pigs in order that they may avoid being made worse-off. Isolated, exceptional cases, such as the lifeboat case, are not practices or institutions, and the judgment one makes about the former is not automatically transferable to the latter. Though, in exceptional circumstances, we are justified in limiting an individual's liberty (say a man has become temporarily deranged and poses a threat to the security of others, a threat we can cancel only by forcibly restraining him), it does not follow that we would be justified in allowing institutions or practices that *routinely* limit individual liberty—that is, that limit individual liberty in *unexceptional, ordinary* circumstances. The justice of a practice or institution is not shown in this way. Its justice is shown by whether all those involved are treated with the respect they are due. Because the practice of animal agriculture as we know it fails to treat farm animals with the respect they are due, that *practice* is unjust. What is permissible on the lifeboat makes no moral difference to what is permissible on a hog farm. And lest the hog farmer be tempted to escape this implication and the general implications of the rights view by seeking refuge in utilitarian theory, it is good to remind him that utilitarianism fails to provide adequate moral protection for *human* beings, himself included.

The dissolution of commercial animal farming as we know it obviously requires more than our individual commitment to vegetarianism. To refuse on principle to buy the products of the meat industry is to do what is right, but it is not to do enough. To recognize the rights of animals is to recognize the related duty to defend them against those who violate their rights (see 8.6), and to discharge this duty requires more than our individual abstention. It requires acting to bring about those changes that are necessary if the rights of these animals are not to be violated. Fundamentally, then, it requires a commitment to contribute to the revolution in our culture's thought about, and in its accepted treatment of, farm animals. Mill's words are again apposite. Recall his observing (8.1) that, when an individual has a valid claim, and thus a right, to something, "society" ought to defend that individual in the possession of that right, "either by the force of law or by that of education or opinion." Our challenge, then, may be conceived in these terms: to help *to educate* those who presently support the animal industry to the implications of their support; to help *to forge the opinion* that this industry, as we know it, violates the rights of farm animals; and to work to bring *the force of law*, if necessary, to bear on this industry to effect the necessary changes. That is no small challenge, to be sure, but to reach the goal of justice for these animals requires nothing less. Merely to content oneself with personal abstention is to become part of the problem rather than part of the solution.

9.2 WHY HUNTING AND TRAPPING ARE WRONG

Since animals can pose innocent threats and because we are sometimes justified in overriding their rights when they do (8.8), one cannot assume that all hunting or trapping must be wrong. If rabid foxes have bitten some children and are known to be in the neighboring woods, and if the circumstances of their lives assure future attacks if nothing is done, then the rights view sanctions nullifying the threat posed by these animals. When we turn from cases where we protect ourselves against the innocent threats wild animals pose, to the activities of hunting and trapping, whether for commercial profit or "sport," the rights view takes a dim view indeed. Standard justifications of the "sport" of hunting—that those who engage in it get exercise, take pleasure in communion with nature, enjoy the camaraderie of their friends, or take satisfaction in a shot well aimed—are lame, given the rights view. All these pleasures are obtainable by engaging in activities that do not result in killing any animal (walking through the woods with friends and a camera substitutes nicely), and the aggregate of the pleasures hunters derive from hunting could only override the rights of these animals if we viewed them as mere receptacles, which, on the rights view, they are not.

The appeal to tradition—an appeal one finds, for example, in support of fox hunting in Great Britain—has no more force in the case of hunting than it does in the case of any other customary abuse of animals—or humans. All that appeals to tradition signal in this case, and all they signify in related contexts, is that it is traditional to view animals as mere receptacles or as renewable resources. These appeals to tradition, in other words, are themselves symptomatic of an impoverished view of the value animals have in their own right and thus can play no legitimate role in defending a practice that harms them. Such appeals are as deficient in Great Britain, when made in behalf of the "sport" of fox hunting, as they are when made in Japan or Russia in defense of commercial whaling,[3] or in Canada in defense of the annual slaughter of seals. To allow these practices to continue, if certain quotas are not exceeded, is wrong, given the rights view, for reasons that will become clearer as we proceed.

Of course, those who hunt and trap sometimes rest their case on other considerations. It is not *their* pleasure that justifies what they do; rather, it is the humane service they perform for *the animals* that does. The situation, we are enjoined to believe, is this: If a certain number of animals are not hunted or trapped, there will be too many animals belonging to a given species for a given habitat to support. That being so, some of these animals will die of starvation because of their inability to compete successfully with the other animals in the habitat. To cull or harvest a certain number of these animals thus has the humane purpose and achieves the humane goal of sparing these animals the ordeal of death by starvation. How can the rights view, or any other view that is sensitive to the welfare of animals, find fault with that?

The rights view finds fault with this defense of hunting and trapping on several counts. First, the defense assumes that the death endured by hunted and trapped animals is always better (i.e., always involves less suffering) than the death these animals would endure as a result of starvation. This is far from credible. Not all hunters are expert shots, and not all trappers tend their traps responsibly or use traps that exhibit their "humane" concern for animals, the infamous leg-hold trap being perhaps the most notorious example to the contrary. Is it obvious that animals who experience a slow, agonizing death as a result of a hunter's poor shot or a poorly tended trap have a "better death" than those who die from starvation? One looks for an argument here and finds none. Unless or until one does, the defense of hunting and trapping on the grounds that they kill "more humanely" is specious.

Second, appeals to "humane concern" are dramatically at odds with the philosophy of current hunting and trapping practices, as well as with wildlife management generally. This philosophy, or the creed of maximum sustainable yield, applies to hunting and trapping in the following way. Those who hunt and trap are legally permitted, within specified seasons, to "harvest" or "crop" a certain number of wildlife of various species, the quota for that season, both collectively and for each individual hunter, to be fixed by determining whether, together with the best estimates of natural mortality, those who hunt and trap will be able to "harvest" the same number next season, and the next, and so on. In this way the maximum sustainable yield is established. If this philosophy is applied successfully, hunters and trappers will be legally licensed to do the same thing in future seasons as others were licensed to do in the past—namely, kill up to a certain number (a certain quota) of animals. If, that is, restraint is exercised in each season, the *total* number of animals that can be harvested over time will be larger, or, to put the point in its simplest, starkest terms, if fewer animals are killed now, future generations of hunters will be able to kill a larger (aggregate) number of animals in the future, which will be better. This implication of the creed of maximum sustainable yield unmasks the rhetoric about "humane service" to animals. It must be a perverse distortion of the ideal of humane service to accept or engage in practices the explicit goal of which is to insure that there will be a larger, rather than a smaller, number of animals to kill! With "humane friends" like that, wild animals certainly do not need any enemies.

Essentially the same point can be made regarding the aggregate amount of suffering animals will endure if the creed of maximum sustainable yield is successful. If successful, the total number of animals who will die an agonizing death as a result of the poor shooting of hunters, plus those who die in similar agony as a result of poorly tended "humane" traps, plus those who die by natural causes will be larger than if other options were adopted. It is a moral smokescreen, therefore, to defend sport hunting and trapping by appeal to their humane service. The actions allowed by the philosophy of maximum sustainable yield speak louder than the lofty words uttered in its defense. The success of this philosophy would guarantee that more, not fewer, animals will be killed, and that more, not fewer, animals will die horrible deaths, either at the hands of humans or in the course of nature.

But it is not only the inconsistency between what it proclaims and what it implies that marks the undoing of the creed of maximum sustainable yield. That approach to decision making regarding wildlife management policies profoundly fails to recognize or respect the rights of wild animals. No approach to wildlife can be morally acceptable if it assumes that policy decisions should be made on the basis of aggregating harms and benefits. In particular, these decisions should not be made by appeal to the minimize harm principle (see 8.10). That principle sets before us what seems to be a laudatory goal—namely, to minimize the total amount of harm in general and suffering in particular. But that principle lacks the moral wherewithal to place any limits on how this laudatory goal is to be achieved; it lacks the means to assess the means used to achieve this end. If the rights of individuals are violated, that simply does not compute morally, given the minimize harm principle, if violating these rights is instrumental in achieving the goal of minimizing total harm. The rights view categorically denies the propriety of this approach to decision making. Policies that lessen the total amount of harm at the cost of violating the rights of individuals, whether these individuals are moral agents or patients, and, if the latter, human or animal, are wrong. Even if it were true, which it is not, that the philosophy of maximum sustainable yield would lead to a reduction in the total amount of death and suffering for undomesticated animals, it still would not follow that we should accept that philosophy. As it systematically ignores the rights of wild animals, so does it systematically violate them.

The rights view categorically condemns sport hunting and trapping. Though those who participate in it need not be cruel or evil people (recall the earlier discussion of cruelty, 6.1), what they do is wrong. And what they do is wrong because they are parties to a practice that treats animals as if they were a naturally recurring renewable resource, the value of which is to be measured by, and managed by reference to, human recreational, gustatory, aesthetic, social, and other interests. Animals do renew themselves. Normally, they do not require human assistance to reproduce, any more than do trees, for example; but wild animals are not natural resources *here for us*. They have value apart from human interests, and their value is not reducible to their utility relative to our interests. To make a sport of hunting or trapping them is to do what is wrong because it is to fail to treat them with the respect they are due as a matter of strict justice.

Shorn of their appeal to their "humane concern" for wildlife, defenders of hunting and trapping are likely to protest that what they do is no different in kind from what other animals do in the state of nature. Animals routinely kill members of other (though only infrequently members of their own) species, and the death they suffer at the hands of other animals is gruesome enough to make even the most hardened heart wince. When it comes to interspecies relations, nature *is* red in tooth and claw. If the rights view professes to condemn sport hunting and trapping, it might be claimed, then it should do the same when it comes to the fatal interaction between animals themselves.

The rights view rejects this argument. Animals are not moral agents (see 5.2) and so can have none of the same duties moral agents have, including the duty to respect the rights of other animals. The wolves who eat the caribou do no moral wrong, though the harm they cause is real enough. So it is that, according to the rights view, the overarching goal of wildlife management should not be to insure maximum sustainable yield; it should be to protect wild animals from those who would violate their rights—namely, sport hunters and trappers, commercial developers who destroy or despoil their natural habitat in the name of economic interest, and the like. *It is, in short, human wrongs that need managing, not the "crop" of animals.* Put affirmatively, the goal of wildlife management should be to defend wild animals in the possession of their rights, providing them with the opportunity to live their own life, by their own lights, as best they can, spared that human predation that goes by the name of "sport." We owe this to wild animals, not out of kindness, nor because we are against cruelty, but out of respect for their rights. If, in reply, we are told that respecting the rights of animals in the wild in the way the rights view requires does not guarantee that we will minimize the total amount of suffering wild animals will suffer over time, our reply should be that this cannot be the overarching goal of wildlife management, once we take the rights of animals seriously. The total amount of suffering animals cause one another in the wild is not the concern of morally enlightened wildlife management. Being neither the accountants nor managers of felicity in nature, wildlife managers should be principally concerned with *letting animals be*, keeping human predators out of their affairs, allowing these "other nations"[4] to carve out their own destiny.

When we move from sport to the commercial exploitation of wildlife, the moral scene is the same, only worse because the number of animals involved is greater. The rights view condemns the business of killing wild animals. Even if it is true that those whose present quality of life is tied to commerce in wild animals would be made worse-off if their business failed, that is no reason why we should continue to allow it. Like anyone else who enters the world of business, those whose business it is to kill wild animals must understand that they waive their right not to be made worse-off if their business fails. We have no duty to buy their products, and they have no right to require that we keep either their business or their present quality of life afloat. To appeal to the risk of diminished welfare in the case of their dependents is as lame in the present case as it was in the case of animal agriculture, as a defense in support of those whose business it is to kill wild animals. Moreover, while those in this business, like the rest of us, have the right to do what they can to avoid being made worse-off, they, like the rest of us, exceed this right when what they do violates the rights of others. And the commercial exploitation of wildlife does this—with a vengeance. Animals in the wild are treated as renewable resources, as if they had value only relative to the economic interests of those who feed off their dead carcasses. The rights view categorically condemns the commercial harvesting of wild animals, not because those embarked on this business are, or must be, cruel or evil people, but because what they do is wrong. Justice will be done when, and only when, we refuse to allow these commercial ventures to continue.

One can imagine someone accepting the letter but not the spirit of the foregoing. For there are, after all, many nonhumans who are killed, either for sport or commerce, who are not animals in the limited sense in which this word has been used throughout this and earlier chapters—who are not, that is, normal mammalian animals, aged one year or more. A voice might be heard in support of duck hunting, for example, or in defense of the commercial exploitation of baby seals. Because similar protests might be raised in different contexts (for example, one might claim that what one does to nonmammals in science or to poultry in agriculture should not be covered by the same principles that apply to what is done to mammals), a review of this defense of hunting and trapping will be deferred until later (see the final paragraphs of 9.4 and note 30).

Here it will suffice to raise a simple question. Let us assume that newly born *wild mammalian animals* (e.g., baby seals) do not yet meet the subject-of-a-life criterion; still, they clearly have the potential to do so. Why, then, should the moral standards that apply to how they may be treated differ in any way from those that apply to how human infants should be? The rights view denies that there is a nonarbitrary difference one could cite to justify treating the two differently. Unless one would be willing to approve of harming human infants in pursuit of sport or profit, one cannot approve of the similar treatment of infant mammalian animals.

No even partial assessment of hunting and trapping could be adequate if it failed to mention the matter of predator control. Sheep farmers in the southwestern United States, for example, are troubled by predatory animals, most notably coyotes, who attack grazing sheep, sometimes killing more than they need to subsist. The economic loss suffered by these farmers occasions their public outcry, and they have taken steps, with the assistance of federal funds and personnel, to control these predators.

Those who accept the rights view must work to bring an end to such predator control programs. The official justification of these programs assumes that the predators cause losses to persons engaged in a justified enterprise—namely, the animal industry. Since the rights view denies that this industry's treatment of animals is morally justified, the harm done to predatory animals in the name of minimizing the financial losses of those engaged in this industry is morally to be condemned. In the struggle between those involved in the animal industry and those predatory animals who inhabit the lands used in the name of this industry, it is the industry, not the predators, that ought to go. And if in response those in this industry appeal to their legal rights to the land and their legal ownership of the animals in their business, those who accept the rights view should reply, first, that the appeal to legal rights by itself never settles any moral question and, second, that the present legal status of farm animals, as owned property, is itself one of the traditions the rights view seeks to change.

9.3 HOW TO WORRY ABOUT ENDANGERED SPECIES

The rights view is a view about the moral rights of individuals. Species are not individuals, and the rights view does not recognize the moral rights of species to anything, including survival. What it recognizes is the prima facie right of individuals not to be harmed, and thus the prima facie right of individuals not to be killed. That an individual animal is among the last remaining members of a species confers no further right on that animal, and its right not to be harmed must be weighed equitably with the rights of any others who have this right. If, in a prevention situation, we had to choose between saving the last two members of an endangered species or saving another individual who belonged to a species that was plentiful but whose death would be a greater prima facie harm to that individual than the harm that death would be to the two, then the rights view requires that we save that individual. Moreover, numbers make no difference in such a case. If the choice were between saving the last thousand or million members of the species to which the two belong, that would make no moral difference. The aggregate of their lesser harms does not harm any individual in a way that is prima facie comparable to the harm that would be done to this solitary individual. Nor would aggregating the losses of other interested parties (e.g., human aesthetic or scientific interests) make any difference. The sum of these losses harms no individual in a way that is prima facie comparable to the harm that would be done to the single individual if we chose to override his right.

The rights view is not opposed to efforts to save endangered species. It only insists that we be clear about the reasons for doing so. On the rights view, the reason we ought to save the members of endangered species of animals is not because the species is endangered but because the individual animals have valid claims and thus rights against those who would destroy their natural habitat, for example, or who would make a living off their dead carcasses through poaching and traffic in exotic animals, practices that unjustifiably override the rights of these animals. But though the rights view must look with favor on any attempt to protect the rights of any animal, and so supports efforts to protect the members of endangered species, these very efforts, aimed specifically at protecting the members of species that are endangered, can foster a mentality that is antagonistic to the implications of the rights view. If people are encouraged to believe that the harm done to animals matters morally *only when* these animals belong to endangered species, then these same people will be encouraged to regard the harm done to *other* animals as morally acceptable. In this way people may be encouraged to believe that, for example, the trapping of plentiful animals raises no serious moral question, whereas the trapping of rare animals does. This is not what the rights view implies. The mere size of the relative population of the species to which a given animal belongs makes no moral difference to the grounds for attributing rights to that individual animal or to the basis for determining when that animal's rights may be justifiably overridden or protected.

Though said before, it bears repeating: *the rights view is not indifferent to efforts to save endangered species. It supports these efforts.* It supports them, however, not because these animals are few in number; primarily it supports them because they are equal in value to all who have inherent value, ourselves included, sharing with us the fundamental right to be treated with respect. Since they are not mere receptacles or renewable resources placed here for our use, the harm done to them as individuals cannot be justified merely by aggregating the disparate benefits derived by commercial developers, poachers, and other interested third parties. That is what makes the commercial exploitation of endangered species wrong, not that the species are endangered. On the rights view, the same principles apply to the moral assessment of rare or endangered animals as apply to those that are plentiful, and the same principles apply whether the animals in question are wild or domesticated.

The rights view does not deny, nor is it antagonistic to recognizing, the importance of human aesthetic, scientific, sacramental, and other interests in rare and endangered species or in wild animals generally. What it denies is that (1) the value of these animals is reducible to, or is interchangeable with, the aggregate satisfaction of these human interests, and that (2) the determination of how these animals should be treated, including whether they should be saved in preference to more plentiful animals, is to be fixed by the yardstick of such human interests, either taken individually or aggregatively. Both points cut both ways, concerning, as they do, both how animals may and how they may not be treated. In particular, any and all harm done to rare or endangered animals, done in the name of aggregated human interests, is wrong, according to the rights view, because it violates the individual animal's right to respectful treatment. With regard to wild animals, the general policy recommended by the rights view is: *let them be!* Since this will require increased human intervention in *human* practices that threaten rare or endangered species (e.g., halting the destruction of natural habitat and closer surveillance of poaching, with much stiffer fines and longer prison sentences), the rights view sanctions this intervention, assuming that those humans involved are treated with the respect they are due. Too little is not enough.

Rights and Environmental Ethics: An Aside

The difficulties and implications of developing a rights-based environmental ethic, alluded to in an earlier context (7.5), should be abundantly clear by now and deserve brief comment before moving on. The difficulties include reconciling the *individualistic* nature of moral rights with the more *holistic* view of nature emphasized by many of the leading environmental thinkers. Aldo Leopold is illustrative of this latter tendency. "A thing is right," he states, "when it tends to preserve the integrity, stability, and beauty of the biotic community. It is wrong when it tends otherwise."[5] The implications of this view include the clear prospect that the individual may be sacrificed for the greater biotic good, in the name of "the integrity, stability, and beauty of the biotic community." It is difficult to see how the notion of the rights of the individual could find a home within a view that, emotive connotations to one side, might be fairly dubbed "environmental fascism." To use Leopold's telling phrase, man is *"only* a member of the biotic team,"[6] and as such has the same moral standing as any other "member" of "the team." If, to take an extreme, fanciful but, it is hoped, not unfair example, the situation we faced was either to kill a rare wildflower or a (plentiful) human being, and if the wildflower, as a "team member," would contribute more to "the integrity, stability, and beauty of the biotic community" than the human, then presumably we would not be doing wrong if we killed the human and saved the wildflower. The rights view cannot abide this position, not because the rights view categorically denies that inanimate objects can have rights (more on this momentarily) but because it denies the propriety of deciding what should be done to individuals who have rights by appeal to aggregative considerations, including, therefore, computations about what will or will not maximally "contribute to the integrity, stability, and beauty of the biotic community." Individual rights are not to be outweighed by such considerations (which is not to say that they are never to be outweighed). Environmental fascism and the rights view are like oil and water: they don't mix.

The rights view does not deny the possibility that collections or systems of natural objects might have inherent value—that is, might have a kind of value that is not the same as, is not reducible to, and is incommensurate with any one individual's pleasures, preference-satisfactions, and the like, or with the sum of such goods for any number of individuals. The beauty of an undisturbed, ecologically balanced forest, for example, might be conceived to have value of this kind. The point is certainly arguable. What is far from certain is how moral rights could be meaningfully attributed to the *collection* of trees or the ecosystem. Since neither is an individual, it is unclear how the notion of moral rights can be meaningfully applied. Perhaps this difficulty can be surmounted. It is fair to say, however, that no one writing in this important area of ethics has yet done so.[7]

Because paradigmatic right-holders are individuals, and because the dominant thrust of contemporary environmental efforts (e.g., wilderness preservation) is to focus on the whole rather than on the part (i.e., the individual), there is an understandable reluctance on the part of environmentalists to "take rights seriously," or at least a reluctance to take them as seriously as the rights view contends we should. But this may be a case of environmentalists not seeing the forest for the trees—or, more accurately, of not seeing the trees for the forest. The implications of the successful development of a rights-based environmental ethic, one that made the case that individual inanimate natural objects (e.g., *this* redwood) have inherent value and a basic moral right to treatment respectful of that value, should be welcomed by environmentalists. If individual trees have inherent value, they have a kind of value that is not the same as, is not reducible to, and is incommensurate with the intrinsic values of the pleasures, preference-satisfactions, and the like, of others, and since the rights of the individual never are to be overridden merely on the grounds of aggregating such values for all those affected by the outcome, a rights-based environmental ethic would bar the door to those who would uproot wilderness in the name of "human progress," whether this progress be aggregated economic, educational, recreational, or other human interests. On the rights view, assuming this could be successfully extended to inanimate natural objects, our general policy regarding wilderness would be precisely what the preservationists want—namely, let it be! Before those who favor such preservation dismiss the rights view in favor of the holistic view more commonly voiced in environmental circles, they might think twice about the implications of the two. There is the danger that the baby will be thrown out with the bath water. A rights-based environmental ethic remains a live option, one that, though far from being established, merits continued exploration. It ought not to be dismissed out of hand by environmentalists as being in principle antagonistic to the goals for which they work. It isn't. Were we to show proper respect for the rights of the individuals who make up the biotic community, would not the *community* be preserved? And is not that what the more holistic, systems-minded environmentalists want?

9.4 AGAINST THE USE OF ANIMALS IN SCIENCE

Debates over the use of animals for scientific purposes have traditionally been waged in terms of being for or against vivisection. But this term, *vivisection, is ill suited for our purposes.* To vivisect an animal is to dissect it, to cut it, while it is alive. Not all practices that demand our attention involve vivisection. There are three major areas of science in which animals are routinely used. These are (1) biological and medical education; (2) toxicology testing, where the potential harmful effects for human beings of new products and drugs are first tested on animals; and (3) original and applied research, including not only research into the causes and treatment of various diseases but also into the basic biochemical nature and behavior of living organisms.[8] All of us are familiar with the use of animals in education from our time spent in laboratory sections in biology, for example, and most of us have an outsider's inkling of what goes on in original and applied research from what we read in the newspapers and are exposed to by the other media. As for the use of animals in toxicity testing, that will become clearer below, when we discuss various toxicity tests, including the so-called LD50 test.

It is possible that some people might object to including all three uses of animals under the general heading of the use of animals in science. In particular, some scientists might have a narrower view of science, according to which only original and applied research count as "genuine science"; the use of animals in educational contexts or in toxicological testing isn't science, on this view, or not "real science" at any rate. This narrower conception of science is understandable, if science is viewed exclusively in terms of devising and testing original hypotheses. The fact remains, however, that it is not by witchcraft or astrology, say, that the toxicity of pesticides, food additives, hair sprays and oven cleaners is determined; it is a matter of applied science. And it is not to turn out persons educated in, say, philology or accounting that lab sections are held in connection with standard courses in biology; it is to educate persons in biological science. So, while there may be a sense in which neither toxicity tests nor instructional labs are science, there is certainly another sense in which they are a recognized part of those activities carried on by scientists, in their capacity as scientists or as teachers of science. For these reasons, then, to inquire into the morality of how animals are used in science or for scientific purposes requires assessing their use in all three areas—in biological and medical education, in toxicology testing, and in original and applied research. Each area will be considered in the order just given.

The Use of Animals in Educational Settings

Animals of many kinds and descriptions are used in a variety of ways in educational settings, including science fairs, standard laboratory sections for high school and university courses in biology, zoology and related disciplines, in student-conducted research projects, in practice surgery in both medical and veterinary schools—the list goes on. Nothing approaching a complete examination of the many uses is possible. By concentrating on one use (namely, the dissection of live animals in high school and university lab sections), what the rights view's position would be regarding these remaining uses should be clear enough not to require separate treatment, especially in light of this view's position about the use of animals in toxicology and research.

As farm and wild animals are not to be viewed as mere receptacles or renewable resources whose rights can be overridden on the basis of aggregating human benefits, so mammalian laboratory animals are not to be viewed in these ways. The acquisition of knowledge is a good thing, but the value of knowledge does not by itself justify harming others, the less so when this knowledge is obtainable by other means. In the case of knowledge of the anatomy and physiology of mammalian animals studied in lab sections in high school and university biology, zoology and related courses, this knowledge is obtainable without relying on hands-on experience. Students do not need to dissect any known animals to learn facts about their anatomy and physiology. Detailed drawings of animal anatomy and physiology exist in abundance and are usually included in the very texts used in such courses. On the rights view, to continue to include standard lab sections involving dissection of live mammalian animals is as unnecessary as it is unjustified.

Three objections can be anticipated. (1) The first claims that, while these facts can be obtained without dissecting any living animal, *the experience of dissecting* cannot be had by this means. That experience can only be had by dissecting. This is true, but not to the point. Morally, one cannot justify doing something merely on the grounds that one cannot have the experience of doing it without doing it. If that were sufficient, one could justify doing anything and everything, from rape to murder; for it is only if I participate in a rape or if I murder someone that I can have the experience of doing so. The general point is the simple one—namely, that to justify doing something, one has to justify what one does independently of pointing out that one could not experience it without doing it. Thus, while it is true that students could not have the experience of dissecting a living animal without dissecting one, that fact by itself goes no way toward justifying their doing it, let alone requiring that they do it. One must ask whether there are any reasons for viewing what is done as wrong, or as not wrong, and this will involve asking whether the value of having the experience is sufficient to justify doing what is necessary to have it. The rights view holds that the reasons against doing it outweigh the reasons for. Since dissecting a living mammalian animal harms that animal, frequently causing it pain and customarily being a prelude to that animal's untimely death, to defend dissection by appeal to the value of the experience of dissecting commits one to viewing these animals as if they were mere receptacles or renewable resources, a profound mistake according to the rights view. It is wrong because unjust to dissect living animals so one can have the experience of dissecting.

(2) In reply, the following might be urged. Even granting that the harm done to *mammalian* animals in lab sections is unjustified, most of the animals used in such courses are *not* mammals. Now, since, on the rights view, nonmammalian animals are not claimed to be the subjects-of-a-life,

in the sense in which this notion is understood by the rights view, the proponents of that view should have no principled objection to the use of these animals.

The rights view's response begins by noting that even if nonmammalian animals are not the subjects-of-a-life in the sense explained (8.5), it is possible that many of these animals are conscious and capable of experiencing pain. As has been conceded on more than one occasion in the above (3.8, 8.5), *where one draws the line* regarding the presence of consciousness is in some ways analogous to where one draws the line in other cases (e.g., how tall one has to be to be tall, or how old one must be to be old). There is no precise height or exact age one must be to be tall or old, respectively; but there are clear cases nonetheless. Similarly, it may not be possible to say, with anything approaching certitude, whether a given individual is or is not conscious or does or does not experience pain, despite the fact that there are clear cases where individuals are conscious and sentient. But though analogous in some respects, the two cases differ in others. Normally, nothing of moral significance turns on whether an individual is tall or is old. A great deal that is morally significant turns on whether an individual is conscious and can experience pain. Because we are uncertain where the boundaries of consciousness lie, it is not unreasonable to advocate a policy that bespeaks moral caution. Such a policy would have us act *as if* nonmammalian animals are conscious and are capable of experiencing pain unless a convincing case can be made to the contrary. In the absence of the case to the contrary, that is, it is not unreasonable to advocate a policy that gives the benefit of the doubt to animals that, though not mammals, nevertheless share relevant anatomical and physiological properties with mammalian animals (for example, a central nervous system). The adoption of this policy would make a significant difference to whether we should permit or require dissection of live, unanesthetized animals that are relevantly like paradigm conscious beings. If we give these animals the benefit of the doubt, we will operate on the assumption that these animals are conscious and do experience pain; and if we operate on that assumption, we will view dissection, when they are unanesthetized, as causing them pain and thus as standing in need of moral defense. That defense is not supplied by pointing to the knowledge gained. Since this knowledge is obtainable without causing pain to anyone, the presumptive pain caused those animals to whom we have given the benefit of the doubt, caused in the name of acquiring knowledge, is morally too great. Nor is the required justification supplied by alluding to the value of having the experience of dissecting, when this causes presumptive pain, since that experience can be had without risking causing any pain. Without the use of anesthetics, the policy of giving these animals the benefit of the doubt assumes that the animals *are* caused pain *and* pain that is unnecessary. To require or allow students to dissect "lower" animals without the use of anesthetics is morally unjustified.

But what of cases where "lower" animals are anesthetized? The same considerations apply. Though nonmammalian animals differ from us anatomically and physiologically in some respects, they resemble us in others, and it may be that the resemblances in some cases are more important than the differences. We simply do not know enough to justify dismissing, *out of hand*, the idea that a frog, say, may be the subject-of-a-life, replete with desires, goals, beliefs, intentions, and the like. When our ignorance is so great, and the possible moral price so large, it is not unreasonable to give these animals the benefit of the doubt, treating them *as if* they are subjects, due our respectful treatment, especially when doing so causes no harm to us. Adoption of this policy would make a difference, one that taking care to administer anesthesia to frogs, say, would not fully accommodate. For since the untimely death of an animal who is the subject-of-a-life *harms* the animal, the routine death caused those animals in lab sections becomes morally relevant. If we are genuinely to give the frog the benefit of the doubt, we will not only take care to spare frogs unnecessary pain by using anesthesia, we will also take care not to kill them, or allow them to die, unnecessarily. We will, that is, not use them for purposes of dissection.

(3) A critic might protest that frogs *just aren't worth* giving the benefit of the doubt to, claiming that stirring our conscience over the remote possibility that "frogs have rights" is to carry things too far. Let us, then, this critic maintains, prohibit use of mammalian animals but allow unlimited use of those who are not mammals, though with the recommendation that anesthesia be used. This reply occasions the third point. What transpires in, say, a biology lab doesn't occur in a vacuum. It is both an effect and a contributing cause of prevailing cultural beliefs, attitudes, and traditions about nonhumans. The acquisition of these beliefs and attitudes and the introduction into these traditions are part of our acculturation. The rights view has implications that challenge some of these beliefs, attitudes, and traditions. It rejects the view that mammalian animals, at least, are mere receptacles or convenient renewable resources and affirms that they have a value of their own, independent of human interests. Now, the cultural acceptance of the rights view obviously in part turns on how well it is received and transmitted in our culture's system of education, including courses in science. Indeed, it is these

courses, more than any others, that have the greatest potential to encourage cultural acceptance of the rights view. Pedagogically, how might
this potential be developed most fully? Not by continuing to require
students to dissect living animals, whether anesthetized or not, and
whether mammalian or not, especially when the knowledge gained is
obtainable without doing this. To require this is to help encourage the
belief that *nonhuman animals don't count morally,* a belief that the dominant
cultural influences outside the lab encourage enough without the need of
any further assistance. Outside the lab is the world of Big Macs, Kentucky
Fried Chicken, the weekend hunting trip, commercial whaling, fur coats,
rodeos, cock fights, animal shelters—all symptoms of our culture's
throw-away attitude toward animals, as if these sensitive creatures were
commodities or *things.* To require students to dissect animals, when the
knowledge acquired can be gained without doing this, is to feed into this
throw-away attitude. To cease to require this is to take an important step
in the opposite direction.

A variant of Kant's psychological speculations is apt in this regard.
Kant's position, it will be recalled (6.5), is that "cruelty to animals" ought
to be discouraged, not because we owe it to animals themselves not to be
cruel to them, but because people who are cruel to animals develop habits
of cruelty that in time lead them to maltreat human beings. However
likely Kant's speculation about the connection between "cruelty to animals" and "cruelty to human beings" might be, it is more likely that
requiring students to treat some animals as if they were of no direct moral
significance will encourage them to form this habit of thought and action
toward animals generally, the more so given that the dominant cultural
influences already are heavily inclined in this direction. Even if it is true,
then, that the animals most frequently dissected in high school and
university lab sections lack rights, to continue to require dissecting them
is likely to help foster habits that will lead persons to engage in practices
that violate the rights of those animals who do have them—or to acqui-
esce by supporting those who do so. One way (and this a not unimportant
way) to check the development of these habits is to cease to require
students to dissect *any* animal, explaining that the knowledge acquired by
doing it is obtainable without doing it and pointing out that the sciences of
biology, zoology, and the like do not take the view that the animals they
study are so insignificant, so "valueless," that they may be dissected and
disposed of when it is unnecessary to do this. (Considerations analogous
to [2] and [3], above, form part of the basis of the rights view's case against
treating chickens and turkeys as if they are renewable resources; see
p. 349; see, too, n. 30.)

These judgments are unlikely to meet with much enthusiasm on the part of some of those who teach high school and university courses in the life sciences. Like academicians generally, they will treasure their academic freedom, and rightly so. To challenge what they require or permit in their laboratories is likely to be viewed as an invasion of this freedom. "We don't tell philosophers how they should teach their courses," it may be said, "so philosophers shouldn't tell us how we ought to teach ours!" The point is well taken, up to a point. Philosophers obviously are not in a position to select what text should be used in science courses, or what scientific ideas should be stressed, or in what order these ideas should be presented. Nothing said in the above implies otherwise. What a philosopher may legitimately do is challenge common practices on moral grounds, with reasons that do not require expertise in one or another scientific discipline. And scientists can do the same, if they find practices in the classrooms of philosophy that they consider morally objectionable. *It is the soundness of the moral arguments given, not who gives them, that should be decisive.* The preceding attempts to show how, by relying on the rights view, a commonly accepted practice in scientific education can be challenged. Reasons for accepting the rights view have been set forth at length in the preceding chapters. If that view has reason on its side, and if its application in the present case is sound, then lab sections that require or permit dissection of live animals ought to cease. For teachers to call a halt to this customary part of our education in the life sciences would not be to abdicate their academic freedom; it would be to exercise it.[9]

Toxicology

Animals are routinely used to test for the possible toxicological (literally, poisonous) threat posed by a variety of commercially manufactured items intended primarily for human use or consumption. Two kinds of substances are tested: therapeutic and nontherapeutic. The former are drugs that may alleviate or cure pathological conditions (e.g., gout, ulcers, high blood pressure). The class of nontherapeutic products includes everything else. The following is a representative list of nontherapeutic products tested for toxicity: insecticides, pesticides, antifreeze chemicals, brake fluids, bleaches, Christmas tree sprays, church candles, silver cleaners, oven cleaners, deodorants, skin fresheners, baby preparations, bubble baths, freckle creams, depilatories, eye makeup, crayons, fire extinguishers, inks, suntan oils, nail polish, mascara, hair sprays and rinses, zipper lubricants, paints, thermometers and children's novelties.[10] For simplicity's sake, therapeutic items will normally be referred to simply as *drugs*, while nontherapeutic items will be referred to as *products*.

Kinds of Toxicity Tests

Dallas Pratt, an American medical doctor, offers the following definition of a toxic substance.

> A substance is defined as toxic if, when eaten, inhaled or absorbed through the skin, it causes by its chemical action either damage to structure or disturbance of function, or both.[11]

Standard test procedures include (1) acute toxicity, (2) subacute toxicity, and (3) chronic toxicity. Acute toxicity tests Pratt characterizes as a "search for untoward reaction at a high dose level,"[12] while subacute tests "in general . . . define the biological activity of a compound, an estimate of the 'no effect' dosage, and the maximum tolerated dosage."[13] The latter tests are generally conducted over a three-month period; the former take a shorter amount of time. The long-term, small dosage toxic effects of a substance are assessed in chronic toxicity tests that normally take about two years. Carcinogenicity tests on animals fall in this last category. In addition, there are other standard tests for some products (e.g., cosmetics), including eye and skin irritancy tests.

The number of animals used in toxicity tests in the United States is unknown, but using available British statistics Pratt estimates that about 20 percent of his estimate of 100 million animals used for scientific purposes in this country are used in toxicology. That works out to about 20 million animals. Among the common signs of a substance's toxic effects on test animals, Pratt lists the following: "unusual vocalization, restlessness; twitch, tremor, paralysis, convulsions; . . . rigidity, flaccidity; salivation, lachrymation; swelling of sex organs and breasts; skin eruptions; discharge, including hemorrhage, from the eye, nose, or mouth; unusual posture, emaciation."[14] Toxicity tests, in short, harm animals, not only if and when they cause them acute or chronic suffering or distress, but also because they deprive them of opportunities for obtaining the satisfactions their capacities make available to them. Animals who are paralyzed may not be in pain, but that does not mean they are not thereby harmed.

A number of books have chronicled these tests at length.[15] We will have to be content with a slightly fuller description of only one test—the acute toxicity test known as the LD50 test. No one can improve on the description Singer gives:

The standard test for toxicity, or the extent to which a substance is poisonous, is the "Lethal Dosage 50" test, commonly abbreviated to LD50. The aim of this test is to determine the dosage level at which 50 percent of the test animals will die. Usually this means that all the animals will become very sick before half finally succumb and the other half survive. In the case of fairly harmless substances it is still considered good procedure to find the concentration that will make half the animals die; consequently enormous quantities have to be force-fed to the animals, and death may be caused merely by the large volume or high concentration given to the animals. . . . It is also normal to let the process of poisoning take its full course, until death occurs. To put dying animals out of their misery might give a slightly inaccurate result.

Similarly to be discouraged, for similar reasons, is the use of anesthesia in standard toxicity tests. The effects of the anesthetic "might give a slightly inaccurate result." The information obtained from LD50 tests forms the background basis for the "DANGER: POISON," "WARNING," and "CAUTION" labels on many products[16].

The *legal* requirement to perform *particular* tests, such as the LD50, is murky at best in the case of some products (e.g., cosmetics). As Pratt observes, however, "even when the test is not mandated by government regulations, it is frequently used by manufacturers of drugs and consumer products on the supposition that it is a protection against proceedings for negligence."[17]

With these brief remarks serving as background, let us now turn to the task of morally assessing toxicity tests on animals, beginning first with products.

Toxicity Tests of Products

Animal toxicity tests of products can be, and have been, challenged on the basis of their limited scientific validity.[18] The problem of extrapolating test results from animals to humans is notorious—for example, some products (e.g., benzene and arsenic) have no discernible toxicological effect on test animals and yet are highly toxic for human beings. Why this is so is not clear, but test results have been shown to vary depending on the time of day the test was performed, what the animals ate, and other subtle variables.[19] Moreover, since much already has been learned about the toxicity of strong acids and alkaloids, new products that contain either are known to be highly toxic for humans before conducting any further test, while others, such as many cosmetics, because they contain chemicals known to be benign, are known to be nontoxic without additional testing. In such cases the tests can be disputed on the grounds that they are unnecessary.

Both these ways of attacking toxicology tests of products on animals can create the unintended and, from the rights view's perspective, the unwarranted impression that toxicity tests on animals *would* be morally acceptable *if only the unnecessary* tests were eliminated or *if only the problem of extrapolation* could be surmounted. On this latter point, those who conduct and support such tests, acknowledging the present limitations, could argue that the very unreliability of present tests justifies conducting further tests in order to overcome the shortcomings of existing methods. And if those who would defend laboratory animals were to object that these present scientific liabilities *cannot* be overcome, they would be accused, and rightly so, of prejudging a very complicated scientific question in advance, without adequate knowledge, and in a way that invites and deserves the charge of being "antiscientific." The reasons one must mount against such tests, if one is to defend laboratory animals, cannot be confined to citing some blatantly unnecessary tests (though such tests there are) or to exposing the stark deficiencies of the methodology as presently applied (though the exposure is deserved). The very institution of administering these tests must be attacked at its moral foundations.

How might someone attempt to justify these tests, given the principles identified and defended by the rights view? The following line of argument seems the most plausible by far. If new products were introduced into the market without having pretested their toxicity by using animals, the risks of harm humans would run would be greatly increased, and the harms in question would be prima facie greater than the harm done to any test animal. For example, use of a hair spray might cause blindness, or inhalation of an untested oven cleaner might cause incapacitating respiratory defects, either of which would make a human being worse-off than any test animal. Moreover, since, according to the rights view, the aggregate of lesser harms does not harm any particular individual, we cannot add up the lesser harms done to test animals and suppose that we arrive at a greater harm than, say, the harm that blindness is for a human. What we must do, in order to minimize the risk that a human will be made worse-off by using a product that turns out to be toxic for humans, is pretest for toxicity by using animals.

The rights view attacks this defense on two main grounds. The first contests the permissibility of placing animals at risk of harm, or harming them, in order to identify or reduce the risks that humans would run if they use something new. Since this argument applies to *any* toxicity test carried out for this purpose, not just to tests on new products, a statement and defense of this argument will be postponed until toxicity tests of new drugs are examined. The second ground applies specifically to testing new products for their toxicity by using animals. It begins by noting that the defense of these tests, offered by appeal to the worse-off principle, assumes that *pre*market toxicity tests that harm animals can be justified by appealing to what might happen *after* new products are marketed, if these premarket tests were not performed. But morality does not work in the way this defense assumes it does. *After* the mine cave-in has occurred, to refer back to that earlier example (8.9), I am justified in saving the fifty even though this will cause certain death to the one miner; but it does not follow from this that I would have been justified in causing the mine cave-in in the first place. Analogously, even if it were true that employing harmful toxicity tests on animals could be justified by appealing to what might happen assuming a product already is on the market, it would not follow that the decision to *develop and market* the product is justified. In this latter case, what is wanted is a moral justification for developing the product in the first place, a justification that, in the nature of the case, cannot be given by appealing to the harm that might happen after the product already has been introduced.

Now, the very principle (the worse-off principle) to which manufac-turers are most likely to appeal, in an effort to defend these tests, shows that these tests are unjustified. The defense of this claim begins by noting that there *already are plenty* of lipsticks, eyeshadows, oven cleaners, paints, brake fluids, crayons, and other products competing in the market and readily available to consumers. There is no demonstrable human need that would be served by having new products from which to choose (excluding, of course, the economic interests of the manufacturers, about which more momentarily), nor is there any credible basis for believing that any consumer would be harmed by being deprived of yet another Christmas tree spray or nail polish from which to choose, least of all that this deprivation in any given case would be prima facie comparable to the harm done to animals in, say, the LD50 test. Moreover, since the aggre-gate of these lesser harms endured by consumers, even assuming that consumers would be harmed by being deprived of new products from which to choose, harms no particular individual in a way that is prima facie comparable to the harm done to the test animals, appeal to the worse-off principle shows not that these tests are justified, but the very reverse. Since the issue is whether the *pre*market development of a new product can be justified if it harms animals, and since this is a question *about the decision to develop a new product in the first place*, the harm that might result *after* the product has been marketed is irrelevant, just as, analogously, what I would be justified in doing *after* the mine cave-in is irrelevant to determining whether I would have been justified in causing the cave-in in the first place. The central moral point, then, is this: no consumer will be made worse-off than any test animal if no new products are introduced. Assuming, then, that all those involved are treated with respect, and assuming that no special considerations obtain, what we ought to do is *not* introduce new products, if their premarket development involves making animals worse-off relative to any consumer. Rather than justifying harmful toxicity tests on animals, appeal to the worse-off principle shows that they are unjustified.

The economic interests of those involved in businesses that manufacture these products may be cited as a reason for allowing toxicity tests on animals. The rights view denies the moral relevance of these considerations when questions about overriding basic moral rights are at issue. Even if it were true that those involved in the cosmetic industry, for example, would lose some future profits when barred from doing toxicity tests on animals, that would make no moral difference, first, because their loss of profits would not represent a harm that is prima facie comparable to the harm done to the test animals, and, second, even if it were true that someone involved in this industry would be harmed in ways that are prima facie comparable to the harm done to these animals—indeed, even assuming this individual was made worse-off relative to the condition of the animals—that would not justify continued use of these tests. Those who voluntarily participate in a business venture voluntarily take certain risks, including the risk that they might be made worse-off if their business fails. Thus, even if someone involved in, say, the cosmetic industry would be made worse-off if toxicity tests of cosmetics on animals ceased, that would not justify their continued use.

Harmful toxicity tests of products on animals *are* wrong, then, according to the rights view, not because they are an unreliable means for assessing what is toxic for humans (though the limitations of these tests, relative to establishing what is safe for humans, are real enough); nor are they wrong only when, because the results are predictable before the tests are done, certain tests are unnecessary (though this is true also); fundamentally, these tests are wrong because they violate the rights of laboratory animals. Since the only humans who might claim, however implausibly, that they would be made worse-off if these tests were not done (namely, those associated with the manufacture of new products) are the very ones who voluntarily waive their right not to be made worse-off as a result of their voluntarily participation in a relevant business venture, and since no consumer would be made worse-off than any of the test animals if these tests were stopped and consumers were "deprived" of new products, appeal to the worse-off principle shows that these tests are morally unjustified. These harmful tests violate the basic moral right of these animals not to be harmed. Morally, they ought to cease.

The rights view is not anticonsumer or anti−worker protection. It is not opposed in principle to efforts to minimize the health risks individuals run in the work- and marketplace. Consumer and worker safety is a laudatory aim, and, human nature being what it is, perhaps it is not unreasonable for society to impose regulations on manufacturers whose products are intended for the public's use, in the hope of protecting the public against unscrupulous businesses out to make a quick buck at the public's expense. What the rights view opposes is practices that violate the basic rights of individuals in the name of "the public interest." Toxicity tests of new products that harm animals fall into this category. Anyone who objected to the rights view on the grounds that it is "morally indefensible" to release untested products into the market would miss the central point. What *is* morally indefensible is to rely on tests that violate anyone's rights. The options, then, are not *either* to continue to use these tests *or* to release untested products. A third option is *not to allow products on the market if they were pretested for toxicity on animals.* That is the option those who would dispute the rights view in the way currently under review fail to recognize.

The rights view's denunciation of standard toxicity tests on animals is not antibusiness. It does not deny any manufacturer the liberty to introduce any new product into the marketplace, to compete with the others already there, and to sink or swim in the waters of free enterprise. All that the rights view denies is that the toxicity of any new product may be pretested on animals in ways harmful to them. *Nonanimal alternatives* are not ruled out by the rights view. On the contrary, their development should be encouraged, both on the grounds of the public interest and because of the legitimate legal interests of the manufacturers. Commercial firms should begin to devote their not inconsiderable financial and scientific resources toward the development of such tests. If, in reply, we are told that it is government regulatory agencies, such as the Food and Drug Administration, that require these tests, and that the manufacturers are only doing what the law requires, then the rights view's principal reply is that *these regulatory agencies do not require that any new product be produced.* To take refuge in what these agencies require neither provides a moral justification for introducing new products nor for testing their toxicity on animals. Moreover, in denouncing the present practice of testing the toxicity of new products on animals, the rights view does not bid cosmetic manufacturers, for example, to remove all their present products from the shelves. The wrong that has been done in the past cannot be undone. The vital point is not to let it continue in the future. Manufacturers can hardly complain that this is antibusiness or against the spirit of the free enterprise system. Let those companies competing in the marketplace compete with the products they already have or, even more in keeping with this economic philosophy, let them outdo one another by developing nonanimal alternatives and, as also befits this philosophy, let them labor to have the scientific validity of these tests recognized by the appropriate regulatory agencies. That sort of competition would be a paradigm of the free enterprise system at its finest.

In reply it will be claimed that no valid nonanimal alternatives exist. This is false. In the case of cosmetics, for example, the pioneering work of Beauty Without Cruelty demonstrates beyond any reasonable doubt that it is possible to manufacture and market attractive, reliable products whose toxicity for humans has not been pretested on animals.[20] Moreover, in areas where no nonanimal tests presently exist, there is no reason why they cannot be explored, and to claim in advance that there *are none* to be found is to be guilty of being just as antiscientific as some of those who criticize animal toxicity tests. None are so blind as those who will not look. Whether found or not, whether looked for or not, the rights view's position is uncompromising: *Harmful toxicity tests of new products violate the rights of laboratory animals and ought to be stopped.* The least we, as consumers, can do to help achieve this goal is henceforth to refuse to buy any new product, including so-called new, improved varieties of old ones, when they hit the market, unless we know that they have not been pretested for their toxicity on animals. That is a modest deprivation anyone who respects the rights of these animals ought to be willing to endure.

Toxicity Tests of New Drugs

Someone might accept the preceding critique of toxicity tests on animals in the case of new products and claim that the case of doing such tests on *new therapeutic drugs* differs in morally relevant respects. No human being will be harmed in a way that is prima facie comparable to the harm caused test animals in an LD50 test, for example, by being deprived of a new brake fluid or paint. Some humans are harmed, however, right now, as a result of a variety of pathological conditions, and many more will be harmed if we fail to investigate the causes, treatments, and cures of these conditions. Indeed, some will today lose their lives as a result of these maladies, and many more will lose theirs in the future if we fail to investigate their causes and cures. Now, one thing we must do, it may be claimed, is reduce the risk that the treatment prescribed for a given malady will make patients worse-off than they otherwise would have been, and this will require establishing the toxic properties of each new drug before, not after, humans take them. Thus arises the need to test the toxicity of each new drug on test animals. If we do not test the toxicity of all new drugs on animals, humans who use these drugs will run a much greater risk of being made worse-off as a result of using them than they would if these drugs were pretested on animals. In the nature of the case, we cannot say which drugs are toxic for humans *in advance* of conducting tests on animals (if we could, there would be no need to do the test in the first place). Indeed, we cannot even eliminate all risks *after* the drug has been extensively pretested on animals (thalidomide is a tragic example). The best we can do is minimize the risks humans who use drugs face, as best we can, and that requires testing for their toxicity on animals.

The rights view rejects this defense of these tests. *Risks are not morally transferable to those who do not voluntarily choose to take them in the way this defense assumes.* If I hang-glide, then I run certain risks, including the possibility of serious head injury, and I shall certainly, if I am prudent, want to minimize my risks by wearing a protective helmet. You, who do not hang-glide, have no duty to agree to serve in tests that establish the safety of various helmet designs so that hang-gliders might reduce their risks, and hang-gliders, or those who serve the interests of these enthusiasts, would violate your rights if they coerced or forced you to take part in such tests. *How much* you would be harmed is not decisive. What matters is that you would be *put at risk of harm, against your will*, in the name of reducing the risks that others voluntarily undertake and so can voluntarily decide *not* to undertake by the simple expedient of choosing not to run them in the first place (in this case, by choosing not to hang-glide). That tests on you would make it possible for those who hang-glide to lessen the risk of being made worse-off goes no way toward justifying placing you at risk of harm. As hang-gliders are the ones who stand to benefit from participation in this sport, they are the ones who must run the risks involved in participating. They may do all that they can to reduce the risks they run, but only so long as they do not coerce others to find out what these risks are or how to reduce them.

It would be a mistake to suppose that what is true in the case of high-risk activity is not true in the case of low-risk activity. Whenever I plug in my toaster, take an elevator, drink water from my faucet or from a clear mountain stream, I take some risks, though not of the magnitude of those who, say, sky-dive or canoe in turbid waters. But even in the case of my voluntarily taking minor risks, others have no duty to volunteer to establish or minimize my risks for me, and anyone who would be made to do this, against her will, would have her rights unjustifiably overridden. For example, the risks I run when I drive my car could be minimized by the design and manufacture of the most effective seat belts and the most crash-proof automobile. But it does not follow that anyone else has a duty to take part in crash tests in the name of minimizing my risks, and anyone who was coerced to do so, whether injured or not, would have every reason to claim that her rights had been violated or, if the test subject is incapable of making the claim, others would have every reason to make this claim on the subject's behalf. "No harm done" is no defense in circumstances such as these.

To minimize the risks humans who use new drugs would run by testing them on animals is morally no different. Anyone who elects to take a drug voluntarily chooses to run certain risks, and the risks we choose to run or, as in the case of moral patients for whom we choose, the risks we elect to allow them to run are not morally transferable to others. Coercively to harm others or to put others, whether human or animal, at risk of harm in order to identify or minimize the risks of those who voluntarily choose to run them, is to violate the rights of the humans or animals in question. It is not *how much* the test subjects are harmed (though the greater the harm, the worse the offense). What matters is that they are coercively used to establish or minimize risks for others. To place these animals at risk of harm so that others who voluntarily choose to run certain risks, and who thus can voluntarily choose not to run them, may minimize the risks they run, is to fail to treat the test animals with that respect they are due as possessors of inherent value. As is true of toxicity tests on new products, similar tests of new drugs on animals involve treating them as *even less* than receptacles, as if their value were reducible to their possible utility relative to the interests of others—in this case, relative to the interests humans who voluntarily take drugs have in minimizing their risks. Laboratory animals, to borrow an apt phrase from the Harvard philosopher Robert Nozick, "are distinct individuals who are not resources for others."[21] To utilize them so that we might establish or minimize our risks, especially when it is within our power to decide not to take these risks in the first place, *is* to treat them as if they were "resources for others," most notably for us, and to defend these tests on the grounds that animals sometimes are not harmed is as morally lame as defending fox hunting on the grounds that the fox sometimes gets away.

The rights view is not in principle opposed to efforts to minimize the risks involved in taking new drugs. Toxicity tests are acceptable, so long as they violate no one's rights. To use human volunteers, persons who do not suffer from a particular malady but who give their informed consent as a test subject, is, though possible, not generally to be encouraged. To tie the progress of pharmacology and related sciences to the availability of healthy, consenting human subjects itself runs significant risks, including the risk that some may use deceptive or coercive means to secure participation. Moreover, few, if any, volunteers from the affluent classes are likely to step forward; the ranks of volunteers would likely be comprised of the poor, the uneducated, and those human moral patients whose relatives lack sufficient "sentimental interests" to protect them. There is a serious danger that the least powerful will be exploited. More preferable by far is the development of toxicity tests that harm no one— that is, tests that harm neither moral agents nor patients, whether humans or animals. Even at this date promising alternatives are being developed.[22] To validate them scientifically is no small challenge, but it is the challenge that must be met if we continue to desire or require that new drugs be tested for their toxicity prior to being made available on the market. To test them on healthy human volunteers is dangerous at best; to test them coercively on healthy animals and human moral patients is wrong. The moral alternative that remains is: find valid alternatives.

A number of objections can be anticipated. One claims that there are risks and then there are risks. If we stopped testing new drugs for their toxicity, think of the risks people would run if they took them! Who could say what disastrous consequences would result? The rights view agrees. People would run greater risks if drugs were not pretested. But (a) the rights view does not oppose all pretesting (only those tests that coercively utilize some so that others may reduce those risks they may choose to run or choose not to run), and (b) those who had the choice to use an untested drug, assuming it was available, could *themselves* choose not to run the risks associated with taking it by deciding not to take it. Indeed, prudence would dictate acting in this way, except in the direst circumstances.

Of course, if untested drugs were allowed on the market and if people acted prudently, sales of new (untested) drugs would fall off, and we can anticipate that those involved in the pharmaceutical industry, people who, in addition to their chosen vocation of serving the health needs of the public, also have an economic interest in the stability and growth of this industry, might look with disfavor on the implications of the rights view. Four brief replies must suffice in this regard. First, whatever financial losses these companies might face if they were not permitted to continue to do toxicity tests on animals carry no moral weight, since the question of overriding basic moral rights is at issue. That these companies might lose money if the rights of animals are respected is one of the risks they run. Second, there is mounting evidence that these companies could save, rather than lose, money, if nonanimal tests were used. Animals are an expensive proposition. They must be bred or purchased, fed and watered, their living quarters must be routinely cleaned, their environment controlled (otherwise one runs the scientific risk of an uncontrolled variable), and so forth. This requires employing trained personnel, in adequate numbers, as well as a large and continued outpouring of capital for initial construction, expansion, and maintenance. Tissue and cell cultures, for example, are cheaper by far. So the economic interests of commercial pharmaceutical firms are not necessarily at odds with the changes that will have to be made, as the rights of laboratory animals are respected. Third, anyone who defends present toxicological practice *merely* by claiming that these tests are required by the involved regulatory agencies (e.g., the Food and Drug Administration) would miss the essential moral point: though these agencies have yet to recognize nonanimal tests as meeting their regulations, these agencies themselves do not require that any pharmaceutical firm manufacture any new drug. That is a moral decision each company makes on its own and for which each must bear responsibility. Fourth, appeals to what the laws require can have no moral weight if we have good reason to believe that the laws in question are unjust. And we have good reasons in the present case. Laboratory animals are not a "resource"[23] whose moral status in the world is to serve human interests. They are themselves the subjects-of-a-life that fares better or worse for them as individuals, logically independently of any utility they may or may not have relative to the interests of others. They share with us a distinctive kind of value—inherent value—and whatever we do to them must be respectful of this value as a matter of strict justice. To treat them *as if* their value were reducible to their utility for human interests, even important human interests, is to treat them unjustly; to utilize them so that humans might minimize the risks we voluntarily take (and that we can voluntarily decide not to take) is to violate their basic moral right to be treated with respect. That the laws require such testing, when they do, does not show that these tests are morally tolerable; what this shows is that the laws themselves are unjust and ought to be changed.

One can also anticipate charges that the rights view is antiscientific and antihumanity. This is rhetoric. The rights view is not antihuman. We, as humans, have an equal prima facie right not to be harmed, a right that the rights view seeks to illuminate and defend; but we do not have any right coercively to harm others, or to put them at risk of harm, so that we might minimize the risks we run as a result of our own voluntary decisions. That violates their rights, and that is one thing no one has a right to do. Nor is the rights view antiscientific. It places the *scientific* challenge before pharmacologists and related scientists: find scientifically valid ways that serve the public interest without violating individual rights. The overarching goal of pharmacology should be to reduce the risks of those who use drugs without harming those who don't. Those who claim that this cannot be done, in advance of making a concerted effort to do it, are the ones who are truly antiscientific.

Perhaps the most common response to the call for elimination of animals in toxicity testing is the benefits argument:

1. Human beings and animals have benefited from toxicity tests on animals.
2. Therefore, these tests are justified.

Like all arguments with missing premises, everything turns on what that premise is. If it read, "These tests do not violate the rights of animals," then we would be on our way to receiving an interesting defense of toxicity testing. Unfortunately for those who countenance these tests, however, and even more unfortunately for the animals used in them, that premise is not true. These tests do violate the rights of the test animals, for the reasons given. The benefits these tests have for others are irrelevant, according to the rights view, since the tests violate the rights of the individual animals. As in the case of humans, so also in the case of animals: overriding their rights cannot be defended by appealing to "the general welfare." Put alternatively, the benefits *others* receive count morally only if no *individual's* rights have been violated. Since toxicity tests of new drugs violate the rights of laboratory animals, it is morally irrelevant to appeal to how much others have benefited.[24]

A further objection is conceptual in nature. "Animals cannot volunteer or refuse to volunteer to take part in toxicity tests," it may be claimed, "and so cannot be forced or coerced to take part in them either. Thus the rights view's opposition to using them is fatuous." Now it is true that, unlike *some* humans, animals cannot give or withhold their informed consent, relative to participation in a toxicity test. But this is because they cannot be informed in the relevant way. It is no good trying to inform them about pH factors or carcinogens. They *will not* understand because they *cannot* understand; but it does not follow from this that animals cannot be forced or coerced to do something they do not want to do.

Because these animals are intelligibly viewed as having preference-autonomy (see above, 3.1), we are able intelligibly to say, and confirm statements made about, what they want, desire, prefer, aim at, intend, and so forth. We can, therefore, give a perfectly clear sense to saying that they are being forced or coerced to do something they do not want to do. Beyond any doubt, those animals used in the LD50 test, for example, are not doing what they want to do, and those who use them in these tests do so by means of force or coercion.

To establish the scientific validity of nonanimal toxicity tests is a difficult challenge certainly, one that can only be met by scientists. No moral philosophy can do this. What a moral philosophy can do is articulate and defend the morally permissible means of conducting science. If the rights view has the best reasons on its side, this is the view we ought to use to assess what is and what is not permissible in the case of toxicity testing. And the implications of this view are clear. *Toxicity tests of new products and drugs involving animals are not morally justified. These tests violate the rights of these animals. They are not morally tolerable. All ought to cease.*

Scientific Research

One can imagine someone accepting the arguments advanced against toxicity tests on animals but putting his foot down when it comes to scientific research. To deny science use of animals in research is, it might be said, to bring scientific and allied medical progress to a halt, and that is reason enough to oppose it. The claim that progress would be "brought to a halt" is an exaggeration certainly. It is not an exaggeration to claim that, given its present dominant tendency, the rights view requires massive redirection of scientific research. The dominant tendency involves routinely harming animals. It should come as no surprise that the rights view has principled objections to its continuation.

A recent statement of the case for unrestricted use of animals in neurobiological research contrasts sharply with the rights view and will serve as an introduction to the critical assessment of using animals in basic research. The situation, as characterized by C. R. Gallistel, a psychologist at the University of Pennsylvania, is as follows:[25] "Behavioral neurobiology tries to establish the manner in which the nervous system mediates behavioral phenomena. It does so by studying the behavioral consequences of one or more of the following procedures: (a) destruction of a part of the nervous system, (b) stimulation of a part, (c) administration of drugs that alter neural functioning. These three techniques are as old as the discipline. A recent addition is (d) the recording of electrical activity. All four cause the animal at least temporary distress. In the past they have frequently caused intense pain, and they occasionally do so now. Also, they often impair an animal's proper functioning, sometimes transiently, sometimes permanently."[26] The animals subjected to these procedures are, in a word, harmed. When it comes to advancing our knowledge in neurobiology, however, "there is no way to establish the relation between the nervous system and behavior without some experimental surgery," where by "experimental surgery" Gallistel evidently means to include the four procedures just outlined. The issue, then, in Gallistel's mind, is not whether to allow such surgery or not; it is whether any restrictions should be placed on the use made of animals. Gallistel thinks not.

In defense of unrestricted use of animals in research, Gallistel claims that "most experiments conducted by neurobiologists, *like scientific experiments generally,* may be seen in retrospect to have been a waste of time, in the sense that they did not prove or yield any new insight." But, claims Gallistel, "there is no way of discriminating in advance the waste-of-time experiments from the illuminating ones with anything approaching certainty."[27] The logical upshot, so Gallistel believes, is that "restricting research on living animals is certain to restrict the progress in our understanding of the nervous system and behavior. Therefore," he concludes, "one should advocate such restrictions only if one believes that the moral value of this scientific knowledge and of the many human and humane benefits that flow from it cannot outweigh the suffering of a rat," something that, writing autobiographically, Gallistel finds "an affront to my ethical sensibility."[28]

Even those unpersuaded by the rights view ought to challenge Gallistel's argument at every point. Is it true, as he claims, "that there is *no* way to establish the relation between the nervous system and behavior without some experimental surgery"? Can we learn nothing whatever about this connection from, say, clinical observation of those who have been injured? Again, is it true that *we can never say in advance* that a given proposal has been drawn up by an incompetent researcher who doesn't know what he is looking for and wouldn't recognize it if he found it? What could be the grounds for peer review of research proposals if Gallistel's views were accepted? Why not draw straws instead? Those stirrings in the scientific community, away from unrestricted use of animals toward the refinement of one's protocol (thereby eliminating so-called unnecessary experiments) and reduction in the number of animals used, will find no support from the no-holds-barred approach Gallistel advocates. Since there is, in his view, no way to separate the scientific wheat from the chaff in advance of experimenting, why worry about refinement? Why worry about reduction?

These matters aside, the rights view rejects Gallistel's approach at a more fundamental level. On the rights view, we cannot justify harming a single rat *merely* by aggregating "the many human and humane benefits" that flow from doing it, since, as stated, this is to assume that the rat has value only as a receptacle, which, on the rights view, is not true. Moreover, the benefits argument that Gallistel deploys is deficient. Not even a single rat is to be treated as if that animal's value were reducible to his *possible utility* relative to the interests of others, which is what we would be doing if we intentionally harmed the rat on the grounds that this *just might* "prove" something, *just might* "yield" a "new insight," *just might* produce "benefits" for others.

It bears emphasizing that the rights view's critique of the use of animals in research is unlike some that find favor in the literature on this matter. Some object on methodological grounds, arguing that the results of such research offer very little hope of benefits for humanity because of the by-now well-established difficulty of extrapolating results from animals tests to the species *Homo sapiens*; others challenge the necessity of a variety of experiments, cases where animals have been cut, blinded, deformed, mutilated, shocked into "learned helplessness," and so on, all in the name of research. Neither of these critical approaches, though each has clear validity as far as it goes, gets to the moral heart of the matter. It is not that the methodology is suspect (though it is), nor that a great deal of research is, Gallistel's opinion to the contrary notwithstanding, known to be a waste of time before it is undertaken. The point to note is that both these challenges *invite the continuation of research on animals*, the latter because it would rule out only that research known to be a waste of time before it is conducted, and the former because it gives researchers a blank check to continue animal experiments in the hope of overcoming the deficiencies in the present methodology. If we are seriously to challenge the use of animals in research, we must challenge the *practice* itself, not only individual instances of it or merely the liabilities in its present methodology.

The rights view issues such a challenge. Routine use of animals in research assumes that their value is reducible to their possible utility relative to the interests of others. The rights view rejects this view of animals and their value, as it rejects the justice of institutions that treat them as renewable resources. They, like us, have a value of their own, logically independently of their utility for others and of their being the object of anyone else's interests. To treat them in ways that respect their

value, therefore, requires that we *not* sanction practices that institutional-
ize treating them as if their value was reducible to their possible utility
relative to our interests. Scientific research, when it involves routinely
harming animals in the name of possible "human and humane benefits,"
violates this requirement of respectful treatment. Animals are not to be
treated as mere receptacles or as renewable resources. Thus does the
practice of scientific research on animals violate their rights. Thus ought it
to cease, according to the rights view. It is not enough first conscientiously to look for nonanimal alternatives and then, having failed to find
any, to resort to using animals.[29] Though that approach is laudable as far
as it goes, and though taking it would mark significant progress, it does
not go far enough. It assumes that it is all right to allow practices that use
animals as if their value were reducible to their possible utility relative to
the interests of others, provided that we have done our best not to do so.
The rights view's position would have us go further in terms of "doing
our best." *The best we can do in terms of not using animals is not to use them.*
Their inherent value does not disappear just because we have failed to
find a way to avoid harming them in pursuit of our chosen goals. Their
value is independent of these goals and their possible utility in achieving
them.

A variant of the lifeboat case discussed earlier (see 8.6, 8.13, 9.1) is
likely to surface at this point, if not before. Let us suppose that the lifeboat
contains four normal adults and a dog. Provisions are plentiful this time,
and there is more than enough room. Only now suppose the humans
have a degenerative brain disease, while the dog is healthy. Also on
board, so it happens, is a new medicine that just might be the long-
awaited cure of the disease the humans have. The medicine has not been
tested. However, it is known to contain some potentially fatal compounds. The means exist to give the degenerative disease to the dog. In
these dire circumstances, would it be all right to do this and then to
administer the medicine to the animal to assess its curative properties?

Quite possibly most people would give an affirmative reply, at least
initially—but not those who subscribe to the rights view. Animals are not
to be treated as if their value were reducible *merely* to their possible utility
relative to human interests, which is what the survivors would be doing if
they made the healthy animal (who, after all, stands to gain nothing and
lose everything) run their risks in their stead.

Some might sieze upon this verdict of the rights view as a basis for
urging what they regard as a fatal objection: since most people think it
would be all right to give the medicine to the dog, since the rights view
allows appeals to what most people think as a basis for testing alternative

moral principles and theories, and since what most people think in this case conflicts with the verdict of the rights view, it follows, some may think, that the practice of using animals in harmful research is justifiable.

Three replies must suffice. First, just because most people think the dog should be treated as described, assuming that most do so, it does not follow that most people think well in this case. Our prereflective intuitions, as was explained in an earlier chapter (see 4.3ff.), must be tested reflectively to determine how well they stand up under the conscientious attempt to reach an ideal moral judgment. Without making this attempt, those who are content to appeal to "what most people think" have no rational basis to assume that what most people think in any given case is not based on their shared ignorance, their shared prejudices, or their shared irrationality. *Merely* to appeal to "what most people think," in other words, is not decisive in this, or in any other, moral context.

Second, even in those cases where a given belief continues to be held by most people *after* they have made a conscientious effort to remove the insidious effects of ignorance, prejudice, and the like, the possibility still remains that the belief in question stands in need of revision or abandonment. For if a given belief cannot be squared with moral principles that themselves pass the relevant tests for assessing their validity (namely, scope, precision, consistency, and conformity with a host of other intuitions that stand up on reflection), one must come to doubt the rational grounds of that belief and others like it in the relevant respects. Again, then, *merely* to announce that, after having given the matter one's conscientious attention, one still thinks that the dog should be treated as described in the lifeboat case, is not to mount a serious challenge to the rights view or its verdict in this case. A serious challenge can be raised only if, in addition to citing one's belief in this case, one also adduces the general principles that would support it and shows that these principles are equal or superior to the rights view when these principles are themselves subjected to the tests of scope, precision, and the like.

But third—and here we echo earlier observations (9.1)—the justice of policies or practices are not guaranteed by generalizing on one's judgment in exceptional cases; and lifeboat cases, as was mentioned earlier, are exceptional cases. To make the danger of generalizing on such cases clearer, imagine that the lifeboard contains four exceptional and one average human. Suppose the four are preeminent scientists, each on the verge of making discoveries that portend enormous health benefits for humanity. The fifth man delivers Twinkies to retail stores in Brooklyn. The four scientists have the degenerative brain disease. The Twinkies deliveryman does not. Would it be permissible to give the disease to him and then test for the drug's efficacy by administering it to him first? No doubt many people would be inclined to reply affirmatively (though not, again, those who subscribe to the rights view). Even among those who think the deliveryman should serve as the proverbial guinea pig in these exceptional circumstances, however, none with the slightest egalitarian tendencies would be willing to generalize on the basis of this unusual case and favor a policy or practice of doing research on average humans so that humans who are very bright or who make large social contributions might benefit. Such a practice leaves the bad taste of perfectionism in our mouths (see 7.1). The rights view categorically rejects perfectionism as a basis for assessing the justice of practices involving humans, whether in science or elsewhere. And so should we all. But just as perfectionism is not an equitable basis for assessing the justice of practices involving humans, so it is an unacceptable basis for assessing the justice of practices involving animals. And it is implicit allegiance to perfectionism that would tempt one to sanction the harmful use of animals in research, their "lesser" value being "sacrificed" for the "greater" value of humanity. Grounded in the recognition of the equal inherent value of all those who have inherent value, the rights view denies that a distinction between lesser and greater should be made where the perfectionist defense of the use of animals in research requires it. Thus does it deplore the continuation of this practice.

The rights view does not oppose using what is learned from conscientious efforts to treat a sick animal (or human) to facilitate and improve the treatment tendered other animals (or humans). In *this* respect, the rights view raises no objection to the "many human and humane benefits" that flow from medical science and the research with which it is allied. What the rights view opposes are practices that cause intentional harm to laboratory animals (for example, by means of burns, shock, amputation, poisoning, surgery, starvation, and sensory deprivation) preparatory to "looking for something that just might yield some human or humane benefit." Whatever benefits happen to accrue from such a practice are irrelevant to assessing its tragic injustice. Lab animals are not our tasters; we are not their kings.

The tired charge of being antiscientific is likely to fill the air once more. It is a moral smokescreen. The rights view is not against research on animals, if this research does not harm these animals or put them at risk of harm. It is apt to remark, however, that this objective will not be accomplished merely by ensuring that test animals are anaesthetized, or given postoperative drugs to ease their suffering, or kept in clean cages with ample food and water, and so forth. For it is not only the pain and suffering that matters—though they certainly matter—but it is the *harm* done to the animals, including the diminished welfare opportunities they endure as a result of the deprivations caused by the surgery, *and* their untimely death. It is unclear whether a *benign* use of animals in research is possible or, if possible, whether scientists could be persuaded to practice it. That being so, and given the serious risks run by relying on a steady supply of human volunteers, research should take the direction away from the use of any moral agent or patient. If nonanimal alternatives are available, they should be used; if they are not available, they should be sought. That is the moral challenge to research, given the rights view, and it is those scientists who protest that this "can't be done," in advance of the scientific commitment to try—not those who call for the exploration— who exhibit a lack of commitment to, and belief in, the scientific enter- prise—who are, that is, antiscientific at the deepest level. Like Galileo's contemporaries, who would not look through the telescope because they had already convinced themselves of what they would see and thus saw no need to look, those scientists who have convinced themselves that there can't be viable scientific alternatives to the use of whole animals in research (or toxicity tests, etc.) are captives of mental habits that true science abhors.

The rights view, then, is far from being antiscientific. On the con- trary, as is true in the case of toxicity tests, so also in the case of research: it calls upon scientists *to do science* as they redirect the traditional practice of their several disciplines away from reliance on "animal models" toward the development and use of nonanimal alternatives. All that the rights view prohibits is science that violates individual rights. If that means that there are some things we cannot learn, then so be it. There are also some things we cannot learn by using humans, if we respect their rights. The rights view merely requires moral consistency in this regard.

The rights view's position regarding the use of animals in research cannot be fairly criticized on the grounds that it is antihumanity. The implications of this view in this regard are those that a rational human being should expect, especially when we recall that nature neither re- spects nor violates our rights (see 8.2). Only moral agents do; indeed, only moral agents *can*. And nature is not a moral agent. We have, then, no basic right against nature not to be harmed by those natural diseases we are heir to. And neither do we have any basic right against humanity in this regard. What we do have, at this point in time at least, is a right to fair treatment on the part of those who have voluntarily decided to offer treatment for these maladies, a right that will not tolerate the preferential treatment of some (e.g., Caucasians) to the detriment of others (e.g.,

Native Americans). The right to fair treatment of our naturally caused maladies (and the same applies to mental and physical illnesses brought on by human causes, e.g. pollutants) is an *acquired right* we have against those moral agents who acquire the duty to offer fair treatment because they voluntarily assume a role within the medical profession. But those in this profession, as well as those who do research in the hope that they might improve health care, are not morally authorized to override the *basic rights* of others in the process—rights others have, that is, independently of their place in any institutional arrangement and independently of any voluntary act on the part of anyone (see 8.3ff.). And yet that is what is annually done to literally millions of animals whose services, so to speak, are enlisted in the name of scientific research, including that research allied with medical science. For this research treats these animals as if their value is reducible to their possible utility relative to the interests of others. Thus does it routinely violate their basic right to respectful treatment. Though those of us who today are to be counted among the beneficiaries of the human benefits obtained from this research in the past might stand to lose some future benefits, at least in the short run, if this research is stopped, the rights view will not be satisfied with anything less than its total abolition. Even granting that we face greater prima facie harm than laboratory animals presently endure if future harmful research on these animals is stopped, and even granting that the number of humans and other animals who stand to benefit from allowing this practice to continue exceeds the number of animals used in it, this practice remains wrong because unjust.

A further objection has a distinctively contractarian flavor. As a society, it might be claimed, we have decided that the use of animals for scientific purposes, even their harmful use, is permissible. Anyone who becomes a scientist in a nation that supports science by the use of public funds *acquires the duty to serve the public will*, and the public has a right against scientists to do so. Since the harmful use of animals in pursuit of scientific purposes is necessary if science is to fulfill the terms of its contract with society, the existence of this contract is a special consideration that justifies the continued use of animals in science.

The rights view is not unsympathetic to appeals to contracts and other voluntary arrangements as a basis for validating acquired duties and correlative rights. As was observed in an earlier discussion of these issues (8.12), however, the moral validity of a contract or other voluntary arrangement is not shown just by establishing that certain individuals voluntarily entered into a given agreement. Moral validity depends upon the respectful treatment of all those involved, not just those who enter into the agreement. A slave-trader does not do what is right by supplying his client with a promised slave, and he has no valid moral duty to do so, despite his promising to do so. Since the institution of slavery treats slaves with a lack of respect, promises made in the name of the perpetuation of this institution are morally null and void. The same is true regarding society's "contract" with science and the supposed duty of scientists to carry out their end of the agreement by harming some animals so that others, both humans and animals, might benefit. This "contract" has no moral validity, according to the rights view, because it fails to treat lab animals with the respect they are due. That science that routinely harms animals in pursuit of its goals is morally corrupt, because unjust at its core, something that no appeal to the "contract" between society and science can alter. What is required is a new contract, one that takes account of, and respects, those currently exploited by the existing one, a contract that, if it cannot be drawn up and enforced by education and opinion, will have to take the form of law. Only then will society's contract with science constitute a valid special consideration.

Though the efforts of many are needed to forge the terms of this new contract, the efforts of veterinarians are especially important. Veterinarians are the closest thing society has to a potential role model for the morally enlightened care of animals. It is, therefore, an occasion for deep anguish to find members of this profession increasingly in the employ of, or rendering their services to, the very industries that routinely violate the rights of animals—the farm animal industry and the lab animal industry, for example. On the rights view, veterinarians are obliged to extricate themselves and their profession from the financial ties that bind them to these industries and to dedicate their extensive medical knowledge and skills, as *healers*, as *doctors of medicine*, to projects that are respectful of their patients' rights. The first signatures in the new contract involving justice and animals should be from those who belong to the profession of veterinary medicine. To fail to lead the way in this regard will bespeak a lack of moral vision or courage (or both) that will permanently tarnish the image of this venerable profession and those who practice it.

A final objection urges that the rights view cannot have any principled objection to using mammalian animals for scientific purposes generally, or in research in particular, before these animals attain the degree of physical maturity that makes it reasonable to view them as subjects-of-a-life, in the sense that is central to the rights view (see 7.5). For example, use of newly born mammalian animals must stand outside the scope of the proscriptions issued by the rights view.

This objection is half right. *If certain conditions are met*, the rights view could sanction the scientific use of mammalian animals at certain stages of their physical development. As has been remarked on more than one occasion in the preceding, however, where one draws the line, both as regards what species of animals contain members who are subjects-of-a-life and as regards when a given animal acquires the abilities necessary for being such a subject, is controversial. We simply do not know, with anything approaching certainty, exactly where to draw the line in either case. Precisely because we are so palpably ignorant about a matter so fraught with moral significance, we ought to err on the side of caution, not only in the case of humans but also in the case of animals. Though during the earliest stages of development it is most implausible to regard a fetal mammalian animal as conscious, sentient, and so on, it becomes increasingly less implausible as the animal matures physically, acquiring the physical basis that underlies consciousness, perception, sentience, and the like. Although throughout the present work attention has been for the most part confined to normal mammalian animals, aged one or more, it does not follow that animals less than one year of age may be treated in just any way we please. Because we do not know exactly where to draw the line, it is better to give the benefit of the doubt to mammalian animals less than one year of age who have acquired the physical charac-teristics that underlie one's being a subject-of-a-life. The rights view's position concerning those animals, then, is against their use for scientific purposes.

There are Kantian-like grounds that strengthen the case against using newborn and soon-to-be born mammalian animals in science. To allow the routine use of these animals for scientific purposes would most likely foster the attitude that animals are just "models," just "tools," just "resources." Better to root out at the source, than to allow to take root, attitudes that are inimical to fostering respect for the rights of animals. Just as in the analogous areas of abortion and infanticide in the case of humans (8.12), therefore, the rights view favors policies that foster re-spect for the rights of the individual animal, even if the creation of these attitudes requires that we treat some animals who may not have rights as if they have them.

Finally, even in the case of mammalian animals in the earliest stages of fetal development, the rights view does not issue a blank check for their use in science. For though, on the rights view, we do not owe a duty of justice to these fetuses, we do owe justice to those animals who would be enlisted to produce them in the number researchers are likely to desire. Were mature animals used as "fetal machines" and, as a result, were they housed in circumstances conducive to their reproducing at the desired rate, it is most unlikely that the rights of these mature animals would be respected. For example, it is very unlikely that *these* animals would be provided with a physical environment conducive to the exercise of their preference autonomy, or one that was hospitable to their social needs; and it is equally unlikely that they would avoid having their life brought to an untimely end, well in advance of their having reached a condition where killing them could be defended on grounds of preference-respecting or paternalistic euthanasia. Once they had stopped reproducing, they would likely be killed. To the extent that we have reason to believe that these mature mammals would be treated as if they had value only relative to human purposes, to that extent the rights view would oppose the scientific use of fetal mammalian animals, not because these latter have rights that would be violated, but because this would be true in the case of the mature animals used as breeders. Those who would use mammalian animals in the earliest stages of their fetal development, then, may do so, according to the rights view, but only if they ensure *both* that (1) the lab animals used to produce the fetuses are treated with the respect they are due *and* that (2) reliance on mammalian fetuses does not foster beliefs and attitudes that encourage scientists to use mature mammalian animals for scientific purposes, including research. It is unclear that science could institute policies that satisfied the first condition. It is clear that a policy could be introduced that satisfied the second. This would be for science to cease using mammalian animals who are subjects-of-a-life in ways that harm them directly, or that put them at risk of harm, or that foster an environment in which their harm is allowed. That is a policy the rights view could allow,[30] but one science has yet to adopt.

Animals in Science, Utilitarianism, and Animal Rights

The fundamental differences between utilitarianism and the rights view are never more apparent than in the case of the use of animals in science. For the utilitarian, whether the harm done to animals in pursuit of scientific ends is justified depends on the balance of the aggregated consequences for all those affected by the outcome. If the consequences that result from harming animals would produce the best aggregate balance of good over evil, then harmful experimentation is obligatory. If the resulting consequences would be at least as good as what are otherwise obtainable, then harmful experimentation is permissible. Only if harmful experimentation would produce less than the best consequences would it be wrong. For a utilitarian to oppose or support harmful experimentation on animals, therefore, requires that he have the relevant facts—who will be benefited or harmed, how much, and so on. *Everyone's* interests, including the interests of those who do the tests or conduct the research, their employers, the dependents of these persons, the retailers and wholesalers of cages, animal breeders, and others, must be taken into account and counted equitably. For utilitarians, such *side effects count*. The animals used in the test have no privileged moral status. Their interests must be taken into account, to be sure, but not any more than anybody else's interests.

As is "almost always" the case, utilitarians simply fail to give us what is needed—the relevant facts, facts that we must have, given their theory, to determine whether use of animals in science is or is not justified. Moreover, for a utilitarian to claim or imply that there must be something wrong with a given experiment, if the experimenter would not be willing to use a less intelligent, less aware human being but would be willing to use a more intelligent, more aware animal, simply lacks a utilitarian basis. For all we know, and for all the utilitarian has thus far told us, the consequences of using such an animal, all considered, might be better than those that would result from using the human being. It is not *who* is used, given utilitarian theory, that matters; it is *the consequences* that do.

The rights view takes a very different stand. No one, whether human or animal, is ever to be treated as if she were a mere receptacle, or as if her value were reducible to her possible utility for others. We are, that is, never to harm the individual merely on the grounds that this will or just might produce "the best" aggregate consequences. To do so is to violate the rights of the individual. That is why the harm done to animals in pursuit of scientific purposes is wrong. The benefits derived are real enough; but some gains are ill-gotten, and all gains are ill-gotten when secured unjustly.

So it is that the rights view issues its challenge to those who do science: advance knowledge, work for the general welfare, but not by allowing practices that violate the rights of the individual. These are, one might say, the terms of the new contract between science and society, a contract that, however belatedly, now contains the signature of those who speak for the rights of animals. *Those who accept the rights view, and who sign for animals, will not be satisfied with anything less than the total abolition of the harmful use of animals in science—in education, in toxicity testing, in basic research.* But the rights view plays no favorites. No scientific practice that violates human rights, whether the humans be moral agents or moral patients, is acceptable. And the same applies to those humans who, for reasons analogous to those advanced in the present chapter in regard to nonhumans, should be given the benefit of the doubt about having rights because of the weight of our ignorance—the newly born and the soon-to-be born. Those who accept the rights view are committed to denying any and all access to these "resources" on the part of those who do science. And we do this not because we oppose cruelty (though we do), nor because we favor kindness (though we do), but because justice requires nothing less.

9.5 SUMMARY AND CONCLUSION

This chapter traced some of the implications of the rights view. On this view, animal agriculture, as we know it, is unjust (9.1), and it is unjust because it fails to treat farm animals with the respect they are due, treating them instead as renewable resources having value only relative to human interests. Animal agriculture, as we know it, is wrong, not only when farm animals are raised in close confinement in factory farms, but also when they are raised "humanely," since even in this case their lives are routinely brought to an untimely end because of human interests rather than on grounds of preference-respecting or paternalistic euthanasia. Those who support current animal agriculture by purchasing meat have a moral obligation to stop doing so. There is no credible basis for claiming that consumers would be made worse-off than the animals involved if consumers became vegetarians, and though those whose quality of life currently is tied to the vitality of the animal industry might be made worse-off if that industry fails, their voluntary participation in that business signals that they waive the right not to be made worse-off if the business fails. We do not owe it to any farmer, meat packer, or wholesaler to buy their products, and neither do we owe this to their dependents. It is no criticism of the rights view, moreover, to note that, once deprived of a suitable economic incentive to raise farm animals, farmers will raise few (if any) animals for commercial gain, since it is the justice of how individual animals are treated, not the number of domesticated animals there are, that is morally central. To protest that farm animals, as legal property, may be treated in whatever way their legal owners see fit is lame, first, because what is legal is not necessarily moral, and, second, because the rights view challenges the very conception of animals as legal property. In sharp contrast to the utilitarian basis of the obligation to be vegetarian, the rights view holds that the individual has a duty to lead a vegetarian way of life independently of knowing how many others are doing so and independently of knowing how large or small is the vegetarian impact on the market in meat. *The individual is right to withhold support from institutions that violate the rights of others, even if the individual is the only one to do so.* Like utilitarian advocates of vegetarianism, however, those who subscribe to the rights view call upon individual vegetarians to do more than simply abstain. *The rights view will not be satisfied with anything less than the total dissolution of the animal industry as we know it.*

Hunting and trapping, whether for sport or commerce, were assessed from the perspective of the rights view (9.2). Both were roundly condemned. The pleasures derived from these sports (e.g., communion with nature) can be secured without killing animals, and the commercial exploitation of wildlife erroneously assumes that the value of wild animals is reducible to their utility relative to human interests, especially economic interests. To attempt to avoid these criticisms by taking refuge in the philosophy of maximum sustainable yield is unsuccessful. That philosophy perpetuates the view that wild animals are a renewable resource, having value only relative to human interests; thus does it perpetuate, rather than correct, an impoverished view of the value of these animals. Moreover, the successful implementation of the philosophy of maximum sustainable yield would actually maximize, rather than reduce, the total number of animals that would be killed and the total number that would endure a "bad death" as a result of starvation, a hunter's poor shot, and so on. Sport and commercial hunters and trappers do not do wildlife any favor, are not "friends of wildlife," by practicing the philosophy of maximum sustainable yield. Wildlife managers who subscribe to this philosophy are part of the problem, not part of the solution. *In general, the rights view's position is to let wildlife be. Wildlife management ought to be designed to protect wild animals against hunters, trappers, and other moral agents.* This will require the abolition of the traditions of legalized hunting and trapping as well as the dismantling of all commerce in wild animals (e.g., the fur industry and whaling).

Because paradigmatic right-holders are individuals, and because individuals do not acquire any further rights if they belong to rare or endangered species, the rights view does not acknowledge any privileged moral status on the part of members of rare or endangered species of animals (9.3). However, the rights view is not opposed to efforts to save rare or endangered animals. It only insists that these animals be protected because they are animals, not because they are rare or endangered. Moreover, to the extent that efforts to protect rare and endangered species foster beliefs and attitudes that place less importance on the value of plentiful animals, to that extent the rights view must lodge its strong moral dissent. All animals are equal, both the plentiful and the rare.

The central importance of *the individual*, given the rights view, poses unresolved questions about the ability of those who subscribe to it to develop an environmental ethic. At least at the level of theory, the rights view is at odds with the holistic or systems approach that characterizes much of contemporary thought about the environment (environmental fascism, so-called). In particular, the rights view rejects the aggregative implications of a theory like Leopold's, an approach that would have us assess the morality of what we do by summing the consequences for members of the biotic community, approving of what brings about "the best" consequences for the community, disapproving of what brings about less than "the best." The rights view rejects this approach to moral decision making and the theory of the value of the individual on which it rests. At the level of practice, however, the implications of the rights view, especially regarding wilderness preservation, could well be in harmony with the causes championed by environmentalists. Though a rights-based environmental ethic has yet to be formulated, let alone adequately assessed, such an ethic remains a live theoretical option. It should not be dismissed out of hand.

The use of animals in science was the final area for which the major implications of the rights view were set forth (9.4). For a variety of reasons, the rights view takes a principled stand against the use of animals in educational contexts, in toxicity testing of new products and drugs, and in research. Dissection of living mammalian animals in high school and university lab sections is to be condemned, all the more so since the relevant knowledge obtained by this practice can be secured without engaging in it. To anesthetize these animals will not avoid the rights view's condemnation, since it is the animals' untimely death, not merely their pain or suffering, that is morally relevant. To the objection that most animals used in high school and university labs are not mammals and so do not fall within the scope of the principles advocated by the rights view, it was noted that (1) where we draw the line between those animals that are, and those that are not, subjects-of-a-life is far from certain, so that we ought to err on the side of caution, giving animals the benefit of the doubt in many cases, including the present one, and that (2) routine use of even nonmammalian animals fosters beliefs and attitudes that contribute to acceptance of acts and institutions that fail to show respect for, and thus violate the rights of, mammalian animals. Both reasons provide compelling grounds for discontinuing standard lab sections in high school and university courses in the life sciences.

Among the reasons offered against using animals in toxicity tests, the principal one is that risks are not transferable in the way reliance on this use of animals assumes. Whether in the case of new products or new drugs, individuals do not have a right to have the risks they can voluntarily choose to run or not run established or minimized by forcing others to find out what risks there are. The good consequences for others that do (or might) result are not relevant to the moral justification of toxicity tests any more than they are relevant in other cases where laudable ends are secured by reprehensible means. We are not to do injustice that good may come, not coercively to put others at risk of harm, or harm them, so that others might establish or minimize their risks. *To approve toxicity tests on laboratory animals is to sanction the routine violation of their rights. On the rights view, all such tests must be stopped.* This is not to say that toxicity tests should come to an end. On the contrary, inasmuch as it is desirable to minimize the risks we run if we choose to use a new product or new drug, the rights view applauds the development of valid scientific procedures that protect our interests in this regard, calling upon the involved commercial interests and the affected government regulatory agencies to make a conscientious commitment to protect humans in the home and workplace. *All that the rights view prohibits are procedures that violate the rights of individuals. It is not reduction of the number of animals that is required, nor refinement of one's protocol. The rights view calls for the total elimination of the use of animals in toxicity tests.*

The same call is made by the rights view when it comes to the use of animals in research. To harm animals on the chance that something beneficial for others might be discovered is to treat these animals as if their value were reducible to their possible utility relative to the interests of others, and to do this, not to a few, but to many millions of animals is to treat the affected animals as if they were a renewable resource—renewable because replaceable without any wrong having been done, and a resource because their value is assumed to be a function of their possible utility relative to the interests of others. *The rights view abhors the harmful use of animals in research and calls for its total elimination.* Because animals have a kind of value that is not the same as, is not reducible to, and is incommensurate with their having utility relative to the interests of others, because they are owed treatment respectful of their value as a matter of strict justice, and because the routine use of laboratory animals in research fails to treat these animals with the respect they are due, their use in research is wrong because unjust. The laudatory achievements of science, including the many genuine benefits obtained for both humans and animals, do not justify the unjust means used to secure them. As in other cases, so in the present one, the rights view does not call for the cessation of scientific research. Such research should go on—but not at the expense of laboratory animals. The overarching challenge of scientific research is the same as the similar challenge for toxicology and all other facets of the scientific enterprise: to do science without violating anyone's rights, be they human or animal.

The rights view does not deny in principle that use of mammalian embryos in science, including research, might be justified. Fetuses in the early stages of their development can be used, according to the rights view, if we have good reason to believe that allowing their use will not foster beliefs and attitudes that sanction treatment violative of the rights of those animals who have rights, in particular the rights of those animals used as breeders. Though it is not clear that this challenge can be met, it is clear that it cannot be met if scientists themselves continue to use *both* mammalian embryos *and* mature animals. An essential part of the evidence necessary to justify use of mammalian embryos, therefore, consists in scientists not using mature mammalian animals (or other mammalian animals who, though less than one year old, ought to be given the benefit of the doubt). As such, the rights view will take seriously a defense of the use of mammalian embryos only when scientists themselves cease using mammals at later stages of their life. But not until then. The onus of proof is where it belongs.[31]

Epilogue

*I*n issuing its condemnation of established cultural practices, the rights view is not antibusiness, not antifreedom of the individual, not antiscience, not antihuman. It is simply projustice, insisting only that the scope of justice be seen to include respect for the rights of animals. To protest against the rights view that justice applies only to moral agents, or only to human beings, and that we are within our rights when we treat animals as renewable resources, or replaceable receptacles, or tools, or models, or things—to protest in these terms is not to meet the challenge the rights view places before those who would reject it. On the contrary, it is unwittingly to voice the very prejudices it has been the object of the present work to identify and refute.

But prejudices die hard, all the more so when, as in the present case, they are insulated by widespread secular customs and religious beliefs, sustained by large and powerful economic interests, and protected by the common law. To overcome the collective entropy of these forces-against-change will not be easy. The animal rights movement is not for the faint of heart. Success requires nothing less than a revolution in our culture's thought and action. At this moment in our cultural evolution we are as far removed from having an accurate conception of the moral status of animals as Stefan Lochner was from having an accurate image of a lion. How we change the dominant misconception of animals—indeed, whether we change it—is to a large extent a political question. Might does not make right; might does make law. Moral philosophy is no substitute for political action. Still, it can make a contribution. Its currency is ideas, and though it is those who act—those who write letters, circulate petitions, demonstrate, lobby, disrupt a fox hunt, refuse to dissect an animal or to use one in "practice surgery," or are active in other ways—though these are the persons who make a mark on a day-to-day basis, history shows that ideas do make a difference. Certainly it is the ideas of those who have gone before—the Salts, the Shaws, and more recent thinkers—who have helped move the call for the recognition of animal rights, in the words of Mill that serve as this book's motto, past the stage of ridicule to that of discussion. It is to be hoped that the publication of this book will play some role in advancing this great movement, the animal rights movement, toward the third and final stage—the stage of adoption. To borrow words used in a different context by the distinguished American photographer Ansel Adams, "We are on the threshold of a new revelation, a new awakening. But what we have accomplished up to this time must be multiplied a thousandfold if the great battles are to be joined and won."

Notes

1: ANIMAL AWARENESS

1. See, for example, Plato *Republic* 9.571C.

2. Father Joseph Rickaby, S.J., "Ethics and Natural Law," *Moral Philosophy* (1901; reprint in *Animal Rights and Human Obligations*, ed. Tom Regan and Peter Singer [Englewood Cliffs, N.J.: Prentice-Hall, 1976]), p. 180.

3. Mary Midgley, *Beast and Man* (Ithaca: Cornell University Press, 1979), p. 1.

4. René Descartes, *Discourse on Method* (portions reprinted in *Animal Rights*, ed. Regan and Singer), p. 62.

5. John Cottingham, " 'A Brute to the Brutes?': Descartes' Treatment of Animals," *Philosophy* 53, no. 206 (October 1978): 551—559.

6. From *Descartes: Philosophical Letters*, trans. and ed. Anthony Kenny (Oxford: Oxford University Press, 1970; reprint in *Animal Rights*, ed. Regan and Singer), p. 66.

7. E. Haldane and G. Ross, eds., *Philosophical Works of Descartes* (London: Cambridge University Press, 1911) 2, 251: AT 7, 436—437.

8. Cottingham, "Descartes' Treatment of Animals," p. 557.

9. Ibid., p. 551.

10. Quoted in Leonora Rosenfield, *From Beast-Machine to Man-Machine* (New York: Columbia, 1968), p. 54.

11. As reported in Keith Gunderson, "Descartes, La Mettrie, Language and Machines," *Philosophy* 39, no. 149 (July 1964): 202.

12. From a letter to Henry More (5 February 1649), in Kenny, *Descartes: Philosophical Letters* (reprint in *Animal Rights*, ed. Regan and Singer), p. 66.

13. Ibid., p. 65.

14. For a fuller discussion of and a comparison between the views of Descartes and La Mettrie, see Gunderson, "Descartes and La Mettrie."

15. Kenny, *Descartes: Philosophical Letters*, p. 208 (reprint in *Animal Rights*, ed. Regan and Singer, p. 64).

16. La Mettrie suggests that Descartes's views on the human mind (soul) was

a concession he made to the powerful theologians of his day. Descartes's teaching regarding the human mind, La Mettrie writes, is "plainly but a trick of skill, a ruse of style, to make theologians swallow a poison hidden in the shape of an analogy. . . . For it is this, this strong analogy (between human and animal behavior), which forces all scholars and wise judges to confess that these proud and vain beings (i.e., theologians in particular and humans in general), more distinguished by their pride than by the name of men however much they wish to exalt themselves, are at bottom only machines which, though upright, walk on all fours." Quoted in Gunderson, "Descartes and La Mettrie," p. 212.

17. From a letter from Descartes to the Marquess of Newcastle, in Kenny, *Descartes: Philosophical Letters* (reprint in *Animal Rights*, ed. Regan and Singer), pp. 63–64.

18. For additional relevant passages, see the selections by Descartes in *Animal Rights*, ed. Regan and Singer. It is not clear that Descartes always held the same view about language and consciousness. The passage just quoted seems to support interpreting him as believing that the inability to use a language proves that that individual lacks consciousness. That is the view examined here. On at least one occasion, however, Descartes seems to soften this hard line position, writing that "though I regard it as established that we cannot prove there is any thought in animals, I do not think it is thereby proved that there is not, since the human mind does not reach into their hearts. But when I investigate what is most probable in this matter, I see no argument for animals having thoughts except the fact that since they have . . . sense-organs like ours, it seems likely they have sensation like us; and since thought is included in our mode of sensation, similar thought seems to be attributable to them" (from Descartes's letter to Henry More, *Philosophical Letters*). Descartes then proceeds to undermine this argument by, among other things, arguing that animals cannot use a language. The direct criticism offered in the pages that follow contests the hard line position. The subsequent argument advanced in this chapter, in favor of an evolutionary understanding of animal nature, provides an alternative to his view concerning what is most probable in this matter.

19. *New York Times*, 29 May 1974, p. 52. For a similar, fuller account, see Peter Jenkins, "Ask No Questions," *The Guardian* (London) 10 July 1973; reprint in *Animal Rights*, ed. Regan and Singer.

20. Herbert S. Terrace, *Nim: A Chimpanzee Who Learned Sign Language* (New York: Random House, 1979), p. 210.

21. Ibid., p. 215.

22. Ibid., p. 218.

23. Ibid., p. 221.

24. Charles Darwin, *The Descent of Man* (London: 1871; excerpted in *Animal Rights*, ed. Regan and Singer), p. 72.

25. Ibid., p. 80.

26. D. R. Griffin, *The Question of Animal Awareness: Evolutionary Continuity of Mental Experience* (New York: The Rockefeller University Press, 1976), p. 85.

27. Ibid., p. 74.

28. Descartes, *The Meditations* (New York: The Liberal Arts Press, 1951), p. 25.

29. D. O. Hebb, "Emotion in Man and Animal," *Psychological Review* 53 (1946): 88 (quoted in Gareth B. Matthews, "Animals and the Unity of Psychology," *Philosophy* 53, no. 206 [October 1978]: 440).

30. Ibid.

31. Cottingham, "Descartes' Treatment of Animals," p. 558.

32. For some thoughtful suggestions in this regard, see Griffin, *Animal Awareness*, chap. 7.

33. Ibid., p. 104. Emphasis added.

34. To the best of my knowledge this expression originates with Val and Richard Routley. See, for example, their essay, "Against the Inevitability of Human Chauvinism," in *Moral Philosophy and the Twenty First Century*, ed. K. Goodpaster and K. Sayre (Notre Dame University Press, 1979). I do not mean to imply that the Routleys use "human chauvinism" in precisely the same way as I do.

35. George Pitcher saved me from a number of errors in this and the next chapter by offering helpful criticisms. I am grateful to him for his assistance. I have, however, clung to some ideas he counseled letting go of, so I do not mean to imply that he would agree with all that I maintain. Also to be thanked is my colleague Harold Levin who discussed various aspects of animal awareness with me.

2: THE COMPLEXITY OF ANIMAL AWARENESS

1. Unless otherwise indicated, the word *animal* is used to refer to mammalian animals. For further discussion of this usage, see 2.5.

2. Griffin, *Question of Animal Awareness* (see chap. 1, n. 26), p. 74.

3. On the attribution of beliefs, desires and intentions to wild animals, see Thomas A. Long, "Hampshire on Animals and Intentions," *Mind* 72, no. 287 (July 1963): 414—416.

4. Stephen P. Stich, "Do Animals Have Beliefs?," *Australasian Journal of Philosophy* 57, no. 1 (March 1979): 17—18.

5. Ibid., pp. 15—17.

6. Ibid., p. 17.

7. Ibid., p. 18.

8. Ibid.

9. Tom Regan, "Frey On Why Animals Cannot Have Simple Desires," *Mind* 91 (1982): 277—280.

10. That beliefs of these forms figure in the analysis of desires is suggested by Joel Feinberg in "The Rights of Animals and Unborn Generations," *Philosophy and Environmental Crisis*, ed. W. T. Blackstone (Athens: University of Georgia Press, 1974), pp. 43—68 (reprint in Joel Feinberg, *Rights, Justice, and the Bounds of Liberty:*

Essays in Social Philosophy [Princeton: Princeton University Press, 1980], pp. 159—184). Frey writes approvingly of this analysis in R. G. Frey, *Interests and Rights: The Case Against Animals* (Oxford: The Clarendon Press, 1980), pp. 55ff.

11. See, e.g., Frey, *Interests and Rights*, pp. 108—110.

12. Ibid., p. 87.

13. The grounds for anticipating that Frey is likely to reply as depicted here are provided by the way he responds to a similar challenge to his analysis of desire. See ibid., pp. 55ff.

14. See, e.g., ibid., p. 58.

15. Ibid., pp. 57—58.

16. See ibid., pp. 89—91. For a similar argument, see Donald Davidson, "Thought and Talk," in *Mind and Logic*, ed. S. Gutterplan (Oxford: The University Press, 1975), pp. 7—23.

17. Ibid., p. 90.

18. Ibid., p. 91.

19. Ibid.

20. Stich, "Do Animals Have Beliefs?" p. 25.

21. Ibid., p. 26.

22. Ibid.

23. Ibid., p. 28.

24. Ibid., pp. 18—19.

25. Richard Routley makes this point in his critical discussion of Stich. See his "Alleged Problems in Attributing Beliefs and Intentionality to Animals," *Inquiry* 24, no. 4 (December 1981): 385—417.

26. Stich, "Do Animals Have Beliefs?" p. 19

27. Frey, *Interests and Rights*, pp. 111—112.

28. Ibid., p. 113.

29. Ibid., p. 108.

30. Stich, "Do Animals Have Beliefs?" pp. 23—24.

31. Frey would think otherwise, since Fido lacks language and so, Frey believes, lacks beliefs. Thus Frey would flatly deny that Fido has any particular belief (e.g., the preference-belief). Frey's grounds for his denial were found wanting in the preceding (2.3).

32. Stich, "Do Animals Have Beliefs?", p. 23.

33. Jonathan Bennett, *Linguistic Behavior* (Cambridge: Cambridge University Press, 1976), p. 118.

34. David Hume, *A Treatise Concerning Human Nature*, ed. L. A. Selby-Bugge (Oxford: The Clarendon Press, 1941), p. 176.

35. Thomas Nagel, "What Is It Like to Be a Bat?" in *Mortal Questions* (Cambridge: Harvard University Press, 1979), p. 168.

36. Frey, *Interest and Rights*, pp. 114—115. Frey gives a second argument that I do not discuss because it is deficient in the same way and for the same reasons as the one I do consider—viz., it asks an improper question about animal behavior because it treats behavior atomistically rather than holistically.

37. Frey is not alone in deploying an atomistic view of behavior and then arguing that we cannot say what someone believes on the basis of how he or she behaves. Bernard Harrison, to whom Frey acknowledges a debt, argues similarly against Johnathan Bennett's position that behavior constitutes grounds for attributions of belief. See Harrison's review of Bennett's *Linguistic Behavior* in *Mind* (October 1977), pp. 600—605.

38. Frey, *Interests and Rights*, writes that "perception involves not only sensory detection but comprehension by the mind . . . (or) . . . subsuming and thereby classifying the data of sense under concepts" (p. 119). Thus, where there are no concepts, Frey argues, there is no perception either—only "sensory detection." And since, on Frey's view, we cannot say what concepts animals have, or even that they have any, we also should be skeptical regarding whether they can or do perceive anything. If the argument presented in the foregoing is sound, Fido and similar animals must have general concepts, and we can say, at least in some cases, something about the content of their concepts. Even accepting the distinction between "perception" and "sensory detection," we are entitled to say that Fido, as well as many other animals, perceive. If they did not, they could not form preference-beliefs.

39. Gareth Matthews, "Animals and the Unity of Psychology," *Philosophy* 53, no. 206 (October 1978): 440.

40. This is not to deny the reality of, say, free-floating anxiety, only to insist that such phenomena are unusual precisely because they deviate from normal cases of emotions and feelings, cases that do involve beliefs of the kind characterized in the above.

41. Frey, *Interests and Rights*, p. 122.

42. Charles Darwin, "Comparison of the Mental Powers of Man and the Lower Animals," chaps. III and IV in *The Descent of Man* (London: 1871, reprint in *Animal Rights*, ed. Regan and Singer), pp. 72—81.

43. Hebb, "Emotion in Man and Animal" (see chap. 1, n. 29, p. 88).

3: ANIMAL WELFARE

1. R. B. Perry, *Realms of Value* (Cambridge: Harvard University Press, 1954), p. 7.

2. Nicholas Rescher, *Welfare: The Social Issues in Philosophical Perspective* (Pittsburgh: University of Pittsburgh Press, 1972), p. 16.

3. John Kleinig, "Crime and the Concept of Harm," *American Philosophical Quarterly* 15, no. 1 (January 1978): 38.

4. There is a use of the word *benefit* that allows us to say that satisfying a desire is a benefit (i.e., is beneficial) to the individual whose desire is satisfied. *Benefit* is not used in this way in the text since to do so would require that we distinguish between 'benefit$_1$' (what makes finding satisfaction possible, or expands the opportunity for satisfaction) and 'benefit$_2$' (the beneficial effect of finding satisfaction in one thing or another). On this distinction, see T. M. Benditt, "Benefit and

Harm," *Philosophy and Phenomenological Research* 37, no. 1 (1976): 116—120.

5. Jeremy Bentham, *The Principles of Morals and Legislation*, chap. XVII, Sec. I (1789; reprint, New York: Hafner, 1948), p. 311n.

6. For further remarks on these points, see, for example, my "The Moral Basis of Vegetarianism," *The Canadian Journal of Philosophy* 5, no. 3 (1975); reprint in Tom Regan, *All That Dwell Therein* (Berkeley, Los Angeles, London: University of California Press, 1982).

7. The claim is not being made that Bentham himself held the views that follow, only that what he says in the quoted passage would have permitted him to do so.

8. John Kleinig, "Crime and Harm," p. 27. Kleinig himself does not limit harm in this way.

9. Thomas Nagel appears to hold a similar position. See his essay, "Death," in *Mortal Questions* (see chap. 2, n. 36).

10. Now-classic accounts of factory farming are Ruth Harrison, *Animal Machines: The New Factory Farming Industry* (London: Stuart, 1964), and Peter Singer, *Animal Liberation* (New York: A New York Review Book, distributed by Random House, 1975, cloth, and New York: Avon Books, 1978, paper). A more recent and, in my view, the best study yet to be produced, is Jim Mason and Peter Singer, *Animal Factories* (New York: Crown Publishers, 1980).

11. See, for example, Barry Holstum Lopez, *Of Wolves and Men* (New York: Scribners, 1978).

12. See Mason and Singer, *Animal Factories*, pp. 21ff.

13. Ruth Cigman, "Death, Misfortune and Species Inequality," *Philosophy and Public Affairs* 10, no. 1 (Winter 1980): 47—64.

14. Bernard Williams, "The Markropolous Case," in *Problems of the Self* (Cambridge: Harvard University Press, 1973).

15. Cigman, "Death, Misfortune," p. 58.

16. Ibid., p. 57.

17. Ibid., p. 59. I assume that misfortunes and harms, when applied to humans and animals, are coextensive. It would not make any clear sense to say that something was a misfortune to Mary but that she was not harmed by it, or that, though she was harmed by something, she suffered no misfortune. Thus I assume that when Cigman denies that death is a misfortune for animals, she implies that it is not a harm for them either. My viewing matters in this way, whether sound or not, at least is not eccentric. In addition to Nagel ("Death"), see L. W. Sumner, "A Matter of Life and Death," *Nous* 10 (May 1976): 145—171.

18. Lopez, *Of Wolves and Men*, gives a number of examples of such behavior by wolves.

19. Ibid., p. 55.

20. Those who work to save the whale, for example, are unlikely to change how they talk because philosophers argue that "tragedy" is an idea that does not apply to the death of animals. These persons are likely to continue to think, and say, that the killing of whales by commercial whalers is tragic indeed. It must be a

somewhat narrow analysis of tragedy that would preclude the propriety of using language in this way.

21. Bernard Gert and Charles M. Culver, "Paternalistic Behavior," *Philosophy and Public Affairs* 6, no. 1 (Fall 1976): 53, emphasis added.

22. Ibid., p. 50.

23. Ann Palmeri, "Childhood's End: Toward the Liberation of Children," in *Whose Child?: Children's Rights, Parental Authority, and State Power*, ed. William Aiken and Hugh LaFollette (Totowa, N. J.: Littlefield, Adams & Co., 1980), p. 107. Culver and Gert also cite acting "for the good of one's plants" as a case where "paternalism" cannot literally be applied.

24. Ibid., p. 54.

25. Ibid., p. 53, emphasis added.

26. The present discussion of euthanasia owes much to James Rachel's essay, "Euthanasia," in *Matters of Life and Death*, ed. Tom Regan (New York: Random House, 1980), pp. 28—66.

27. John Stuart Mill, *Utilitarianism* (New York: The Liberal Arts Press, 1957), p. 14.

28. I have benefited from discussing the major ideas explored in this chapter with Sidney Gendin.

4: ETHICAL THINKING AND THEORY

1. Aristotle, *Nicomachean Ethics*, 1094: 25.

2. George Edward Moore, *Principia Ethica* (Cambridge: Cambridge University Press, 1903), p. x.

3. W. D. Ross, *The Right and the Good* (Oxford: The Clarendon Press, 1930).

4. John Rawls, *A Theory of Justice* (Cambridge: Harvard University Press, 1971).

5. See, for example, R. M. Hare, "Justice and Equality," in *Justice and Economic Distribution*, ed. John Arthur and William H. Shaw (Englewood Cliffs, N. J.: Prentice-Hall, 1978).

6. Peter Singer, *The Expanding Circle: Ethics and Sociobiology* (New York: Farrar, Straus & Giroux, 1981), p. 70.

7. Ibid., pp. 70—71.

8. Peter Singer, "Utilitarianism and Vegetarianism," *Philosophy and Public Affairs* 9, no. 8 (Summer 1980): 326. Singer argues this point at greater length in his "Sidgwick and Reflective Equilibrium," *The Monist* 58, no. 3 (July 1974): especially 515—517.

9. Dan W. Brock, "Utilitarianism," in *And Justice for All*, ed. Tom Regan and Donald VanDeVeer (Towota, N. J.: Rowman and Littlefield, 1981), p. 223.

10. Singer, "Sidgwick and Reflective Equilibrium," p. 494.

11. Singer, "Utilitarianism and Vegetarianism," p. 327.

12. See Peter Singer, *Practical Ethics* (Cambridge: Cambridge University Press, 1980), p. 87.

13. Most, but not all, utilitarians favor one of these two views. Moore provides an important counterinstance, maintaining that the intrinsic value of certain states of consciousness is not reducible to the pleasure or satisfaction they contain. This version of utilitarianism is not examined in the sequel. For a critique, see my "A Refutation of Utilitarianism," *Canadian Journal of Philosophy*, in press.

5: INDIRECT DUTY VIEWS

1. A reminder: unless otherwise indicated, the word *animal* refers to normal mammalians, aged one or more.

2. The view that our duties involving works of art, architecture, and nature are indirect duties to mankind, including future generations of human beings, is to be found, for example, in Feinberg, "The Rights of Animals and Unborn Generations" (see chap. 2, n. 11). Feinberg does not hold an indirect duty view with respect to animals.

3. Richard D. Ryder was the first to introduce this term as a way of capturing the kind of prejudice toward animals that he and others believe is essentially comparable to the prejudices of racism and sexism. See his *Victims of Science: The Use of Animals in Research* (London: Davis-Poynter, 1975). For further comments on speciesism, see 8.11.

4. Jan Narveson, "Animal Rights," *The Canadian Journal of Philosophy* 7, no. 1 (March 1977): 177.

5. Ibid.

6. Ibid.

7. Ibid., p. 177.

8. Ibid., p. 178.

9. Ibid.

10. Ibid., p. 177.

11. Ibid., p. 164.

12. John Rawls, "The Sense of Justice," *Philosophical Review* 72 (1963): 284.

13. Rawls, *A Theory of Justice* (see chap. 4, n. 4), p. 512.

14. Ibid., emphasis added.

15. Edward Johnson, *Species and Morality*, Ph.D. dissertation, Philosophy, Princeton University, July 1976 (University Microfilms International, 1977: Ann Arbor, Michigan), pp. 155–156. I have benefited from this work and commend it to the attention of others.

16. Rawls, *A Theory of Justice*, p. 511.

17. Ibid., p. 517.

18. It may be that a reinterpretation of the original position could provide a Rawlsian-like basis for our having direct duties to animals who have a welfare. On this, see Donald VanDeVeer, "Of Beasts, Persons, and the Original Position," *The Monist* 62 (1979): 368–377. I owe much to this paper. I believe, however, that VanDeVeer's position, like Rawls's, is vulnerable to the objection raised below (see 8.12) against all forms of contractarianism.

19. Though I have objections to speaking of a direct duty not to be cruel to animals, I shall allow this way of speaking in the discussion that follows. For my objections, see the discussion of the cruelty-kindness view at the beginning of the next chapter (6.1).

20. Rawls, *A Theory of Justice*, p. 512.

21. Ibid., pp. 114—115.

22. Ibid., p. 114.

23. Ibid., p. 115.

24. Ibid., p. 512.

25. Cf. ibid., p. 506.

26. Immanuel Kant, *The Groundwork of the Metaphysic of Morals*, trans. by H. J. Paton (New York: Harper and Row, 1964), p. 96.

27. Ibid., p. 70.

28. Ibid., p. 76.

29. Immanuel Kant, "Duties to Animals and Spirits," in *Lectures on Ethics*, trans. Louis Infield (New York: Harper and Row, 1963), pp. 239—241; reprint in *Animal Rights*, ed. Regan and Singer (see chap. 1, n. 2).

30. As quoted in John Vyvyan, *The Dark Face of Science* (London: Michael Joseph, 1971), p. 29.

31. Alexander Broadie and Elizabeth M. Pybus, "Kant's Treatment of Animals," *Philosophy* 49 (1974): 345.

32. Ibid., p. 382.

33. Ibid., p. 383.

34. "Kant and the Maltreatment of Animals," *Philosophy* 53 (1978): 560.

35. I believe it was my colleague, W. R. Carter, who, in discussions about Kant's views, first made this point clear to me.

36. Ross, *The Right and the Good* (see chap. 4, n. 3), p. 49.

6: DIRECT DUTY VIEWS

1. Locke writes as follows:

> One thing I have frequently observed in Children, that when they have got possession of any poor Creature, they are apt to use it ill: They often *torment*, and treat very roughly, young Birds, Butterflies, and such other poor Animals, which fall into their Hands, and that with a seeming kind of Pleasure. This I think should be watched in them, and if they incline to any such *Cruelty*, they should be taught the contrary Usage. For the Custom of Tormenting and Killing Beasts, will, by Degrees, harden their Minds even towards Men; and they who delight in the Suffering and Destruction of Inferior Creatures, will not be apt to be very compassionate, or benign to those of their own kind. . . .

(John Locke, *Some Thoughts Concerning Education*, 5th ed. (London: printed for A. and C. Churchill, 1905). See also James Axfell, ed., *The Educational Writings of John Locke* (Cambridge: Cambridge University Press, 1968), sec. 116, 225—226.

2. Here and throughout the discussion that follows so-called total utilitarianism is at issue. To discuss other forms (e.g., so-called average utilitarianism) would be to complicate the argument unnecessarily. The difficulties endemic to all forms of utilitarianism are perspicuously highlighted in Dan W. Brock, "Utilitarianism" (see chap. 4, n. 9).

3. Bentham, *The Principles of Morals and Legislation*, chap. XVII, sec. 1.

4. Ibid., p. 264.

5. Singer, *Practical Ethics* (see chap. 4, n. 12), p. 124.

6. Ibid., p. 12.

7. Peter Singer, "Animals and the Value of Life," in *Matters of Life and Death*, ed. Tom Regan (see chap. 3, n. 26), p. 238, emphasis added.

8. Singer, *Practical Ethics*, p. 81.

9. Singer, "Animals and the Value of Life," p. 235.

10. Ibid. Singer makes a comparable claim in "Killing Humans and Killing Animals," *Inquiry* 22, nos. 1–2 (1979). "Self-conscious beings . . . are not mere receptacles for containing a certain quantity of pleasure, and are not replaceable" (p. 153).

11. H. L. A. Hart, "Death and Utility," *The New York Review of Books*, 27 no. 8 (15 November 1980), p. 30.

12. Ibid.

13. Singer, *Practical Ethics*, pp. 10–11.

14. Peter Singer, "All Animals Are Equal," *Philosophical Exchange* 1, no. 5 (Summer 1974); reprint in *Animal Rights*, ed. Regan and Singer (see chap. 1, n. 2), p. 148. Page references are to the latter appearance of this essay. In a more recently published work, Singer continues to characterize equality as a moral or ethical principle. See his *Practical Ethics*, p. 18, where he writes that "equality is a basic ethical principle, not an assertion of fact."

15. Ibid., p. 152.

16. Ibid.

17. I assume that the problem of the *logical* relationship between the principles of utility and equality can and will arise for "cognitivist" and "noncognitivist" utilitarians alike, and thus that this problem could not be avoided by a Singer-type utilitarian who advocates a noncognitivist meta-ethic. In assuming that noncognitivist utilitarians can and will accept that logical relations hold between different moral prescriptions, I assume what noncognitivist utilitarians themselves profess. On this point, see R. M. Hare, *The Language of Morals* (Oxford: The Clarendon Press, 1952), especially chaps. 2, 3; and J. J. C. Smart's contribution to *Utilitarianism: For and Against* (Cambridge: The University Press, 1973), especially pp. 7–9.

18. Singer, "Utilitarianism and Vegetarianism" (see chap. 4, n. 8), pp. 328–329.

19. Ibid., p. 329.

20. Though a *possible* option, I know of no utilitarian who has chosen it. Certainly Singer, much to his credit, does not. To do so would, among other things, undermine his case for animal liberation, since the utility of counting the

interest animals have in avoiding pain as equal to the interest humans have in avoiding it might differ quite markedly.

21. Singer, *Practical Ethics*, p. 12.

22. On one occasion Hare observes that utilitarianism is "consistent" with his views on the meanings of the moral use of terms like 'right' and 'ought,' thus suggesting that he would accept what I have termed "the weak option." See his "Principles," *Proceedings of the Aristotelian Society*, 1972—1973, p. 15. On another occasion he argues that what I have termed the principle of conditional equality "leads to" or "yields" utilitarianism, thereby suggesting that he would accept "the strong option." See his "Ethical Theory and Utilitarianism," in *Contemporary British Philosophy*, ed. H. D. Lewis (London, 1976), pp. 116—117. I believe, though I shall not argue the point here, that Hare's arguments are open to all the same (and more) objections raised against Singer's attempt to generate utilitarianism out of the conditional equality principle. It is also worth noting that Singer, for one, though acknowledging a debt to Hare for the use of the idea of getting utilitarianism from conditional equality, makes it clear that he does not think the argument shows as much as he thinks Hare supposes. "The tentative argument for a utilitarianism based on interests or preferences owes most to Hare's 'Ethical Theory and Utilitarianism,' although it does not go as far as the argument in that article" (*Practical Ethics*, p. 222). Singer, then, evidently interprets Hare as selecting what I have labeled "SO_1"—i.e., "Strong Option$_1$." I believe this is the most reasonable interpretation of Hare.

23. Singer, *Practical Ethics*, p. 13.

24. Ibid., pp. 12—13.

25. For reasons I advance elsewhere, I do not think anyone does commit himself to this consequentialist principle, even granting we concede Singer his assumptions. Indeed, to the extent that preference utilitarianism relies on a preference theory of value, not only does Singer's consequentialist principle not follow from the reasons he gives in its support, but that principle actually is inconsistent with the preference theory of value. On these matters, see my "Equality and Utility: Some Neglected Problems," *The Journal of Value Inquiry*, in press. Even if I am mistaken about the charge of inconsistency leveled in that paper, there are more than enough reasons for refusing to accept the consequentialist principle Singer defends. See, for example, the argument given below, 8.12.

26. Singer, "All Animals Are Equal," p. 148.

27. Singer, *Animal Liberation* (see chap. 3, no. 10), p. 21.

28. Peter Singer, "The Parable of the Fox and the Unliberated Animals," *Ethics* 88, no. 2 (January 1978): 122.

29. Singer, "All Animals Are Equal," p. 155.

30. See Garrett Hardin, "Lifeboat Ethics: The Case Against Helping the Poor," *Psychology Today* (September 1974); Peter Singer, "Famine, Affluence and Morality," *Philosophy and Public Affairs* 1, no. 3 (Spring 1972). Both are reprinted in *World Hunger and Moral Obligation*, ed. W. Aiken and H. LaFollette (Englewood Cliffs, N. J.: Prentice-Hall, 1977).

31. See, e.g., Singer, "All Animals Are Equal."

32. Singer, "Utilitarianism and Vegetarianism," p. 335.

7: JUSTICE AND EQUALITY

1. The discussion of justice and equality in this chapter owes a debt to an essay on this topic by David A. J. Richards. See his "Justice and Equality," in *And Justice for All*, ed. Regan and VanDeVeer (see chap. 4, n. 9). I do not mean to suggest that Professor Richards would agree with the conclusions of the present chapter.

2. Singer has a stimulating essay entitled "All Animals Are Equal" (see chap. 6, n. 14). The equality Singer has in mind is the equality set forth in his equality principle and thus concerns counting equal interests equally. The equality of individuals—their having equal inherent value in their own right—is not what Singer means when *he* says "all animals are equal." It is what is meant here.

3. In an earlier essay I set forth views that are inconsistent with those advanced here. "It is not implausible," I wrote, "to suppose that normal, adult humans, because they can lead a life which can have a range of values (e.g., moral virtues) not obtainable by the severely mentally enfeebled, can themselves be regarded as having greater inherent value than the enfeebled" ("An Examination and Defense of One Argument Concerning Animal Rights," *Inquiry* 22, nos. 1−2 [1978]: 210; reprint in Regan, *All That Dwell Therein* [see chap. 3, n. 6], p. 137. This is unwittingly to commit me to a perfectionist theory of justice, a view that I now reject and should have rejected earlier.

4. Albert Schweitzer, *Civilization and Ethics*, pt. II of *The Philosophy of Civilization*, trans. C. T. Champion, 2d ed. (London, 1929), pp. 246−247.

5. Regan, "The Nature and Possibility of an Environmental Ethic," *Environmental Ethics* 3, no. 1 (Spring 1981): 19−34; reprint in Regan, *All That Dwell Therein*, pp. 184−205.

6. These points are argued at length in my "Feinberg on What Sorts of Beings Can Have Rights," *The Southern Journal of Philosophy* 14, no. 4 (1976): 485−498; reprint in Regan, *All That Dwell Therein*, pp. 165−183.

7. I am confused about this point in the essay cited in the previous note and have tried to clarify this muddle in the essay cited in note 5.

8. A particularly lucid survey of standard objections to rule utilitarianism is provided by Fred Feldman, *Introductory Ethics* (Englewood Cliffs, N. J.: Prentice-Hall, 1978), pp. 61 ff.

9. Hare, "Justice and Equality" (see chap. 4, n. 5), p. 126.

10. Ibid., pp. 124−125.

8: THE RIGHTS VIEW

1. D. G. Ritchie, *Natural Rights* (London: Allen & Unwin, 1894). Relevant passages are included in *Animal Rights*, ed. Regan and Singer (see chap. 1, n. 2), p. 182.

2. Hare, "Justice and Equality" (see chap. 4, n. 5), p. 130.

3. Jeremy Bentham, "Pennomial Fragments," in *The Works of Jeremy Bentham*, ed. John Bowring (Edinburgh: W. Tait, 1843—59, V. III), p. 221.

4. Jeremy Bentham, "Anarchical Fallacies," in *The Works of Jeremy Bentham*, ibid., V. II, p. 501.

5. Mill, *Utilitarianism* (see chap. 3, no. 27), p. 66.

6. David Lyons "Human Rights and the General Welfare," in *Rights*, ed. David Lyons (Belmont, California: Wadsworth Publishing Co., 1979), p. 183.

7. Mill, *Utilitarianism*, p. 66.

8. Lyons, "Human Rights," p. 182.

9. Joel Feinberg, "The Nature and Value of Rights," *The Journal of Value Inquiry* 4 (Winter 1970); reprint in *Rights*, ed. David Lyons, p. 90, and in Feinberg, *Rights, Justice, and the Bounds of Liberty* (see chap. 2, n. 11). I have expressed my great debt to Professor Feinberg's work on more than one occasion in the past and do so again here. The analysis of claims-to, claims-against, etc., that is given in the pages that follow is, I believe, essentially the same as Feinberg's. It is the adequacy of this analysis, however, not its faithfulness to the spirit and letter of Feinberg's views, that is of cardinal importance. Moreover, though my own views on rights have been considerably influenced by my interpretation of his, it is unclear that Feinberg would agree with the conclusions I reach, especially in the case of animal rights. Feinberg argues that they *can* have rights—i.e., that attributing rights to them is not conceptually absurd. To my knowledge, however, he has never argued that animals *do* have rights.

10. Rawls, *A Theory of Justice* (see chap. 4, n. 4), pp. 114—115.

11. Ibid., p. 115.

12. In fact this is to concede more to opponents of the rights view than is required, since there are alternative analyses of moral rights, distinct from their analysis as valid claims, that are compatible with the argument for recognizing the moral rights of moral agents *and* patients.

13. H. J. McCloskey, "Rights," *Philosophical Quarterly* 15 (1965): 118. The analysis of rights as entitlements is defective. Whether you are entitled to do something must depend on whether it is permissible for you to do it (i.e., whether you would be doing wrong in doing it), and whether you are entitled to do it (i.e., whether you are within your rights to do it) must depend on whether, in doing it, you would be violating any right others have against you. The analysis of "what you are entitled to do" thus *uses* the notion of rights rather than *analyzing* that notion.

14. Feinberg, "The Nature and Value of Rights," p. 91.

15. Ross, *The Right and The Good* (see chap. 4, n. 3), p. 50.

16. For tokens of this argument in print, see Ritchie, *Natural Rights* (London: Allen & Unwin, 1916, 3d edition), pp. 107ff.; reprint in *Animal Rights and Human Obligations*, ed. Regan and Singer, pp. 181ff. See also Michael Martin, "A Critique of Moral Vegetarianism," *Reason Papers* 3 (1976): 13ff.

17. See, for example, W. R. Carter, "Once and Future People," *American Philosophical Quarterly* 17, no. 1 (1980): 66.

18. For stylistic reasons, "one's causing harm," "one's harming another," and other expressions sometimes will be used in place of the more cumbersome "one's doing something that harms another."

19. Jan Narveson, "Pacifism: A Philosophical Analysis," *Ethics* 75 (1965).

20. This point is argued at greater length in Tom Regan, "A Defense of Pacifism," *The Canadian Journal of Philosophy* (September 1972).

21. For a reply to the defense of pacifism just outlined, see Jan Narveson, "Violence and War," in *Matters of Life and Death*, ed. Tom Regan (see chap. 3, n. 26), pp. 117ff.

22. This example embellishes a similar one sketched by Robert Nozick, *Anarchy, State, and Utopia* (New York: Basic Books, 1974), p. 35.

23. For further comments on the innocence of moral patients, see Dale Jamieson and Tom Regan, "On the Ethics of the Use of Animals in Science," in *And Justice for All*, ed. Regan and VanDeVeer (see chap. 4, n. 9). I have benefited from discussing these ideas with Sidney Gendin.

24. "Should the Numbers Count?" *Philosophy and Public Affairs* 6, no. 4: 293–316.

25. Ibid., p. 306.

26. Ibid., pp. 307–308.

27. Ibid., p. 308.

28. In saying that the harms are prima facie comparable it is assumed that no one individual would be made worse-off than any other. Cases where someone, or some number, would be made worse-off are discussed below.

29. I must confess that I have not always been clear about this myself, since on more than one occasion I have stated or implied that individual rights can be justifiably overriden by appeal to the minimize harm principle. On this, see, for example, my "Animal Rights, Human Wrongs," *Environmental Ethics* (Summer 1980); reprinted in Regan, *All That Dwell Therein* (see chap. 3, n. 6) and in *Ethics and Animals*, ed. Harlan Miller and William Williams (Clifton, N. J.: Humana Press, 1982).

30. Gareth Matthews draws attention to some of the relevant empirical and conceptual issues regarding the psychological abilities of the fetus in "Animals and the Unity of Psychology" (see chap. 1, n. 29).

31. Conversations with my colleague Maurice Wade helped me work through some of the implications of the respect principle.

9: IMPLICATIONS OF THE RIGHTS VIEW

1. A number of reliable nutritional guides are readily available. See, for example, Francis Moore Lappe, *Diet for a Small Planet* (New York: Ballentine Books, 1975). For a spirited general discussion of vegetarianism, see Jon Wynne-Tyson, *Food For A Future: The Complete Case for Vegetarianism* (London: Centaur Press, 1975).

2. For a fuller discussion of the legal status of animals, see my "Animals and

the Law: The Need for Reform," in Regan, *All That Dwell Therein* (see chap. 3, n. 6).

3. A fuller argument critical of commercial whaling is contained in my "Why Whaling is Wrong," in Regan, *All That Dwell Therein*.

4. The suggestion that we view wild animals as "other nations, caught with ourselves in the net of life and time, fellow prisoners of the splendour and travail of the earth," comes from Henry Beston, *The Outermost House: A Year of Life on the Great Beach of Cape Cod* (New York: Viking Press, 1971), p. 25.

5. Aldo Leopold, *A Sand County Almanac* (New York: Oxford University Press, 1949), p. 217.

6. Ibid., p. 209, emphasis added.

7. For further remarks on these matters, see my "What Sorts of Beings Can Have Rights?" and "The Nature and Possibility of an Environmental Ethic," both in Regan, *All That Dwell Therein*.

8. These three areas are identified and discussed more fully by Andrew W. Rowan in *Alternatives to Laboratory Animals: Definition and Discussion* (Washington, D.C.: The Institute for the Study of Animal Problems, 1980). I have benefited from discussions with Dr. Rowan, which is not to say that he would agree with my position regarding the use of animals in science. It is possible that others might wish to refine the three categories. Such refinement would not affect the argument advanced in the sequel.

9. In April 1981, the American Institute of Biological Sciences announced its endorsement of the *Guidelines for the Use of Live Animals at the Pre-University Level* as set forth by the National Association of Biology Teachers (NABT) (*Bioscience* 31, no. 4 [April 1981]: 330). These guidelines call for a discontinuance of painful experiments on vertebrate animals in elementary and secondary schools. Though this is welcome progress, it does not go as far as it should if the preceding argument is sound. To discourage experiments that cause "unnecessary pain or suffering" is not enough; to engage in activities that bring about the untimely death of an animal also matters morally, something no amount of anesthesia will numb. Nevertheless, the position of NABT does illustrate how one can exercise one's academic freedom by saying no to a tradition; and that is important. It remains to be seen what, if any, analogous steps will be taken by comparable university-level scientific organizations.

10. Gleason, Gosselin, Hodge, and Smith, *Clinical Toxicology of Commercial Products* (London: Williams and Wilkins, Ltd.), as quoted in Ryder, *Victims of Science* (see chap. 5, n. 3), pp. 39—40. I have benefited from Dr. Ryder's work.

11. Dallas Pratt, *Alternatives to Pain in Experiments on Animals* (New York: Argus Archives, 1980), p. 202. Those who say there are no alternatives to using whole animals are encouraged to read Dr. Pratt's work.

12. Ibid., p. 203.

13. Ibid., p. 208.

14. Ibid., p. 205.

15. In addition to Pratt, see Ryder, *Victims of Science*, and Peter Singer, *Animal Liberation* (see chap. 3, n. 10).

16. Singer, *Animal Liberation*, p. 50.

17. Pratt, *Alternatives to Pain*, p. 206.

18. See, for example, Ryder, *Victims of Science*.

19. See, for example, H. Magalhaes, ed., *Environmental Variables in Animal Experimentation* (New Jersey: Associated Universities Presses, Inc., 1974).

20. Beauty Without Cruelty is a British-based firm that manufactures and markets cosmetics that have not been pretested on animals and contain no animal products. A list of their offerings is available by writing Beauty Without Cruelty, 175 West 12th Street, New York, NY 10011.

21. Nozick, *Anarchy, State, and Utopia* (see chap. 8, n. 22), p. 33. Nozick does not have animals in mind when he says this.

22. On this matter, see Ryder, *Victims of Science*, and Pratt, *Alternatives to Pain*.

23. It is not only in animal farming that animals are treated as renewable resources. The same is true in the case of laboratory animals in general and of their use in toxicity testing in particular. This theme will be developed more fully in the discussion of the use of animals in basic research that follows.

24. The benefit argument sometimes is advanced, especially by veterinarians, in defense of testing for the toxicity of drugs on some animals in the hope that *other animals* might benefit. It is true that some animals have benefited because these tests have been done on others, but this does not provide a moral justification of these tests. Just as animals used in the laboratory are not resources to be used in the name of obtaining *human* benefits, so they are not to be viewed as a resource to be used in pursuit of benefits for *other animals*.

25. C.R. Gallistel, "Bell, Magendie, and the Proposal to Restrict the Use of Animals in Neurobehavioral Research," *American Psychologist* (April 1981), pp. 357—360.

26. Ibid., p. 357.

27. Ibid., p. 358.

28. Ibid., p. 360.

29. This is the view recommended in Jamieson and Regan, "On the Ethics of the Use of Animals in Science" (see chap. 8, n. 23). In disassociating myself from this earlier view, I speak only for myself. I am in no position to speak for Professor Jamieson.

30. Note that replies analogous to those given in the last three paragraphs could be given in response to the view that it is all right to eat farm animals or to hunt or trap wild animals less than one year old, including those who are newly born and soon-to-be-born. Concerning farm animals first, since (1) we do not know with anything approaching certainty that these young animals are not subjects-of-a-life; since (2) whether they are or not, we want to encourage the development of beliefs and attitudes that lead to the respectful treatment of those animals who are subjects-of-a-life; and (3) since the adult animals who would be used as "fetal machines" in agriculture would in all likelihood not be treated with the respect they are due, the rights view opposes this defense of meat eating. Points (1) and (2) apply to hunting and trapping newly born wild animals and are

the principal (but not the only) sorts of reason the rights view gives against the slaughter of newly born seals, for example. The rights view offers reasons of the same kind in support of its condemnation of killing nonmammalian animals (e.g., birds and fish of all kinds) in the name of sport or in pursuit of a profit. Even assuming birds and fish are not subjects-of-a-life, to allow their recreational or economic exploitation is to encourage the formation of habits and practices that lead to the violation of the rights of animals who are subjects-of-a-life.

31. Comments by Henry Shapiro, professor of psychology at Bates College, helped me see the relevance and importance of the idea of risk-taking in assessing the morality of our treatment of animals. Helpful discussions about rights with my colleague Donald Van De Veer inched me forward to a better understanding of what rights are.

Index

Designer:	UC Press Staff
Compositor:	Trend Western
Text:	10/12 Palatino
Display:	Palatino Italic
Printer:	Vail-Ballou Press
Binder:	Vail-Ballou Press